Information Technology Strategies

This book is published as part of the
Alfred P. Sloan Foundation program on
Centers for Study of Industry

Center studies published by Oxford University Press include

The Renaissance of American Steel: Lessons for Managers in Competive Industries
  Roger S. Ahlbrandt, Richard J. Fruehan, and Frank Giarratani

A Stitch in Time: Lean Retailing and the Transformation of Manufacturing
  Frederick H. Abernathy, John T. Dunlop, Janice H. Hammond, and David Weil

Information Technology Strategies

*How Leading Firms Use IT
to Gain an Advantage*

William V. Rapp

OXFORD
UNIVERSITY PRESS

2002

OXFORD

UNIVERSITY PRESS

Oxford   New York
Auckland   Bangkok   Buenos Aires   Cape Town   Chennai
Dar es Salaam   Delhi   Hong Kong   Istanbul   Karachi   Kolkata
Kuala Lumpur   Madrid   Melbourne   Mexico City   Mumbai   Nairobi
São Paulo   Shanghai   Singapore   Taipei   Tokyo   Toronto

and an associated company in Berlin

Published by Oxford University Press, Inc.
198 Madison Avenue, New York, New York 10016

www.oup.com

Oxford is a registered trademark of Oxford University Press

Library of Congress Cataloging-in-Publication Data
Rapp, William V.
Information technology strategies : how leading firms use IT to gain an advantage / by
William V. Rapp.
p.   cm.
Includes bibliographical references and index.
ISBN 0-19-514813-4
1. Information technology—Management.   2. Business—Data processing.   3. Strategic
planning.   4. Information technology—Management—Case studies.   5. Business—Data
processing—Case studies.   6. Strategic planning—Case studies.   I. Title.
HD30.2.R36 2002
658.4'038—dc21   2001044796

9 8 7 6 5 4 3 2 1

Printed in the United States of America
on acid-free paper

Foreword

Hugh Patrick

How do successful firms use information technology as a key element in their strategic planning and implementation, and what can be learned from them? In *Information Technology Stratagies* William Rapp has distilled the strategies and practices of successful users of IT in the United States, Japan, and Europe into a book that is of great value to corporate executives, entrepreneurs, and academics alike. The distillation is presented as a rigorous conceptual framework for evaluating and implementing IT strategies. That conceptual material is drawn from, and illustrated by, case studies of leading IT users in a variety of industries.

Bill effectively generalizes from these company and industry studies to provide both important analytical insights and practical guidance on how to use IT as an important component of an effective business strategy. A key theme is that firms can develop IT strategies and techniques that are not easily emulated, thereby differentiating products and services so as not only to add value but also to raise a sustained competitive barrier.

Information Technology Strategies is the product of the Software to Achieve Competitive Advantage Project, a five-year study of how firms in the United States, Europe, and Japan make use of information technology. Supported by the Alfred P. Sloan Foundation and Columbia University's Center on Japanese Economy and Business, that research grew out of a study of the Japanese software industry undertaken by Bill in the early 1990s.

Case studies of 18 firms from around the world identified in consultation with the various Sloan industry centers and others as leading, successful IT users were prepared. These firms were in automobiles, finance, pharmaceuticals, retailing, semiconductors, steel, and telecommunications. Bill then analyzed the cases for commonalities, especially ones that are applicable and transferable out of a firm-specific context. The framework presented here, combined with other insights from the case studies, provides a sharper understanding of IT strategies that work as an integral component of strategic planning, so as to actually shape the marketplace.

In the 1970s and 1980s Japan's economic prowess and management styles were over-lionized. Bill's analysis shows that many may now be under-estimating the skill and expertise of leading Japanese firms in using IT to strengthen their competitiveness.

Bill is especially qualified to have undertaken this project. Following his Ph.D. in economics at Yale, he promptly plunged into the "real world." Over the next three decades he worked in consulting (Boston Consulting Group), banking (Morgan Guaranty Trust and Bank of America), and as counselor of commercial affairs at the US embassy in Tokyo. But he also remained on the academic scene, participating in seminars and conferences. He has been, in the words of an associate, "a breath of fresh air, or a blast of cold air, to his business and academic colleagues as he shuttled ideas and experiences between the two groups." A decade ago he returned to academe with positions at Columbia, Victoria, and Yale. He currently is Henry J. Leir Professor of International Trade and Business at the School of Management, New Jersey Institute of Technology.

Hugh Patrick is Director of the Center for Japanese Economy and Business, and RD Calkins Professor of International Business in the Columbia Business School.

Why Read This Book?

The firms featured in this book are changing the competitive dynamics of their industries, the way their customers see their products and services, their supplier relations, and many aspects of our lives. They are achieving strategic goals and profitability superior to those of their rivals. Explaining how they are managing and using information technology to attain these results is the foundation of this book.

The case studies are of interest in their own right, but of more immediate importance to executives and entrepreneurs—and hence the ultimate purpose of the book—is drawing from the practices of these leading IT users an understanding of how to use information technology strategically.

Information technology offers unique opportunities, but it also poses risks. When used ineffectively—with insufficient attention to training, quality, or systems and organizational integration—software can confound seemingly routine operations. The "bleeding edge" that symbolizes the forefront of technological change thus has been joined by a "bleeding tail" of strategic stumblers—with many of the failed dot-coms demonstrating that a firm easily can be both.

In contrast, the firms successfully directing the transformation recognize that a viable business strategy is a necessary condition for an effective IT strategy. This is unremarkable. What is notable is that the IT strategies the companies are pursuing have evolved from existing cultures and organizational structures, and build on doing better what the firm already does well (their "core competencies," in 1990s jargon).

By deriving broadly applicable insights into the strategic use of IT from what leading firms in Japan, Europe, and the United States are doing, and using the case studies to illustrate and elaborate the points, this book provides the reader with the strategic tools for gaining an edge in the competitive environment of the 21st century.

Consider: it is 2010. You have arrived at the local 7-Eleven to begin a vacation—with an extra day because you will be able to work in the car for several hours en route. A rented ultra-low-emission Toyota van is waiting but, to give the family maximum traveling room, the night before, you brought some bulkier items to the store to be sent ahead by a package delivery service. Although not noticeable, the van's exterior paint and steel were bonded together at the steel mill, reducing potential scraping and chipping damage.

The clerk at 7-Eleven processes the rental with your on-line bank account while you use another terminal to check your Citibank balance, pay some last-minute bills, and place some stock trades. It is the same terminal used to reserve the car the week before. You note an alert for a new financial product as well as a stock purchase recommendation. The kids have been picking out the latest video games to play in the van from a console that loads the games directly from a central computer onto a Sony CD-ROM supplied by the store. Alerted by the computer, the clerk reminds you of Merck drug prescriptions that will run out during your trip.

In the van, pressing a few buttons displays a video screen of the best route, based on the latest traffic and weather reports. It also gives the coordinates and access code for the traffic control system that will drive the van for most of the trip on an expressway that uses Toyota's new Intelligent Transportation System. Because you have to drive only to and from the access ramps, you will be able to work on the way, using the on-board computer, fax, and global telecom connections. The only distraction will be the children playing in the back, mitigated by the sound system's use of headsets. After answering your Nokia cell phone—a call from Citibank that your trades were executed—you are off, covered by travel insurance provided on-line by Travelers as part of the rental package.

This is not science fiction. Versions of these systems are in place or have been announced for completion by 2010. Further, the way businesses deal with each other are being changed by information technology at least as fundamentally as for consumers, as the case studies show.

Acknowledgments

The Alfred P. Sloan Foundation has been instrumental in making this work possible, and I wish to thank it and the other funding sources for their support.

Hirsh Cohen at the Sloan Foundation is due special thanks for his support of the project, and especially for his insight that the research team should avoid trying to confirm any specific IT strategy model. Rather, it should complete its study of the leading IT strategists and from the material thus assembled (which became a set of working papers) see what common approaches there might be.

From 1993 through 2001, Columbia University's Center on Japanese Economy and Business (CJEB) received grant funding from the Japan-U.S. Friendship Commission and the Sloan Foundation to examine and analyze the Japanese software industry, as well as strategic and competitive developments in Japanese, European, and U.S. companies' use of information technology.

Additional funds were received from the Center on Japanese Economy and Business, the Center on International Business Education and Research at the University of Washington, the Centre for Asia Pacific Initiatives at the University of Victoria, the New Jersey Institute of Technology, and the Ridgefield Foundation. This book is based on those studies, including the results of interviews and meetings with industry experts, analysts, government policy makers, large systems houses, large software developers and large IT customers in Japan, the United States, and Europe.

The Sloan industry centers (listed in the appendix) provided invaluable assistance. This included advice on the industries and firms selected for case studies, and assistance in conducting the studies. Peter Burns, Charles Cooney, Stanley Finkelstein, Robert Leachman, Chelsea White, David Mowery, Robert King, and Roger Ahlbrandt were especially helpful with their comments and advice.

The views expressed here, however, are solely those of the author and not necessarily those of the other case writers, the industry centers, the participating firms, or the project sponsors.

Thanks are due a number of individuals.

Hugh Patrick, who has been my economics and Japan mentor since I was a graduate student at Yale in the 1960s, gave full support, including helping with fund raising. Without him, this study would never have emerged.

Larry Meissner diligently read the last two drafts, and provided queries and comments that helped sharpen the points and make the presentation more transparent. An anonymous reader provided extensive comments and encouragement that have improved the book. Josh Safier struggled with editing the various working papers on which the initial draft was based, and acted as the point person at CJEB during the process of turning draft into final manuscript into book.

At Oxford University Press, Martha Cooley helped shape and focus the manuscript after Paul Donnelly and (earlier) Herb Addison had prodded me to finish it.

Christos Cabolis, Nobuhiko Hibara, and Hiroshi Amari are due special thanks for writing the initial cases on semiconductors (NEC and AMD), retailing (Ito-Yokado), and pharmaceuticals (Takeda and Merck) respectively. David Hawk at the New Jersey Institute of Technology helped develop the chapter on Nokia. Mazhar ul Islam updated the industry and firm data in the tables and collected material on corporate consolidations and reorganizations.

Staff at the Japan Fund, Nikko Securities, and Scudder Kemper International, especially Miyuki Wakatsuki, were generous with their time, advice, and contacts. Many executives generously shared their insights and experiences, giving me a better understanding of their industries, their companies, and their strategic use of IT.

Colleagues at Yale, Ritsumeikan University, the New Jersey Institute of Technology, the University of Victoria, and the Fulbright Commission in Japan helped me have the time needed to complete the software study and the cases, and to write this book. Ritsumeikan University and Fulbright especially gave important support that allowed me to spend a large part of 1999–2000 in Japan completing the research, the initial draft and several case studies.

Among the numerous other individuals who have given time and provided comments on the study and this book are Akira Kawanami, Akikazu Kida, Takeshi Murakami, Tom Hout, Charles Brody, Hiromitsu Kaneda, Kazuo Otsuka, Fumio Kobayashi, John Giovenco, Charles Popper, Alan Young, Cathy Grant, Perry Pickert, Akihiko Morino, Seung Kwak, Kiyofumi Sakino, Haksoo Ko, Hajime Inomata, Masaaki Toda, Yoshihiro Iketani, Glen Fukushima, Peter Taylor, Yoshinobu Noguchi, Philip Chapman, John Plum, Kensuke Nagane, Kevin O'Brien, Takeo Dazai, Robert A Feldman, Kazuhiro Harada, Masayoshi Suzuki, Steve Connell, Kenzi Tsukazawa, Carl Taeusch, Noriyuki Matsushima, Richard Nelson, Hidekazu Ohe, Frederick Abernathy, Katsuhito Sasajima, Nelson Fraiman, Kozo Yamamura, and Arthur D'Arcy.

Then there is Japan itself, which continues to offer fascinating examples and serious challenges to conceptions of the way business should be pursued.

My wife and children inevitably deserve my special thanks. Diane and our children—Stacy, Christina, and Jordan—provided moral and spiritual support, particularly during the year I was away from them in Japan completing the research and writing.

William V. Rapp

August 2001

Contents

Terminology

"Information technology (IT)," "computer systems," and "systems" are used interchangeably. "Software" is a subset of IT that includes "firmware" unless a distinction is noted explicitly.

Cellular (telephony) is, strictly speaking, a subset of mobile communications, and care has been taken to preserve the distinction. "Wireless" is an even broader term than "mobile communications."

A firm is "it," and its management is "they."

Some of the terms in this book are new because the concepts are original. In some cases, new terms are used for existing concepts because the current terminology has been muddied by careless use or was never well-defined.

Acronyms

AIDS	acquired immunodeficiency virus
API	application program interface
ARP	audio-radiophone
ASEAN	Association of Southeast Asian Nations
ASIC	application-specific integrated circuit
CAD	computer-assisted design
CAM	computer-assisted manufacturing
CDMA	code division multiple access
CEM	contract electronics manufacturers
CEO	chief executive officer
CEPT	Commission for European Post and Telecommunications
CIM	computer-integrated manufacturing
CIO	chief information officer
CSR	customer service representative
CVS	convenience store(s)
DRAM	dynamic random-access memory
DRM	(distributed) digital rights management
ECN	electronic commerce network
ECR	efficient consumer response
EDI	electronic data interchange
EDP	electronic data processing
EDS	electronic data system
EMR	electronic management response
EMS	electronic management system
ERP	enterprise resource planning
EU	European Union
FDA	Food and Drug Administration (United States)
FDI	foreign direct investment
FMA	frames multiple analysis
GEML	gene expression mark-up language
GMS	general merchandise store(s)
GPRS	general packet radio service
GSM	Group Special Mobile (mobile communication system)

HCR	hot-charge rolling
HIV	human immunodeficiency virus
HMO	health maintenance organization
HR	human resources
HTML	hypertext mark-up language
IC	integrated circuit
ICE	improved chemical entity
IMTS	intelegent multimode transit system
IND	investigational new drug
ICH	International Conference on Harmonization of Technical Requirements for Registration of Pharmaceuticals for Human Use
IP	Internet protocol
ISP	Internet service provider
IT	information technology
ITS	Intelligent Transportation System (Toyota)
JIT	just-in-time
LAN	local area network
MBS	mortgage-backed securities
MHW	Ministry of Health and Welfare (Japan)
MIS	management information system
MITI	Ministry of International Trade and Industry (Japan)
MOF	Ministry of Finance (Japan)
MONET	Mobile Network (Toyota)
MPT	Ministry of Post and Telecommunications (Japan)
MRP	material resource planning
MSS	Meiji System Service
nav	net asset value
NCE	new chemical entity
NDA	new drug application
NHP	National Health Plan
NPV	net present value
NTE	new therapeutic entity
OEM	original equipment manufacturer
OES	order entry system
OLAP	online analytical processing
OTC	over-the-counter
PAC	project approval committee
P&G	Procter & Gamble
PBM	pharmacy benefit manager
PC	personal computer
PCM	pulse code modulation
PE	production engineering
PMS	production management system
POS	point-of-sale
PSS	Postal Savings System
R&D	research and development

ROA	real options analysis
SKU	stockkeeping unit
SMS	short message service
SQL	structured query language
SULEV	super ultralow-emission vehicle
SUV	sport-utility vehicle
TCM	total cost management
TDMA	time division multiple access
TETRA	terrestrial trunked radio system
3G	third generation (telecommunications)
THS	Toyota Hybrid System
TIM	totally integrated management
TOA	total office automation
24×7	twenty-four hours a day, seven days a weeek
UL	universal life insurance
ULEV	ultralow-emission vehicle
VAN	value-added network
VICS	Vehicle Information and Communication System
WAN	wide area network
WIM	wireless identity module
WML	wireless mark-up language
Y2K	year 2000

Information Technology Strategies

Introduction

Information technology (IT) is being strategically managed by a group of U.S., Japanese, and European companies in ways that improve their competitive position and, in some cases, also affect their competitive environment advantageously. The implications of this, and how the firms do it, are analyzed in this book. Explanations are given of how they have woven specific industry and information technologies and routines into their organizations and business strategies in order to achieve definite business purposes that spill over into their long-term competitiveness.

The book began as a series of case studies on leading users of IT. The resulting material then was reviewed to see what common approaches there might be. Thus, the project used a pragmatic research technique and, as a result, the book represents a "bottom-up" approach to mastering information technology as a competitive tool.

A key goal of the strategies of sophisticated IT users is to make the specifics of what they are doing difficult to emulate. This means fast following will not work as a competitive response. To profit from the experience of leading IT strategists, it is thus essential to understand the why behind the how. With this material, the reader can move toward being a Level 3 IT strategist, able to recognize and select "best practice" IT for whatever industry you compete in.

Focus

Focusing on strategic principles emerged during the project as the best way to explain the findings in ways that readers can use and apply in their own situations. The specific software a firm is using generally is noted only when directly relevant to IT strategy. These firms manage their IT decision-making by following a set of strategic principles integrated with their view of their competitive environments. Therefore, strategy was the focus of managers in their responses in our interviews and conversations. Further, when the material was presented in various forums, discussants commented favorably on the approach. (For more on the choice of focus, see box 1.)

Although leading firms use customized and semi-customized vertical ap-

Box 1

WHY THE FOCUS ON IT STRATEGY

Strategy as the focus was not specified when the project began, but it emerged as the project progressed for several reasons. Primarily, strategy was the focus of managers' responses in our interviews and conversations. There are three other reasons.

First, at a detailed level, all the firms have unique software and IT systems as a result of the way each combines organization with packaged and custom software. There is thus little that others could learn if a case merely explained a firm's detailed IT system. Further, the reader would quickly drown in data, because IT pervades all aspects of these corporations. This was apparent when the project team tried to develop IT organization charts.

Second, at a general level, differences in firm IT systems can be almost trivial, because there are a limited number of operating systems.

Third, IT changes very rapidly and each firm is constantly upgrading and evolving its systems, thus rendering detailed descriptions rapidly obsolete.

plication software, I strongly believe that their use of IT demonstrates several common principles that are applicable across a wide range of manufacturing and service sectors. This is the origin of the best-practice IT strategy paradigm derived from the case studies and set forth in this book. Indeed, any firm implementing this paradigm and its principles should benefit competitively and improve its ability to control its own future.

The general IT theories, fads, and practices discussed are topics for critical analysis. However, because the book's purpose is to distill and synthesize the *best* practices of firms considered outstanding strategists in using IT to achieve a competitive advantage, critical analysis of possible mistakes and the like generally is outside the scope of the case studies. In other words, beneficial selection determined the firms studied and, especially, the particulars of what is presented in the case studies. The intention is to help readers better understand how to use IT to gain an advantage.

The best-practice IT strategies presented in this book emerge directly from studying the actions of leading strategists. During seven years of research on IT users and their strategies, not once did a manager indicate in an interview or in a questionnaire that the firm's actions or IT decisions were driven by any specific management theory, research, or paradigm. Nor was any reference made to particular studies or proponents of specific approaches to management issues. All this suggests that best practices can be understood and implemented without reference to management literature or consulting-firm practices. This is not to say that leading strategists are unaware of and not influenced by models and paradigms from the literature, only that they have not explicitly commented on such connections. Thus, works are cited for further reference where the research results support or reflect these firms' actions and ideas.

Outline

An in-depth case-study approach was used to provide the raw material from which general lessons were drawn. The methodology is explained further in the appendix to this chapter. In part I the general lessons have been distilled and used to create a framework for thinking about and using IT as a competitive tool. Part II presents some of the case studies, with emphasis on best practices that are more specific to each of the industries examined. Further details on the methodology and questions posed are presented in Appendix 1. Part III summarizes the ways in which best practices are being applied by leading users—and can be applied by others.

For each case in the project, the goal was to establish the firm's perception of its industry, its competitive position and business strategy, and its advantages in developing and using IT. The team sought firms in an industry where software is a significant factor in competitive performance, selecting firms widely considered to be using software successfully. All the firms thus are recognized by their industry as being good at using IT to improve competitiveness. The firms were selected with the advice of the Sloan industry centers, with the exception of Nationwide Financial Services and Nokia (there was no Sloan center for telecommunications at the time research began). The Introduction to part II lists the firms featured in the industry chapters, as well as other companies, groups, and institutions that cooperated with the study.

The last part of this introduction outlines the supporting concepts used and animated by the analysis, and also provides an overview of aspects of the interaction between IT and a firm's managers and workers.

Evolutionary Approach

An important premise of this book is that a firm's corporate management is founded on an evolutionary process that reflects the development of company-specific sets of rules and routines. In business terminology, this means that path dependency matters. The firm's rules and routines govern strategic and operational decisions, and also their implementation, which means they affect R&D, production, human resources, finance, and market expansion. Although economists wedded to the theory of perfect competition might argue that any innovation will be immediately adopted, evolutionary analysis shows that, from a practical standpoint, adoption of radical changes in organization and technology is difficult. (For re-engineering as an example, see box 2. A seminal study of evolutionary theory is Nelson and Winter 1982.)

Radical changes are to be viewed skeptically even when it is recognized that failure to change is not efficient or best practice. This is because any proposed change must accommodate the existing organization, practices, and routines. Such a notion seems common-sensical, but in fact it has been rather late coming to the economics and business literature.

Box 2

RE-ENGINEERING

Re-engineering was *the* hot management concept in the early-to-mid-1990s. The idea was that, in looking at ways to make a process more efficient, one should ignore the existing organization and start with a blank piece of paper on which one outlines the "best" approach to managing the process. This is a variation of the much older economic point that one should ignore sunk costs in making decisions. But it went further, as re-engineering called for abandoning the old method completely and putting the "ideal" organization and process in place. This included introducing the IT systems needed to support and institutionalize the new. Such discontinuity reflected a major tenet of re-engineering: that successful IT use requires substantial corporate reorganization to achieve large productivity improvements. Leading users examined in this volume indicate otherwise.

Revolutions are not costless. Even assuming one had found the "ideal," the disruption resulting from re-engineering routinely swamped any benefits. Moreover, the ideal is continually evolving as new technologies and competitive responses appear. It is not surprising that in 1997 the MIT Systems Dynamics Group estimated that 70% of re-engineering efforts had failed.

It is critical in understanding leading users' IT strategies that they have handled IT using routines similar to the ones they have developed to introduce other innovations. Thus, evolutionary analysis offers the best assessment of how they are affecting their industry structures in ways that are difficult for competitors to follow. Each case-study chapter stresses the path dependency and historical evolution of the industry and specific users to explain the competitive and business context in which each firm has developed its approach to using IT strategically.

Generally, these evolutionary analyses indicate that past competitive successes resulted from adaptations to business, economic, and political circumstances over many years. An implication is that rivals will find it difficult to copy an organizationally integrated IT system that is best practice, and thereby to become equally efficient and cost-competitive. First, each firm and its competitive challenge are moving targets. More important, successful firms formulate their IT-linked strategies so that competitors will not be able to follow easily. However, even though one cannot copy the specifics, it is useful to know what one is up against, and the general lessons still apply.

Further, legacy systems notwithstanding, leading firms do not select IT simply for compatibility with existing machines and systems. Instead, the necessary hardware and software are chosen for their ability to provide what is required after assessing the associated costs and benefits. They then are integrated into the overall system, using customized middleware as necessary.

Overall Strategy Subsumes IT Strategy

All the leading software users in this study have a thorough understanding of their business, their industry, and their firm's competitive strengths. They also are creating large, proprietary interactive databases that promote automatic feedback among various stages and players in the production, delivery, and consumption process. Especially important is the recognition that these factors are related, and the firms are acting on this understanding.

To facilitate strategic integration of IT into their overall business strategy, they have made IT's strategic role an explicit part of their mission statements. In doing so, the firms recognize that successful performance is not based solely on software. Although it is integral to their management strategy and plays a key role in serving corporate goals, IT must be coupled with an appropriate approach to R&D, manufacturing, and marketing. It is this vision that has enabled them to select, develop, and use the type of software they require for each business function and to integrate the software into a total IT support system that achieves corporate goals.

As part of this, the CIO (Chief Information Officer) and the IT group actively participate in the firm's business and decision-making structure—as facilitators and support staff driven by the needs of the actual users. A Management Information Systems (MIS) department determining the needs of other departments, and the IT resources available to them, is inherently inconsistent with this. So, too, is extensive IT outsourcing.

The Customization Imperative

An IT strategy is a necessary part of a leading firm's business strategy. However, the business strategy must drive the IT strategy. That is, successful IT codifies and institutionalizes existing culture and organizational structures. The use of technology to improve product or service development and delivery must already be part of the firm's philosophy or ethos (corporate culture). This is because deploying IT cannot of itself improve anything—as exemplified in "garbage in, garbage out."

While leading users will adopt software packages available to competitors if there is no advantage to developing their own, they assign significant positive value to customization. This is because customization provides improved integration and enhanced control from both intellectual property and management perspectives. Thus, they select their own software and do their own systems integration. Extensive outsourcing is seen as surrendering strategic options because systems service companies generally have an incentive to develop increasingly standardized products to improve their own efficiencies.

IT's greatest value added comes from semi-customization and customization. Opening cans and microwaving frozen foods provide something to eat: making packaged goods into a real meal requires more.

Because of the perceived benefits of controlling the integration and use of information technology in their basic business and organization, leading software users have come to rely primarily on customized and semi-customized software. Primarily, but not exclusively: packages are used for particular tasks, such as payroll and running a specific manufacturing process. The overriding criterion is what works strategically and is cost-effective; the firms are not wedded to either customization or packages for their own sake. But they are concerned that the ultimate result achieves business goals, and they have established mechanisms to track and confirm this. That is, each business and IT problem is addressed on its own terms, so that the firms' IT systems evolve incrementally in response to their users' requirements. There are no grand firmwide IT solutions such as enterprise management systems (EMS).

Customization is dealt with extensively in chapter 2 and in the specific context of Japan in chapter 4.

A New Strategic Paradigm

Mass production improved on craft production through economies of scale and the use of standardized parts. Lean production has made the production line more continuous, reducing inventories and tying output more closely to actual demand. Now, from firms that are particularly good at using IT, a new strategic paradigm is emerging: totally integrated management (TIM). TIM is proactive. It significantly improves productivity through monitoring, controlling, and linking every aspect of producing and delivering a product or service, including suppliers, design, distributors, after-sales service, and repair. Moreover, it can actually alter a firm's competitive environment.

This is an evolutionary enhancement of the production process, so lean manufacturers implementing TIM retain lean characteristics if those production functions remain cost-effective, just as they have retained the scale effects of mass production when those remain cost-effective. What changes is the precision with which a firm can monitor and control different aspects of its business. TIM allows both greater flexibility and greater control, just as numerical control improves the scope and precision of what a machine tool can do within a flexible manufacturing system.

Broader than lean production, TIM applies to service providers as well as manufacturers. The concept is developed further in chapter 3.

The Overriding Theme

From the analysis, an overriding theme emerges: the leaders in using IT to improve their competitive position do so by developing IT systems that improve the processes and structures that provide the firms' products and services, improve the products and services themselves, and influence their suppliers, customers, and competitors. They, along with many of their suppliers, are investing aggressively in a mix of customized and semi-customized software adapted to their needs and developed as part of a clear strategic vision.

Although the specific competencies and organizational structures needed to succeed vary by industry and by country, the logic of using IT to improve them cuts across all firms and industries. Leading users in the United States, Japan, and Europe have converged on similar approaches. Moreover, these best practices significantly reflect Japanese practices. The United States may have the most dynamic, innovative IT industry, but IT is a tool; what matters to a firm is how that tool is used. Here, along with the leading US and European users, we have much to learn from the Japanese.

Supporting Concepts

There are several management concepts that are relevant to the analysis of IT strategy use by leading firms: user-based economics, beneficial loops, tacit knowledge, vortex strategies, real option analysis, and total cost management. They are summarized here.

User-Based Economics

Each additional user or sale reduces the average cost of delivering products by spreading the fixed costs over more and more users or output. This is especially important in IT, where development costs are significant and the marginal costs are small. And, within IT, it is especially true for software, where an additional copy of a program costs almost nothing to produce. (Training the user and providing hardware can be very expensive, and historically firms have not paid as much attention to these costs as they perhaps should have, but the benefits of spreading fixed costs remain.) Expanding a user base can create a beneficial loop.

User-base economics is related to concepts such as positive network externalities, first-mover advantage, returns to scale, marginal costs, public goods, critical mass, and positively reciprocal production functions. All of these are covered in any good textbook on applied intermediate microeconomics.

Beneficial Loops

A beneficial loop is a situation in which, after the initial change, future changes come naturally and lead naturally to further improvements. These are similar to "positive feedback effects," but with a clearer implication of being repetitive, although not necessarily self-reinforcing. Perhaps the simplest example is greater customer satisfaction leading to repeat sales. The economic concept of increasing returns to scale is also a beneficial loop in that lower costs lead to lower prices that increase sales, lower costs, and decrease prices. Successful application of IT can create beneficial loops that increase productivity or decrease costs in areas as diverse as R&D, production, delivery, and after-sales service.

As a complex example, NEC has integrated marketing and production considerations into the design of some types of semiconductors so that the precise final product is determined farther along in the production process than is usually the case. This enables NEC's manufacturing plants to schedule production more efficiently, thus reducing in-plant inventories and the time for order-to-delivery (cycle time). Customer satisfaction is improved through on-time delivery and awareness of NEC's ability to offer short lead times in the face of changing demand. Improved cycle time reduces costs and increases the reliability of NEC's demand forecasts because the projections need to cover a shorter period. This means NEC can satisfy customer demand shifts more quickly at lower costs, thereby improving price performance in an industry whose economics are driven by better yields and lower costs. Thus NEC is constantly improving costs, customer satisfaction, and market share, which further improves costs.

Loops are not always benign to competitors. Indeed, that is often the intention! Software in particular is subject to user-base economics that can create beneficial loops by adding users, which reduces development costs per unit. Where it is protected by copyright or patent (as most is), there can be increasing returns and monopoly rents. All that is needed is to become the industry standard. Others will write programs to the standard, expanding demand for it by making it more useful. This has been termed the Microsoft model. It is important to note that a loop can emerge to a firm's benefit even if it scrupulously adheres to laws on antitrust and unfair practices. Further, open standards that are widely adopted can favor the industry leader if it is a low-cost producer. Such recognition of competitive dynamics is a key part of Nippon Steel's, Citigroup's, and Nokia's approach to IT strategy.

Tacit Knowledge

At all firms, many things simply are taken for granted by those who have been there a while. This is called tacit knowledge. It can include procedures, contacts, and point people inside and outside the company. It can even include institutional history that gives context and meaning to explicit rules and routines. There usually is no formal, or even explicit, training involved in disseminating tacit knowledge: it is simply absorbed as part of being on the job. Yet, it is real and is used to explain why low turnover and having an experienced long-time work force can be beneficial to the bottom line not only by keeping training costs low but also by having a smoothly running organization that can efficiently adopt innovations such as new or improved IT systems.

Tacit knowledge is thus a way of knowing and understanding something independently of its specific context. This contrasts with levels of knowledge specificity (see box 3), which relate just to the content of what is known.

Specific knowledge can be held tacitly, but much is not; and much tacit knowledge falls outside the classification of specific knowledge. Importantly, information and understanding regarding a firm's relationships with outside parties often is held tacitly. (Such information is in some ways an aspect of firm-specific knowledge, but that term generally refers only to internal aspects of a company, whereas here there is an emphasis on how the company relates to its suppliers, customers, regulators, and even competitors.)

A seminal paper on the concept of tacit knowledge is Richard Nelson's "Why Do Firms Differ and How Does It Matter?" (1991), which discusses how the different historical origins of firms, including their relationships with universities, result in competitive and behavioral norms that are unique to those firms and institutions, and yield lasting competitive advantages.

Box 3
KNOWLEDGE SPECIFICITY

The work-related knowledge (or skills) an individual has that is relevant to a job can be viewed as a set of nested circles, from the more general to the more specific.

Types of knowledge and the content they include:

General. Basic work habits (such as coming in on time) and schooling (the "3 Rs") that can be used in any job.

Occupation-specific. Specialized skills that can be used at any firm requiring those skills. For example, a C++ language programmer could work at any software house using C. (This sometimes, especially in older literature, is called industry-specific knowledge.)

Firm-specific. Things one needs to know to work at a given firm, but are of little use at another firm. (Note that knowledge *about* a firm is different, and is relevant to a much broader group than employees. These include shareholders, analysts and consultants, suppliers, customers, and competitors.) Beyond the mundane, this is exemplified by knowing the person to call to solve a specific problem related to the firm's IT systems. This often is tacit knowledge.

Job-specific. Firm-specific ways in which particular occupation-related skills are utilized. By definition, very little of such information can be transferred to another job.

Tacit knowledge is important because firms that have significant amounts can use that fact as a competitive advantage in a number of ways, as discussed in the case studies. Further, their IT systems often are an important codification of what otherwise is tacit knowledge.

E-Commerce and Vortex Businesses

Gurley (1998) is an excellent analysis of the requirements to establish a strategically effective e-commerce system. (Another useful study is Evans and Wurster 1999.) Such a system must address both industry and IT issues. Gurley stresses that "the companies that will do well . . . are the ones that take the time to understand the context of the industry in which they operate. Rather than aggregate technology, they must aggregate context . . . [T]he hard part is aggregating context." For this reason, "the home-run opportunities belong to companies with people who deeply understand how a particular industry works; who understand how the Internet as a channel can serve that industry. These companies will build Websites that aggregate buyers and sellers to help facilitate both the decision-making process and the subsequent delivery of products or services."

Kevin Jones of *Interactive Week* illustrates a service that aggregates buyers and sellers as two triangles touching at the web source, leading him to call them butterfly businesses. Gurley prefers to "call these [web] sites vortex businesses, as their success involves aggregating not just buyers and sellers, but also technology, content, and commerce." A key element in this regard is "understanding the features and specifications a customer would typically evaluate to make a purchase decision." In addition, the system must reflect "a complete understanding of the way products or services are moved in each industry. How are products ordered? How are they delivered?" Finally, the vortex must make "the information generated at the Website . . . available in various forms to the industry community."

Gurley continues, "Vortex businesses are likely to have one very powerful edge over traditional distribution and manufacturing operations: They will get increasing returns rather than diminishing marginal returns. As a site becomes successful, the chances of its becoming more successful increase. The more buyers are attracted, the more sellers will be drawn in, and the more products that are available, the more customers will be drawn in. That, in turn, makes content aggregation easier—vendors must bring you content, rather than your having to gather it. Everything gets drawn to the center of the vortex. The implication is clear. Great vortex businesses will tend toward monopolies, and there will be no such thing as second place" (Gurley 1998, pp. 146–48).

Microsoft is the archetype for his contention but, although there are industries that have had a very dominant player for extended periods—IBM in mainframes and Intel in microprocessors come quickly to mind—there are very few industries of any size without a number of viable direct competitors. Indeed, Gurley simply has taken the concept of natural monopoly and wrapped it in the World Wide Web. This is ironic, in that technological advances have broken most "traditional," "natural" monopolies except where regulators have kept them in place (utilities) or antitrust action has failed. One market that should be turning into a vortex business à la Gurley is stock trading, but that is not happening, perhaps because no single guiding force is behind it.

In fact, precisely because of the Microsoft experience, most industries will vigorously try to avoid the "Gurley gurgle" of being sucked into a vortex business. This is well demonstrated by Nippon Steel's attempt to create an e-commerce network in Japan (chapter 6). Still, the concept behind the vortex can offer firms powerful strategic benefits. The key element is the "tendency toward" monopoly because, even though it is likely to fall (far) short of a monopoly, this tendency implies a competitive advantage, a barrier to entry, and economic rent. This situation is especially helpful for a firm in a capital-intensive industry vulnerable to diminishing returns due to product commoditization (such as steel) where it is difficult to differentiate oneself from the competitive pack.

Real Options Analysis (ROA)

Opportunity is a key concept in economics, and grasping opportunity is the driving force behind the success of entrepreneurs and firms. Until the early 1990s, how one assessed opportunity was very much an art—supported by some mathematics one could not do in one's head, but could (by the mid-1970s) do on a high-end pocket calculator. This has changed with the spread of the use of options. Options are a way to look at (and price) opportunities.

An option is the right, but not the obligation, to do something. Here, we are addressing pursuit of a business opportunity. There is some *discretion in timing* as to when pursuit is begun and, once begun, most projects can be terminated at any time (*partial reversibility*). (Note that the last feature violates the assumption of traditional net present value [NPV] analysis that the project is irreversible once begun. However, termination may have costs.)

These features give an option on a business opportunity a positive value that should not be ignored. There are five generic implications of the options approach.

- Delay is often valuable.
- Projects that create information and new options should be expedited.
- Actions that exercise options should be valued less than NPV suggests.
- The desire to retain options may encourage corporate inertia.
- Traditional accounting that values only projects actually undertaken overstates return on assets employed in those projects, especially if they are undertaken after extensive trial and error.

Delay has value because it avoids immediate expenses. Thus, because all projects require committing at least some resources that cannot subsequently be transferred to other purposes, it is often beneficial to wait and observe more about a project's prospects. Waiting also can clarify possible alternatives as conditions change for competitive and technological reasons. The discounted value of undertakings that create new options tends to be underestimated because it does not account for the value of flexibility.

This type of decision-making was first extensively used in financial markets (such as hedging foreign exchange exposures), but has spread to general project analysis, evaluating acquisitions, and R&D planning.

R&D offers ample opportunities for using such decision criteria. Traditional accounting does not measure the reduction in project risk as a project progresses. To calculate the real present value, a Monte Carlo simulation can be used to predict the value under different scenarios. Using pharmaceuticals as an example, each scenario is generated from a unique set of random draws from probability distributions based on the odds of a drug's discovery, pipeline survival, and commercial success profile. R&D decisions are sequential, so real options analysis (ROA) takes into account the flexibility of not making a resource commitment as having value. (A good analysis of its application to pharmaceuticals is Myers and Howe 1997.)

ROA can be used to manage contingent progress payments to outside researchers where, after initial funding, the payer retains the right to stop pursuing a project at any time.

The literature on ROA has become quite large, and it is covered in basic textbooks on corporate finance. A useful compendium of readings on various aspects is Schwartz and Trigeorgis (2000).

Total Cost Management (TCM)

Total cost management (TCM), sometimes called total cost analysis, is a concept employed by IT users to assess the actual costs and benefits arising from an IT initiative. Under TCM, costs include not only the direct expense of programming and developing a system or purchasing a package, but also the ancillary expenses of the meeting time between the business and IT units, integrating the program into the system, training, and demands on the hardware (including any new equipment required). It also includes projections of maintenance and upgrade costs and considers such issues as speed with which the initiative can be implemented.

Once the comparative total costs of customizing versus buying a package have been determined, they are compared and the prospective benefits each offers are determined. Cost reduction, revenue enhancement, faster cycle times, improved customer satisfaction, and fewer product defects are among the areas in which benefits are sought.

Looked at from a TCM perspective, the direct cost of an IT package often becomes a relatively small component in the overall picture. If it takes longer for the organization to learn to use, must be semi-customized and integrated into the corporate system, or does not deliver the same user benefits, a generic package actually will be more expensive than a customized approach.

TCM has been considered by economists who identify various sunk, shadow, and transformation costs.

Life-Cycle Models

Customer life-cycle models have emerged as key elements in the strategic thinking of many leading firms in various industries in different countries. Indeed, some have exploited them creatively by incorporating the concepts into their IT strategies. This is happening globally.

The economic concept of lifetime savings models has a long history in the academic literature, such as Milton Friedman's permanent income hypothesis (1957). However, the use of life-cycle models to tailor products for the individual consumer on a mass basis is a relatively new phenomenon and appears to be a direct result of increased IT capacity.

Life-cycle concepts and related data-gathering and analysis have occurred to the greatest degree in financial services. Citibank (chapter 10) is applying such models worldwide. They are particularly important in Japan, where the world's most rapidly aging population, deregulation of financial markets, and a huge asset base together have created a need and an opportunity. It is in this context that Meiji Mutual Life Insurance (chapter 9) and Sanwa Bank (chapter 10) are using their visions of the customer life cycle in combination with innovative IT delivery systems to alter the future of financial services in Japan.

The approach can be applied even in product markets. Thus Ito-Yokado (chapter 8) has developed sophisticated IT systems that track changes in tastes and lifestyles by age to develop new sales and services such as "meals on wheels." Using similar techniques, the company tracks daily, even hourly, purchases of different products by different customer groups.

Toyota (chapter 7) works to stay aware of how tastes in cars and options shift as people's lives develop. Further, knowing these tastes can change quickly has increased the importance for Toyota of gathering and assessing data in an organized and timely manner in order to speedily develop and deliver auto products and services that appeal to these evolving tastes. This has been a prime driver behind many of Toyota's "smart" IT initiatives.

IT, Managers, and Workers

This section looks at the relationship between IT and managers and workers that is needed to implement the basic IT strategy framework.

IT Fluency

An important distinction is between managers who are IT-fluent and those who are merely IT-literate. The first level of understanding of IT on the part of executives is a simple grasp of what IT means and what their choices are. More important, as Dr. Charles Popper, at one time CIO of Merck, has noted, executives have to become involved. IT-fluent executives are willing to engage in discussions about some key IT issues, including whether to be on the leading edge of IT development and utilization, and are comfortable doing so. This matters because IT specialists cannot be expected to know an industry or company as well as a firm's managers. Managers do not need to understand the mechanics of IT, any more than they need to understand telephony to use a telephone. But they do need to know what IT can do for their company, and to see that the company's business needs drive IT selection and use.

When Merck did a strategic plan for its basic research operations in the late 1990s, the IT staff asked the leadership of the laboratories "Do you want the information technology to be bleeding edge, leading edge, or trailing edge?" and explained the differences. In basic research, all said they would have to be bleeding edge. In this area, the firm needs every possible advance in IT that can be applied. On the other hand, when it came to clinical trials, what is needed is something really good, but that will not fail. That means just behind the leading edge. In administrative and other systems, they wanted the oldest and most reliable stuff, that they would not even need to think about. These are the kinds of issues that executives have to deal with, and when you get to IT fluency, you can have these kinds of discussions.

Workers and IT

Hunter and Lafkas (1998) note two approaches to using IT in the workplace. One automates existing practices to reduce the skills needed to perform a task, which I term "task simplifying." (Hunter and Lafkas label it "deskilling"; others call it "dumbing.") The second enhances employees' existing skills, extending capabilities and making them more productive. This I term "employee enhancing" (Hunter and Lafkas use "upskilling").

In evaluating the performance of customer service representatives in terms of IT support to see how these two alternatives apply in practice, Hunter and Lafkas found that IT systems generating information (as opposed to just automating existing tasks) tend to support high-performance work practices. Such IT systems usually improve existing skills, create new ones, and lead to greater worker autonomy—that is, they are employee enhancing.

Middle Managers and IT

Improved information systems have led to flattened organizations. For most companies in this book the motivation has been that existence of fewer layers allows clearer accountability, as well as quicker, more informed decisions. That is, IT has enabled firms to reduce the number of middle managers because they are no longer required to process information or to manage and set objectives for subunits. However, having fewer managers does not inherently mean more work for those remaining. Aided by IT, each manager is able to process work more easily. The idea is to use IT to expand managers' capabilities: managers need greater skills and have broader responsibilities than before.

This more nuanced approach differs from the view that flattening occurs simply because it is easier for top management to communicate with lower levels, and thus easier for each level to monitor subordinates. That approach often leads to greater workloads and stress for the remaining managers.

Integrating Technology and Personnel Practices

Successful firms have an articulated, conscious strategic link between technology and market objectives based on technology, people, and organization. This means technology and personnel practices must be closely integrated.

As an example, Nippon Steel's integrated IT strategy corresponds to the important criteria for success in steel (but relevant in other industries) emphasized by Ahlbrandt and colleagues (1996). As they point out, each IT investment decision is "made in light of a focused market strategy" and fits with the totality of the firm's investments, including links to steelmaking technology and the employees' knowledge base. The company and its IT subsidiary's managers at all levels "understand and take advantage of the interlocking nature of investments" in the broadest sense (machines, IT, employee skills, human-resource practices, and organization) as well as the complementary relationships. This includes the recognition that "new technology and human capital must be developed in use at the same time." Further strategy and practice are aligned "in the same direction so they reinforce one another," and improvement is continuous (*kaizen*). The basis for this is "a conviction about where they want to go that is rooted in a deep understanding of products and markets" while "setting a very high goal: to pursue quality and efficiency simultaneously." This includes the commitment of the CEO, another key element in the Ahlbrandt group's analysis, and a critical element in managing IT successfully to gain a sustainable competitive edge.

Appendix: Methodology

The cases were developed using questionnaires in combination with a review of existing data and studies. For each case, the project team sought to answer key questions while recognizing firm, country, and industry differences. The goal was to establish the firm's perception of its industry, its competitive position and business strategy, and its advantages developing and using IT. This was achieved by using a common approach in the methodology and questions asked each firm.

The research technique used to develop the "best-practice" studies combined questionnaires and direct interviews with an analysis of existing research results developed by other analysts, such as those at the Sloan industry centers. To relate these materials to previous work, the team talked with experts at the various industry centers. To obtain data comparable to earlier research, the questionnaire and interview material were related to materials gathered in a 1995 study, done at the Center of Japanese Economy and Business under the auspices of the U.S.-Japan Friendship Commission, that compared the Japanese software industry to the U.S. and European industries.

The team worked with the Sloan centers to develop questions specifically relating to each firm's business strategy and IT's role in that strategy. Some questions address issues that are relatively general across industries, such as inventory control. Others, such as managing integrated circuit production, are more industry-specific.

To determine if other industry participants recognized the competitive benefits and effects that the firm perceived, customers, competitors, and industry analysts also were contacted. Interviews and meetings were held with industry experts, analysts, government policy makers, large systems houses, large software developers, and large customers in Japan and the United States. These sources provided additional data on measures of competitiveness, as well as on industry strategies and structure.

PART I

A STRATEGIC FRAMEWORK FOR USING IT

Part I provides the framework for thinking about and using IT as a competitive tool, a distillation of what can be learned from the case studies in part II about the IT practices and strategies of leading users. It also presents an overview of Japanese approaches to IT that are influencing the best-practice IT strategies that leading users around the world are converging toward.

Chapter 1 defines three levels of IT strategy, based on the skill and sophistication with which firms utilize information technology. The characteristics of IT use by firms using higher-level IT strategies are outlined in terms of their general business strategies, and with respect to the role and interactions of IT with the firms' overall strategies and organizational structures.

Chapter 2 provides insights into how leading firms manage IT.

Chapter 3 introduces totally integrated management (TIM) and efficient customization, practices that characterize especially successful IT users. It also summarizes the distinctions between Level 3 and other IT strategists.

Chapter 4 is an overview of how competition and industry evolution are forcing convergence in the strategic practices of leading IT users, regardless of where they are based. Understanding the dynamics of IT use in Japan is important because Japanese practices and their strong competitive impact are affecting IT strategy formulation globally. Thus, the chapter also provides an overview of the software industry in Japan, how it has evolved, and how it has contributed to the IT strategies of its leading users.

(The last part of the Introduction summarizes some key supporting concepts used in the analysis and an overview of important aspects of the interaction between IT and a firm's managers and workers. That material provides a consistent approach to the analysis of the diverse practices of the firms studied, and helps form the framework for the distillation of ideas that can be used in crafting an IT strategy that is specific and appropriate to the reader's organization and competitive environment.)

1

Basic Strategic Framework

Drawing on the lessons learned from the firms examined in this book, this chapter constructs a basic strategic framework for thinking about and using IT as a competitive tool. The framework defines three levels of IT strategy, based on the degree of skill and sophistication with which firms utilize IT.

The basic elements that determine the level of IT use are introduced, followed by a closer look at the characteristics of IT use by higher-level firms. This is done first in terms of general business strategies, then as regards the specific role and interactions of IT with strategies and organizational structures.

The Strategic Levels of IT Use

For comparative convenience, the IT strategies that firms follow can be classed by how firms treat IT and what they expect from using it. Each of the levels is a general characterization of what is a continuum, with Level 1 not being a strategy in any meaningful sense. Level 3s are using totally integrated management (TIM) as their overall strategic paradigm.

The basic attributes that define strategy levels are the extent to which IT is integrated into a firm's overall business strategy, the use of IT to create functional benefits and to establish competitive advantage, and the mix of customized and packaged IT used to enhance firm-specific advantages to create value and competitive barriers that rivals cannot emulate easily. That is, firms using higher-level strategies successfully use IT to differentiate their products and services from competitors' in terms of kind, quality, or price on a long-term basis in ways that cannot easily be replicated, thus establishing a competitive advantage relative to others.

Point List 1.1
Strategy Level Determinants

- Extent IT is integrated into overall business strategy
- Extent and nature of how IT is used to create functional benefits

- Extent and nature of how IT is used to create competitive advantage
- Nature of mix of customized and packaged IT

The Minimalist Approach

In terms of IT strategy, despite the Internet revolution, there are still firms that use IT only for minimal functions, such as spreadsheets and word processing, technologies that are generally available to any high school or college student. From this book's perspective, such companies have no IT strategy at all and are not in the game. At the basic or first level are corporations that have linked various IT packages together to provide integrated IT support for most or all corporate functions, including personnel, order tracking, billing, and accounting.

Such a first-level approach includes outsourcing to IT integrators that provide comprehensive IT support. It also includes packaged or outsourced enterprise management systems (EMS) that provide a total integrated IT system covering all aspects of a company's operations. Such systems are first-level even when they are presented as adaptable to any industry or are focused on a particular sector, such as finance, retailing, or medical services. This is because, despite the fact that they may cover all aspects of a firm's activities and may even have a clear industry focus, they are open to easy emulation. Indeed, they encourage it. Therefore, any business benefits are quickly competed away.

Level 1 firms use a minimal strategy that does not address the issue of how to use IT to differentiate their products and services, including new ones, from those offered by competitors. Differentiating is important because having a competitive edge comes down to price and features. If a firm forfeits features, it is left with just price. And even being low-price is not enough in the many markets where innovative producers can add features or enhance service without increasing price, as is shown in several of the case studies.

Box 1.1
RELATED LITERATURE

The strategic importance of IT has been widely recognized for some time. For example, Porter (1980, 1986), as part of his overall analysis of strategy, refers to using IT to increase entry costs and raise competitive barriers, and to alter other organizations' competitive environment. However, he does not address the strategic use of IT in specific competitive situations. Benefits of customized IT compared to cost-cutting efficiencies that are not sustainable as competitive advantages were identified by Davidow and Malone (1993). For the strategic importance of evolutionary growth, technological change, and barriers to entry for international competition, an early work is Rapp (1973).

Moving to a Higher Level

Level 2 and Level 3 strategists see IT as integral to their corporate strategies and competitive success, and use IT as an important competitive tool to help them own the future of their industry's evolution. The case studies indicate that they make IT and software choices for rationally explainable business reasons, and use proprietary software as an essential input into virtually all aspects of their businesses. They realize that although packaged IT systems are readily available and seem cost-effective, pure off-the-shelf IT solutions give little advantage because any benefits can be competed away by easy emulation.

Therefore higher-level firms use semi-customized and customized vertical application software. Packaged solutions available to all cannot improve competitive advantage unless linked to a larger proprietary system. The key to success depends on effectively mixing physical production and delivery with the use of IT systems to achieve a result satisfactory to customers. The point is that software closely related to a firm's organization and business strategy is not easy for competitors to emulate, and thus can establish a competitive barrier. Done properly, this use of IT adds value and creates competitive barriers that more than cover the cost of using and developing the customized IT systems.

Overview of Higher-Level IT Use

This section summarizes IT use by Level 2 and Level 3 firms in terms of general business strategies and as regards the role and interactions of IT with overall strategies and organizational structures.

Basic Strategy

A good business strategy includes IT as an integral element. There is no freestanding IT strategy or purely IT-based business strategy. The general business strategy (and thus its IT component) emerges from the firm's competitive environment and reflects the need to differentiate its products and services from those of rivals. That is, the ultimate goal is to give customers a reason to do business with you—and in so doing, achieve (and sustain) some competitive advantage. Often, firms meld IT into business strategies that already are successful, thus extending and enhancing the value of those strategies.

The ability to use IT in the basic business is fundamental. Thus, IT is integrated not just into the firm's business strategy but also into its operations and organization. Moreover, IT is seen as a means to the real end: the success of the business. The firm recognizes that success depends on a good understanding of its own business and industry, including its own and rivals' competitive strengths. With such a clear competitive vision, the firm

Table 1.1 Differentiating Strategic Levels of IT Use

Level 1	Level 2	Level 3
IT is treated as a cost. Organization must conform to the IT used. This means there is a real risk of organizational sabotage (lower levels undercutting the commands of supervisors).	IT is recognized as a strategic tool with a customer and user focus. The goal is to improve one's competitive position not only via cost reduction but also through product and revenue enhancement.	IT is fully integrated into a clearly conceived overall business strategy, as well as into operations and organization, but remains subservient to them. Managers are IT- and strategically fluent.
Lasting functional benefits are not sought and should not be expected.	Creation of functional benefits and competitive barriers is pursued, but on a somewhat ad hoc basis. IT development is constant, incremental, and evolutionary.	Creation of functional benefits and competitive barriers is pursued systematically and proactively, and involves customers and suppliers.
The goal (actually, more an intention) is to maintain perceived competitive parity by constantly upgrading IT packages available to everyone in the industry.	Aims are focused vertically within the firm and do not try to create industry standards.	Developing and controlling industry standards affecting the competitive environment is an explicit goal. Customers and suppliers are encouraged to make firm-specific IT investments.
Packaged IT is used.	Customized and semi-customized IT inputs, which cannot be emulated easily, are used. IT supports the organization and enhances firm-specific advantages.	Customized inputs are used extensively, limiting competitive emulation.

can properly select, develop, and use the IT required for each business function.

Achieving a competitive advantage is essential. Absent that, or at least parity, all other goals and ideals are unachievable or unsustainable: the firm simply will lack the resources to meet them.

IT's Role

The role of IT is to enable the user to do better what already is done well (that is, in 1990s management literature parlance, enhance core competencies). IT systems thus are coupled with marketing, sourcing, customer service, new product development, inventory control, and constant cost reduction to support the firm's services and products in accord with its business goals and objectives. The effect is to create higher competitive barriers, leading to greater returns, which give the firms more strategic flexibility in pricing, IT development, and product R&D.

All business elements must be in place and working together in the same direction for IT to be used successfully. That is, personnel organization, the physical plant, and the IT must mesh, and the IT must be coupled with appropriate approaches to marketing, customer service, and new product development. This is why a higher-level user typically uses IT to build on existing competencies. Adding IT does not inherently add competency—it may even be disruptive and alienating for both staff and customers.

Indeed, the use of IT to enhance existing competitive advantages has itself become an important competitive advantage (core competency), one that, over time, further facilitates and improves the ability to closely integrate IT with organizational and business strategies. This undercuts competitors' ability to follow with a quick adoption of best practice because doing so involves not only copying the specific IT but also emulating the related organization.

A higher-level user's strategies are two-pronged, combining cost containment with revenue enhancement. Thus, not only does IT help control costs by improving overall consistency, performance, and productivity, it also is used to improve product quality and value, leading to more revenues.

Continuous, active monitoring of various business functions is a natural use of IT. Thus, the data needed to link strategic elements are systematically collected, managed, and analyzed. The information then is integrated with the firm's supply, production, and delivery systems in order to improve productivity and increase customer satisfaction. Building proprietary databases and data-mining techniques is a widely recognized way of establishing a competitive advantage, so the real edge comes from integrating the collection and utilization of the data into the overall business strategy and operation of the firm. Among the cases, Citibank is particularly expert at using its global credit card database to monitor customer expenditure patterns by product and merchant in order to develop new financial services.

IT can be part of the product or service the company sells. That is, the IT is embedded. This can be an efficient way to sell existing and new customers a wider range of specialized or even unique products and services. As when IT is used within the firm, embedded software alone is not enough—it must be coupled with marketing, product design, customer service, and constant cost reduction in ways that appeal directly to customers. Toyota's new Intelligent Transportation System (ITS) does this by incorporating both functional and service features into its on-board computer and navigation system. In combination these not only control different aspects of the car, such as acceleration and distance to the next car, but also travel services.

Effective IT not only must add value, it also must frustrate emulation. This is a fundamental aspect of Level 2 and Level 3 IT strategies.

IT's Place

IT is subservient to people. Thus, a higher-level user has good human-resource characteristics and employs IT to simplify tasks and to increase worker skills. This allows increased productivity, through greater output or reductions in personnel, without overwhelming staff. (See the Introduction, section "IT, Managers, and Workers" for more on this.)

As part of a general attention to detail and quality, a leading IT user puts sound basic strategies and organizational structures in place and continuously seeks to improve their efficiency in a variety of ways. IT is just one aspect of this. Not only does a user need to drive IT initiatives, the business units that will use an IT system are closely involved in its design and development. The result is a coevolution of technology and organization. There is an overall corporate evolution rather than the revolution of re-engineering or a major reorganization.

To a higher-level user, IT is something that assists change and development but does not compel organizational adjustment. If existing structures or strategies need to be changed, this is done for its own sake. This rule simplifies fixing problems that may arise from the introduction of new software, because IT difficulties are not confused with organizational or product problems.

IT Interactions

A critical element separating Level 2 and Level 3 IT strategists from firms using Level 1 strategies is the use of a mix of customized and packaged IT to create value and competitive barriers in ways that rivals cannot emulate easily. To do this well, the firms have developed cultures that are positively oriented toward using technology to improve product and service development and delivery. This involves training and developing personnel who understand the production system, know the product or service, and are (at the least) IT-literate. All three aspects are critical to strategic success because all three technical streams are needed to develop new products, new production technologies, and new IT support systems.

Close integration of organization, personnel, and technology improves employee satisfaction—and it is well known that when conflicts arise among managers and employees in setting goals, employees can sabotage the system and productivity improvements become limited. Successful managers understand this, and take advantage of the interlocking and complementary nature of investments in machines, IT, employee skills, human-resources practices, and organization.

Organizational structure and IT support one another on an interactive basis. Thus, just as business units determine a firm's need for and use of IT, so the CIO and IT support group actively participate in the firm's general decision-making. This is logical because the CIO's charge is to oversee the development and maintenance of IT systems that are integrated into the overall business strategy and organizational structure. To do this effectively, the CIO has the full support of the CEO. This support is demonstrated in such things as mission statements and actions that explain that IT is important to achieving the firm's goals and long-term success. The mission statements generally explain that because IT is an integral part of business strategy, its development and implementation are driven by the business units, often in response to customer demand.

This integration, and the involvement of users in the design and selection of IT, help ensure that purchase decisions are made for business suitability rather than the convenience of IT specialists.

Controlling IT

A higher-level user clearly understands that the economics that places packaged software at an advantage in common horizontal applications can have negative aspects for a user shifting its IT usage toward vertical applications within a product, firm, or industry. That is why a strategic principle of adding real net value is an important company goal in selecting IT. Achieving this goal manifests itself in retention and expansion of the customer base through IT in ways competitors cannot meet with their own IT, or even with a discounted price. Often the value added is from aligning IT with nonprice variables, such as time and quality management. These reduce the ease with which competitors can emulate IT-supported technical and product advances with "me, too" responses using benchmarking or reverse engineering.

The objective is to develop an IT mix that supports firm strategies and differentiates them from competitors in ways that enhance existing strengths. This means recognizing that functional and market gains frequently justify the initial expense of customizing systems, integrating them into a single firmwide IT system, and training workers to use it. The standard procedure to do this is, first, to determine the purpose of the system within the organization and its operations, with the focus on IT's role in enhancing the firm's ability to efficiently develop, produce, and deliver many different qualities and types of products or services. Next is to create a system that serves that purpose.

In short, strategically a firm retains control over its software through an integrated IT department or captive subsidiary. Outsourcing is limited to captives or firms with close historical links. Such a proprietary IT mix is seen as helping to create a competitive barrier. (This topic is more fully developed in chapter 2.)

Appropriate IT

At all firms, consciously or not, organizational structures drive software product choices and the understanding of IT's use and benefits. That in turn determines IT demand and system evolution within a firm. A high-level IT strategist proceeds in an evolutionary manner by building on the company's specific advantages and existing business strategy. Such an approach emphasizes pragmatic implementation as an important rule.

The basic philosophy of Toyota's approach to all types of technology is relevant to IT users:

- Emphasize total cost-effectiveness and reliability.
- Prefer equipment with "just enough" functions.
- Keep things simple and rely on skilled labor.
- Avoid technology for its own sake.

Funds spent on an IT project are not available for other purposes, so evaluation is important. Expectations need to be clear about what the project is to do, and objective ways of measuring success should be determined in advance. (Also see the Introduction, subsection "Total Cost Management.")

Point List 1.2
Attributes of Firms Using Level 2 and Level 3 IT Strategies

Business Strategy

- Focus on customer and customer satisfaction
- Clear competitive vision
- Conscious quest to build competitive advantages
- IT an integrated element

Organizational Structures

- Evolutionary change
- Attention to detail and quality
- Continuous improvements in efficiency

IT Strategy

- Sees IT as a tool and, as such, subordinate to people
- Supports organizational structures interactively
- Develops and grows databases that are intensely used and analyzed
- Relies on customized software
- Focuses on limited, realizable goals and results
- Is judged on results, ease of use, and overall cost-revenue benefits

IT Functions

- Extend and enhance human resources
- Contain costs
- Increase capabilities and improve products

IT Interactions

- Technology, organization, and personnel closely integrated
- IT design and selection driven by user needs
- IT group participates in general decision-making

2

Managing Information Technology

How Level 2 and Level 3 IT users decide and implement software strategies, how they measure success, and how they select software for achieving specific goals vary with each firm's particular competitive situation and business strategy. In addition, within the context of IT being an integral element of an overall business strategy, there are differences among the companies in how they link IT strategies with corporate goals. One feature is common, however: software development and selection are driven by the needs of the users. This means extensive customization of software and a considered gradualism in implementation.

The overriding criterion is what works strategically and is cost-effective. Leading firms are not wedded to either customization or packages for their own sake. Nor do their criteria include using the latest software or IT technology just because it is new.

Because the software must fit into the firm's organizational structure, it is selected on a case-by-case basis. Packaged software is used where appropriate—typically, in manufacturing and accounting. (Two examples are specific production equipment processes and payroll.) When used, packages are adapted to the firm's needs (semi-customized) and integrated into the larger IT system through proprietary middleware. This is because packaged solutions available to all cannot improve competitive advantage unless linked to, or made part of, a larger, proprietary system that contains features that enhance performance and act as barriers to entry. The result is a mix of customized and adapted packaged software integrated with existing systems and organizational structures.

Evaluation

Most leading IT users have evaluation systems to ensure that the costs of customization or of a new package are recovered directly through reduced costs or indirectly through business benefits. The benefits can be easily quantifiable (such as faster cycle times) or intangible (better market information, more consistent organizational performance).

Costs and benefits typically are tracked through cross-functional approval and review committees. NEC, Nippon Steel, and Merck are particular examples of this. NEC has committees of managers and engineers that examine and review the software used in each part of the design and production processes. This is a critical function because NEC cannot afford to fall behind a competitor in production efficiency. This means the software (almost always packaged) controlling each machine in the production process is constantly being upgraded. At the same time, NEC does not want to upgrade an existing package if another package is better, or if the benefits are marginal. Its management thus looks carefully at cost, functional benefit, and the elapsed time to full efficiency improvement. Nippon Steel has joint committees of staff from its captive IT subsidiary and the actual users at the parent. They work together to budget, manage, and develop the IT system.

Merck has cross-functional committees involving people from manufacturing, R&D, finance, IT, and marketing, as well as top managers. Often using the same return criteria Merck demands for a dollar invested in drug development, these committees examine each dollar of IT investment. This often involves application of real options analysis. This forces the committees to examine the potential cost of not doing something relative to the cost and benefits of proceeding. The model also considers the likelihood during the development period of technology advances that could improve results. (For further details, see the Introduction, subsection "Real Options Analysis.")

Leading firms specifically reject the notion it is acceptable to buy a package if it delivers some base ("sufficient") level, typically 80%, of the functionality needed by the firm's users because the missing percentage may be what achieves a real and lasting competitive advantage. That is, some CIOs follow a corporate rule or routine in purchasing packaged software under their annual IT budgets in which they poll other corporate users regarding items on their IT wish list. They then find the least expensive IT support that will deliver at least the base percentage of the items on the users' lists. Over time, most of the users' IT needs will thus be filled. Unfortunately, however, this approach may never fulfill important user needs, because there may not be any IT package that meets a given user's requirements. This clearly is a Level 1 IT strategy.

More significantly, the leading firms' approach of supporting their business units' requirements as long as the cost is justified by the competitive benefits, which they track, means that rivals using such a first-level, budget-driven wish list approach will fall behind in new, critically competitive areas. This is because these are frequently the areas where an IT package does not exist. If these initiatives by the leaders are subject to beneficial loops as well, the Level 1 firm's competitive position will erode quickly. This is why Merck's managers, for example, require the IT supporting the firm's drug pipeline to be at the bleeding edge.

Best Practices

The foregoing runs counter to the best-practice hypothesis posed by traditional economic theory, where users are expected to quickly and easily introduce the technical and organizational changes necessary to take maximum advantage of changes brought on by new IT technologies. That
hypothetical view provides a theoretical foundation for the fast-follower
strategy, which suggests that one does not need to lead in the introduction
of a new technology because it is easy to follow quickly once a competitor
has adopted it. But the hypothesis assumes most innovations are going to
be in packaged software. In fact, best-practice IT is driven by user strategies
in combination with industry evolution and economics, and that implies
customization.

The leading users' evolutionary approach recognizes that various markets
have developed differently and are not growing equally. There are large,
mature markets (such as steel), medium-growth markets (autos), and high-
growth markets (electronics, finance, pharmaceuticals). Each market
and industry has its own strategic and competitive imperatives. Each user
is responding to the situation it faces with the business and IT strategies it
deems appropriate. In some cases there may be overlaps that require different IT support for different segments. For example, Nippon Steel is
working with Toyota on automobile sheet steels that are easier to recycle.
Thus, of necessity, the strategies are different for each firm, although, as explained in this book, they share many common strategic principles and approaches.

Outsourcing

Leading users question the benefits of extensive IT outsourcing, a Level 1 IT
strategy pursued by many U.S. firms. While the firms providing outsourcing
services will link various packages together to serve a particular customer's
IT requirements, their economic incentive is to reuse as much software as
possible and to provide similar solutions to companies in the same industry.
Thus the leading users perceive that firms focused heavily on outsourcing
are pursuing a first-level approach that overemphasizes the cost side of
software investment, rather than analyzing its possible organizational and
operational benefits. In determining what is cost-effective for themselves,
leading firms will not sacrifice user functionality or revenue enhancement
merely to reduce short-term costs.

Extensive outsourcing is seen as surrendering strategic options because
systems service companies generally want to develop increasingly standardized products to improve their own efficiencies. Outsourcing also puts
the user one step from its customers and suppliers, which means a loss of

beneficial loops. In addition, the leaders question outside firms' knowledge of their industry and organization, and thus outsiders' ability to design and integrate new IT into the leader's basic business. The leading IT strategists also are concerned about the system integrators' commitment and operational understanding to make the IT work on a fail-safe basis. Given these leading firms' clarity of vision, customer focus, and strong supplier relations, these seem to be legitimate concerns.

As an example of picking-and-choosing, both Takeda and Merck use systems from SAP, one of the world's largest software firms and a specialist in enterprise management systems (EMS) and electronic management response (EMR) (box 2.1). However, they have not adopted SAP's entire EMS or EMR integrated system because that would require substantial reorganization. Rather, they have selected pieces of SAP's system that they thought would be useful, and which could be adapted to their existing proprietary systems more cost effectively and quickly than developing in-house programs.

Nippon Steel and Toyota both commented that a major reason even the new EMR and EMS systems would not work for them is that their systems have developed over many years and involve hundreds of millions of lines of code. They are so complex and tightly integrated with their organizations that the new enterprise software packages simply cannot replicate the benefits and functionality of their current systems. This is because their propri-

---

Box 2.1

SAP

SAP AG, based in Germany, has the largest (roughly one-third) share in the world market for enterprise applications. Its success is based on its holistic approach. Rather than combining many specialized software packages, all potentially from different vendors, SAP offers an integrated bundle that facilitates information exchange among its modules to make better, quicker business decisions. Its R/3 software is especially suited for multinational companies because SAP wrote it to handle multiple languages, currencies, and regulations.

R/3 consists of modules that handle asset management, controller functions, financial accounting, human resource management, industry specific solutions, plant maintenance, production planning, project systems, quality management, sales and distribution, materials management, and business work flow.

Introduced in 1992 (with a Japanese version in 1993), R/3 is client-server oriented, is designed for open systems (UNIX), and permits semi-customization. Thus, some Japanese pharmaceutical manufacturers, including Takeda, are collaborating with SAP to develop IT packages that will be used specifically in Japan's pharmaceutical industry.

The company was started in 1972 by four software engineers from IBM. The name is the acronym of the project they had been working on.

etary systems are closely tailored to the needs of specific units within their organizations, and are continually being modified in response to those units' business needs.

They therefore eschew the prepackaged integration of a purchased EMS in order to maintain and extend the very effective end-to-end solutions they have created and connected, using their own proprietary middleware in combination with IT solutions developed in response to their business units' specific requirements. Even a company newer to information technology, such as Nokia, without such a historical IT legacy, has limited its adoption and use of such packages because it feels it needs "99.99999% reliability in terms of managing its demand supply structure for its mobile phones end-to-end."

A preference for sourcing software in-house is not surprising with respect to Japanese firms, as they historically have viewed software as an integrating element in their production and delivery of a good or service. However, it was a surprise to see how adamant leading U.S. and European software users were that developing and using customized software makes sense if the increased cost of customization results in competitive benefits. (On the convergence of approach by leading users to employing IT and the origins of customization in Japan, see chapter 4.)

Customizing IT

IT customization is used to capture and institutionalize corporate goals. The rules and routines leading firms use to achieve these objectives often are based on routines used to introduce other innovations, and will be linked to the existing customized system. Budgets and benefits are used to minimize costs and to measure advantages to users. IT improvements are steady and incremental, and use proven technology, because these large system users are risk-averse.

Leading users' strong demand for customization runs counter to the expectation in the 1990s that customization, especially in Japan, would fade in the face of technical convergence, including the trend toward open systems, and downsizing. (In the United States downsizing often has meant contracting out computer services on a large scale, as well as the movement within organizations to LANs supported by servers linked to a mainframe. By having terminals and PCs only indirectly connected via servers to the corporate or outside provider's mainframe, a system's size requirement is reduced.) Instead, customization in vertical and embedded applications has persisted and grown, and many leading users are employing mainframes as servers. Furthermore, a large part of the packaged software leading firms use is semi-customized.

Firms that have invested heavily in IT customization believe that for them, software development economies are generated mostly through commonalities and the use of object-oriented software that can be used in multiple programs within the firm or group.

Choosing Software: An Example

In the semiconductor industry, software and information systems are used extensively in all activities from design through marketing. As with leading firms in other industries, the choice between customized and packaged software (with and without a customized interface) depends on how it is to be used. A good example is NEC.

When choosing chip design programs, the criteria NEC uses are technology (functioning and performance), price, and interoperability, in that order. This selection process has resulted in its adapting various packaged software programs that are managed by a customized interface. NEC internally develops only 20% of the software used in chip design. This emphasis on packaged systems is due to NEC's realization that, for chip design, specialized firms have a comparative advantage in developing efficient, technically superior software products. NEC develops only the software that serves to tighten the linkage between the design and production processes, that is, the part that must be closely allied with its own organization and business strategy.

This situation is reversed, however, for production and marketing. Here NEC perceives that its tacit knowledge, business philosophy, and corporate culture have to be directly integrated into its IT systems. In other words, the software must reflect and facilitate the transfer of NEC's unique strategic approach. Thus, the IT has to be customized. Because there must be seamless integration between marketing and operations, 90% of such IT is developed by NEC or its affiliates. The packages it does purchase are mostly database management systems, application software used in overseas subsidiaries, and software particular to a specific piece of production equipment. In the last case, machinery manufacturers develop the controlling software and upgrade it on a regular basis. NEC's proprietary system links these machines and their programs.

Innovation

Once a user has a program that accomplishes its needs and has developed the skills needed to use or improve the system, there is little incentive to switch to a different system, and a large incentive to improve and expand the existing system. For this reason, substantial changes usually occur only when new hardware and software are purchased to address a problem the existing system cannot accommodate. The firm then links these with its existing system to maintain the integrity of its proprietary systems.

Users must keep their systems technologically current, which often means using new or specialized software. But often they will accept, and even desire, a certain time lag in adopting and customizing such software in order to make sure the serious bugs are worked out. (An example is Merck's experience in choosing software for its research operations, which is detailed in the Introduction, subsection "IT Fluency.")

This is part of an incremental approach to software innovation that clearly works well in established business environments—such as steel, automobiles, and retailing—where it is unlikely there will be a profound technological transformation that completely alters an industry's cost structure. But it also appears to be the approach of the established leaders in dynamic, rapidly changing industries such as banking, insurance, pharmaceuticals, semiconductors, and telecommunications.

The cases suggest that the principles of *kaizen* are applicable to IT systems development and strategies. (*Kaizen* is the introduction of innovations and new developments incrementally, but constantly, as the organization and related technologies evolve. See Imai 1986.)

Innovative Customization

At the frontier of an industry's IT needs there can be no leading-edge software because exactly what it should do is only just being explored. This can give firms with the capacity to customize an advantage over firms that must wait for packages. Thus, where there is no suitable IT to give the company the capabilities it wants, it will consider developing innovative customized software. This can be considered high-risk, but the large functional and market gains, including possible first-mover advantages, justify the customization and total system integration expense.

As with customization in general, this provides the firm an opportunity to capture and perpetuate tacit knowledge, and corporate features that account for its success.

Integration

Differences among software programs and operating systems affect user purchase and development decisions, but there is no indication that having a certain system prevents the introduction or integration of new hardware and software if that is what is required to achieve a certain business or functional result. However, users will not relearn or rewrite particular programs every time they purchase a new machine or attach a new program, so it is fundamental that the new must be compatible with the existing application programs, middleware, and operating systems.

As users switch more of their IT activities to network servers, workstations, and PCs, the need for integration into a firm's overall system increases. This is because leading users indicate that, except for word-processing and spreadsheet programs, almost all the packaged software they buy, even for PCs and workstations, has to be adapted to their systems. These semi-customization expenses can run two to three times the cost of the packaged software. From an evolutionary perspective, these conditions are being perpetuated because of the high cost and organizational difficulty that users face in significantly changing their existing systems. Users also do not want to risk a possible disruption of the smooth functioning of their IT and business operations. This perspective is exacerbated by suppliers' desire to continually maintain and not upset their client relationships.

Because users want their various hardware and software configurations to communicate, and their applications to work on disparate systems, they must develop appropriate middleware. This middleware stands between the operating systems, the network software, and various applications, and is key to understanding how firms use complex IT systems to achieve their corporate objectives and how their proprietary IT systems function.

The middleware contains the various standard protocols and communications programs that allow programs written for other operating systems or on other machines to communicate and interact. Networking programs, including those making use of the Internet, are thus middleware. The middleware also provides the application program interface (API), which is what lets a program run on a particular machine with a particular operating system.

Leading users generally have multivendor systems in order to control costs, give them more solution flexibility, and avoid excessive dependence on their mainframe suppliers. To maintain flexibility and facilitate communication across these multiple platforms, there is a desire for open systems, network flexibility, and easy middleware interfaces.

Limiting Objectives: An Example

Advanced Micro Devices (AMD) entered the microprocessor business in 1982 because IBM insisted that Intel provide a second source for its microprocessors. Intel and AMD very quickly became embroiled in lawsuits. By the mid-1990s AMD recognized that it either had to exit the microprocessor business or design its own Wintel-compatible chip. AMD decided to stay the course, which is the origin of the K6 processor, introduced in 1997.

The company had never designed a microprocessor before and did not realize that there was a very close relationship between the design problem and manufacturing. (Nor did NextGen, the microprocessor developer AMD bought in 1996.) When transferring designs to AMD, Intel had withheld how those designs were created and their relationship to production. The K6 had serious yield problems, and AMD went from being considered a consistent and very reliable producer to being seen as inconsistent and un-reliable. Moreover, the K6 did not meet customers' expectations regarding speed.

One source of difficulties was that AMD was trying to do too many things to keep up with Intel in particular and changes in chip technology generally. This related to both design and production. Thus, in addition to having to design its own microprocessor, it had to shift from a 0.30- to a 0.25-micron geometry and to ultraviolet lithography. It thus was difficult to identify pre-cisely what and where specific problems were. To avoid such situations, leading IT practitioners limit the number of objectives they set for any IT initiative. Then, when there are problems, it is easier to identify and fix them. In preparing for the next generation, AMD tackled technical problems one at a time, prioritizing and solving one issue before moving on to the next.

AMD's solution to its design and production problems did involve more than just shifting strategies. The company hired a new president from Mo-torola, who had experience producing microprocessors reliably in volume, and the design team from Digital Equipment (DEC) that had created the highly regarded Alpha chip. However, the strategic shift was a necessary element in the company's recovery.

Networks

Because users' IT strategies are heavily dependent on effective communi-cation or networking within the firm, there is a desire for open systems, network flexibility, and easy middleware interfaces. At the same time, be-cause its IT systems often involve mission-critical databases and key opera-tions, system integrity is paramount and any threat is unacceptable. This drives a risk-averse approach with respect to security and promotes adopt-ing new technology on an incremental basis.

A firm's interest in communicating with external entities and tying them into the firm's network, whether directly or via the Internet, varies according to the firm and the situation.

For financial services in particular, security is always a paramount con-cern. Their business generally is client, transaction, and product specific. Thus, in addition to capturing contextual specificity, there is confidentiality and fiduciary responsibility. These considerations force financial service firms to take a cautious approach to developing and adding system software, and to allowing any access that might compromise the system. At many firms, employee usage is carefully monitored and passwords are changed frequently.

Citibank has established standard protocols that permit outside vendors to access certain information from Citi's system, such as for credit card checks, but does not allow access to customer accounts. Meiji Life requires agents to physically sign in on their laptop screens to access the system, and does not permit them to load other software on the laptops.

Toyota has direct communication links with its suppliers to inform them about production schedules, but those suppliers cannot access Toyota's design engineering programs. Nippon Steel's customers can send e-commerce orders by e-mail or a web site, and can track order flow through the production process. However, they cannot make entries directly affecting Nippon Steel's IT scheduling, shipping, or billing processes.

Thus, firms allow limited horizontal access among system users depending on the situation and the need to share information in real time. Such access requires horizontal system compatibility (the ability of different systems to communicate across various organizations), as opposed to vertical compatibility within a production process. In this way user-base impacts can create external benefits and competitive effects by persuading various users to share information with clients or others outside the firm. The impacts depend on customer economics, supplier relationships, and competitive interactions that vary by industry. Establishing these external benefits thus relies on getting customers or suppliers to make firm-specific investments that improve the firm's competitive position and that can be emulated by rivals only if they adopt the firm's system as the industry standard. This gives the firm more control over the industry's evolution.

Extensions outside the firm raise security issues because of the need to get and share information. There also are questions of compatibility, communication, and interoperability of software among diverse operating systems and configurations of hardware and software. When necessary, leading IT users are able to develop the appropriate middleware needed to address these strategic considerations, often using a hub-and-spoke strategy that actually extends their control over their business environment and introduces an essential element in a TIM strategy. Citibank has been particularly adept in using this process to link its products and customers with other financial service providers. (See chapter 10, subsection "Hub and Spoke.")

This process has been facilitated by the fact that leading users' IT systems usually have evolved into hierarchical three-tier systems where mainframes manage network servers that manage workstations and PCs. They thus can manage contacts with outside PCs or mainframes that are separate from their own internal vertical systems. These users are interested in the contribution of each system and type of hardware to their total system, including horizontal compatibility externally with customers, suppliers, and systems providers. However, even vertical links are provided only on a selective basis. Affiliated software developers and hardware providers in turn take their cue from their close relationship with these major customers.

To maintain the integrity, security, and confidentiality of interconnections and prevent unauthorized data or system access, the system's customization and networking must be done in-house or at closely affiliated software development subsidiaries. This is another indication of these large users' commitment to using software as part of controlling their business processes and improving productivity.

Software Efficiency

Software efficiency for a user is in utilizing IT as a strategic tool to advance business objectives, such as improving the making and delivery of a product, rather than efficiency in the creation of software. The cost of software in a unit of output is usually not so large as to justify buying it off the shelf if that means sacrificing the benefits of a firm's unique procedures.

Toyota's vaunted production system, for instance, is based on highly integrated computer systems that begin with the order from the customer, then schedule the production run, notify the appropriate suppliers, and on through the production and delivery cycle. Although Toyota is widely studied and used as a benchmark, no U.S. auto company has developed a system that can deliver a car produced to the customer's specifications as fast as Toyota's current two to three weeks. Toyota's information system cost per car is around ¥10,000 (1998 data), on average only 1% to 1.5% of the ex-factory price. This is small relative to the importance of maintaining a production and organizational technology advantage. Toyota does not see cost savings from using packaged software as large relative to the productivity and revenue gains of customization. Indeed, any downtime resulting from implementing a totally new production system, rather than making incremental improvements to the existing one, is totally unacceptable.

No retailer is as close as Ito-Yokado to being able to predict what a particular customer will order at a local convenience store at a particular time on a specific day, given particular weather. It already uses IT systems based on point-of-sale data to specify the delivery of highly perishable snack foods by day and time of day. Indeed, whenever IT competitiveness emerges in the product—whether a car or a rice ball—rather than as a shrink-wrapped software package, Japan has software users that are quite successful and very competitive. This concept includes, but goes beyond, "embedded software" (the proprietary IT in a product such as the software that controls a camcorder).

Customized Japanese application software in areas of existing competitive strength (autos, steel, and consumer electronics) seems particularly effective globally in terms of improving product and production competitiveness. Similarly, several firms in the United States and Europe, especially in financial services and telecommunications, are using IT and their ability to rapidly develop product support systems as a competitive lever into global markets. Such advanced IT strategies are a conscious and important element in their continuing success.

3

Advanced Strategy

Several characteristics distinguish Level 3 users from other IT strategists. These are summarized in this chapter. From the study of the IT practices of successful firms, a new strategic paradigm can be seen: totally integrated management. Related to TIM are lean production and new forms of customization.

What Makes a Level 3 Strategist

The strategy-level attributes discussed in chapter 1 are a continuum on which quantitative differences can become qualitative. That said, there are three important distinctions between Level 3s and other strategists.

A commitment by senior executives, especially the CEO, to provide resources for IT projects is essential, but not sufficient. Level 3s have IT fluency throughout the top ranks of management. This is more than a simple grasp of what IT means and what the choices are; this is IT literacy. IT fluency means senior executives are willing to discuss IT in terms of what you do to be on the leading edge and being comfortable doing so. This is important because IT specialists cannot be expected to know an industry or company as well as a firm's managers do. Managers do not need to understand the mechanics of IT. But they do need to know what IT can do for their company, and to see that company needs drive IT selection and use.

Level 3s fully understand the imperative of differentiation and have been successful at extending the paradigm to influence the behavior of their customers and suppliers in ways that change their industry's competitive dynamics to their advantage. That is, their actions affect the competition. This usually involves other firms either joining a real-time, on-line network that the lead strategist controls or strongly influences, or adopting the Level 3 firm's systems as actual or de facto industry standards. The firms make investments specific to the network or standard, which ties them to it and gives them an interest in its success.

Suppliers or customers often are willing to do this because of their feeling of support during a long-standing business relationship. In any case, it requires providing incentives to participate (a "fair" sharing of benefits). In these cases, IT strategy is intertwined with the leading firms' business structures and interactions with customers and suppliers, because these affect areas such as the willingness to invest in new designs or systems to improve cycle times.

Firms operating at Level 3 are using totally integrated management as their overall strategic paradigm. This concept is developed in the next section.

Point List 3.1
What It Takes to Be a Level 3 IT Strategist

- IT fluency
- Ability to influence the competitive environment to one's advantage
- Use of totally integrated management (TIM)

Totally Integrated Management (TIM)

Totally integrated management (TIM) involves linking and influencing every segment of a firm's supply, production, distribution, and service chains into a coherent whole using information technology. This became feasible only in the 1990s with increases in computing power and advances in database management. Not only do cost savings flow directly from TIM, there also are better-designed, more quickly delivered products, and increased customer satisfaction.

TIM originated in leading firms' quest for more efficient responses to changes in the level and structure of demand. Based on IT's ability to monitor and coordinate data on orders and production, the TIM concept has been formulated from actual practices that have emerged at leading firms. I have created it only in the sense of structuring a set of best practices, indicating some rules, and providing a name.

TIM is more comprehensive than what is termed "lean production." Lean production developed within manufacturing to increase efficiencies—ultimately, to reduce costs. It is essentially a manufacturing concept, although its inventory aspects are relevant in distribution, and thus in wholesale and retail trade. TIM is applicable to service firms as well. A TIM firm need not be a lean producer, but probably is if it is a manufacturer. Thus, Toyota, the original lean producer, also is becoming a TIM firm. IT was not an integral part of Toyota's production system (TPS) as it evolved in the 1960s, and the firm did not use TPS to control all aspects of its business. Now that the IT tools are available, Toyota is implementing TIM.

TIM has led to a seemingly radical departure from lean principles: the use of breaks in a production line, with a resulting increase in process inventory. Manufacturers such as Toyota and NEC found that certain assembly line points had constrained potential for improved productivity, and these reduced the possibility of improvements in continuous manufacturing. But by breaking the line and having small buffer stocks, it is possible to make improvements on parts of the line in ways that increase overall productivity. Overseeing and controlling the buffer stocks is done using information technology. How Toyota has modified traditional assembly is covered in chapter 7, and box 3.1 outlines what NEC has done.

First-level IT strategies, even those employing an EMS enterprise management system approach, fail to achieve TIM because they expect the firm, its customers, and its suppliers to adopt, learn, or interact with the IT system selected. The IT system does nothing directly to extend the user's influence over customers and suppliers. A Level 2 strategy goes further, but usually stops at adapting a common interface with suppliers and customers. In

---

Box 3.1
REFINING LEAN PRODUCTION

Japan's leading semiconductor maker, NEC, has deviated from stylized lean manufacturing by using buffer stocks to shorten the production cycle, and increase the accuracy and precision of information sharing so that equipment is used more intensively. The result has been smaller overall inventories, lower production costs, and faster response to changes in demand.

In semiconductors, batch size has been limited by the capacity of the least productive piece of equipment, with the result that more productive equipment was always underutilized. As the cost of semiconductor equipment has risen, the opportunity cost of this unused capacity has become significant. Therefore, NEC runs each piece of equipment or assembly segment closer to its capacity, even if this means some increase in in-process inventory compared to a traditional assembly line approach. Controlling this process, including the size of the buffer stocks, requires sophisticated data processing. Once in place, such IT can help to schedule production and orders from suppliers, thus building on existing lean production methods.

A particular strategic benefit was NEC's discovery that certain initial aspects of its production process are common to a variety of devices. This is particularly true for ASICs (application-specific integrated circuits). Thus, by increasing buffer stocks at these stages of production, NEC has more flexibility when demand shifts, because it can switch final production from one device to another in less time.

Integrated circuit demand and prices can change very rapidly, so NEC's ability to alter production more quickly than competitors means it is less likely to experience severe price erosion or be stuck with large inventories of obsolete devices when demand changes. Better margins in turn improve the cash flow available to support R&D, marketing, and capital investment. The power of this concept was demonstrated in 1995 and 1996 when NEC was the only large Japanese IC producer to avoid a loss due to the reduced demand for DRAMs. NEC had the ability to switch to ASICs, for which demand was still relatively good.

contrast, capturing externalities is a key concept in a Level 3 IT strategy's approach to an end-to-end business solution.

By definition TIM affects a firm's environment in terms of after-sales service and repair, supplier relationships, and industry standards. Cambridge Technologies advises corporations on this concept as an "extended firm" because such control and influence can redefine the normal microeconomic relationships we assume among firms, suppliers, and customers. However, while the concept of the "extended firm" captures the idea of externalities, it does not address the fact that the firm does not fully control these externalities. They are not an integral part of the firm. The firm can only influence them. It is in this respect that IT can play a critical role in a TIM approach by encouraging firm-specific investments and tying customers and suppliers more closely to the firm's IT system and related strategies. This is a key principle in Level 3 IT strategies.

In addition, by capturing and sharing previously unexploited externalities, firms using TIM can improve their competitiveness and increase their market shares, establishing beneficial loops that can substantially alter an industry's existing competitive relationships. Such changes then create ripple effects that have an impact on customers and suppliers, and on those firms' customers and suppliers. To the extent that such IT systems are protected by copyright or patent, or are subject to user-base economics (where high development costs per unit are continuously reduced by adding users—customers, employees, or suppliers), a beneficial loop emerges. Market expansion and greater usage lower unit costs, thus creating increasing returns to scale. This increases market share through lower prices and increased user benefits. The user base is then expanded further and unit costs are again lowered. And so on.

Efficient Customization

Customized offerings at lean-production costs—that is, individually tailoring services and what have been mass-produced products, and doing it at a low price—is being made feasible by advanced IT that allows managing different products and production processes more easily than was previously possible. The concept applies to intermediate goods as well consumer goods. In the consumer market, the concept is very much in fashion, the buzzwords being "mass customization" and "mass individualization," best defined as "customization for the masses." The term used here is "efficient customization." This is preferred because it captures the point that the customization that actually occurs for the specific customer is being accomplished efficiently on a large scale, and the concept applies to more than final consumers.

There is nothing new in the idea—car buyers long were able to select from a wide range of options. Ironically, in the 1990s the profusion of car models and the cost of providing options (an aspect of "fat design") led to a significant narrowing of choices—to the point that some luxury car buyers get to choose only color, wheel style, and whether to take an "options" package that once was less bundled.

Many of the IT practices of leading users presented in this book are relevant to achieving the goal of wedding customization to mass production, and this is noted as appropriate. Moreover, most of the case-study firms are engaged in efficient customization. Thus, the discussion will stress a few key points.

Essential Elements

Knowing the cost of each product or service being sold is an absolute requirement. Average cost of some grouping is the minimum proxy if the items are sufficiently similar—for example, they differ only in color. But in these cases such things as the cost of offering different colors need to be included. These range from inventorying paint to cleaning the equipment between color runs. IT can provide the mechanics to do this, but it is the organizational structure that makes it work. Nippon Steel is one of the leaders in this, having begun in the mid 1990s to refine a cost accounting system that allows it to custom-cast and properly price color-coated steel.

Particularly when offering services, efficient customization relies on databases that are both specific to customers (and prospects) and broadly capable of being mined to identify relationships that allow cross-marketing. The various life-cycle models in financial services are major examples (see the Introduction to this volume, and chapters 9 and 10). Using IT-based analysis of the data, leading firms develop and promote what they believe is demanded by each customer segment, while constantly testing this view and the system in the market.

Efficient customization is IT-intensive. Indeed, it is possible only because cheap IT can be substituted for expensive people. But everything is relative: IT is especially expensive if it does not work or alienates customers. Thus, for example, the better leading users avoid customer DIS-service phone lines that require callers to work through "please note our menu has changed" messages or key in 16-digit account numbers (at least if they are targeting older customers; it is generally maintained that "the young" do not mind).

The philosophy of leading users is that it is easier and more efficient to align delivery and human-resources systems with their customers' psychology, goals, and interests than to try to get the customers to align themselves with a different and more narrowly defined cost-driven strategy.

Point List 3.2
Requirements for Efficient Customization

- Efficient existing sourcing, production, and delivery structures
- Precise cost accounting

- Intensely used and analyzed databases
- IT-intensive delivery structure tempered by customer needs
- End-to-end IT, highly integrated with all business functions

The application and development of advanced IT strategy principles such as TIM and efficient customization can be seen in the way many leading Japanese firms have evolved in terms of the use of IT to achieve an advantage. This is taken up in the next chapter in terms of competition's push of these firms toward a common approach to IT usage.

4

Convergence, Competition, Evolution

The specialized requirements of each user's industry, combined with different countries' varying software and IT development structures, has interacted with unique historical legacies and competitive environments to put Japanese, U.S., and European software users on different evolutionary paths. Yet, as this book shows, the paths are converging for successful users. That is, how leading strategists select and use IT is becoming independent of a firm's geographical base. That means understanding the dynamics of IT use in Japan is important. After explaining why Japanese firms are affecting IT strategy formulation globally, this chapter provides a brief overview of the software industry in Japan, how it has evolved, and how it has contributed to the IT strategies of its leading users.

Convergence

Interviews with managers at leading IT strategists in the United States and Europe indicate that these firms are using more customized software to create value and establish competitive barriers. At the same time, leading Japanese users are using more packaged software but heavily customizing it to work with their proprietary systems, something called semi-customization.

An important reason for this convergence is competitive pressure, as leading users across a range of industries have begun to recognize that using customized IT is the way to create competitive benefits that cannot be emulated easily or competed away. This approach contrasts with cost-cutting through layoffs or reductions in R&D expenditures. Further, leading Japanese strategists' successful use of proprietary IT to improve competitiveness has pressured global rivals to understand and counter these activities.

The evolution of Japanese IT has coincided with the evolution of Japanese firms and industries. Understanding this evolution is an important component in appreciating how Japanese firms have become very strong in vertical application software (software specific to a firm or industry, including software embedded in a product or service, such as Canon camcorders or Meiji's life-cycle insurance policy). It is especially vital as an antidote to the general perception that U.S. and European firms are more sophisticated and creative users of IT than their Japanese counterparts and are particularly adept at adopting best practice.

There are several things wrong with that self-serving perception. First, it is not always clear what the best practice is strategically, even after the fact. More important, even when something is clearly better, it may not be possible to copy it. Consider how long it has taken rivals to emulate Toyota's production system even partially.

Not being able to emulate or catch up is consistent with an evolutionary analysis, which argues that only certain users can combine software with other business elements in the ways necessary for strategic success. As the case studies show, Japanese emphasis on customization and forming software development subsidiaries favors intra-industry software advances—and hence strategic success in those businesses—which is why leading U.S. and European users pragmatically have adopted a similar approach.

In other words, Japanese firms often already have what is becoming recognized as the best practice for strategically using IT for specific industries. Moreover, these firms are in industries (autos, steel, electronics) already favored by Japan's competitive strengths. Similarly, leading IT users in the United States are firms in finance and pharmaceuticals that already are global powerhouses, while European firms were early leaders in mobile communications.

The Origins of Customization in Japan

In Japan large users account for most software use, and their heavy use of customized software has resulted in such software being about 85% of the total market. Most software is for mainframes and minicomputers. Although the percentage of Japanese households with a PC increased substantially during the late 1990s and is reported to have exceeded 50% as of March 2001, PC use still is primarily in offices. Packaged PC software sales thus depend largely on big customers' purchase and use decisions. This situation is expected to change only slowly. A large percentage of the software that consumers buy is games. The pattern of large software users and customization dominating Japan's IT development, except for games, emerged during an earlier study of Japan's software industry (see Rapp 1995).

The preference for customization in Japan is due largely to historical accident. MITI (Ministry of International Trade and Industry) promoted development of a Japanese computer industry by subsidies and by sponsoring multiple alliances with overseas producers. This means that each major Japanese computer company has had a different antecedent for its operating system: Hitachi with RCA and then IBM, NEC with Honeywell, Oki with Sperry Rand, Toshiba with General Electric, Mitsubishi with TRW, and Fujitsu first on its own and then with IBM. The IBM-compatible producers hardwired the IBM instruction set into their mainframes, paying IBM a royalty.

Still, the operating systems, while able to run potential customers' existing IBM programs, were different enough that application programs written for one system would not run on the operating systems of IBM-compatible competitors. To keep customers dependent on them for support, upgrades, and application development, suppliers did little to encourage interoperability between the disparate systems, except to the extent of facilitating an initial transfer to their proprietary system.

In addition, government subsidies for mainframe development and sales encouraged suppliers to offer customers highly customized software packages, using their proprietary operating systems as a further subsidy and lock-in device. IBM was required by a 1960s U.S. antitrust decree to unbundle its software and hardware sales on a global basis; Japanese firms were not. One informed observer notes that "In the 1960s, Japanese companies almost gave us their computers. They wanted us to work with them and give them feedback to improve their systems. If we wanted new software, they would give it to us for free. They were losing money, but they looked at it over the long-term" (quoted in Anchordoguy 1989, p. 42).

This resulted in large, highly integrated but unique systems for large users. Although this can be perceived as an expensive legacy, it gradually was recognized by several major Japanese users as being advantageous in promoting operational consistency and tying the organization and its culture together in ways that could not be emulated. In response to their competitive environments, the leading U.S. and European producers examined in this book are now utilizing this concept as well. That is, competition has pragmatically pushed leading IT strategists toward similar rules and routines in formulating their IT strategies.

Software Choices

Most leading IT strategists, and especially the leading Japanese users, buy operating systems and middleware to connect those systems to their proprietary systems from hardware vendors or specialized software developers. But most develop applications and networking middleware internally or through IT subsidiaries rather than purchasing standardized packages. This is especially true when the software is used to support a new service or product, or is unique to the firm's customer base or supplier network. Citibank and Nokia, for example, both take this approach. In Japan the need to maintain and integrate developments with existing systems has also meant that the increased use of smaller servers and workstations, though progressing, is happening slowly and mostly in new IT uses. There remains a heavy reliance on mainframes even as network servers.

Further, captive IT units are part of the parents' vertical *keiretsu*, and their rapid growth is an important element in Japan's industrial development, in contrast to the United States and Europe, where companies such as Electronic Data Systems Corp (EDS), Computer Associates, SAS, and SAP hold sway. This is because these leading Japanese firms' IT strategy is to reduce development costs per software system developed for the *keiretsu* by selling software to other group members, as well as to customers and suppliers. The captives also sell noncompeting IT services to third parties, particularly small and medium firms, to spread corporate overhead. A specific example is presented in chapter 6 for Nippon Steel and its software subsidiary. An exception that proves the rule is Ito-Yokado (IY) and Nomura Research Institute (NRI), discussed in chapter 8. IY does not own NRI, but the two firms have a close, decades-old IT support relationship as well as joint ventures. Similar practices also are found in the United States. For example, in 2000, Citigroup created Citi Technologies Inc as a specific subsidiary for group IT support functions (see chapter 10).

The top 10 software companies in Japan are affiliates of larger companies and mostly of large users. Besides helping control costs, these affiliates offer careers to specialized personnel outside the parent's personnel system. Furthermore, they expand the firm's IT user base to reduce the overall cost of maintaining a proprietary software system. (The long-term employment system typical of most large Japanese firms has helped them train and retain the industry- and firm-savvy IT personnel needed to manage, upgrade, and expand the systems.)

When the leading firms do buy application or system packages, they or their captives extensively customize them or develop special middleware to integrate them into a firm's total system. Because this semi-customization can run three times the cost of the basic package, in Japan most software developers and systems integrators are forced to specialize by industry, resulting in dependence on specific customers in particular industries, each with its own large proprietary system. When combined with long-term employment, this has made large numbers of Japanese programmers and software engineers heavily specialized by firm, industry, and system, with limited skills or interest in developing more generalized packaged software solutions or learning new programming languages. But when firm-specific advantages are paramount, this situation helps to maintain those advantages in the face of intense competition.

Japanese job stability promotes and facilitates customization, because workers can spend the time to fully learn a company's proprietary system, its organization, and its industry with little employment risk. Although many U.S. firms similarly would like to retain experienced and skilled IT personnel knowledgeable about their firms and industries, the high demand for such talent and U.S. job mobility has worked against this. Japanese firms therefore have an advantage in pursuing long-term proprietary IT strategies, especially in less rapidly growing industries such as steel and automobiles. This will force their global competitors to move toward more proprietary systems and changes in human-resource policies.

Japanese programming and software engineering resources for industry thus focus on developing and maintaining large proprietary systems, and on localizing and adapting (usually foreign) packaged software to specific firm uses. Large development costs and low reproduction costs generally make spreading costs across an expanding internal user base a primary goal for proprietary software producers. This means software for large proprietary system users—whether Japanese, U.S., or European—should produce visible gains in productivity, customer service, or some other identifiable area of the firm's business. That is, an expanded user base is achieved through improvements related to the firm's products or services rather than in greater software sales as such.

An Evolutionary Path

Some observers have hypothesized that Japan's transition to the Information Age will be difficult because of its weakness in developing packaged software. But the results of this large-scale study indicate that leading Japanese IT user firms, along with their leading U.S. and European counterparts, are taking a different path. This has important competitive implications for rivals. Because the leaders' initiatives are based on proprietary systems, organizational integration, and copyright protection, competitors will find it difficult to emulate them.

The leading strategists' approach exploits two major trends. The first is the technical development of the computer industry, the second is the users' increasing sophistication and administrative heritage. In Japan these developments have promoted customized systems in the vertical application software market as opposed to the EMS-type solutions typical of the U.S. and European markets. Yet leading U.S. and European users, like their Japanese counterparts, have turned toward customized systems that support the user's desire for compatibility between its software needs and its basic management goals. This is why the evolutionary examination of the motivations and successes of the major participants presented in later chapters is key to understanding and appreciating how these firms are developing and achieving industry best practice.

For Japanese firms this IT administrative heritage and firm evolution includes the fact that since the 1950s, these leading users have developed programs involving millions, even billions, of lines of customized code, mostly written using COBOL. Since the programs continue to accomplish their basic business goals, the management view is that there is little reason to spend the time, effort, and money to convert them to newer systems, even though there may be some loss of efficiency, operating flexibility, and interoperability from not shifting.

This pragmatism is based on the fact that conversion of existing programs to newer programming languages would divert large numbers of scarce systems engineers and programmers from the more important task of developing programs for new business requirements and maintaining existing ones. Further, due to Japan's long-term employment system, the firms have knowledgeable personnel who can maintain and adapt the existing systems at relatively low cost compared to conversion. Although many firms outside Japan replaced programs in anticipation of Y2K, Japanese firms generally preferred to modify their existing software.

They find, in short, no compelling reason to shift totally and rapidly to newer systems. That said, many Japanese industry associations have a regular technical group meeting to discuss the latest software and the best way to introduce it into industry practice.

The pattern of leading Japanese, U.S., and European users each pursuing their own IT goals therefore will persist, which means their use of IT will continue to be heavily customized and development will be evolutionary. For Japanese firms, especially, there is little incentive to end customization, given the huge sunk costs and strong desire to support unique operating advantages in their basic businesses, which are not software. But this rationale generally extends to leading U.S. and European IT strategists as well. It is thus important to recognize that these major companies are developing and using very advanced IT to maintain and improve their global competitiveness. Further, their customization approach represents an alternative way for them to participate in the Information Age. Judging by the examples presented in this book, they are doing this quite successfully, with significant future implications for their corporate rivals.

Successful users of IT in general, and successful Japanese firms in particular, view IT as an input, a tool like any other for pursuing whatever their real business is. Understanding this perspective is important because too often, especially in the United States, where IT frequently is in the hands of IT specialists with only limited knowledge of the industry and company, IT is seen almost as an end in itself. Instead of becoming sufficiently knowledgeable (IT-fluent) to make IT serve the firm's overall needs, managers too often become hostage to what IT providers (both internal and external) dispense.

The cachet of IT as a gee-whiz source of solutions has had serious negative consequences in the United States, the disruptions of re-engineering (see box 1.2) being just one. It has also tended to perpetuate a producer-dominated software industry to which any trend toward customization is a direct challenge. This is because customization reduces the ability of software producers to force the pace of the industry's evolution, including frequent "upgrades."

While Japanese firms have borrowed much of their IT from the United States, they have in some ways deployed it with greater skill and success. This perception is reinforced by leading U.S. and European strategists' adoption of a similar approach. That is, successful users of IT are converging on a path that differs from what many users have done traditionally in the

United States and Europe, and that is actually closer to Japanese practice. This is because to the extent that leading firms already treat IT as a tool, customizing it to their needs and introducing it as required, they have a distinct, demonstrated advantage over firms that have not moved in this direction. The rationale and its competitive implications for their industries are described in more detail in the cases that follow.

PART II

CASE STUDIES

There is a fountain of youth—at least for firms. Companies that can evolve by refining their technologies, organizational structure, rules, and routines in ways that attract and retain customers can be said to stay young. Conversely, a firm (an entire industry) can be using the latest technology (even be the technology) and still shrivel if it fails to be important to users. Thus, although much is said about an "old" and a "new" economy, the really interesting distinction is between firms that evolve and those that do not. The second part of this book looks at a group of firms that are among the best at using IT to stay "young"—and the future belongs to the young.

Five manufacturers in two process industries are analyzed. The IT needs of process industries are different in many ways from those of assembly industries, but both provide lessons for all IT users. Merck and Takeda in pharmaceuticals are the topic of chapter 5; Nucor, Tokyo Steel, and Nippon Steel of chapter 6. (As "old economy" as steel is perceived to be, Nucor is among the youngest of the firms examined.)

Toyota, the developer of the lean-production paradigm for assemblers and (by incremental response to changing circumstances) a leading developer of the totally integrated management (TIM) paradigm, is covered in chapter 7.

Ito-Yokado and its Seven-Eleven Japan subsidiary, retailers with projects under way to offer a wide range of services, including banking, are taken up in chapter 8 along with their major IT partner, the Nomura Research Institute. Financial services are very IT-intensive. Leading firms include Meiji Mutual Life and Nationwide Financial Services (chapter 9) and Sanwa Bank and Citigroup (chapter 10).

Founded in the mid-19th century as a papermaker and now aiding communications as a telecom company, Nokia is the subject of chapter 11. It was added after the project began because of its connection to several leading users' IT-based strategies and telecommunication's strong interactions with IT.

Each of these chapters includes background material on the industry and the firm generally, as well as analysis of its use of IT. This is in keeping with a key point of the study: context matters.

A list of all the firms studied in connection with this and a predecessor project is provided below.

Industries and Firms Included in This Book and the Software to Achieve Competitive Advantage Project

---

Automobiles
   Toyota Motor Corp.† (Toyota Jidosha)

Finance, Investment banking
   Credit Suisse First Boston (CSFB)[1]
   Nomura Shoken†[2]

Finance, Retail banking
   Citigroup†
   Sanwa Bank†

Finance, Life insurance
   Meiji Mutual Life (Meiji Seimei Hoken)
   Nationwide Financial Services

Pharmaceuticals
   Takeda Chemical Industries (Takeda Yakuhin Kogyo)
   Merck & Co

Retailing, Food
   Ito-Yokado† (Seven-Eleven Japan)

Retailing, Apparel
   Bloomingdale's (part of Federated Dept Stores)
   Isetan

Semiconductors
   Advanced Micro Devices (AMD)
   NEC† (Nippon Denki)

Steel, Integrated
   Nippon Steel† (Shin Nippon Seitetsu)

Steel, Minimills
   Nucor Corp
   Tokyo Steel Manufacturing (Tokyo Seitetsu)

Telecommunications Equipment
   Nokia Corp.†[3]

Note: The seven firms in italics are Level 3 IT strategists.
†Indicates a member of an *e-retsu* (discussed in chapter 12).
[1]Case study not written due to extensive reorganization.
[2]Most of the study was of Nomura Research Institute (NRI), a subsidiary; it is NRI that is a member of an *e-retsu*.
[3]Added for this book; not part of the original study.
Copies of Software Project working papers are available at *gsb.columbia.edu/japan/ publications/index.html*

5

Pharmaceuticals

Takeda, Merck

For millennia people have used drugs in the quest for health and longevity. The modern pursuit of these goals may be as mysterious to the layperson as the ruminations of Taoist sages 2300 years ago, but the uses of IT strategies and practices can provide accessible insights even for those outside the industry. After providing an overview of the industry context, this chapter looks at two firms. Takeda, Japan's largest ethical drugmaker, is a Level 2 IT user. Merck, one of the world's pharmaceutical giants, is a Level 3.

INDUSTRY CONTEXT

Pharmaceuticals are a part of health care, which is heavily regulated in high-income economies for both patient safety and costs. Even in the face of cost containment, if drugs are more effective in reducing aggregate costs compared to other treatments, pharmaceutical firms can benefit, at least relatively. Determining cost and therapeutic effectiveness is IT-intensive, and some of the ways drug firms have developed to use IT for this and other purposes are relevant to other industries.

The major firms, all large multinationals, are listed in table 5.1. Only firms that primarily develop ethical drugs (box 5.1) are considered here.

Overview

Two critical aspects define the industry's competitive context. One is technological change arising from the convergence of life and biological sciences. The other is political.

Lawmakers and regulators are considering various measures to reduce health-care costs in response to budgetary and political pressures. For pharmaceuticals, these actions include substituting generic drugs for branded versions. That can mean lower returns for discovering and developing new drugs. Still, new drugs are the key to the industry's competition for health-

Table 5.1 Major Global Pharmaceutical Companies, Ranked by Global Market
Share (percent)

1996	2000	
4.4	7.0	Pfizer, Inc. (U.S.) [PFE][1]
7.1	6.9	GlaxoSmithKline plc (UK) [GSK][2]
3.9	5.0	Merck & Co. (US) [MRK][3]
3.6	4.4	AstraZeneca plc (UK)[4]
3.4	4.1	Bristol-Myers Squibb Co. (US) [BMY][5]
4.4	3.9	Novartis AG (Switzerland)[6]
3.3	3.8	Johnson & Johnson (US) [JNJ]
4.8	3.7	Aventis SA (France) [AVE][7]
3.1	3.2	American Home Products Corp. (U.S.) [AHP]
2.5	3.1	Pharmacia Corp. (U.S.) [PHA][8]
3.1	3.1	Abbott Laboratories (U.S.) [ABT][9]
3.1	2.9	Roche Holding, Ltd. (Switzerland)[10]
2.2	2.9	Lilly (Eli) & Co. (U.S.) [LLY]
1.9	2.4	Schering-Plough Corp. (U.S.) [SGP]
2.2	1.9	Bayer AG (Germany)[11]

Country of incorporation is in parentheses. Ticker symbols of U.S.-traded firms are in
brackets.
    Motivated in large part by a desire to achieve scale, there has been a rash of mergers
since the late 1980s. Many of these have been across borders. Because the mergers have
extinguished many familiar names, the notes list significant combinations. Rankings for
1996 are pro forma for subsequent mergers.
    A number of the major pharmaceutical producers in Europe—particularly in Germany
and Switzerland—are part of very large chemical companies, reflecting the industry's historical development and the fact that most drugs are chemicals. In the United States,
several are part of diversified medical supply companies.

care expenditures. Finding a drug that works and bringing it to market over
the hurdles and through the maze of regulatory requirements is complex and
expensive. The process takes years. Merck estimates the cost of bringing a
new drug to market in the United States is $350 million to over $500 million
for drugs starting in 2000. This development cost compares to $250 million
to $350 million for drugs that came to market in 1998–99. Then there is the
need to recover the cost of pursuing R&D on compounds that do not reach the
market. Reducing drug prices thus hinges on reducing the high fixed cost of
new drug development, including reducing the number of dead ends.
    The industry and its required skill mix are changing. By the 1990s, ad-
vances in technology and scientific understanding meant a convergence of
life and biological sciences that has transformed the competitive landscape.
As a result, in creating new drugs, pharmaceutical firms have faced new
entrants. For some four decades after World War II the drug industry grew
steadily and, except for mergers, the major players remained unchanged for

Table 5.1 Notes

[1]On 19 June 2000, Pfizer merged with Warner-Lambert.

[2]Formed 27 December 2000 by merger of GlaxoWellcome, plc, and SmithKline Beecham plc. GlaxoWellcome was formed by a 1995 merger of two U.K. companies. SmithKline Beecham was the result of a 1989 merger between U.S.-based SmithKline and U.K.-based Beecham.

[3]During World War I the U.S. operations of the German company Merck (founded in the 17th century and today known as Merck KGaA) became independent. Merged with Sharp & Dohme in 1953.

[4]Formed by 6 April 1999 merger of Astra AB (Sweden) and Zeneca plc (U.K.), which had been formed in 1993 from drug-related business of Imperial Chemicals Industries plc.

[5]Formed by 4 October 1989 merger of Bristol-Myers and Squibb Corp.

[6]Formed in late 1996 by the merger of Sandoz AG and Ciba-Geigy AG, reuniting three Basel-based firms. The name means "new arts." Ciba and Geigy merged in 1970, and in 1994 bought just under half of the U.S. biotech Chiron Corp., a joint venture partner since 1986. (Also see note 10.)

[7]Formed by December 1999 merger of Hoechst AG (Germany) and Rhône-Poulenc, S.A. (France). See *aventis.com* for details of the subsequent restructuring. Hoechst AG had been the ultimate acquirer, sometimes after joint ventures, of several U.S. firms, including Marion Laboratories, and the drug business of Dow Chemical Co. Rhône-Poulenc merged its drug business with U.S.-based Rorer Group, Inc., in 1990, taking majority control; in 1997 minority holders were bought out.

[8]Successor, after the 31 March 2000 purchase of Monsanto Co. (U.S.), to Pharmacia & Upjohn, which had been formed by the 2 November 1995 merger of Pharmacia AB (Sweden) and Upjohn Co. (U.S.). Pharmacia was created by the 1993 merger of Kabi Pharmacia and Carlo Erba. Monsanto, then primarily a chemical company, acquired the drugmaker G. D. Searle & Co. in 1985.

[9]In early 2001 Abbott agreed to buy Knoll, BASF A.G.'s pharmaceutical business, part of which BASF had acquired in 1995 from Boots Co plc, a U.K. retailer. Knoll is included in determining Abbott's global share.

[10]In early May 2001, Novartis purchased 20% of Roche. In 1990 Roche purchased a majority position in Genentech (U.S.), and on 30 June 1999 merged it into a subsidiary. Subsequent public offerings of Genentech [DNA] mean that about 40% trades publicly. Roche acquired Syntex Corp (U.S.) in 1995.

[11]During World War I the U.S. assets of Bayer were seized by the U.S. government and sold to Sterling Drug, which ultimately became part of SmithKline Beecham. Bayer regained the U.S. rights to its name in 1994.

Sources: Compiled by the author from various public sources, except that market shares are as estimated by IMS Health Global Services.

years. Now, new players and many disciplines are working to uncover the mechanisms by which diseases and our bodies function and interact.

Biotechnology companies have proven very good at basic research, and this has caused pharmaceutical firms to re-evaluate how they conduct research, including more alliances and more focus on biotechnology. As scientists observe life from new chemical and physical viewpoints, the ability to represent, process, and organize the mass of data accumulated becomes especially important. High-level IT skills, accompanied by large investments in software and hardware systems, are needed to take advantage of the opportunities this implies. No single company, even among the new mega-companies, is large enough to cover all the areas of expertise and therapeutic interest. Thus, firms have had to form strategic alliances to learn or access new technologies and capture new markets. A stand-alone company has a lot to lose if it fails to keep up.

Box 5.1

TYPES OF PHARMACEUTICAL PRODUCTS

Ethical drugs are biological and medicinal chemicals advertised and promoted primarily to the medical, pharmacy, and allied professions. They include products available only by prescription, as well as some over-the-counter (OTC) drugs in certain countries. (A drug that requires a prescription in one country may not in another. Some drugs available OTC also come in dosages or formulations that require a prescription—for example, Tylenol with codeine.)

Although "prescription drug" is not synonymous with "ethical drug," it is common to see the terms used interchangeably even by industry analysts because historically all prescription drugs were ethical drugs. This is changing (see "Prescription drugs," below). An ethical drug can be either branded or generic (see "Generic drugs," below).

Generic drugs are drugs sold by their chemical name rather than by a brand name. When introduced, a drug inevitably is given a brand name by its producer to aid in promoting it. After the patent expires, other firms can get approval to market the drug, which generally is done under its chemical name. A prescription may or may not be required.

Over-the-counter (OTC) drugs mostly are remedies for common ailments (such as upset stomachs and headaches) and palliatives for the symptoms of allergies and illnesses (such as colds and flu). They generally are promoted directly to consumers by brand names or (to the price conscious) as house brands or unbranded copies with active ingredients similar to branded drugs. As the designation OTC makes explicit, they do not require a prescription, although many began as prescription drugs (such as ibuprofen, now sold by its original brand name Motrin and generically).

Prescription drugs require a doctor to prescribe them. However, some are being advertised directly to consumers in the United States to encourage potential users to "Ask your doctor." The Internet also has spawned increased awareness (if not understanding) of specific drugs. The change in the balance between doctor and patient resulting from this customer use of IT is significant but beyond the scope of this book.

The earlier stability in industry participants reflected entry barriers that still exist. Principal of these are the costs and complexities of bringing a drug to market, starting with R&D and continuing on through expensive clinical trials. It remains difficult and costly for a new company to acquire the needed combination of skills to do this. Marketing also is important, because even most patented drugs have competitors for their indicated uses.

The challenge is how fast and effectively a firm can move to foster both technological innovation and cost containment. Normal business risk is amplified by political and budgetary considerations, as companies cannot be certain anyone actually will pay the full cost of new drug development and expensive R&D technologies (although they can be certain a drug's users will be happy to have someone else pay).

There also is the impact of increased international coordination among regulators. In 1990 the International Conference on Harmonization of Technical Requirements for Registration of Pharmaceuticals for Human Use (ICH) was first held. Its aim has been to harmonize clinical trials in order to exchange data internationally and introduce drugs into various markets more quickly. Many large international drugs firms will benefit from this, as it reduces the cost of introducing drugs to new markets while helping to expand markets and speed cash-flow receipts.

Other significant characteristics of the market for pharmaceuticals are summarized in box 5.2.

Box 5.2
CHARACTERISTICS OF THE MARKET FOR PHARMACEUTICALS

Once a drug is on the market, the cost of manufacturing, marketing, and distribution is relatively small. Too often industry critics and politicians look only at the marginal cost of production and marketing, and ignore the much higher average cost (which includes research, development, testing, three phases of clinical trials, the approval process, and monitoring after sales begin).

The market is highly segmented, both domestically and internationally, and price discrimination between and within national markets is common. Research studies cannot even agree on a common measure for the wholesale price because hospitals and large chains (such as Wal-Mart) buy on a different basis than the local druggist. Indeed, no measure captures the actual transaction prices including discounts and rebates).

For all but the most simple ailments, a doctor must prescribe the drug because consumers are, with good reason, assumed by the legal and medical systems to be incapable of choosing the appropriate drug and dosage or of evaluating the interactions with other medicines.

Governments, HMOs, and other managed-care plans can negotiate substantial discounts because they control the prescription decisions made by participating physicians and because they buy in large quantities. They are highly price sensitive, and this means drug prices are substantially determined by purchaser demand elasticity.

Regulatory approval does not mean a new drug is better than an old one, only that it is safe and therapeutically effective. This has pressured companies to demonstrate to patients and payers that a drug is effective as regards both cost and quality of life.

There are many drug classes for which only a few products exist. Reasons for this include limited understanding of possible cures (for example, Alzheimer's, disease), the disease being new (AIDS), and there being only a small number of patients (many examples).

The Drug Pipeline

The drug discovery and approval process is very lengthy, leading to its being termed a pipeline—albeit one that discards much of what enters it. Governments support pharmaceutical R&D, especially in the United States, but the industry's economics ultimately are driven by its drug pipeline. It is profit from the drugs that have emerged successfully into the market that drives and supports the flow of new drugs into and through the pipeline.

Chemists and biologists used to decide which drugs to pursue, but R&D now is more systematic and is a collective company decision, because it can involve expenditures of $350 million to $500 million or more prior to market launch. Key factors in the process are the expected costs and returns, the behavior of competitors, potential liability from side effects, and possible government policy changes.

Just how unrewarding even massive R&D efforts can be is illustrated by Bristol-Myers Squibb. The company is reported to have spent $11 billion on R&D during 1993–2000 without a single "blockbuster" drug (currently, one with sales of over $1 billion a year). The two "most promising products" are variations of a diabetes drug that went off-patent in September 2000 and was first developed before World War II (*Wall Street Journal*, 21 May 2001, p. 1).

New therapeutic products fall into four broad categories (see box 5.3).

From the viewpoint of major pharmaceutical firms, new chemical entities (NCEs) are the most important source of the innovative drugs that drive industry success. Because finding and developing NCEs is a risky and very

---

Box 5.3
CATEGORIES OF THERAPEUTIC PRODUCTS

There are four broad categories of therapeutic products.

1. New chemical entities (NCEs), new therapeutic entities (NTEs), and new therapeutic molecular compounds never before used or tested in humans.
2. Drug delivery mechanisms that are new approaches to delivering therapeutic agents at the desired dose to the desired part of the body.
3. Improved chemical entities (ICE), which are new combinations, formulations, dosing forms, or dosing strengths of existing compounds that must be tested again in humans before market introduction.
4. Generic products that are copies of drugs not protected by patents or other exclusive marketing rights, but that still require some testing to prove they are equivalent to the existing drug and that are subject (in the United States) to Food and Drug Administration (FDA) approval based on best-practice ethical drug manufacturing standards, as well as periodic inspections and certification by the FDA.

expensive process, understanding a company's R&D and drug pipeline process is critical to understanding its strategy and competitiveness. According to Merck, drug discovery statistics indicate that only about 1 in 60,000 compounds synthesized by laboratories can be regarded as "highly successful." (The ratio of drugs that make it to market is higher: 1 in 10,000 is a still widely cited figure from the early 1990s. But making it to market does not mean a drug is successful, or even profitable.)

It thus is very important to stop the R&D process whenever the firm recognizes that success is not likely. For this reason, reviews (called "stage reviews" in the industry) during drug R&D are common as the drug passes (or does not pass) critical milestones. Past experiences in finding, developing, manufacturing, managing approvals, and marketing can provide important guidance in evaluating a drug's prospects relative to the cost of remaining stages.

By refining a drug, making it an improved chemical entity (ICE), patent protection or marketing advantage can be extended. An example is the complexity of manufacturing single-isomer (right-handed and left-handed) drugs that have been created through molecular modeling. Some of these production processes are new and can be patented. In addition, they often require several steps in different manufacturing facilities because of the equipment or special processes involved. This complexity limits potential competitors.

Through the Pipeline

NCEs are discovered through screening existing compounds or designing new molecules. Once synthesized, they go through a rigorous testing process. Their pharmacological activity, therapeutic promise, and toxicity are tested using isolated cell cultures and animals, as well as computer models. A promising NCE is then modified to optimize its pharmacological activity with fewer undesirable biological properties.

Once preclinical studies are completed and the NCE has been proven safe on animals, the drug sponsor applies for investigational new drug (IND) status. If it receives approval, phase I clinical trials are started to establish the tolerance of healthy human subjects at different doses and to study the effects on humans of anticipated dosage levels. The firm also studies the NCE's absorption, distribution, metabolism, and excretion patterns. This stage requires careful supervision, as it is not yet certain if the drug is safe for humans.

If phase I results are favorable, phase II is authorized. A relatively small number of patients participate in controlled trials to establish the compound's potential usefulness and short-term risks. Depending on these results, phase III trials are approved. The firm gathers precise information on the drug's effectiveness for specific indications and to determine whether it produces a broader range of adverse effects than those exhibited in the smaller phase I and II trials. Phase III can involve several hundred to several thousand subjects, and is extremely expensive. Reviews occur before and during each phase, and drug development may be terminated at any point if the risk of failure and the added cost needed to prove effectiveness outweigh the probability of success.

There is a data and safety monitoring board in the United States under the Food and Drug Administration (FDA). This group of experts in given therapeutic areas has access to "unblinded data" throughout the conduct of a trial, but does not let anyone else know what the data show until it is necessary. For example, the board will not divulge efficacy data unless a point is reached where it seems appropriate to recommend stopping the trial because the drug's basic efficacy has been either accepted or rejected. The FDA usually insists on the drug proving its efficacy with respect to ameliorating a disease before giving approval to sell it.

If clinical trials are successful, the sponsor seeks FDA marketing approval by submitting a new drug application (NDA). If approved, the drug can be marketed immediately, although the FDA often requires some amendments before marketing can proceed. The amendments are based on recommendations from the FDA's outside advisory panels. These include such things as what potential side effects should be explained to the patient and other information that must be given to doctors regarding how to prescribe the drug.

A drug's manufacturing process must meet stringent best-practice standards. Scaling up from making a drug in the research phase to producing it in large quantities is difficult. In the lab, processing is done in small batches. In commercial production, significantly greater quantities are being produced, so ingredients generally go into a flow process that produces output continuously. (These are still batches in the sense that after the desired quantity is produced, the run stops, the equipment is cleaned, and a different drug is made.) Variations from the mean in a dose's chemical make-up must be very small (the FDA constant-dosage requirement). Such uniformity of output is difficult in continuous processing because many parameters and conditions have to be kept constant. This requires a good understanding of optimizing the chemical process and maintaining safeguards against abnormal conditions. Thus, experience often helps achieve purer output in the intermediate processes, and this better output reduces problems in later processes (see box 5.4).

U.S. regulations also require phase IV trials, where manufacturers selling drugs must periodically notify the FDA about the performance of their products. This postmarketing surveillance is designed to detect uncommon, yet serious, adverse reactions that typically are not revealed during premarket testing. It is especially important when phase III trials are completed under the smaller-sample, fast-track reviews that apply to drugs treating diseases with a small number of potential patients or other special considerations. These additional studies and data-gathering usually include use by children and by those taking multiple drugs, where potential interactions can be important.

Box 5.4
PROCESS R&D

Drug production is a process, an important distinction from industries where output is assembled (such as automobiles and electronics). For process industries, the knowledge required for innovation tends to be more specialized because one must understand both complex molecular interactions and the physics of the material being continually processed. However, less coordination in production is required due to its flow from one step (process) to another.

Finding ways to improve manufacturing in chemical pharmaceuticals involves what is called process R&D, which involves three stages.

1. Process research, where basic process chemistry and possible synthesis are explored and chosen.
2. Pilot development, where the process is run and refined in an intermediate-scale pilot plant
3. Technology transfer and start-up, where the process is run at a commercial manufacturing site.

Computer simulations are used more extensively in drugs made by chemical synthesis than for biotech-based drugs. This reflects the fact that the scientific base of chemistry is more mature than that of biotechnology. In chemistry, many scientific laws are available for such process variables as pressure, volume, and temperature. This means computer models can do simulations to predict cost, throughput, and yield.

By contrast, biotechnology has many aspects that are more art than science. This is particularly true for large-scale biotechnology processes. Simulation is thus less reliably extrapolated to commercial production in biotechnology. An additional factor is the importance of purification after large-scale production in bioreactors. Contamination is fatal, so extracting and purifying a small amount of the desired materials from a large amount of broth is critical. This is done using filters, chromatography, and other methods specific to organisms. At the stage of extraction and purification, commercial application is sometimes found to be impossible, even though the scale-up is otherwise successful.

Other Aspects

Among the things that make clinical trials and data gathering complex and expensive are patent issues, fast-track reviews, and quality-of-life issues. All put a premium on a firm's ability to manage its pipeline efficiently, including creating and using large patient and treatment databases.

Because drug development costs are so high relative to production costs, patent protection is a critical aspect of a company's strategy. Under U.S. law, a patent application must be filed within one year of developing the idea, or else it enters the public domain. Therefore, filing usually is done early in the development cycle or prior to the filing of the NDA. Because filing begins a patent's life, shortening a drug's approval period extends its effective revenue life under patent protection. This makes efficient management of clinical trials and the drug-approval process a very important strategic variable.

Companies are constantly pressuring the authorities to reduce NDA review times. As a consequence, the FDA introduced an accelerated approval process for new drugs in oncology, HIV (AIDS), and other life-threatening illnesses. A feature of these fast-track reviews is the use of surrogate end points, or proxies for clinical end points that are measured by laboratory values but lack supporting clinical data on actual results. Such accelerated approval speeds new drugs to market, thus providing positive cash flow. However, it does not generate the clinical values that insurers and managed-care organizations demand. To address this situation, drug firms have increased the complexity of the analyses during clinical trials. This responds to the need to include an analysis of cost-effectiveness in the evaluation of new drugs and to integrate such analysis into the clinical trials. Continued use of an existing drug or therapy also is assessed.

Governments and other payers are demanding data on cost-effectiveness in terms of "outcome," which involves not just basic efficacy but also the quality of life during and after treatment. In response, pharmaceutical companies have sought to show how their drugs will, for example, help patients go back to work sooner. Trying to capture quality-of-life measures, such as how patients perceive their lives while using the new drug, is not easy because there are no consistently applicable, let alone universal, measures. Firms must vary their analysis by country, as measures of effectiveness shift according to clinical practice, accessibility to doctors, and what different cultures value as important. The components measured depend largely on the objectives of each researcher, but some companies are trying to introduce more systematic measures. No matter what components are chosen, capturing, storing, and using the data requires sophisticated software and database management techniques that must be correlated with various families of molecules.

Getting outcome data adds to the cost and complexity of clinical trials, but the underlying reason for seeking it reflects recognition of an awareness of the importance of having relevant metrics when doing cost-benefit analysis.

Biotechnology

All scientific frontiers affect pharmaceutical companies. No company can be an expert on everything, so what technology to develop in-house and what to license or subcontract are important strategic issues. Pharmaceutical companies were skeptical at first about developments at small biotech firms. Now, the biotechs are providing promising areas of drug research and potential products, as well as new techniques in basic research and fermentation, to the established drug makers. Typically these are contract research projects or joint ventures, with the drug companies providing capital and other expertise.

Although many biotech companies are developing new drugs more quickly than established firms, they often have difficulty managing the clinical trials and the approval process. This is an area where large firms have considerable experience and skill, including sophisticated software for tracking the large databases and handling the computerized application procedure. In addition, biotechnology demands skills in large-scale commercial production that small firms may not possess. Thus, close association with a larger firm is logical and efficient, and more alliances are probable. Finally, there is need to track phase IV data.

Working against this is outsourcing to organizations that specialize in managing clinical trials, and then contracting production to another specialized firm. Variations of this model have worked in simple assembly industries, especially apparel and consumer electronics. How well it will work in pharmaceuticals is less clear, and so far seems unlikely to replace the advantages and expertise of the large drug firms.

Another important factor encouraging specialization within a network of companies is the industry's heavy use of information technology, although specialization in and of itself results in at best a Level 2 IT strategy because it limits the areas in which proprietary systems can add value and create barriers. At the same time, specialization can focus Level 3 strategies on areas where the firm has more critical advantages, or may enable Level 3 strategies when a firm can influence the standard being used by the network. An example of the latter is Merck's influence on the medical lexicon and the automated drug approval application process.

Still, the trend toward greater use of web-based technology in R&D and other operations may change our notion of a firm and its boundaries, as firms may eventually be characterized by their knowledge-creating capabilities. In any case, having more ways to communicate with other companies makes frequent communication with greater nuance possible, and will at the least support more strategic alliances.

Idea Creation and Information Sharing

A science-based industry generally is driven by knowledge creation, and that is dependent on human resources. This means new drug development depends more on the nature and ease of information exchange between individuals than on asset ownership, especially when the relevant knowledge is increasing rapidly and becoming more diverse. Scientists who move across disciplines carry concepts and tools with them, cross-fertilizing the various fields of science. Thus, creating access and information-sharing mechanisms so that the complementary capabilities of different groups can be exchanged and used efficiently is part of a successful strategy in knowledge-based industries. This includes computational expertise.

There is evidence that when innovation is dependent on trial and error, it is done best when many players can try different approaches, are held responsible for the projects they choose, and can communicate. If the large drug companies successfully form principal-agent relationships with biotech companies doing advanced research in particular areas, there may be major breakthrough opportunities without drug companies having to do such trial and error.

In general, significant input in the design and running of phase I and II trials must come from the bench scientists who built the molecule. However, classical pharmacology models often are irrelevant to biotech-based drugs. Clinical trials for biotech drugs lack tested models because of limited experience, so in-house communication among those involved in drug discovery, preclinical trials, and clinical trials is necessary, especially due to the increased use of transgenic animals bred to examine inherited diseases. This is because, although some proteins express their activities across other species, others are more species-specific. Animal trial results thus are not necessarily predictive for humans. Particularly difficult problems are those related to toxicology, as some animals develop neutralizing antibodies.

"Rational" Drug Design

Drug design (molecular modeling) has relied on theoretical chemistry and experimental data, which are used either to analyze molecules and molecular systems or to predict molecular and biological properties. During the last third of the 20th century, a range of computerized techniques were developed to implement both of these approaches.

Drug discovery historically consisted of taking a lead structure (molecule) and developing a chemical program to find analog molecules exhibiting the desired biological properties. In the 1970s and 1980s, discovery thus was grounded in organic chemistry. Initial lead compounds often have been found by chance or random screening, and the process has involved trial-and-error cycles developed by medicinal chemists using intuition to select a candidate analog for further development.

This method now is supplemented by structure-based drug design that tries to use the molecular targets involved in a medical condition. The underlying principle is that a molecule's biological properties are related to its structure. This reflects the better understanding of biochemistry that has developed beginning in the 1970s.

Rational drug design provides customized drugs, targeted specifically to activate or inactivate particular physiological mechanisms. That is, one is working from demand rather than trying to find a use for some new molecule. This technique is most useful in therapeutic areas where the starting point is a molecular target in the body. For example, histamines were among the first areas where rational design was applied, because the underlying mechanisms were understood very early.

This jump in research capability and analysis has depended on computer software and hardware becoming more powerful and less costly. Many scientists now access computational techniques that are easier to use than mechanical models. Three-dimensional graphics particularly suit the needs of a multidisciplinary team because each participant has different chemical intuition.

Universities, research institutes, and commercial laboratories have developed packages for molecular modeling. However, no one system meets all the modeler's needs, so those who want to take advantage of this technology must develop their own software. The better that firms can select systems, develop their capabilities, and manage their use, the better they will be in drug development and in managing other aspects of their drug pipeline.

Rational design has opened a wide range of new research options based on a firm's understanding of biochemical mechanisms. This means tremendous opportunities to enter new therapeutic areas. However, rational design is very expensive, contributing to the increased cost of new drugs through higher R&D and systems-support spending, so it has raised entry costs and the minimum effective size of pharmaceutical firms. It favors firms with a sequence of cash-generating drugs and broader product lines, able to spread the costs of equipment over many projects and to transfer knowledge across therapeutic areas. A similar analysis applies to major drug companies' use of other new technologies to discover and develop drugs systematically, such as computational biology, combinatorial chemistry, robotic high-throughput screening, advances in medical genetics, and bio-informatics.

The Industry in the United States

Widespread dissatisfaction notwithstanding, the trend in the United States is toward managed care, including HMOs, with closely controlled costs. This means physicians are losing some autonomy in drug selection. The market share of generic drugs increased from 15% to over 41% between 1983 and 1996. This forced branded ethical drug producers to communicate more effectively with managed-care organizations and to demonstrate the greater efficacy of their products compared to generic versions.

Acquisition of pharmacy benefit managers (PBMs; see box 5.5) by pharmaceutical companies was an important development in this regard. As of 1993 the five largest PBMs controlled 80% of a PBM market that covers about 100 million people. Many physicians have to prescribe drugs listed in a managed-care organization's formulary, and PBMs suggest lower-cost alternatives for a given therapeutic benefit to save money. As PBMs and mail-order companies have expanded, local pharmacies have lost the data

---

Box 5.5
PHARMACY BENEFIT MANAGERS (PBM)

PBMs, of which Merck's subsidiary Merck-Medco is the largest, help their plan members (health benefit organizations, corporations, etc.) manage and control the cost of drugs for their members (patients, employees). They do this in several ways.

They provide health management programs that assist payers such as insurance companies and providers such as hospitals, as well as patients, to manage the drug costs related to various diseases, especially diseases that are high-risk and high-cost. Thus, they educate doctors and patients about lower-cost generics.

They electronically review millions of patient prescriptions. This review not only looks for generic alternatives but also is keyed to avoid prescriptions that might cause adverse side effects for particular patients.

In addition, they provide on-line or mail-order pharmacy services to their members' members. By buying and processing on a large scale, they can substantially reduce costs (and pass some of this on in the form of lower prices).

---

necessary to examine various drug interactions that can be important in phase IV clinical trials or in protecting against large lawsuits.

The Industry in Japan

Japanese are the largest per-capita users of prescription drugs in the world. However, this reflects government policies more than drug efficacy. Historically, the industry has not been particularly innovative—IMS Health Global Services, a consultancy, reports that only 2 of the 15 fastest-growing products globally in 2001 originated in Japan. Companies are much smaller than the leading global firms, and also than the large Japanese chemical and food producers that began to move into pharmaceuticals during the 1990s. The market is highly fragmented. Of the roughly 1000 drug companies, only some 200 have significant revenues from ethical drugs, and among these, several purchase in bulk from contract manufacturers. These companies are thus packagers that do not discover or develop drugs. Table 5.2 lists the five largest firms that develop ethical drugs.

Table 5.2 Five Largest Japanese Ethical Drug Makers, Ranked by 2000 Revenue

---

Takeda Yakuhin Kogyo (Takeda Chemical Industries Ltd.) (4502)

Sankyo Co. Ltd. (4501)

Yamanouchi Seiyaku (Yamanouchi Pharmaceutical Co. Ltd.) (4503)

Daiichi Seiyaku (Daiichi Pharmaceutical Co.) (4505)

Eisai Co. Ltd. (4523)

Note: Tokyo Stock Exchange codes are in parentheses.

Global technical trends are reinforced in Japan by significant changes in the domestic economy and the regulatory environment. Demographics argue for rising medical and drug costs, both in total and per capita. Japan's population is growing older faster than any other country's: between 1970 and 1998 the percentage of Japanese over 65 jumped from 7.1% to 16.2%; it is projected to rise to over 25% by 2025 and to over 32% by 2050. Medical costs in 1997 were 6.5% of national income—some ¥25.3 trillion. This is projected to increase to 9% of national income by 2010 and 13% by 2025. Thus the Ministry of Health, Labor, and Welfare (successor to the Ministry of Health and Welfare [MHW]) is under pressure to control National Health Plan (NHP) costs.

Because Japan's NHP pays for virtually all pharmaceuticals sold in Japan, trends affecting drug reimbursement have a substantial impact on the country's ethical drug producers. To limit the rising fiscal burden of health care, the government acted to limit drug costs by cutting the prices it will pay for a drug by 4% to 10% each year beginning in 1990. This has contributed to poor revenue growth for Japanese firms, and thus their declining share of the global drug market.

Lack of Innovation

MHW historically gave weak incentives to produce truly innovative drugs, as its main task has been to provide and ensure good health-care services to all Japanese, regardless of their ability to pay. The system in place in the 1990s was criticized for excessive drug prescription, so a principal MHW objective became a more efficient distribution of medical services (such as using regional or teaching hospitals for expensive procedures) and fewer drugs. Because drugs are just one way to improve health, coordinated price adjustments for health care are necessary, such as the payment for doctor service versus payment for drugs. This has led to more centralized decision-making by the ministry.

Doctors benefit financially from writing a prescription in Japan because many run clinics that also sell drugs. Because the old pricing scheme allowed higher prices for "new" drugs, doctors preferred to prescribe them. The drug companies routinely turned out "new" drugs that may have had weak therapeutic value and interactions with other medicines that were not clear. It is possible that existing drugs, proven safe and effective over a long period, have been forced out by the reimbursement scheme.

Due to such regulatory lapses, the public now is pushing for more rigorous scientific analysis and greater accountability.

Cost Controls

In 1996 MHW began to address the issue of drug companies introducing "new" products to circumvent cost-containment efforts. Official drug prices have been eliminated. In their place the ministry introduced a reference-price system that reflects the market price for all drugs in a therapeutic category. The plan pays on the basis of the reference price. If patients pay more for any reason, they have to bear the difference. Truly innovative drugs still enjoy higher prices, but prices of new drugs that are not innovative are curbed.

Drugs accounted for about 28% of total health-care costs in fiscal 1995, but only 20% in fiscal 1999. The Ministry of Finance has budgeted for no increases through 2001, resulting in the government's increasing patient copayments and fees, as well as further drug reference-price reductions and separate copayments for drugs.

Other Reforms

To meet the requirements of increased international coordination among regulators, firms need to reassess how they manage clinical trials in Japan. Japan's past approach to treating certain diseases has been different than in the United States and Europe because diseases affecting its population have a different profile. For example, due to factors such as different diet, Japanese have fewer cases of heart disease compared to the United States, but a higher incidence of cancer. Further, among cancer patients, the profile is different.

In addition, clinical practices vary, and often are structured or adapted to suit the dominant drug available to treat a given condition. Therefore, the data that companies gather in other countries may not be helpful in assessing a drug's effectiveness in Japan, and conversely. Companies have to reassess data when feedback from doctors suggests that further investigation is required.

Japan made good post-marketing surveillance practice a legal obligation for pharmaceuticals in 1993. This reflects the government's more aggressive enforcement of regulations requiring information on the side-effects experienced by all patients. The elderly are more likely to take multiple medicines and to experience complications, so an aging population is forcing firms to gather data on complex interactions that are not always available during clinical trials. The trials cannot cover long-term effects, nor can they test groups taking all potential drug combinations. Therefore feedback from doctors who administer drugs to seniors after their commercial introduction has become more important.

Industry Response

Japanese drug companies now are subject to price and therapeutic efficacy pressures similar to their US and European counterparts, and so have a similar need to gather data on therapeutic effects in order to get better prices. This puts pressure on the firms to place more relative focus on R&D (especially on drugs related to aging), drug development for the global market, and care in gathering information on clinical trials and side effects. Given these trends, firm strategies and related IT strategies are being driven by industry economics determined by drugs' very lengthy R&D process, combined with cost-containment policies in global markets. Japanese drug companies that have good R&D and data-gathering capabilities can benefit, while those that do not, will suffer from increased foreign competition and be shaken out.

TAKEDA

Takeda Yakuhin Kogyo (Takeda Chemical Industries Ltd.) is Japan's largest pharmaceutical company, although globally it ranked only 16th in terms of 2000 sales. In fiscal 2000, drug sales of ¥680 billion (out of total revenue of ¥923 billion) provided virtually all of operating profit. This compares to 1995 numbers of ¥361 billion in drug sales and ¥772 billion in total revenue.

Historically, it has been a diversified company. Takeda reorganized its product divisions into "companies" in the mid-1990s, each with its own president in charge of that company's operations. At the end of 1999 these divisions were consumer health care, vitamins and food, chemical products, agro-business, and life environment. They replaced divisions established in 1960: pharmaceuticals (68% of fiscal 1991 revenue, including 2% from veterinary drugs), pharmaceutical sales, food, chemical products, and an overseas division.

Although the "companies" remain organizational functions within Takeda, they operate separately. In fact, the vitamin company was sold to BASF, a German chemical group, in 2000. The corporation's president directly manages the ethical drug business, indicating its strategic importance, while the other businesses have become semi-autonomous profit centers.

International presence has been increased by building on joint ventures established in France and Germany in the late 1970s, plus foreign subsidiaries. Takeda also has expanded its U.S.-based R&D partnership with Abbott Laboratories, begun in the 1980s, and its Abbott joint venture formed in 1985, TAP Pharmaceuticals, which markets drugs in the United States. Sales outside of Japan rose from ¥135 billion in 1998 (16% of sales) to ¥215 billion (23%) in 2000.

Since the early 1990s Takeda has focused primarily on ethical drugs. This has required it to increase the role of basic research, which it first undertook in 1988 when it established a research laboratory at Tsukuba. Earlier, most of its drugs had been made under license from foreign companies. With the opening of the Japanese market, licensing became more difficult because foreign drugmakers could sell their drugs through their own operations.

Organizational Innovation and Strategy

In responding to the global industry's common problems, Takeda is moving away from typical Japanese management methods and is starting to emphasize globalization to spread R&D costs, individual creativity to stimulate new drug development, and the use of IT to handle expanded data management and R&D requirements. The company believes IT should be used to improve the quality of decisions by enhancing managers' experience and judgment—that is, to improve the firm's existing decision-making skills, which, after all, have produced reasonable success. Even though an important use of software is to facilitate better communication, Takeda still believes in face-to-face communication among managers in formulating strategies.

Takeda's president, Kunio Takeda, has introduced organizational changes in corporate governance and human-resource management that are very different from the past. In 1996 the company announced plans to reduce its 11,000 employees to 7500 by the year 2005 through attrition, and is introducing performance-based pay, especially in ethical drug R&D, where there has been intense competition for innovative researchers. Under this new pay system, raises depend heavily on individual performance. For middle managers and above, annual goals are set, and each manager is evaluated in absolute terms based on achieving those targets. If managers cannot achieve their objectives within four years, they have to leave the position.

Like its competitors, during the late 1990s Takeda became slimmer and flatter. Although done in reaction to competition, it was implemented with an eye to making each person's responsibilities clearer, rather than simply reducing the head count. Any flattening effects from increased IT use have been indirect.

Takeda also has instituted special rewards for discovering innovative drugs that generate significant sales. These can reach ¥50 million over five years and apply only to R&D employees as a reward for individual creativity. This is an exceptional bonus in any Japanese industry.

Another part of Takeda's strategy has been to transfer production of mature products in its pipeline to related companies while keeping the parent slim. It plays a wholesaler's role for these companies, and that accounts for 40% of its pharmaceutical sales. This approach is changing as Takeda shifts production facilities to foreign countries, such as the United States, in order to cut costs and create an operational hedge against exchange rate changes.

In general, Takeda's approach to software development and use stresses incremental improvements in its database to improve decision-making, and results that are closely aligned with its basic business procedures. EDP expenditures have averaged about 1% of sales.

IT Selection

Like most Japanese companies developing and selecting IT to implement business and organizational strategies, Takeda historically used outside vendors only rarely. However, it has not relied on a subsidiary specializing in software development, as many other large Japanese companies have.

Rather, it has used internal resources and its own IT group. To handle IT, as of the late 1990s Takeda had 116 people in information systems and 76 in user systems.

In the mid-1990s the IT group began to move away from using only customized software, and has increased its purchase and adaptation of packages for nonstrategic activities. The group explained that writing software had been part of its organizational learning, but the benefits from restructuring Takeda's IT systems now outweigh the organizational learning and accumulation of tacit knowledge that occur through creating all software in-house. This decision is understandable because the government's new regulatory and drug approval processes, combined with international harmonization of clinical trials under ICH, require types of information systems skills and knowledge that are much different from those used in Takeda's previous software development. Nevertheless, new IT, whether packaged or customized, must interface with the legacy system, so there remains substantial maintenance and interface development that requires the group's traditional skill sets in addition to forcing it to acquire new capabilities in software development and semi-customization.

The group's general criteria for choosing software reflect this transition. It tries to select the software that is a de facto standard and is used globally. Still, it must work on Takeda's existing hardware in Japan, which means the package must be capable of becoming part of an open system that promotes compatibility and communication between subsystems. System selection also is influenced by government regulations that apply to manufacturing, clinical trials, and payment. This is because IT systems have to provide sufficient information to meet regulatory standards. Takeda has not adopted any specialized stand-alone hardware to use a particular specialized software package. When the group needs a supercomputer, it rents time on one.

R&D requirements and Takeda's partnering agreements are another factor influencing selection. For example, Takeda has had a technological transfer agreement with GlaxoSmithKline (GSK) under which expertise in combinatorial chemistry is transferred to Takeda. This involves using computers and GSK's database. Researchers of the two companies visit one another to transfer the know-how associated with the technology. (The agreement originated with SmithKline Beecham before the merger forming GSK.)

IT Use

Takeda uses parts of SAP's R/3 (box 2.1), selecting only the pieces that it believes will address specific problems and that it can integrate with its total IT system. The database features particularly help Takeda to see relationships among data in order to make coordinated decisions. Takeda and several other Japanese pharmaceutical manufacturers are collaborating with SAP to develop IT packages that will be used specifically in Japan's pharmaceutical industry.

For communications among employees, the company uses an intranet in addition to e-mail. When certain data or information is relevant to a section, people within the section share that information. Such sharing is traditional in Japan but has been done face-to-face or through circulating memos via well-established but time-consuming routes. The willingness to use e-mail and the intranet substantially increases the speed with which this process can occur, leading to significant increases in office productivity. Still, Japanese face-to-face communication in making decisions remains essential. For example, R&D reviews usually are face-to-face.

By using servers for common projects and applications used by multiple groups or individuals, Takeda has avoided the excessive workloads that occur when personnel change or particular projects are on individual PCs.

To manage post-marketing surveillance of its drugs, in the mid-1990s Takeda organized DIONET (a pharmaceutical information system) to collect data about side effects and give feedback to users.

Takeda participates in a system linking Japanese pharmaceutical manufacturers and their wholesalers. Order entry and acknowledgment are processed on-line, substantially reducing paperwork and facilitating prompt delivery. However, because the two systems are accessible by all pharmaceutical companies and Takeda has not organized itself to take special advantage of them, the company is not a Level 3 IT user.

An important IT tool for Takeda is the information exchange between sales and manufacturing, called the "sales-manufacturing balance table." This report shows past monthly sales, past monthly production, planned monthly sales, planned monthly production, finished inventory, and intermediate goods inventory for each product. This provides a basis for daily production schedules, and the IT group creates them using artificial intelligence software. Then, based on this data, the group meets monthly with manufacturing to review the previous month and to set the general plan for subsequent production. The software helps the firm adjust production to accommodate volatility in schedules within a month, given changes in actual customer demand. The company analyzes volatility, using 10 days as a planning period.

Conclusion

Through a creative mix of customized, semi-customized, and packaged software, Takeda has created an IT system and organizational support for that system that have significantly improved its competitiveness in several important business areas. One aspect of this is the interactive linking of functions that previously were relatively separate: R&D, the drug approval process, manufacturing, marketing, sales, and after-sales service. Takeda's close association with large hospitals and clinics through DIONET provides such a function. This data gathering and control have established beneficial loops that are self-reinforcing and directly improve costs, quality, and competitive position. For example, better after-sales information builds a data-base that improves future drug design and speeds clinical trials and approv-als. It also directly shortens the time drugs spend in the drug pipeline, improves cash flow, and promotes better R&D, which then lead to better corporate performance.

All in all, Takeda is a successful Level 2 IT strategist. It has created com-petitive advantages that cannot be emulated easily, but it has not substan-tially altered the nature of the competitive playing field to its advantage even within the Japanese pharmaceutical industry.

MERCK

Merck & Co., one of the world's largest pharmaceutical companies, is very much involved in and responsive to the industry's competitive environ-ment. Its history goes back to the 19th century in the United States and to the 17th century in Germany. It thus has seen and managed many business and organizational changes, but has now come to focus almost exclusively on human health, in particular, branded ethical prescription drugs. This is because it has found this is its most profitable business. Also, given the many opportunities that exist, this activity will demand all its capital and energy for the foreseeable future.

Merck sees itself as a growth company with a target of 15% annual in-creases in earnings and revenue. Achieving this requires continual cash flow from existing drugs and a constant flow of new drugs coming through the pipeline. During 1995–99 Merck introduced 15 new drugs and vaccines, and these new products in 1999 represented over 28% of revenues. From the current pipeline, which typically has covered around 15 therapeutic categories, including vaccines, coverage will expand to between 20 and 25 categories by 2005. Because medicines representing about 30% of its drug revenues lose patent protection during 2000–02, it is obvious Merck must run hard just to stand still.

Structural Changes and Alliances

Merck once had a specialty chemical business and had diversified into animal health care. However, in 1995 Merck sold the specialty chemical business and in 1997 sold the crop protection business to Novartis. Also in 1997 it put animal health care into a 50–50 joint venture with Rhône-Poulenc. Called Merial, it is the world's largest company in animal health and poultry genetics. In 1998 Merck sold DuPont its 50% share of their joint-venture pharmaceutical company (formed in 1991) for $2.6 billion.

Like other pharmaceutical companies, Merck continues to sell a drug as long as possible after it is off patent. Because of brand awareness, better quality, and consistency of dosage, some demand for the branded product continues once its price is adjusted downward. However, there is a point at which producing the drug in competition with generic versions no longer justifies using valuable manufacturing capacity. This is especially true when the drug becomes available without a prescription.

The company established a joint venture with Johnson & Johnson in 1989 to market, distribute, and sell the OTC versions of Merck's prescription drugs in the United States and Europe. The manufacturing is done by several firms. In 1996 Merck made a similar agreement covering Japan with Chugai Pharmaceutical, which has significant market reach in OTC drugs.

Merck's clear strategic focus on new ethical drugs is underscored by the active formation of strategic alliances. Its work with Rhône-Poulenc can be seen as a way to improve Merck's competence in genetics. Given developments in biotechnology and the Human Genome Project, this is strategically important. Because biotech-related drugs often are species-specific, more knowledge about the genetic makeup of humans and animals can provide insights into the appropriate animals to use in preclinical trials, thereby increasing the reliability of extrapolation to humans.

Merck-Medco

Merck bought pharmacy benefit manager (PBM; see box 5.5) Medco Containment Services in November 1993 and Systemed, a smaller PBM, in 1996. Several other drug companies became involved with PBMs, but Merck is considered the most successful at integrating and utilizing its acquisition. (Eli Lilly in 1998 sold the PBM it had purchased in 1994.) Merck announced Medco's spin-off in January 2002.

Merck-Medco now serves as a principal distribution vehicle for Merck. In 2000 it represented about half of Merck's $40 billion in revenues, compared to 43% of $27 billion in 1998. It is explicit policy that Medco not favor Merck over other suppliers unless Medco's recommendation of a Merck product is legitimate. Still, Merck has increased its share of Medco's sales from 10% in 1993. Merck does not get any diagnosis information from Medco, part of an agreement Merck made with the industry at the time of the acquisition.

In response to government regulatory concerns and complaints from Merck competitors, Medco has its own IT systems and the interconnections are through firewalls designed to protect competitors' sales information. But the division and the parent share some technical standards, and they have kept the development of their systems parallel, so gradually they can erase the differences. Over time this should reduce costs and facilitate sharing noncompetitive data. For example, Medco will be able to provide information on patients using Merck drugs more efficiently.

This is a potentially important source of data because there is no standard on how patients records are kept in the United States. However, in combination with the medical and disease lexicon Merck has developed (discussed later), the company hopes to use Medco to get more detailed and consistent patient data on Merck products than it can get from the national prescription database maintained by the North American Supply Chain Project. Ultimately, what Merck would like to have is complete patient clinical records collected according to agreed standards, covering a 5- to 10-year period. Merck made some progress in this area in the last half of the 1990s, and this is where Medco could prove helpful going forward.

Merck is using a form of embedded software, in this case prescription data related to its drugs, to develop an interactive database that can affect all aspects of its business. That is, Merck and Medco have established an IT package keyed to a doctor's prescribing of each Merck drug that is being used by a Medco customer. This information is automatically recorded at the time of initial order, plus any refills. Merck uses the data for assessing the drug in a variety of ways, including effectiveness of R&D and marketing, and forecasting manufacturing levels.

Medco's mail-order and Internet businesses are powerful marketing tools. It can sell drugs at a lower price than other pharmacies. At the end of 1999, *merckmedco.com*, with 750,000 plan members, was the world's largest online pharmacy, and Merck sees it as the "Pharmacy of the Future." In 2000 it processed some 110,000 prescriptions per week, representing nearly $450 million in revenue for the year. OTC drugs are now being included in partnership with CVS. (CVS is the largest U.S. drugstore chain in terms of locations, although it operates in fewer states than Walgreen, which is the largest chain in terms of sales.) Through all its channels, in 2000 Medco reached 65 million people and handled 450 million prescriptions.

As the magazine *Datamation* noted in February 1997, Merck "mines its terabyte data warehouse to uncover hidden links between illnesses and known drug treatments, and to spot trends that help pinpoint which drugs are most effective for what types of patients." With the help of Medco Data, the organization that provides Medco with IT system support, Medco has designed a user-friendly system to conduct data-mining and querying of the 76 million patient and treatment records in its database.

Medco spent four years turning this huge database into one of the largest minable, massively parallel data warehouses anywhere, using an NCR Teradata 5100 database platform. Such data warehouses keep related bits of information in storage in ways that can be accessed at the same time—that is, in parallel rather than sequentially. This makes it easier to, for example, generate lists of patients taking certain drugs and the potential side effects associated with the drugs. In the process, Merck and its Medco subsidiary managed to clean out biases hidden in the data because of multiple sources (including different people, collecting at different times, for different purposes) and to standardized conditions. They also were able to enrich the database by integrating additional information on health trends and drug use. They then combine a sophisticated graphical user interface with data-analysis algorithms and database query languages (OLAP products and traditional SQL) to analyze and relate data among patients, drugs, and various therapeutic outcomes.

Linking its customers into its business strategy via IT as a way to change the competitive dynamics of the industry to its advantage is part of what makes Merck a Level 3 IT user. The company can offer personalized services, such as reminders to refill a prescription, at little additional cost to itself.

R&D Overview

Merck's R&D is done internationally. Each of its research centers is focused and typically reflects the local market's comparative strengths in R&D as well as the local therapeutic demand.

No discipline has as blurred a distinction between basic and applied research as biotechnology and pharmaceuticals. This is because applied research often contributes to basic research. Indeed, in molecular biology, science often follows technology. Nevertheless, as a general approach, Merck tries to focus on applied R&D. It relies mostly on universities and smaller biotech firms for the basic science. (Merck has done some basic research related to AIDS, and it was from this that it developed the protease inhibitors that are now a basic part of AIDS therapy.)

Its normal R&D approach is to gather information from published and ongoing research in various life sciences, and then to look for solutions. Any potential solution has to have a potential market that is big enough to justify the investment. If the compound has therapeutic potential, but not a large market, Merck usually seeks another organization to pursue it. Because it means they are unlikely to be competing head-on with major companies, a number of smaller companies are happy to pursue drugs with limited market potential.

As part of its R&D drug evaluation process, Merck also recognizes that even if it is the first to market, other firms may produce drugs in the same therapeutic area. The basic research is available to anyone tracking the basic science. If a later drug is superior in terms of efficacy and cost-effectiveness, it can dominate the market.

Merck's strategy is partly driven by cost-containment pressures in major markets: health-care providers analyze the cost-effectiveness of drugs, and ones that are cheaper and less troublesome to administer are preferred. (Long-term treatment costs depend on how easily patients can follow the prescription and how often nurses have to assist them. One example is Merck's reformulation of Fosamax so that it is taken weekly rather than daily.)

To respond to the challenges of cost containment and regulatory burden, Merck is using management techniques based on consensus decision-making among top functional managers. This is part of an industry trend toward greater parallel decision-making in R&D. (It has replaced sequential decision-making, where manager A must agree before asking B, and so on.) All elements of the firm evaluate a project simultaneously at each stage. This requires better communication support, using e-mail and groupware, combined with face-to-face communication. In this manner, Merck has significantly reduced coordination costs while centralizing and speeding the overall decision-making process.

Drug Development Issues

Besides efficacy, there are two important issues in drug development: bioavailability (the rate and extent to which a dose reaches its destination in the body) and safety.

Researchers use molecular modeling to design particular molecules meant to achieve a certain drug-receptor binding. At Merck, they then combine this information with the results of data-mining a library that represents information collected on various chemicals the company has discovered or knows about. The steadily growing library had about 1 million items in 1998. Each chemical is described, followed by information such as the results of any animal or clinical studies plus side effects. This gives Merck some idea what the new molecule might do, how safe it is, and what should be examined further.

Merck uses IT methods based on combinatorial chemistry. This has become popular at all major pharmaceutical companies because it speeds up the process of generating novel leads and optimizing previously known leads through a very large interactive database management system. Under this system, Merck's biologists develop a set of assays that conform to a particular standard from biological substitutes that they use to test the efficacy of a molecule with respect to a specific disease. Researchers can run a high volume of molecules and tests in this way. Because they have access to Merck's library of similar assays, which is kept in a standard way, they can do a lot of computer-based testing using algorithms that suggest the likely results before doing any animal testing. The underlying idea is that similarity in action often suggests similarity in mechanisms of action, mode of resistance, and molecular structure. To ensure consistency across tests, Merck's researchers have established repeatable procedures.

Merck's development of AIDS drugs involved 32 possible versions of the same chemical molecule. Without a computer's ability to visualize and display complex three-dimensional structures, it would have been extremely time-consuming and difficult, if not impossible, to analyze them.

Thus, the computer, the software, the organized databases, the data collection routines, and the established R&D procedures are highly complementary.

The R&D Process

The choice of what to develop and what not to pursue is important, and the ability to manage this process effectively can determine corporate success. For every candidate compound, the firm has to do an economic analysis.

This is why the manufacturing and marketing groups have members who join R&D personnel on initial assessment panels. Market potential matters. So, too, do the feasibility of scale-up and meeting FDA "best practice" standards in manufacturing.

If a compound looks promising, a contract is written with a development team. It covers who is involved, what resources are needed, and a timetable. During the project, regular reviews are held. These focus on the probability of success and the payoff from success. If it is clear after even just a month that the contract is not being met, there will be a more thorough review, and the contract is adjusted or the project is terminated. Merck sometimes selects difficult projects because it knows other companies face similar difficulties, and thus might be deterred.

Merck in some cases must consider manufacturing and testing complexity, so the review process takes these cost factors into account. Cost differences in testing come primarily from how difficult it is to prove effectiveness. It is relatively easy to show the effects of a drug for infectious diseases, but cancer and cardiovascular drugs require a long observation period and more patients. It is not unusual for such drug trials to involve 4000 to 5000 patients over five to six years. Such trials not only are lengthy and very costly, they necessitate tremendous data-gathering and data management capabilities.

In May 2001, Merck agreed to buy Rosetta Inpharmatics, a company founded in 1997 that uses computers and gene technology to identify compounds that might make worthwhile drugs, including distinguishing any possible toxic side effects. One of Rosetta's products is GEML (gene expression markup language), which provides a consistent format for DNA chip and gene-expression data analysis. This is an emerging engineering standard in the industry, and thus buying the company is very consistent with Merck's Level 3 IT strategy.

Clinical Trials

Merck is well known for its ability to design clinical trials that satisfy FDA requirements, and this has contributed to the relative efficiency and speed with which many of its new drugs have received FDA approval. The company believes that designing trials with good statistical power and managing the post-trial processing prior to submissions are important factors in this success. Before any trial, it develops a protocol that defines the variables to be measured and how it will proceed. The protocol covers what types of patients will be included, what dosage they will be given, how the controls will be managed, and the measurement criteria.

To improve the quality of the trial data, Merck has in the past supplied PCs to the investigators and had them input data directly. This speeded data entry and made investigators more aware of how to do it. But Merck found not all the data were consistent, and it had to do a lot of cross-checking. Thus, its current routine is to send Merck personnel with laptops into the field to enter the data directly from the patients' charts. This makes the Merck personnel sponsoring the trial responsible for gathering accurate data. The cost of correcting misentered data is quite high, and it compounds at each subsequent level of the approval process, so the company has found this to be a cost-effective procedure.

This approach has had an added benefit: it puts the trial's data collection on a real-time basis rather than the previous batch basis. The opportunity cost and revenue impact of faster study execution and higher-quality data are huge if they achieve faster FDA approval, and thus quicker revenues.

Managerial Decision Making

Merck has used real options analysis (explained in the Introduction) in its R&D decision-making since 1993. This is an investment decision process that, at the time of the study, was unique among the leading IT practitioners examined in this book, although the concept is related to Ito-Yokado's concern with lost sales opportunities. The company feels it is misleading to evaluate different drugs using the traditional method (comparing the net present values of discounted cash flows).

In relation to its use of options analysis, Merck has concluded that outsourcing IT may not be a reversible decision. This is because it may shift control over important information outside the company. If Merck does not control how that information is gathered and processed, or is not even aware of it, Merck's flexibility and responsiveness could be constrained, with adverse strategic consequences. Something analogous seems to have happened in late 2000 and early 2001 to some hi-tech companies that had outsourced their manufacturing supply and data management. Having lost direct control over the day-to-day flow of information, they were blindsided by the rapid slowdown in orders and resulting inventory build-up.

Total Cost Analysis

Total cost analysis (explained in the Introduction) can justify development of a customized IT subsystem, provided the proper strategic analysis, metrics, and decision-making criteria are in place. For example, in clinical trials the cost of gathering data directly is secondary compared to receiving FDA approval quickly.

This approach also has been applied to manufacturing and inventory. Because pharmacists may switch to different brands if a firm cannot fill an order quickly enough, Merck kept inventories at levels that enabled it to fill 98% of all orders. Drug companies generally produce enough supply for several weeks, then clean the plant to produce another drug. Combined with a policy of having full availability for all drugs, this builds inventory, and thus cost. Merck has moved away from this supply structure. Instead, it sets sales targets and then, if Merck does not have enough on hand to fill an order, it assesses whether a generic version is available or a competitor can easily supply a similar drug. Based on these data, Merck sets production and drug availability by region. This requires data from other drug companies, which is supplied by the North American Supply Chain Project, started in 1996–97. Each month, the project collects from, and supplies to, the major drug suppliers a standard set of data on physician prescriptions over the previous 24 months.

Setting production and drug availability requires sophisticated calculations for each drug, which Merck does using proprietary formulas. This order management system controls shipments to each pharmacy according to Merck's analysis of needs. The system provides better information regarding actual patient demand for prescriptions. (The data analyzed do not include any patient-specific identification, such as names. Patient-specific data are collected in a separate database to track potential side effects.)

The order system has been very successful, with an unforeseen benefit. Not only has it reduced the number of back orders and lowered inventories more than expected, it has actually increased availability beyond the 98% target. On investigation, field representatives learned that pharmacists had been switching to other providers without notifying Merck when Merck's drugs were not available. Now, better availability means Merck does not lose orders as often. It also has reduced inventory and wastage from drugs passing their discard dates because drugs are held in stock for shorter periods, and marketing forecasts are more accurate because they cover a shorter period.

Information Technology Organization

IT functions except for Medco are centralized under the CIO. At the same time, systems development units are aligned with each business unit and report to the head of the business unit in addition to the CIO. The principal units include R&D, manufacturing, and U.S. sales and marketing. Sales units are generally localized because health-care markets differ across countries due to local laws, regulations, and customs. Manufacturing can be more centralized, because the relevant information on chemical plants is mostly described by data related to their equipment.

IT personnel work with each business partner, as the units are termed, to help implement a functional strategy. To coordinate activities across functions, Merck has a worldwide business team composed of senior functional managers who analyze the market according to disease categories, such as cholesterol-lowering drugs. The teams each conduct reviews, including drug safety. Important information is reported to functional heads and the worldwide business team.

The overall IT centralization reflects the massive amounts and sensitive nature of the data. Although the power of the PC has risen substantially, the mainframe is the workhorse. This is especially true in manufacturing operations, where the mainframe's greater speed and capacity are needed. Supercomputer use is expected to continue indefinitely as a tool for Merck's basic research.

Given its extensive and diverse responsibilities, the IT operation is fairly large. In 1998 there were 750 people doing software development and 350 working on infrastructure and support. Merck does about 60% of its software development internally, purchasing the remainder from unrelated companies on a case-by-case basis. The group develops and maintains the core software supporting clinical trials, basic research, sales force automation, and data warehouse applications. It buys financial, human-resource, and materials resource planning software from outside.

IT Purpose

Merck believes the basic purpose of IT systems is to improve the existing decision-making skills that have been responsible for its success. That is, the systems should help to improve the quality of management decisions by enhancing the experience and judgment of managers. Therefore, although IT is used to facilitate better communication, Merck is a strong believer in face-to-face communication among managers when formulating strategies.

Merck consciously tries to create some barriers among non-R&D employees in order to limit the information flow to those with some need to know. Merck is reluctant, however, to create such barriers among R&D staff because they usually request information only when there is a reason, an impulse that can be important to their creative process. IT enlarges and extends researchers' knowledge domains, allowing them to share part of their chemical intuition, and this is essential in multidisciplinary medical research.

Merck does less job rotation than in the past because IT allows cross-divisional exchange of information electronically and there are more cross-functional committees. Further, by facilitating senior managers' access to information at all levels, the firm has decreased the number of middle managers it requires. Those remaining have more functional areas of responsibility, and thus need an expanded set of skills to do their jobs.

Merck is quite conscious of the relationship between power and information. This makes it alert for possible changes in authority and power among employees when introducing new IT tools. The basic approach of using IT to enhance and improve existing skills and procedures avoids many such organizational dilemmas. This is because people can see their greater effectiveness and the company's improved competitive situation through the greater use of IT.

IT Project Decision-making

Because IT pervades all aspects of Merck's business and operations, IT personnel are intimately involved in helping to control business processes from an organizational and operations standpoint. For example, Merck's CIO sits on several contract evaluation committees that involve marketing and manufacturing working together. IT project selection is subject to the same contract and review discipline used to develop drugs, reflecting the fact that an IT investment dollar means less money available for a new drug.

Merck's CIO during 1991–99, Dr. Charles Popper, saw his major task as putting the appropriate system in place for each situation. Project approval committees (PACs), which review and approve each IT project, are the keys to this process, so he made sure a senior manager was on every one. Getting the managers involved was a major management and strategic breakthrough for the IT group and Merck. PACs are separate from the IT management committees, which manage each project and are composed of personnel from the business unit involved and the IT group.

The first step is an analysis of the project's conceptual feasibility. Then the PAC assesses the project's magnitude in terms of cost and benefits, using monetary and quality measures. This detailed analysis has an allowance for error of ±25%. If the go-ahead is given, those who will work on the project sign a contract for it.

Each IT project has some metric that is identified and agreed to in advance as part of the contract. So the PAC can identify if the project is successful, the metric specifies what is supposed to change. Thus, the PAC tries to express quality in financial terms. The company has found that the quality of medical care a drug offers often can be identified using surveys of customer satisfaction. Drawing on this experience, user surveys also are used for assessing IT projects.

Each individual project is the budget responsibility of the unit utilizing the IT, and the CIO is responsible for managing the portfolio of IT projects as a whole in terms of risk and return. This provides a corporate overview of the firm's IT initiatives and resource commitment. To do this, a bubble matrix that categorizes projects into four types in terms of risk and benefit (or impact) is used. High-risk, high-benefit projects usually require new inventions or systems (that is, often are bleeding edge). Low-risk, high-benefit projects often are found through combining customized and packaged software that has the major bugs already sorted out. IT maintenance, including upgrading, is usually low-risk, low-impact (trailing edge). In an actual report, the bubbles indicate the relative cost of each project, so someone looking at the chart can quickly see the weighting of Merck's IT initiatives.

Merck considers it important to identify instruments to measure failures as well as successes as part of increasing the ratio of successes to failures. This type of planning in numerical terms also makes it possible to compare the desirability of multiple IT projects, taking into account each one's possible consequences from an organizational viewpoint. This requires an element of centralized managerial decision. The PACs make people aware of the externalities that IT creates across various functions. The system and data come full circle because each business function pays for its IT support, and so projects must justify their IT budgets.

As part of putting the appropriate system in place for each situation, in the late 1990s Dr. Popper oversaw a strategic plan for Merck's basic research operations. The IT staff asked the leadership of the laboratories, "Do you want the information technology to be leading edge, bleeding edge, or trailing edge?" and explained the difference. In basic research all said they would have to have bleeding edge. In this area, the firm needs every possible advance in IT that it can apply. On the other hand, when it comes to clinical trials, what is needed is something really good, but that will not fail. That means just behind the leading edge. In administrative and other systems, they want the oldest and most reliable stuff, something they would not even need to think about.

Implementing IT

Some organizations cannot take full advantage of new IT because it can introduce difficulties if it is not fully compatible with how people actually work. Merck addresses this problem by working with each business unit, pilot projects, and careful evaluation.

An example is Merck's worldwide introduction of a new ledger system. First, the IT group identified all the customers (users) for the system, then discussed their requirements of the proposed system. Based on this, it examined a number of packages and asked vendors to discuss and demonstrate their offerings. This approach measured candidates' functionality against user requirements to see which best fit identified user needs. The IT team also interviewed other clients of each vendor to understand the vendor's product implementation approach and possible pitfalls. Such a review can save money and organization time, as software is an "experience good" whose real value and shortcomings are made clear only after introduction.

All the functions and conditions for the vendor short list were tested in a conference room pilot environment prior to going live. Merck planned to first implement the new ledger outside the United States, so the team discussed the software with overseas affiliates and then piloted it in the United Kingdom before worldwide implementation.

This kind of thorough review, assessment, and implementation process is very important for Merck, as IT business development costs are rising faster than the company's overall costs—although IT infrastructure costs are rising only half that fast. Part of this situation is due to the improved cost performance of mainframes and other computers: as a result, many managers think mainframe time is costless. So one task of the CIO is to explain to users how much it really costs and have it included in each manager's budget. In the late 1990s, when the CIO helped the firm's head of human resources (HR) determine if it was cheaper and more efficient to outsource some HR functions, he made sure the HR group included relevant costs. A previous analysis had shown a saving of $1 million by doing it in-house, but ignored the cost of the mainframe and its supporting systems.

This also is true for telecom costs, which are rising in line with IT systems costs, though Merck may increase its telecom investments if it can determine how to control the security issues related to the Internet. Merck has limited Internet access because of the importance of securing R&D data.

Terminology Database

There needs to be consistency in the terms used to describe particular medical outcomes that go into databases. Otherwise, it is difficult to compare results of clinical trials or other observed effects, especially over long periods. However, there are multiple classifications of diseases. Multiple standards for classifying diseases at the World Health Organization and U.S. Food & Drug Administration (FDA), among others, make comparability a problem.

Merck has found that by strongly influencing the IT, it can play a role in increasing the quality of health care by providing good reasons for other firms and medical practitioners to use Merck's perspective on the specific standards that should be applied in determining which terms describe the same things. The need for standards, the extensiveness of Merck's initiative in setting them, and the requirement that its standards be used by those wanting to work jointly with it or to participate in its clinical trials or to access its library are incentives for adhering to Merck's standards. This use of IT as a way to change industry dynamics to its advantage is a key aspect of Merck's Level 3 IT strategy.

To this end, Merck has developed its own lexicon, which is available on the Internet for use by anyone. This lexicon has helped create better descriptive control and consistency for analytical and measurement purposes. It also means information in the database is collected and classified in a consistent way that allows for greater compatibility and comparability, which can feed back into the R&D process. Merck also uses librarians to do reclassifications when someone disseminates data using a different way of classifying a particular disease.

To the extent that Merck can set standards on how data are gathered and classified, it will gain an ongoing strategic advantage in areas such as drug design, expediting clinical trials, and FDA approvals because it will be able to more easily integrate this other material with its own proprietary system and database, to which only it has access, thus leveraging its own R&D and clinical trial data. This in turn affects the number and rate at which drugs enter and exit its pipeline, the core of its business model.

Merck also has proceeded so that, as international standards have emerged and evolved, its system can migrate and easily use the accepted standard. Because this is an interactive process and Merck has been proactive, the company has maintained an advantage. This is an excellent illustration of a Level 3 strategy: creating the opportunity for benefits for others in ways that involve their making firm-specific investments and changing their behavior in ways that benefit the Level 3 firm.

Manufacturing

Though Merck has 30 plants worldwide, because of environmental regulations getting new plants in the United States has become more difficult, which is one reason it stopped producing generics. As Merck expands its product line, it needs to produce as many different drugs as possible in the existing plants. It also has increased effective capacity by making new pills smaller for each dosage level. This requires making the active ingredients more powerful and, if doing this for an already approved drug, getting FDA approval for the change.

The manufacturing process has been broken into three stages: bulk manufacture of the pharmaceutical ingredients, formulation of the product by transforming the active ingredients produced in the first stage, and packaging. Merck manages the first stage through a mix of special-purpose and flexible equipment. In the other two stages, there is an emphasis on special-purpose equipment that permits production to shift between products more easily, thereby reducing inventories and cycle times.

After mass production of a new compound starts, plant workers contribute significantly to efficiency through learning effects that reduce operating costs. Capturing this requires a detailed understanding of the underlying process, as well as information sharing. All processes eventually get into trouble, so local engineers have to interpret the information and act on it. This in turn requires good data systems, such as process data management systems, so that the engineers can track precisely what is happening in various parts of the process when the problem arises. That is, the engineers need to be able to precisely trace and understand what is happening in the plant at the time a production error occurs (thereby producing a bad lot). This means all aspects of each plant need to be monitored continuously.

Drugs typically require between 4 and 17 steps to produce. Reducing the number of production stages increases efficiency because there is always some wastage at each stage, as well as the cost of handling intermediate goods. Merck uses computer-integrated manufacturing (CIM), which means the entire factory is linked under centralized control. Its approach here is "best-of-breed"—seeking the best package available that meets the specified requirements of the various tasks. Selection and integration of these packages into the overall CIM system has been done by

Merck's IT group and manufacturing group working together, using proprietary middleware.

The U.K. tablet manufacturing plant, which is Merck's most advanced
CIM operation, has moved to a paperless operation with regular interfaces
with the plants that supply it with bulk chemical formulations. In this
process, it has reduced cycle times of two to four weeks to just five days,
and in 1999 Merck was almost ready to produce to order on a just-in-time
basis. While so far going paperless has been limited to tablets, Merck is
moving toward trying to do it for all plants.

IT-Based Procurement

Merck saved over $400 million in 1997 through an IT-based procurement
re-evaluation project. Merck is a large organization, covering many regions
and functions, so it is difficult to track and coordinate all transactions, both
internal and with other companies. The procurement project team wanted
to reduce the number of global suppliers from 40,000 to 10,000, and to
consolidate purchases so Merck could improve its bargaining power. The
team also sought to increase the percentage of suppliers under contract from
20% to 80%.

To achieve these goals, the team developed customized data structures
and decision support systems. It used some commercial software packages
but, to get full functionality and impact, it created a proprietary messaging
system that would integrate procurement with other activities. As the basic
procurement module, the team chose SAP's R/3, based on its architectural
flexibility, scalability, functionality, and the supplier's global support capabilities (see box 2.1).

The new system helps Merck order electronically and reduce paperwork,
and also creates order information that can be used for budget approvals. In
addition, the decision support system provides the employees responsible
for ordering with opportunities to ask questions about procurement data,
and they can find cost-saving opportunities through access to this database.

To integrate the SAP package with Merck's other computer applications,
the IT user development team created a "telephone switch" technology using a mix of middleware products which they purchased and integrated
themselves. This is because the final switch system needed to be aligned
with Merck's unique IT system and organizational structure. The switch
used is the Transaction Data Manager from Century Analysis (now part of
IBM). It stores and forwards product supplier information in MQ series. The
switch translates the language of a "sending" application into "Merck Common Business Language" and then into the language of the "receiving" application. Putting this common language in the middle eliminates the need
to translate between local languages, effectively speeding and facilitating
the exchange of information.

Conclusion

At Merck the IT group is an active participant in the firm's business and decision-making structure, but in a role supportive of users. The use of IT to improve corporate performance through monitoring, controlling, and linking every aspect of producing and delivering its drugs and related services, including after-sales services, reflects a Level 3 IT strategy and marks the company as a leader in developing and using the TIM paradigm. As part of its strategic integration, Merck has linked its software strategies with its overall management goals through a mission statement that explicitly includes IT as an important factor in the firm's success. The company's skillful use of IT is seen by it and by industry analysts as important to its exceptional business performance.

As with the other leading users, Merck's use of IT involves a mix of packaged and customized software that supports its business strategies and differentiates it from competitors. In the past the company often relied on packaged software, but now is doing more customization. Functional and market gains justify the additional expense incurred by customization, including the related costs of integrating customized and packaged software into a single information system. Merck knows this because it formally assesses the possible uses of software, as suggested by corporate users, and then sets measures to evaluate the beneficial effects. Although it will use packaged systems if there is no advantage to developing its own software, Merck rejects the idea that IT systems are merely generic packages that are best developed by outside vendors that have lower costs because of scale and access to the latest technologies.

6

Steel

Nucor, Toyko Steel, Nippon Steel

Once *the* symbol of economic might, steel is a small part of the 21st-century global economy. Still, it is an essential product and, as in any industry, the successful firms are those that use technology and organizational structures more effectively than competitors.

Three companies, two Japanese and one U.S., that have been part of the industry's ongoing evolution are taken up here. The chapter begins with an overview of the industry globally and in Japan. Then the strategies and role of IT at two Level 2 users, Nucor Corp. and Tokyo Steel Manufacturing Co. (Tokyo Seitetsu) are taken up. These provide a contrast to how Nippon Steel (Shin Nippon Seitetsu) is using IT strategically to defend and extend its position as the world's premier steel producer.

In variations from the traditional norms, it is the two smaller companies that are endeavoring to be the low-cost producer of high-quality but standard products, while huge Nippon Steel has moved into customization. How Nippon Steel is doing this illustrates many of the best-practice characteristics of IT use and marks the company as a leader in totally integrated management and a Level 3 IT strategist.

INDUSTRY CONTEXT

Steel is a commodity, but a very heterogeneous one: the types of steel and the processes used to produce them are incredibly diverse. As a process industry its manufacturing methods and R&D are quite different from an assembly industry. Thus, in auto assembly, the system is similar for each car, regardless of how different the cars may be, and firms have similar operating systems at each assembly plant. Further, autos usually have only one design division, so the design system is more integrated into the production process. The process and materials flow even for basic steel products within a category can be different, and vary among plants. Thus, each order can have its own unique specifications and associated R&D. Material quality depends on equipment, people, and process control. Japan has been an R&D leader in steel (see Fujitani 1995).

Types of Steel and Steel Products

Basic steel is carbon steel, made from iron ore and coke. Other metals can be added during smelting to make alloy steel. The industry historically is divided into integrated firms, which make steel and either sell it as bars (called raw or crude steel) to others or process it themselves into semi-finished or final products, and specialty firms. The latter are nonintegrated, purchasing crude steel and turning it into various products, or semi-integrated, making purchased pig iron into alloy steel. Scrap steel can be melted down for reuse and, beginning in the 1970s in the United States, the industry was reshaped by the emergence of scrap-using minimills (so called because they are much smaller in scale than integrated mills) using electric furnaces.

Traditionally, steel was cast into ingots which subsequently were made into semi-finished steel identified by the shape of its cross-section. (Slabs are rectangular, blooms are square, billets are blooms with a smaller square.) These in turn become other intermediate shapes or final products. The ingot stage now usually is skipped in what is called continuous casting. Semi-finished steel is rolled into nine principal forms. Slabs become strip and plate. Blooms are made into structural products, tube, pipe, and rails. Billets become rod, wire, and bar.

Strip is rolled into sheets in what are called hot-strip mills (because the process reheats the steel). This is sold flat (hot-rolled sheet) or in rolls (hot-rolled coil). Hot-rolled coils can be further processed into thinner sheets in cold-strip mills, which operate at ambient temperatures. Continuous casting made possible hot-charge rolling (HCR), although HCR still is not very common. Developed by Nippon Steel, HCR links several processes so that steel can flow directly from the continuous caster into cold rolling and finishing. Processes that had taken place over a 21-day period were reduced to a continuous process completed in just 45 minutes! This achievement required combining the company's steelmaking expertise with IT system controls.

Most sheet is used for automobiles and appliances, as well as, in Japan, vending machines. Some sheet is galvanized (coated with zinc) or tinplated (for use as cans and the like). A well-illustrated description of the iron- and steelmaking process is provided by France's largest steelmaker at *usinor. com/english/lacier/acier_p1*.

Alloy (also called specialty) steels include stainless steel (chromium added), silicon steel (used in electric motors, generators, and transformers), and tool steel of various hardnesses.

Automobiles and construction are the two largest users of steel in Japan and the United States. In the 19th century, rails were the major product. An interesting difference between the development of the Japanese and U.S.

> Box 6.1
> MEASURING STEEL
>
> ---
>
> Steel and its ingredients are measured in tons. Just what kind of ton can be confusing. The American Iron & Steel Institute (*steel.org*) reports world pig iron production in short tons (2000 pounds) but U.S. iron ore production in long tons (2240 pounds). Too often writers do not specify—assuming the reader knows the convention for the item in question.
>
> Data here are in metric tons (tonnes) unless noted otherwise, and are from the International Iron and Steel Institute (*worldsteel.org*) or *steelprofiles.com*.

industries in the 1950s and 1960s is that U.S. makers were oriented primarily toward sheet (for automobiles and appliances), while Japanese mills produced relatively more plate (for shipbuilding and machinery) and structural shapes. The emergence of Japan's auto industry in the 1970s has made the two countries' industries more alike in product mix.

Raw and intermediate materials account for about 75% of the cost of producing a tonne of steel in Japan. Companies also need massive amounts of capital. An integrated mill with an annual capacity of 3 million tonnes of crude steel requires around $5 billion in capital. Amortizing this accounts for about 12% of production costs. Labor is about 10% (compared to 25% in labor-intensive industries such as precision instruments.)

Global Overview

Excess capacity has for some time well summarized the steel industry. Steel was long a symbol of a nation's modernity and power, and this has slowed but not stopped the industry's contraction in terms of employment and relative importance in advanced economies. These political-economic problems are outside the scope of this book, but they complicate the actions and weaken even well-managed firms because prices are less than would be the case if the excess capacity were shut down. They also have forced a series of mergers and alliances.

Table 6.1 lists major firms. Note the absence of any U.S. firms in the top 10. More than 10 U.S. firms filed for bankruptcy in the 12 months through June 2001, including LTV, the third largest.

There are cross-border joint ventures; Japanese firms have invested in the United States and Asia; European firms have merged within the EU; and many source raw materials and sell their output worldwide. But firms mostly produce within a single country. Thus, even though the industry has been consolidating for decades, unlike the automobile industry, where truly global firms have emerged, there are no major global steelmakers. Nippon Steel, with affiliates in the United States, Asia, and Brazil probably has come closest.

Table 6.1 Largest Steel Companies, by Output, 1999 (million metric tons of crude steel)

Output	Company	Output	Company
44.4	*Usinor (Luxembourg)*[1,2]	16.7	Baoshan (Peoples Republic of China)
26.5	Pohang Iron & Steel Co. Ltd. (Posco) (Korea)[3]	16.1	ThyssenKrupp Stahl AG (Germany)[8,13]
25.2	Nippon Steel (Japan)[2,3,4]	14.1	Riva (Italy)
23.9	*NKK-Kawasaki (Japan)*[5,6,7,13]	12.8	NKK (Japan)[5,6,13]
22.2	Usinor (France)[1,2,9]	11.3	USX (United States)[14]
22.2	Arbed (Luxembourg)[1,10]	11.1	Kawasaki (Japan)[5,7,13]
21.3	Corus Group plc (United Kingdom)[11]	784.2	World total
20.0	LNM Group (United Kingdom)[4,12]		

Italicized entries are pro forma for pending mergers. Rankings and production changed from year to year but, except for the rapid rise of Baoshan and LMN group, the same firms are on the list as in 1996.

[1]Usinor, Arbed, and Aceralia announced a merger in 2001. The new company will be based in Luxembourg.

[2]Usinor and Nippon Steel have a global "strategic alliance agreement" and a Brazilian joint venture.

[3]In August 2000 Nippon Steel and Pohang formed a strategic alliance that includes joint ventures in third countries and cooperative development of technology and products. Each company acquired shares in the other, with Nippon investing about three times as much (about $229 million) in Posco as Posco invested in Nippon Steel. Nippon initially owned just under 3% of Posco shares and in 2001 increased its stake to 5%.

[4]Nippon Steel and Inland Steel had joint ventures that have continued after Inland's acquisition by part of the LMN Group.

[5]NKK and Kawasaki announced a merger in 2001.

[6]NKK owns 51% of National Steel (U.S.) and has a joint-venture plant with DOFASCO (Canada).

[7]Kawasaki owns 20% of AK Steel Holding (U.S.) and 50% of California Steel Industries (U.S.).

[8]Created by the 1997 merger of Thyssen and Krupp steelmaking operations, under Thyssen AG control. Krupp had acquired the steelmaking operations of Hoesch AG in 1992. Data include 50% of HKM.

[9]During the 1970s the French industry consolidated around two companies. In 1981 the government took control of both, and in 1986 bought out the remaining public shares, merging them into Usinor Sacilor. In July 1995 it was privatized, and in June 1997 shortened its name. Data include Cockerill-Sambre.

[10]Includes Aceralia.

[11]Formed in October 1999 by merger of British Steel and Dutch-based Koninklijke Hoogovens.

[12]Perhaps the most global producer, it is an assembly of firms and plants spread from Trinidad and Tobago to Kazakhstan and Indonesia. Most include Ispat as part of their name. Inland Steel, the sixth largest U.S. producer, was added in July 1998.

[13]Building on talks regarding sheet for automotive use, Thyssen and NKK have been discussing global strategic collaboration. Kawasaki is now included.

[14]In November 2000 USX purchased a plant from East Slovakian Ironworks (VSZ), now called U.S. Steel Kosice (after the town in which it is located). This was preceded by a joint venture.

Sources: The notes are from company web sites and disclosure filings. Production data are from the International Iron & Steel Institute. A longer list, with data for the most recent four years, is at *steelprofiles.com/datacenter/rank.co.html*

In February 2001, Usinor SA of France announced it would absorb a Spanish and a Luxembourg steelmaker by the end of the year, making it the world's largest producer, with output of 44 million tonnes of crude steel in 1999. The new company claims operations on four continents but, although some final products are produced in South America, primary steelmaking is in Europe. The Asian presence is a "growing activity through alliances and joint ventures."

Crude steel production from 1970 to 2000, by country or region is given in table 6.2.

Table 6.2 Crude Steel Production, 1970–2000

1970	1975	1980	1985	1990	1995	2000	
Million Metric Tons							
93.4	102.3	111.4	105.3	110.3	101.7	106.4	Japan
119.3	105.8	101.8	80.1	89.7	93.6	101.5	United States
106.0	123.3	128.0	120.3	118.6	110.9	125.7	Other G7
17.0	23.9	37.1	46.7	66.3	93.0	126.3	China, People's Republic of
0.5	2.5	8.6	13.5	23.1	36.8	43.1	Korea, Republic of
256.7	290.4	329.7	353.0	362.0	313.6	340.7	All others
592.8	648.2	716.3	718.9	770.0	749.6	843.7	World total
Percentage Distribution							
15.8	15.8	15.6	14.6	14.3	13.6	12.6	Japan
20.1	16.3	14.2	11.1	11.6	12.5	12.0	United States
17.9	19.0	17.9	16.7	15.4	14.8	14.9	Other G7
2.9	3.7	5.2	6.5	8.6	12.4	15.0	China, People's Republic of
0.1	0.4	1.2	1.9	3.0	4.9	5.1	Korea, Republic of
43.3	44.8	46.0	49.1	47.0	41.8	40.4	All others

Note: The other G7 are Canada, France, Germany, Italy, and the United Kingdom. Totals may not add due to rounding.

Sources: Absolute data from International Iron and Steel Federation and the 2000 United Nations Statistical Annual. Distribution computed by author.

The Steel Industry in Japan

Steel was one of Japan's early postwar successes, and a prime example of Japanese industrial competitiveness. The industry was rebuilt in the early 1950s, and output grew at an average annual rate of 15% into the early 1970s. In the 1960s and 1970s it was perceived globally as an industrial juggernaut, giving Japanese steel users such as automakers, construction machinery, and shipbuilders a huge competitive advantage. By 1976 annual capacity was nearly 150 million tonnes and Japan had a 16% share of the world market. The competitive benefits persisted through the early 1980s due to the weak yen.

In the mid-1980s, Japan provided over 20% of world steel exports, despite the emergence of aggressive, efficient Korean companies. Even during the 1985–90 bubble when the yen was strong, the major steel producers did fairly well due to buoyant domestic demand. Table 6.3 lists the major Japanese firms. For more on the development of Japan's steel industry, see O'Brien (1992) and Dempster (1969, pp. 213–17).

There is substantial information sharing between Japan's integrated steel producers, and they often cooperate. For example, all domestic orders for both product and raw materials (virtually all imported) traditionally have been handled through trading companies, although this is beginning to change. The Japan Steel Association has a technical committee through which, after a two-year lead, firms generally share new processes. This is one reason Japanese firms have adopted new technologies more rapidly than competitors, thus gaining cost advantage. (Lynn 1982, a classic on Japanese innovation, explains how Japanese steelmakers leaped ahead through quick adoption of basic oxygen furnace technology.) The government has tolerated and participated in this because steel is an intermediate good, and the goal was to make it as cheap as possible for the benefit of such users as shipbuilders, construction companies, automakers, and manufacturers of machinery and heavy equipment.

Industry cooperation usually has not extended to computerization, which is heavily customized and unique to each firm. In the late 1990s major steelmakers started to come together in a joint e-commerce project sponsored by MITI and involving the major trading and appliance companies. Still, each steelmaker was to handle its own interface to the system. While being piloted, the fear that it was being dominated by Nippon Steel contributed to the originally envisioned extension of the project collapsing in late 1999. Nippon thus developed its own Internet-based system in cooperation with two other steelmakers, as described later.

A Declining Industry?

Competitive pressures from two sources began to become significant during the 1990s. One was the emergence of several new, efficient competitors,

Table 6.3 Major Japanese Steel Companies, Ranked by Fiscal 2000 Production (million metric tons)

Output	Company
27.8	Nippon Steel [5401][1,2,3]
13.5	NKK [5402][4,5]
12.1	Kawasaki Steel [5403][4,6]
10.4	Sumitomo Metal Industries [5405][2,7]
6.5	Kobe Steel [5406][8]
3.5	Tokyo Steel Manufacturing [5423][9]
3.3	Nisshin Steel [5407][3,10]
107.0	Japan total

Notes: Fiscal 2000 ended 31 March 2001.
    Data are only for the parent company.
    Tokyo Stock Exchange codes are in square brackets.
    [1]See table 6.1, notes 2, 3, and 4. Ventures in the United States include galvanizing and coating plants with capacity of 3.5 million metric tons. Also owns part of Godo Steel [5410], an electric-furnace steelmaker.
    [2]Nippon Steel has a market-sharing arrangement with Sumitomo Metal; see text.
    [3]Nippon Steel is the largest shareholder in Nisshin (9.7%), reflecting a long-standing relationship.
    [4]Announced merger plans in April 2001. Is discussing global cooperation with ThyssenKrupp (Germany)
    [5]NKK owns 51% of National Steel (U.S.) and has a joint-venture plant with DOFASCO (Canada). Once known as Nippon Kokan, predecessor firms date to 1912. Controls Toa Steel [5447], an electric-furnace steelmaker.
    [6]Kawasaki had a 50–50 operation with Armco (U.S.) that merged into Armco in September 1999 as AK Steel Holdings. As a result, owns 20% of AK. Also owns 50% of California Steel Industries (U.S.).
    [7]Excludes production from two foundries that have been spun off; including them, production was 11.7 million tonnes. Sumitomo has two 40–60 facilities with LTV (U.S.). Has interests in several U.S. firms, including 6% of LTV, which is in chapter 11 bankruptcy.
    [8]Kobe has ventures with U.S. Steel (U.S.).
    [9]Tokyo has a joint venture, Tamco, with Ameron (U.S.) and a research venture with Klockner (Germany).
    [10]Nisshin has two 64–36 operations with Wheeling Pittsburgh (U.S.). Affiliated with Nippon Steel, it has specialized in thin plate and stainless products.
    Sources: *Japan Company Handbook* and company filings.

such as Pohang Iron & Steel (Posco) in Korea and Nucor in the United States. The second was the serious decline in domestic demand as the Japanese economy felt the combined pressures of the bubble collapse and a continuing strong yen. These effects were only partially ameliorated by growth in export demand due to a rapidly expanding Asian economy.

Steel production hit an annual rate of 110 million tonnes toward the end of 1991, but it then fell 15 million tonnes due to the bubble's collapse; only 5 million tonnes were covered by increased demand from Asia.

Some firms have faced declining demand by rationalizing production (shutting, and even completely scrapping, capacity), reducing their labor force, and diversifying into new products. For example, total employment of the five large Japanese integrated producers fell from 150,000 in 1985 to 90,000 in 1995. In comparison, the top five U.S. integrated producers went from 150,000 in 1985 to 77,000 in 1995. Nippon Steel, which had 42,000 workers involved in steel production in 1985 and some 32,000 in 1995, continued to decrease its steel work force to 26,000 in 1997 and 24,000 in 1998. Although helping to maintain competitiveness, this tactic has not raised production or profits at domestic mills because price and cost declines generally were emulated by all the competitors.

Cost reductions of 6% by Nippon Steel during the late 1990s were replicated by other large integrated Japanese producers. Similarly, weak-yen benefits, which helped all steel producers during 1980–85, came to an abrupt halt with the September 1985 Plaza Accord. This resulted in increases in investment in the United States by all Japanese integrated producers. The logical strategy for each was affiliation with U.S. producers through technical assistance and partial or complete acquisition (table 6.1).

Exports have been important for Japanese integrated producers since the 1960s, and continue as an area of intense negotiations with the United States. But the days are gone when Japanese firms always were the low-cost producers internationally or could just move into higher grades of steel. Rather, the yen's relationship to the U.S. dollar (and thus currencies tied to the dollar) drives prices for Japanese steel both overseas and domestically.

Japanese automakers and shipbuilders often compete with users of less expensive steel from Korea, Taiwan, and Brazil. They thus have pressured Japanese producers to reduce prices during periods when the yen is strong. Imports of all steel products into Japan from Korea went from 647,000 tonnes in 1980 to 2,596,000 tonnes in 1996. For 2000 they ran 2,935,000 tonnes, equal to 39% of Japan's steel imports that year.

Attempts to Cope

It is hardly surprising that Japanese steel producers have turned to other activities, including nonsteel products. They included Space World, an amusement park that Nippon Steel opened in 1990 on land in northern Kyushu no longer needed for steelmaking. It was more than four times over budget. The five majors all have semiconductor divisions. However, as with steel, performance in semiconductors has been affected by fluctuations in both demand and exchange rates. DRAM production is just another highly competitive, cyclical business involving an intermediate industrial commodity. In general, diversifications away from activities closely related to steel have not been successful.

Steelmakers have tried to raise the value added in their products. They also have participated in a global proliferation of new capacity and the emergence of competitors through a wide range of acquisitions and affiliations, and through selling engineering services. For example, Nippon Steel participates directly in steelmaking ventures in China, Thailand, and Malaysia. In August 2000 it formed a strategic alliance with Pohang (Posco) of Korea, which is a major supplier of imports to Japan. In mid-2001 it entered an agreement under which Shanghai Steel will supply Honda in China with steel of the same quality that Nippon Steel provides Honda in Japan, which means significant technology transfer. This will replace steel that had been exported from Japan.

It has been difficult for the integrated producers to anticipate prices and demand. Japan's continued weak domestic economy has limited demand generally, which means Japanese companies are not expanding their plants. Thus, along with other major Japanese producers, Nippon Steel's steel assets and revenues have been essentially constant since 1993. Added to this is the assessment of some observers that Japan (and the world) still has too much steel capacity. However, for larger companies, rationalizing operations further means shutting more blast furnaces and concentrating a wider product range in fewer mills, which is not easy, or completely abandoning certain product categories.

Narrowing product range was resisted into the late 1990s, but as the industry's malaise continued, attitudes changed. In April 2000, Nippon Steel and Sumitomo Metal Industries announced a joint marketing and production strategy whereby each would assume responsibility for certain products. Thus, Sumitomo, long Japan's leader in seamless pipe, will run the two companies' operations for this business on an integrated basis while Nippon Steel will do the same for plate and sheet.

In April 2001 the second and third largest firms, NKK Corp. and Kawasaki Steel Corp., announced they would form a holding company and reorganize operations under it by April 2003. In terms of crude steel output, the combined companies are about the size of Nippon Steel, but smaller than a combination of Nippon Steel with Sumitomo Metals.

To cover operating losses, several Japanese steel companies have sold stock they held in various cross-holding relationships, including affiliates. At best this is a temporary, and self-limiting, activity.

In short, the large integrated steel producers have sought similar solutions. Thus, announced and prospective rationalizations simply raise the issue of tit-for-tat cost benefits that will be quickly competed away, as they have in the past.

The Role of Trading Companies

Historically, most steel in Japan has been sold through trading companies, with each standard product having a known set of suppliers. This is different from the role steel distributors have played in the United States. For example, the trading companies do hold inventory, but in most cases they buy steel only against specific user orders. As part of this, a fairly sophisticated ordering and inventory control system for raw materials evolved. Involving Nippon Steel and the other large steel companies, it has helped even out the effects of fluctuations in demand for raw materials among individual producers.

One outcome of the global proliferation of steelmakers has been that the relatively simple structure of Japan's industry has changed significantly. Although most orders for standard products, such as construction rebar, still are placed through a trading company, many products, such as the wire used in a bridge or the sheet used in cars and appliances, no longer are "standard." Rather, more steel is made to non-generic customer specifications. There always had been some product customization for particular projects, but it generally was on a case-by-case basis due to the higher cost compared to buying an off-the-shelf industry-standard product.

Usually the contracts the trading companies manage for automakers and appliance makers are for one year, with specified daily deliveries. This also is true for some heavy equipment makers such as Komatsu.

The other area where the trading companies have been active is in managing steel producers' contracts for iron ore and coking coal from foreign sources such as Australia, Brazil, and the United States. These usually are set years in advance because, while the steel companies do not know the actual future demand for steel by customer or type, they do have a good idea of overall volume. In fact, volume did not change much during the 1990s, so there was a fairly steady demand for raw materials. Actual delivery levels are negotiated about six months ahead.

NUCOR AND TOKYO STEEL

Nucor Corp. and Tokyo Steel Manufacturing Co. (Tokyo Seitetsu) are different from large integrated producers such as Nippon Steel both in product mix and in raw material demand. They both entered the steel business as minimill producers with rebar melted from scrap as their initial major product. Rebar, which is used for reinforcing concrete, is a commodity product sold to the construction industry, and thus historically is subject to volatile swings in demand and price. Thus, only the most efficient producers have been able to grow and prosper. Nucor has been the leader in setting this efficiency standard in the United States, and Tokyo Steel has played this role in Japan. (The evolution of Nucor and its impact on the U.S. steel industry is analyzed in Ahlbrandt et al. 1996, which also contains a brief history and assessment of Tokyo Steel.)

Over time both firms have raised the quality and type of steel they can produce efficiently, and now have the capability to make even high-quality, low-cost sheet for automobiles and appliances. In doing so, they have challenged the large integrated producers, altered the cost of steel production paradigm, and changed the dynamics of the steel industry.

Nucor: Overview

Nucor Steel, a division of Nucor Corp., is the largest scrap recycler in the United States. With its affiliates, it manufacturers carbon and alloy steel products in eight states. Products include joists, girders, decking, and other building components; cold finished steel; and grinding balls, bearings, and fasteners. With capacity of about 12 million tonnes, 2000 revenue of $4.6 billion made it the second largest U.S. steelmaker. For some time its market capitalization has exceeded that of the three leading traded U.S. integrated makers (AK Steel, Bethlehem, and US Steel).

Low costs are achieved by the constant attention to detail at the production level by all employees and by minimizing expenses unrelated to production, including corporate overhead. This is coupled with a bonus program that includes production workers and that is directly related to measurable productivity improvements.

IT at Nucor

Consistent with this corporate vision, Nucor's approach to IT and software usage is the same as the Nucor philosophy in other business areas: "Push the decisions down to the lowest appropriate level." As a result, there is no corporate management information system (MIS) group or anyone at the corporate level with direct responsibility for setting IT policy. Each operating location has its own MIS staff and uses varying combinations of packaged and internally produced software. The diversity and independence are reflected in the company's web site (*nucor.com*), which, while giving corporate and historical information, also indicates that each location has its own Web site and e-mail naming convention.

While the divisions share knowledge, they are very autonomous and independent. At the same time, the overriding focus on production efficiency drives the MIS function to find the most cost-effective solutions to manufacturing problems and to improvements in the current operating systems. Further, division personnel from all departments work together on these projects. Ideas and inputs are sought from operating and maintenance workers alike—and it is frequently from them that the ideas or questions first arise.

Moreover, although actual decisions are pushed down, there is a corporate-level commitment to utilizing IT that makes up part of the environment in which the decisions are made. In the company's 2000 annual report, CEO Daniel R. DiMicco outlines Nucor's overall approach to IT.

> Electronic commerce is a great tool, and it is here to stay. Our E-strategy is to use this technology to make it easier and more efficient to do business both with our customers and our suppliers. We are continuing

to develop and implement these tools across our company. We will use the Web to enhance one of our core values—communications with our divisions and employees. We also have our own Web sites by division and by product group for our customers and suppliers. We do not, however, believe in putting anyone between our customers and us. Therefore, you will not see us joining one of the many and troubled E-trading sites. We will sell through these sites if our customers so desire. But so far, they would rather deal directly with us.

The divisions that have the most important IT programs are Nucor Building Systems in Waterloo, Indiana; Nucor Steel in Darlington, South Carolina; and Vulcraft in Norfolk, Nebraska. But even these divisions tend to outsource anything that does not very directly contribute to increased steel-making productivity. Thus, for example, a major brokerage firm manages all 401(k) and profit-sharing plans.

Nucor Steel announced selection of Datastream's iProcure on-line ordering system for industrial parts on a pilot basis in June 2000. There was no corporate decision on this, nor were other divisions required to do something similar. Nucor Steel says it chose iProcure to coordinate maintenance, repair, and operations purchasing and for access to the network of iProcure suppliers, who list nearly 2 million items, making it the largest e-commerce source for such procurement needs. The company believes the suppliers on iProcure's list are the leaders in their fields, and it is confident that this e-commerce approach will provide the sourcing it needs to maintain full production.

As part of its continual push to seek new methods to improve its efficiency, Nucor Darlington is extending a relationship with Datastream that dates to the early 1990s. Because Darlington's maintenance operations drive the demand for parts, iProcure complements implementation of Datastream's enterprise asset management system. Maintenance-related purchases often are the biggest nonproduction expense, so Nucor believes automation can significantly reduce costs, though the system and its procedures must be configured to meet Darlington's semi-customized specific purchasing requirements.

Tokyo Steel: Overview

Tokyo Steel began to operate in a manner similar to Nucor, with a very lean headquarters and each mill working independently until 1987. However, it has not been able to translate its expanded market share or its operating efficiencies (in terms of man-hours and expenses per tonne relative to other Japanese producers) into a meaningful and long-term strategic benefit.

Although its financial situation is good, with little debt and a positive operating cash flow, its overall business situation deteriorated from exceptionally strong in fiscal 1993 to running losses in 1998 and 1999. During

1993–98 it had to draw down its large cash reserves to cover capital expenditures. As major projects were completed, cash levels subsequently stabilized. For the year ending 31 March 2001 (fiscal 2000), the company reported revenue of ¥106.8 billion ($8.7 billion at then-current exchange rates) and an operating loss of ¥8.5 billion ($690 million).

The company very much recognizes that it needs to improve its cost position even further to defend against price pressures, stagnant demand, and competitive developments. The company's business and IT strategies especially have had to address continued heavy dependence on sales to the construction industry. Although it has entered markets that can use its expanded rolling capacity, including vehicles and appliances, 70% of output is used in construction, which is one of the industries most weakened by Japan's ongoing economic malaise. Although construction in the past has benefited from government attempts to stimulate the economy, there is now widespread recognition that many such projects have been wasteful and have involved various types of corruption.

Tokyo Steel's Strategy

The strategy Tokyo Steel has developed depends on three basic aspects of its business. The first is its very modern and efficient steelmaking capacity and trained labor force. Second is its lean corporate management and production strategy. Third is its sophisticated use of IT to economically manage production and inventories. Tokyo Steel has coupled its strategic technology focus with an IT initiative that integrates data management at the order and corporate levels with an IT system that links the head office with each mill for such things as order allocation. Begun in 1987–88, this is a significant departure from the Nucor-type approach it had been pursuing. As before, each mill's production management system is linked with its equipment controls to enhance that mill's productivity. However, the company has shifted from an independent plant-based strategy to a companywide coordinated strategy using IT.

Key aspects of its strategic solution have been opening the Utsunomiya mill (box 6.2) to produce higher value-added products such as hot-rolled coil; producing products more continuously; and reducing capacity for rebar, a pure commodity product. Altogether, the company makes over 10,000 different steel products, but it is emphasizing sheet steel for construction and autos because, for these products, it competes only with integrated producers and higher-quality minimills. (Still, given the intense competition from these producers, as well as Korean imports, further capacity expansion in sheet and hot-rolled coil has been deemed too risky.)

The company's objectives are to automate and rationalize production so the company can produce and deliver high-quality standard steel products in a timely, cost-effective manner. It also seeks to continue to reduce delivery times so that it can better meet customer supply requirements and pare

---

Box 6.2

UTSUNOMIYA MILL

One of the most advanced in the world, the Utsunomiya mill opened in 1995, two years after construction started. Located 110 kilometers from Tokyo on the main rail line to the north, the mill has an annual capacity of 800,000 tonnes. People working with computers controlled the older mills, but the new plant is controlled virtually 100% by computers.

The mill rolls continuously and rapidly, whereas the older facilities rolled each slab on a batch basis before moving to the next slab. (That was necessary to keep slabs from running into each other.) Continuous rolling is the key to producing the required sheet in a shorter time span and improving productivity. It also saves heat directly and, by allowing for a smaller mill area, indirectly. In this way energy consumption is improved, further increasing overall efficiency. Each worker is producing roughly 5,000 tonnes of steel, a year, double the average rate at the company's older facilities, making it perhaps the world's most productive mill.

However, as part of the company's focused standardized-product strategy, the mill is producing only ordinary steel products, such as H-beams, rebar used in general construction, and sheet that goes primarily into furniture and appliances.

---

its own in-process inventories. This means tracking product requirements by customer group.

Trading companies handle distribution of virtually all of Tokyo Steel's output. Because quality is uniformly high for all producers handled by the trading companies, its customers are targeted by competitors and competition is based largely on price. This intensely competitive environment is a primary driver for Tokyo Steel's focused cost-cutting approach, just as it is for Nucor, and is why the company has put considerable effort into increasing productivity and precisely evaluating costs by product, quality, and customer. Indeed, it believes its focused approach is good at cost-containment, with revenue enhancement dependent on moving to higher value-added products. This is why it is critical for the company to target market segments that have specific standard-product needs, and then be the low-cost provider.

Tokyo Steel's IT System

The basic decision criteria used to make IT selections has been to enhance the mills' capabilities, to increase output through more efficient use of production facilities, and to reduce costs. The objectives of speeding communication, improving mill productivity, and increasing client satisfaction have enabled the company to select, develop, and use the software required for each function, and to integrate it into its IT support system. This is because it is relatively easy to measure whether these objectives have been achieved. Because the systems are development-cost intensive, they are subject to user-base economics, which makes beneficial loops possible.

One indication of the success of its strategy has been the company's ability to expand production while reducing staff. However, it does not blindly expand, but rather always keeps in mind its customers' shifting needs so that it is targeting those who want its higher-quality standard products.

Except for the operating systems, Tokyo Steel generally has developed all its own software. Its basic IT is a three-tier mainframe system similar to most large Japanese companies. The mainframe manages a series of servers that manage the PCs and workstations. A real-time on-line system, it has been totally integrated with the company's business operations. The main computer operation is at the main mill in Okayama. It is connected by a high-speed WAN to the other mills—which are in Wakamatsu (on Kyushu), Utsunomiya, and Takamatsu (on Shikoku)—and the major offices (Tokyo headquarters, Hiroshima, Nagoya, Osaka, and Wakamatsu).

Each mill and office has a local server (from Fujitsu) and LAN, and there is a process computer at each mill. The process computers that control each piece of machinery and equipment at each mill are part of the firm's mainframe-based system, and the equipment makers (such as Hitachi) program and upgrade them. For example, in April 1997 the hot-coil production system at Okayama was upgraded. On balance, once the system has been decided, there is not much change unless the process is changed, which generally is done at the time of regular annual repair and maintenance of the mill.

PCs were introduced in 1991, with a second round in 1996. The company, like Toyota, works on a five-year cycle because of its lease arrangements and also because it then generally is ready for the next version.

While, at the product level, each plant and product has its own control system, certain functions are controlled centrally. These include scrap purchases, transportation, aggregate demand forecasts, order allocation, personnel, and accounting.

Counting just those considered computer experts, the system and network are maintained by just 10 people: 3 in Tokyo, 3 in Okayama, and 1 at each mill. With a support staff, they comprise the company's IT group. In terms of the network, everything is concentrated in Okayama, where the common network is administered.

Until 1987 each mill and office had its own independent program like Nucor, but after 1987 the system was centralized at Okayama. It took the company a year to develop its centralized system from the various stand-alone operations. It designed all the new core system, and then outsourced programming to third parties. That is, essentially all the software for its enterprise management system (EMS) and enterprise resource planning (ERP) was tailor-made from scratch to the company's design requirements. Subsequent upgrades, changes, and modifications have usually been done by the company's IT group.

The overall system, and its close integration with each mill, is so large and complex that only the company has the legacy knowledge to modify it, or to integrate new systems, without disrupting production and delivery. These are the company's major reasons for rejecting packaged EMS concepts in particular and generic-program outsourcing generally.

Managing Orders and Production

Operationally, when Tokyo Steel receives an inquiry (usually from a trading company), it inputs the information into its system. Whether this is done with a specified delivery date depends on the order. (The company was never asked to be part of the integrated producers' short-lived e-commerce system. However, it does plan to use the Internet for receiving orders.) Each day, in-hand orders are checked to determine what processes are required to produce the specified steels. From this, the amount of raw steel required, as well as the timing for producing that steel, is determined. From the company's perspective, the ideal time period from assigning an order to shipment is about 45 days. (Note that this does not include the time to process the order or effect physical delivery, so the time from order to receipt of product by the customer is longer. From receipt of an order; to delivery is about three months.) Although the company is producing a standard set of products, production is in response to a specific order; it is not producing for its own inventory or for speculation.

Based on an analysis of orders and inventories, each month a production schedule is sent to each mill. Each mill uses a three-shift system, and the head office decides the exact shift to which a particular order is assigned. All this is done through computer connections.

The criteria for assigning an order are, first, product (only certain mills produce certain products), then geography (transport costs can be significant). This task is the responsibility of the Planning Adjustment Center, which tracks output and order data and adjusts the orders to even out product flow for each mill. Once an order is assigned to a mill shift, that mill's system takes charge of the subsequent scheduling of the order through the various production processes and shipment.

Tokyo Steel uses an open steel supply chain (box 6.3). However, not all specific orders are tracked through the system because the company produces standard products, which can be placed in inventory by the trading

---

Box 6.3
OPEN STEEL SUPPLY CHAIN

For most major Japanese steelmakers, order and delivery are tracked in real time on their computer systems, so the company knows where a customer's order is at all times. There is a one-to-one correlation between the flow of data and the physical movement of the steel, so that the information flow mirrors the product flow. This is called the open steel supply chain.

companies, and there is no difference in quality from one production run to the next. This means the trading companies only need to access the aggregate amount of a certain product being produced and shipped, and there is no need for the information flow to mirror the product flow precisely.

Still, it is extremely important that the company uses its production facilities efficiently. This is why the company has not adopted an outside ERP or EMS package. These are mission-critical factors, and the IT must be tightly integrated with the mills' physical, technical, and personnel operations, as well as with the corporate systems. No outside vendor would have the detailed knowledge about how the mills and the existing system actually work.

After production is completed, the home office instructs each mill how much of each product should be delivered to each stockyard, with the sale complete at the point of physical delivery to the trading company.

The connection between Tokyo Steel's raw material (scrap purchases) and its order flow is not direct. Rather, the company decides to buy scrap opportunistically, buying if it feels the price is good. Scrap prices reflect cyclical demand, and this is a countercyclical approach that allows the company to control raw material costs. In terms of production flow, the scrap is delivered on a just-in-time basis. The company buys only Japanese scrap, because the local price is cheap and Japan is a net exporter of scrap.

Conclusion

To maintain its low-cost position over the long term, Tokyo Steel is continually revising its IT system on the basis of observed best practice at its mills. This leads to continually increasing production efficiency and improved product delivery. Its IT system achieves these results by simplifying desk work and order tracking; by confirming and allocating the order; and by adding value through supporting each mill's optimal functioning on an integrated basis. This is an ongoing, iterative process involving trial and error. For instance, operational and system control problems at the Utsunomiya Works required system and plant layout modifications that took about a year to resolve and in 1998 quality problems at Takamatsu required a change in the production process.

Management's approach is thus dynamic, in that they are constantly looking for ways to improve cost and operating efficiencies, including the requisite IT support. This is part of the company's continuing strategic upgrading of IT and steel production systems, which has allowed it to shift toward higher-grade products made at lower costs.

Tokyo Steel does not feel its IT system's benefits will be competed away by the industry. The company has integrated the requirements of its primary customer base, mostly construction companies wanting standard products at low cost, into its sales, production, and IT strategy. It believes any IT outsourcing would put the company and its IT support systems one step removed from its mills and the trading companies.

The company's IT initiatives and benefits have been vertically integrated and extended within the firm to enhance its strengths. However, its customers and suppliers are not integrated into an end-to-end demand-supply chain that Tokyo Steel can influence, and its customers and suppliers have not made firm-specific investments that improve Tokyo Steel's competitive position. Thus, scrap is bought on a commodity basis, driven by when prices seem advantageous, while the trading companies control demand. Because of this, Tokyo Steel, like Nucor, is only a Level 2 IT strategist.

NIPPON STEEL

Nippon Steel (Shin Nippon Seitetsu) is Japan's leading steel producer and has been among the largest in the world in since its formation in 1970. The recession induced by the strong yen after 1985 and the collapse of the late 1980s bubble economy adversely affected Japanese steel companies in ways they have yet to recover from. As a result, Nippon Steel, along with other major Japanese producers, has had to restructure. The company, which operates 10 mills, keeps four to five blast furnaces closed; some of these are not expected ever to reopen.

In the year ending March 2001 the company poured about 26% of Japan's total crude steel output, up from 24% the previous year. Its share of total integrated Japanese steel production has been around 40%. During the 1990s Nippon Steel's domestic share of sheet products used by the 11 major Japanese car manufacturers was around 40%, and about 44% for the 8 major appliance makers. It has about 38% of Japan's capacity to produce these products, which is more than twice that of the next largest producer, NKK.

The competitive situation changes somewhat with the merger plans of NKK and Kawasaki, but not in ways that affect this book's concerns. Their combined share in autos is about 36%; in appliances it is about 24%. Sumitomo Metals, which has a cooperative agreement with Nippon Steel, has 14% of autos and 15% of appliances. This is now being managed by Nippon Steel under a cooperative agreement.

Despite its already relatively large size, in the early 1990s Nippon Steel set its sights on gradually increasing its share of the steel market. It has especially pursued this goal in the critical sheet market for cars and appliances, which is part of the flat-rolled products category that provides over 60% of the company's steel revenue and the best overall product-category margins. The strategy it has been following, and the role of IT, are examined in the following sections.

Nippon Steel's History

In January 1934 the government-owned Yawata steel works and six private firms were merged into Nippon Seiketsu Kaisha, with the government owning 70% (the remainder being held mostly by the *zaibatsu* whose mills were included). The new firm made over 90% of the pig iron and about half of the raw steel produced before the war. It was a "national policy" company, reflecting the country's militarization. The Occupation split the company into Yawata Steel and Fuji Steel. Fuji absorbed Tokai Steel in 1967, and Yawata took over Yawata Steel Tube Co. in 1968.

With the encouragement of some career government bureaucrats, an agreement for Yawata and Fuji to merge was reached in January 1968, after several years of negotiations. Fierce opposition by other steel companies and some in the government caused delay. This was quieted when each of the merging companies sold a plant. On 31 March 1970 the firms were reunited as Shin Nihon Seiketsu.

Yawata could trace its origins to the late 19th century. The government built a steel mill at Yawata (in northern Kyushu), convenient to Japan's largest coal field and iron ore from China, that opened in 1901. Through World War II it was the largest steel complex in Japan. The original site is now an amusement park, but the area still has several major steel mills. (See Dempster 1969, pp. 213–17, and Trebartha 1965, pp. 280–4 on the economic geography of Japan's steel industry.)

The company sometimes is called New Japan Steel in English. The characters for "Japan" can be pronounced Nihon or Nippon. The former became the norm after the war, but Nippon is now more common and is used here.

The Need for a New Strategy

In 1996 Nippon Steel recognized that something more than cost-cutting was required to address the cyclical nature of the industry, the increase in global cost-based competition, excess capacity, and accompanying downward price pressure. The company also realized that its ventures outside steel-making, mostly started in the mid-1980s, had been relatively unsuccessful, and a divesting and simplification of structure was begun. In 1996 the company had about 275 subsidiaries and nonsteel products were 35% of revenue.

It is very difficult for a firm to differentiate successfully and create a sustainable competitive edge against large oligopolistic competitors providing commodity products to similar standards. Moreover, the steel industry is crowded with niche players. Nevertheless, if a firm can succeed in efficiently selling existing and new customers a wider range of specialized or custom products, then cash flow should improve as sales and earnings increase. That is what Nippon Steel set out to do.

The strategy has had to address certain fundamental conditions. It had to: (1) be based on the company's existing steelmaking facilities (that is, no green-field plants); (2) accept the existing relationships with trading companies and other Japanese and foreign steel producers; and (3) establish a competitive advantage relative to other producers.

From an overall corporate perspective, the biggest issue was consolidating steel production into fewer mills, which in turn meant the integration of production, accounting, and purchasing that had existed as separate, mill-based systems. Such separation was possible when each mill was associated with a particular set of products and had its own IT system. However, it would not work when mills became less specialized and systems had to be integrated. Thus, in implementing the new strategy, an IT system that had been in place and working well for a decade had to be replaced.

A Multifaceted Strategy

Offering customized steel products tailored to a particular end use or customer product design without the cost premium that previously would have been required for such customization is the core of the company's strategy. Supporting this is an e-commerce strategy that is being implemented to simplify order processing and reduce inventories.

The customization strategy was able to build on a product-specific cost-management system that the company had instituted beginning in 1993. Thus prepared, in 1996 it began implementing procedures by which each mill can produce a variety of customized steels. To do this, Nippon Steel set out to apply lean production principles, and has gone on to utilize the emerging totally integrated management paradigm. Although lean production had become the dominant paradigm (but not practice) in many assembly industries, at the time it had yet to be used in basic materials such as steel.

The company also is seeking to become part of its lean-production customers' design, just-in-time (JIT), and customer-driven production paradigms. An example (which the industry is working toward) is steel sheets tailored specifically to a particular model of car or appliance that can be specified by the design engineers when a standard gauge or quality is not the most suitable.

Point List 6.1
Customized Casting: Implications and Expectations

Implications

- Able to produce a larger variety of products in fewer mills
- Requires gathering and managing a huge database on costs and on actual and potential customers
- Creates a system that is development-cost intensive, and thus subject to user-base economics

Expectations

- Reduce role of price as a selection criterion
- Avoid US dumping allegations

- Build in demand for replacement-part steel
- Retain and expand customer base
- Retain or increase mill efficiency

The first three expectations become possible because customized products are less subject to price pressures when tied to customers' JIT production systems, and are less easy to categorize or emulate. They are aspects of building sustainable competitive barriers between customers and other firms, and help to achieve the fourth expectation.

Implementation

The strategy requires knowing how to cost customized products precisely and how valuable customized production is for particular customers. For example, if lighter, corrosion-resistant steel reduces warranty claims and helps auto firms meet fleet gas mileage requirements, then the steel will add value that can be captured in part by Nippon Steel. Similarly, customized steel helps clients retain the market for "official" replacement parts. Accurately determining costs has meant developing an accounting system to identify specific customer groups and the specific costs of delivering a product to them.

Point list 6.2 summarizes the steps the company has been taking to implement its strategy. These are discussed more fully in the following sections.

Point List 6.2
Nippon Steel's Steps to Implement Its Strategy

- Develop a sophisticated accounting system that can accurately assess the cost of mass-producing customized products (efficient customization)
- Optimally allocate production of the increased variety of products among and within mills
- Work to control inventories for replacement-part steel for customized end products, so they can be competitively but accurately priced
- Explain to customers the benefits to them of the customized casting and e-commerce approaches
- Work to significantly reduce product delivery and production cycle times so that JIT delivery needs do not increase the company's in-process and finished inventories
- Enable customers to track their JIT orders so there is no disruption to the clients' production schedules
- Develop marketing strategies to show that customization adds value or reduces costs for customers, in exchange for which Nippon Steel

gets price stability and becomes a single-source supplier analogous to the customers' relationships with their parts suppliers

Demand Forecasts and Inventory

The collapse of Japan's bubble economy affected industries and even specific products differently. Sheet inventories for automobiles and replacement parts have been particularly critical. (Overall, the company estimates there are some 10,000 different steels for different cars and car parts!) However, Nippon Steel could not just push the issue onto the trading companies. As the channels for physical delivery, they already handle buffer stocks and keep track of available supplies. They also forecast demand on a general, industry-wide basis. However, they do not forecast demand by customer or producer. Rather, they just meet whatever specified customer requirements exist. Thus, Nippon Steel is working with Toyota on a set of mathematical and statistical algorithms that could reduce replacement auto-parts-related steel inventories by $100 million.

Given the strategic requirement of producing a wide range of customized products, Nippon Steel's management recognized they had to do a better job of forecasting specific user demand. Until then, they had been estimating the steel demand likely to result from projections of economic growth. Better forecasts required better networking with users, especially if improved JIT interfaces were going to be used. In particular, it has meant working with the automakers and auto-parts makers to estimate actual new production and replacement-part demand. As a result of this bottom-up approach, the company has gotten better at projecting specific product demand by customer.

Nippon Steel's IT System

Nippon Steel's basic IT system is the three-tier mainframe system typical of most other large Japanese companies. The IBM mainframe controls client servers that manage the PCs and workstations, control the networking system, and communicate with each mill and its equipment. The mainframe has the task of scheduling production and operations, as well as of tracking orders. The client servers are 70% mainframes. Large even by Japanese large-company standards, the system involves over 3 billion lines of code.

Each plant has its own IT systems division because each has its own unique operation as regards what it is producing and the capacity it has to produce it. In fact, each mill decides its own one- to three-month production schedule once it has been assigned orders by the head office. Each mill's mainframe system supports a WAN that delivers and processes both voice and data. (Mills are a collection of production facilities—for example, seven at Kimitsu—spread over a large area, hence a WAN rather than a LAN.)

For each product, each plant has its own legacy control systems, which means it probably is different from the comparable system at other plants. However, certain functions are controlled centrally. These include raw material purchases, transportation, aggregate demand forecasts, personnel administration, and accounting.

The main issue for all systems, particularly those related to production, is that steel plants must operate continuously: 24 hours a day, 7 days a week.

Internal communication, including the internal web site, depends on the company's own fiber-optic system and customized middleware that provides the interface between different users within the company. However, company personnel use the Internet for news, external e-mail, and the external web page. This separation is for security reasons. Not everyone inside the company has access to the internal web site.

Although production operations are fairly efficient, the company feels it needs more "TOA" (total office automation) to speed up the work flow. Thus, the company is looking at doing some benchmarking, as it believes there are several other firms in other industries that are more efficient at TOA (including IT support) than it is. Office operations at its most advanced mill, Kimitsu, in August 1998 were using Windows 3.1 and Windows 95 machines connected using Windows NT. There was no intention to switch to Windows 98 because the older system worked well enough for its purposes. The standard application programs were the Microsoft Office suite. Like Toyota and other leading IT users, Nippon Steel does not confuse buying a newer version with upgrading.

Software Choice and the Role of IT

Nippon Steel has a strong preference for customized software over packaged products, reflecting its specific organizational structures and operating advantages. From the company's perspective, IT is an input, just like iron ore or coking coal. The company has linked its software and IT strategies to overall goals through clear mission statements that explicitly note IT's importance to the firm's success. It has coupled this with active IT support-group participation in the firm's business and decision-making structure. Generally, the company has not changed its organization to use any system. There is no totally independent MIS operation.

Except for the operating systems, it generally has developed all its software and IT systems. Thus, for example, because of the complexity and individuality of each plant and of the company itself, the company does not consider packaged EMS systems suitable for its purposes. However, it does collaborate. For example, when developing the algorithms for the production management system, it worked with IBM.

When the company does buy software, it inevitably heavily customizes the package. This was the case in 1998 for a new accounting system. The vendor was Oracle, with which it already had a relationship. Payroll and billing as they relate to cost accounting for the custom-casting system, as well as the e-commerce and the older ordering systems, are self-developed and closely intertwined with the overall accounting system from Oracle.

System Development

About 150 people are working in the internal Information Systems Division and significantly more at a captive software subsidiary. Most of the company's EDP needs are filled by the subsidiary, which completely manages and maintains the mainframe system. The subsidiary is NS Solutions Corp (NSSC), as successor to ENICOM. References to NSSC are to what was ENICOM unless noted otherwise (box 6.4).

Control of an IT initiative depends on size and impact. Generally, the head office decides what systems are best to use within the head office and the company as a whole, while plant managers decide what is best within their plant to support that plant's particular production system, especially software related to controlling specific equipment. However, even at the plant level, if it is a new system, a very large change, or could affect the company's whole system, the head office is involved.

The head office has responsibility for all changes and systems relating to sales or financial issues. The level at which decisions are made reflects budget and impact. Thus, because the corporate-level accounting system, the IT-based ordering system, and the on-line e-commerce system involve virtually all aspects of the company's steel business, the decisions were made at the highest level.

The head office IT group administers the relationship with NSSC, including monitoring the interaction between NSSC's regional offices and the mills. The group works directly with NSSC on certain projects, such as the integrated, firm-wide accounting system.

For all IT projects, Nippon Steel assigns a budget and an in-house project team. NSSC then assigns its team in consultation with its parent. NSSC never works on a project for Nippon Steel in isolation. NSSC has two ways of organizing projects. One involves groups at the job sites working directly with those producing steel. In this case, the NSSC people join the steel mill conferences. In the other case, NSSC produces a new system to order for a business unit or the corporation. In such cases, it meets with the requesting unit to establish functional requirements and then develops the system. During development, there are regular meetings to discuss progress. The head office oversees testing of new software before it is incorporated into the overall system.

If the budget is exceeded, that is the responsibility of the general project leader, who comes from Nippon Steel. However, overruns do not happen in a vacuum, because the headquarters IT group requires progress and budget reports at least once a month. If a project is behind schedule or is over budget, the reason is sought. If the problem is with NSSC, the head office does not get involved except to identify the problem. NSSC is expected to

Box 6.4

NS SOLUTIONS CORP.

In 1988 Nippon Steel moved virtually all the systems personnel from its internal IT group and its Systems Corporation subsidiary into a separate, wholly owned company named ENICOM. This captive became the principal supplier of IT services to Nippon Steel. In April 2001 a restructuring merged the Electronics and Information Systems division into ENICOM and renamed the operation NS Solutions Corp. (NSSC). The company says NSCC is the fifth largest software and systems integration house in Japan, and that it plans a public offering of a minority interest as early as 2002. The new entity has about 2400 employees and projected fiscal 2001 revenue of ¥30 billion.

A group of NSSC employees works in each mill. Before being merged, Nippon Steel-related projects represented about half of ENICOM's revenue and involved about half of a work force of some 2500. Another 1000 worked in subsidiaries that were handling Nippon Steel projects only indirectly. There were 14 regional offices. On creation of NSSC, many ENICOM employees were transferred to other Nippon Steel ventures rather than to NSSC.

Besides the steel-related activities that are the focus of this chapter, ENICOM has been the top Oracle dealer in Japan. The EI Systems division has been focusing on financial services, including IT support for derivative transactions, stock trading, and liability management. This reflects a belief that some of the mathematical techniques used in steel-making are directly applicable to money management.

Those involved in steel projects have to learn about steel, including steelmaking technology and products, and about Nippon Steel. Projects are initiated at Nippon Steel's request. NSSC and Nippon Steel then address the issue as a joint, interactive effort. This is because there are, in addition to an IT component, a steel technology component and a Nippon Steel business component, and they are never completely and clearly separated. Indeed, this is fundamental to Nippon Steel's IT strategic strength and TIM approach.

In steel-related areas, NSSC works only for Nippon Steel. Other clients include pharmaceuticals and chemicals (Takeda is a client). It also has an electronics business unit in Tokyo with 600 people that does work for the Matsushita group, Daiei (a major retailer that includes supermarkets and the Lawson convenience-store chain), and various small manufacturing companies.

In 1988 almost 99% of ENICOM's revenue was from Nippon Steel; by 1997 it was 37% of total reported revenue of ¥83 billion. However, ENICOM has charged its parent on a cost basis, so Nippon Steel's share of the total business in terms of people and resources is larger. Revenue at other steel companies' captive IT firms is some 60% to 70% steel-related, but they charge their parents at cost plus a profit. Before the planned public offering of NSSC stock, Nippon Steel undoubtedly also will adopt such a practice.

solve its own issues on the computer side. To this extent NSSC operates independently.

Accounting System

During 1998 a new accounting system absorbed most of the head office IT group's time and effort. Before, each mill had its own cost accounting system. Now, the company is applying a common standard to all mills so that it can compare the real cost of producing and delivering various products from different mills. The entire steelmaking operation and the head office had to change to the new system simultaneously, so this was a big effort.

There are two main components to the system. One is a parent-company-only system; the other is the internal accounting system. Both are operated by NSSC. Each mill has its own computer managing the system in conjunction with the main computer at NSSC's office. The software was customized from packages purchased from Oracle, then integrated into the rest of the company's system by NSSC.

Also in 1998–99, Nippon Steel and ENICOM addressed Y2K problems with 30 people. It was not simple to complete, because changes had to be made directly on each of the many process-control computers that run specific pieces of equipment. The programs are date-sensitive because the company tracks the history of each batch of steel it makes. Still, given the huge amount of old code in the company's IT system, the budget of ¥2 billion was not very large.

Electronic Data System

In the 1990s Nippon Steel changed to a dialog-based, on-line management system in its mills. Called EDS (electronic data system), it links the head office, trading companies, and customers, and is intended to distribute orders to the appropriate production lines at each mill. It thus also is the interface with the e-commerce system (discussed later). The company has been working on EDS since 1992, and has done so in conjunction with its e-commerce efforts since 1996.

Reflecting the constant revision of the system based on the observed best practice of its mills, plus trading company and customer feedback, the system evolved from the earlier practice of the major trading companies (such as Mitsui and Mitsubishi) submitting orders in electronic form. Electronic ordering is done daily, usually at night, on a batch basis in an electronic data interchange (EDI) format specified by Nippon Steel that is compatible with its order entry system (OES).

Smaller trading companies traditionally have faxed orders, which are then manually entered into the IT system by Nippon Steel staff using the same OES format. Any modifications to an order, whether originally submitted electronically or by fax, or inquiries regarding status, have been by telephone or fax, although since introduction of the e-commerce system, more can be done on-line.

The number of products and services that the mills can deliver, as well as the required IT supports, have been expanding as the company has shifted toward higher-grade steels and more customized products. The basic decision criteria in this respect have been to enhance the mills' capabilities with systems and machines, to expand the capacity of the system, and to reduce costs, all through extending the use of electronics and, in turn, mill capacity, flexibility, and productivity.

A clear indication of the benefits has been the company's ability to close mills and reduce staff without any efficiency loss or reduced production capacity.

When Nippon Steel receives an order, it is split into two components. One part is order allocation and scheduling to each mill. The other is the actual production instructions to the mill receiving the allocation.

Order Allocation and Scheduling

Order allocation and scheduling probably are the most complex components of the overall system. Utilizing the company's cost-accounting system, the head office calculates the cost of producing and delivering each order. That is, an order's total delivered cost is assessed in advance. There is some human input as it relates to personnel, but otherwise everything from raw material purchasing to equipment usage at a specific mill, including maintenance, is done by the computer.

Six-month, three-month, and one-month schedules are generated. The six-month schedule addresses the processing materials needed to complete the order and helps generate the materials ordering plan; the three-month schedule applies to the production scheduling plan, and the one-month schedule relates to production control at the mill level and direct customer shipment.

The allocation of orders among mills is based on each mill's capacity, territory, and production capabilities. It is a kind of iterative expert system utilizing an analysis of the company's own best-practice operations. An initial allocation is made for a set of orders. Each mill then generates time- and cost-to-delivery estimates, as well as capacity utilization calculations. Iteration proceeds until the best practical allocation, in terms of delivered cost and capacity utilizations, is determined. The system has allowed a reduction in the number of support people—both at the head office and at mills—and an increased focus on systems integration at the plants.

Based on the orders each mill has in hand, the production scheduling process is repeated every week. This weekly schedule then translates into a daily plan and schedule for all mills. The blast furnaces must operate continuously, so raw steel that is not used immediately for specific orders is cast into slabs that go to inventory for use later.

Production Control

Once a mill has been allocated an order, its production management system (PMS) controls how and over what period the steel is made.

There are three levels to PMS: planning, operational control, and process control (which directs mill machinery, such as cranes). Planning involves high-speed computers and large amounts of data to plan the best way to produce the orders. Production is scheduled based on a database of previous experience making such orders, current and expected plant and equipment utilization, and a sophisticated mathematical algorithm developed in cooperation with IBM.

Planning sends its scheduling to the processing control system. This includes having the necessary input materials in the right place at the right time. Each order has its own designated slab from the continuous caster. Thus, the system knows where every order and related materials actually are at any point in time. This means there is a precise match between in-process or finished inventories in the yard and a given order.

The company sees these as mission-critical issues, which its proprietary ERP can perform. The complex optimization model and its associated software are essential to making each mill efficient because each order is handled on a unique basis and must be tightly integrated with the mill's physical, technical, and personnel operations.

Sequencing is the key to economic success in this process and is the hallmark of the company's system. Major cost-efficiency variables appear to be yield, inventory, and delivery. In this manner, the system is constantly balancing costs and physical efficiency.

Other Aspects

Final shipment generates billing information from the mill to the head office, which in turn generates an invoice to the trading company and finally to the customer, while physical shipment is directly to the customer. The usual time from order to delivery is about two months, although it can run three months under certain circumstances. With appliance and auto manufacturers the company is moving toward JIT delivery.

Auto parts makers determine their steel orders from production schedules given them by assemblers. As a result, they do not always have a precise idea of their requirements until very close to the time of actual need. This complicates Nippon Steel's JIT strategy and means that sometimes there are spot shortages of specific products. However, because a defined schedule becomes a regular flow from the plant, Nippon Steel can deliver (modified) JIT if a customer sets a regular time, say once a week. In contrast, when there are single-item orders, the company and the customer may not know about delivery for three months.

Assessment

When Nippon Steel undertook the EDS initiative in the mid-1990s, steel-making IT was very different at each plant because each had its own set of products, involving its own set of specialized equipment and techniques. Consolidating production in fewer plants meant having to introduce more flexibility into swing plants (those that could produce a variety of products) without losing the advantages of focus and scale.

Nippon Steel's successful development and implementation of such a complex and sophisticated system has been aided by Japan's long-term employment system. This is because, for the system to work smoothly, there must be close integration of company, steelmaking, and IT systems knowledge. The company estimates it takes four to five years to train someone to use and develop these systems, so there is a benefit from the staff working for the company for 35 years or more. This supports the observation that successful strategies must closely integrate industry, technology, and personnel practices.

E-Commerce

E-commerce and order-processing systems are examples of how leading users can be on the IT frontier when it is necessary to accomplish strategic aims. A new e-commerce system envisioned in the mid-1990s was to be managed by ENICOM and Nippon Steel for a Japanese steel industry consortium composed of the integrated producers, the trading companies, and the major appliance makers, with cars to be added later.

As implemented and used by Nippon Steel, it would represent an extension of ERP that considers and tries to influence the external environment on the firm's behalf, a TIM strategy. Competitors sensed this, and in late 1999 several major firms withdrew, particularly NKK and Kawasaki. The initial project's failure suggests that competitor awareness will help many industries avoid the "Gurley-gurgle" of being sucked into a vortex dominated or strongly influenced by a single firm. At the same time, Nippon Steel was able to use the expertise it developed to recast the project into an Internet initiative. Moreover, the company believes that its Internet site will emerge as the global leader.

The next section outlines the original project. This is followed by an analysis of the project as recast by Nippon Steel, the remaining participants, and a number of new ones.

ECN: An Attempt at a Japanese Industrywide System

With MITI sponsorship, in 1996 Nippon Steel began laying the foundation for a new e-commerce system, dubbed ECN (electronic commerce network), that would involve the entire industry, including producers, users of the major types of steel, and traditional intermediaries.

The investment needed to access the system was not large, so steel buyers could decide to use it to order directly. This was a threat to the trading companies that have controlled steel marketing in Japan. Despite the risks, they cooperated because they would share in the improved efficiencies. For example, fewer people could run their steel businesses. Also, as holders of buffer stocks and sources of credit, they could concentrate more on the steel service and raw material supply parts of the business, where the value added is more obvious than in merely being a conduit for orders.

Nippon Steel assigned Takeo Dazai, a senior manager, to work with the trading companies and major appliance manufacturers to develop the pilot project. After the pilot, the expectation was that the system would be extended to vending machines (which are very big market in Japan) and, especially, autos. Only steels made to order were being included, because customized products are where the biggest scheduling problems, as well as the best margins, occur. Reflecting what steels are most likely to be customized, the project initially was limited to flat-rolled products.

After an extensive pilot, rollout began during 1997–98. As of the beginning of 2000, about 100 companies had indicated a willingness to join the network, including Honda and Toyota. There was a continuous flow of market information through an Internet connection using PCs and Windows NT. However, the second and third largest steelmakers, NKK and Kawasaki, declined to participate, and so the concept had to be reconsidered.

Kouzai.com

To replace the aborted ECN initiative, Nippon Steel, Sumitomo Metal, and Kobe Steel (through affiliates and in cooperation with several banks) formed kouzai.com in March 2000. This Internet-based electronic marketplace began to register participants in May 2000 and began to trade the next month. Sales through the site reached 20,000 tonnes a month in July 2001, when an upgraded system for tracking and modifying orders on-line was added. That brought in steel service companies that supply auto and appliance parts companies, because these firms have JIT programs that can mean constant adjustments to their near-term steel needs. This was expected based on previous experience. The auto assemblers themselves are not involved directly. The target is 5 million tonnes a year by 2007, more than 20 times the current level but less than 5% of annual steel production in Japan.

As of July 2001, the three steelmakers had been joined as suppliers by 10 steel service centers (including those run by the major trading companies), which obtain steel from myriad steelmakers. Sellers pay 0.5% of the sales price. There are 450 registered buyers, including users, steel wholesalers, and trading companies. Buyers do not pay to participate.

The site takes orders continuously during the day for hot coil, cold-rolled

coil, coated sheet, plate, pipe, H-shaped bar, wire, stainless sheet, and stainless pipe. This is an advantage to the appliance and auto parts producers
that are the ultimate buyers of most of the sheet and coil because it facilitates
JIT ordering compared to the once-a-day ordering of the large trading companies.

Suppliers post prices for many items, and list other stock items without
prices. Quotes on made-to-order items also can be requested. The site does
not perform an auction function. Buyers ask for a quote for specific quantity,
delivery date, and payment terms, and select from among the responses.
Once a buyer has selected the seller, the two communicate directly on-line
concerning other details.

For Nippon Steel the benefits are not as great as they would have been
with the original system, because the orders received must be reformatted
to its internal system. However, it is working on a program that will do this
automatically. The actual seller on Nippon Steel's behalf is Nippon Steel
Trading (NST), which is 45% owned by Nippon Steel; the rest is owned by
various Japanese banks. NST electronically transfers orders to Nippon Steel
daily on a batch basis, just as the major trading houses have been doing
since the late 1980s. However, all follow-up can be done on-line, an improvement compared to the traditional fax and phone system.

There are two competing electronic steel marketplaces in Japan, both
owned by groups of trading companies. Some of them also participate in
kouzai.com. Neither site directly involves a major steel producer, because
NKK and Kawasaki, like Nucor, have in the medium run opted not to participate in any network or e-commerce site. Both marketplaces also have
bought similar sites in the United States. However, neither is doing well,
and kouzai.com expects to be the sole survivor.

NST has a joint venture, called *livesteel.com*, with the trading arm of
South Africa's largest steel producer, Iscor. In the very long run Nippon Steel
sees this being joined with the e-commerce sites of other firms—specifically
Usinor and Posco, with which it has alliances—and merging with
kouzai.com.

Consequences for Processes

Gathering all the required information related to an order (something that
used to take two or three days) now takes two minutes, and the information
is easily utilized. A newly entered order is shown on the system instantly.
The system uses a standard electronic data interchange, which was combined into an open-end standard in 2001. This local standard has been
converted into a web-accessible open-ended database. That is, Nippon Steel
and NSSC have data on each company and order in an on-line order book,
and the relevant data generally are available via the Internet to many customers and the trading companies.

This greatly facilitates order tracking, so customers can know their delivery schedule precisely. Direct results of introducing this system have been

lower inventories, far fewer customer calls, and fewer deferred orders. The company also hopes to reduce time-to-delivery because the system is based on the real demand of users such as appliance makers and auto parts producers.

The system eliminates potential errors from mistaken copying of information from faxes, which were commonly used under the old system and which sometimes caused delays, errors, and frustration. Phone and fax charges (which are especially high in Japan because of NTT's effective monopoly) have been reduced, too.

Databases and e-mail have eliminated a lot of faxes and other paper shuffling. In organizing sales data and forecasts by product, customer, and mill, it also has became easier to compile data for every type of sheet steel and customer. This makes understanding and forecasting shifts in demand easier and more accurate.

The Kimitsu Works

At the mill level, Kimitsu is an excellent example of how Nippon Steel is implementing its linking of electronic data-interchange and e-commerce systems with flexible customized production and the JIT inventory control paradigm for automobiles and appliances. The early 1990s goal of making it one of the most flexible and productive mills in the world before the end of the decade was largely achieved. It is tracking its costs of production and carrying inventory using the new corporate accounting system. It thus represents a microcosm of the firm's emerging TIM strategy. (Similar systems exist at other works—for example, Yawata has the same order-production-flow mainframe system—but as of 2000 none were as completely upgraded to the new overall system.)

Nippon Steel started designing Kimitsu, located in Chiba prefecture facing Tokyo Bay, in 1961. The facility includes docking, unloading, and loading facilities covering a site 5 kilometers in length and 2 kilometers wide (thus, about 2500 acres). It is well positioned near the large Tokyo market and produces 8 million to 9 million tonnes of steel per year, using three of its four blast furnaces. (The number 4 furnace is the largest, and has been replicated in Shanghai under license from Nippon Steel. Number 1 has been shut down because it is too small to operate continuously.) Once a furnace is started, it must run continuously (until shut down for scheduled maintenance, which usually is once a year). The furnaces are designed to use iron ore shot directly into the furnace. This saves the cost of pelletizing the ore. There typically is about 42 days of raw materials on hand, including what is in docked vessels.

Kimitsu can make the broadest range of products of any of the company's facilities. The huge hot strip mill is enclosed due to environmental regulations, which has the benefit of conserving heat. The cold-rolling mill makes thin coils (down to one millimeter thick) and thicker sheet for auto and appliance makers. The pipe mill can produce pipe up to two meters in diameter for the oil industry, building contractors, and water distribution systems. Shaped products for construction, wire and rod (which go into everything from radial tires to rebar), and heavy plate for shipbuilding also are produced.

The company spent the first two decades after Kimitsu opened (that is, until the late 1980s) improving the plant and the IT systems controlling it. This resulted in a 25% improvement in physical labor productivity: crude steel production in 1989 was almost the same as in 1973–74, but the labor force went from 7700 to 6000. With output staying about the same, employment was 3800 in 1997.

IT at Kimitsu

The production control center operates 24×7 using three shifts of four people on each. Nippon Steel's use of computers to control its plants and the steelmaking process dates from the 1950s, so when Kimitsu was designed in 1961 and began operations in 1965, it was all on-line (AOL)—computerized from the start to permit continuous process control using the company's PMS. To run the plant, Nippon Steel developed Kimitsu On-line Computing System. This was combined with office automation and organizing of a computer systems group at the mill level. Giving a mill so much autonomy was a very new idea at the time.

In the plant, the company uses the same three-layer computer structure as at the corporate level, with the process computer system controlling the plant computers, which in turn control the computers that manage each production operation. (Initially these were four IBM 360-M40s, the largest machines then available; by the late 1990s top-of-the-line laptops had equivalent computing power.)

The system currently uses two basic types of software. One involves massive data processing for handling orders, production scheduling, and production flow. The other is a flexible software system that can be used to quickly modify the system controlling a particular machine or activity where frequent adjustments may be necessary. Because it took the company 10 years to fully construct and complete the works, the mill's design and the control systems were modified along the way, and have continued to be changed in response to new steelmaking and data-processing technologies. In conjunction with NSSC, the company, and its local employees, Kimitsu has developed its own groupware to manage the order assignment process (described earlier).

Kimitsu's main IT issues are related to managing a huge data warehouse (500 Gb). These data cover production, quality control, and the history of all the steel ever produced at the works. The production management system is the biggest part, because Kimitsu produces many types of steel. The basic flow always starts with ironmaking, then steelmaking, and then the specific end products. Along with the physical and technical requirements are the General System Administration requirements. These include energy usage, equipment, and accounting (but only for the mill's own costs; head office handles receivables and overhead). In addition, head office manages personnel on a corporate-wide basis.

The mainframes and servers are all IBM, which Kimitsu upgrades roughly every five years as they go off lease. The IT group also uses fault-free Tandem computers to make sure there is never any downtime. The six Tandem computers directly control six nodes and an NCR-5100 that handles the data warehouse, which includes information on order flow and scheduling. Via the nodes, the Tandems control the 100 process computers.

Kimitsu is a significant IT-based operation, although there are only 13 systems people from the parent company at the mill. Besides on-site staff, NSSC maintains a nearby regional office. In total, based on personnel numbers, about 10% of ENICOM's business in the late 1990s was Kimitsu-related.

There also are 900 four-person line crews that are beginning to use PCs on a team basis. From their inputs, Kimitsu's management hopes to develop a database that can be mined to improve production and quality. The in-house staff and NSSC currently are looking at outside data-mining packages to see if there is one suitable for the task. This shows the firm's flexibility in selecting software when the basic functioning of the mill and company system are not involved.

Evaluation

Nippon Steel's integrated IT strategy corresponds to the important criteria for success in steel stressed by Ahlbrandt et al. (1996). Each IT investment decision is "made in light of a focused market strategy" and fits with the totality of the firm's investments, including links to steelmaking technology and the employees' knowledge base. The company and its IT subsidiary's managers at all levels "understand and take advantage of the interlocking nature of investments" in the broadest sense (machines, IT, employee skills, human-resource practices, and organization), as well as the complementary relationships. This includes the recognition that "new technology and human capital must be developed in use at the same time." Further strategy and practice are aligned "in the same direction so they reinforce one another," and so that improvement is continuous (*kaizen*). The basis for this is "a conviction about where they want to go that is rooted in a deep understanding of products and markets" while "setting a very high goal: to pursue quality and efficiency simultaneously." This reflects the IT fluency of the firm's managers.

In addition, successful firms have an articulated, conscious, strategic link between technology and market objectives based on technology, people, and

organization. Indeed, research reported at a Columbia Business School forum in 1997 by Ichniowski shows that organization matters—particularly
the integration of human resources, technology, and plant layout.

Conclusion

The major driver for Nippon Steel's e-commerce and customized-product
strategies has been its need to move away from the foreign exchange impacts
and cost-cutting-only initiatives of the 1990s. To do this, it has had to reduce
the ease with which competitors can emulate its strategic and technical
advances. By coupling steelmaking and organizational skills with proprietary IT systems in creating and implementing its TIM initiative, Nippon
Steel has moved toward this goal.

For although the Japanese industry shares data in the overall demand-
supply chain, including with trading companies and firms supplying materials and support services, such cooperation usually has not extended to
computerization. Given this freedom to act independently relative to IT,
Nippon Steel feels it can continue to retain the benefits generated by combining its customized casting and accounting systems with its links to the
e-commerce and EDI ordering system. That is, the company does not feel
such benefits will just be competed away.

The company hopes to improve customer contact, reduce customer migration, and keep costs low for custom-cast steels (efficient customization).
This includes new steels that are more easily recycled, a major goal of Toyota. Nippon Steel is using IT to influence customer and partner behavior
and expectations and to tie them to the company on an interactive basis at
a time when the competition looks less advanced and sophisticated. Persuading them to make firm-specific IT and organizational investments that
favor Nippon Steel is part of this approach (for example, kouzai.com). This
involves gathering and managing a wide range of information about its client base, its clients' demand for steel, and its mill operations on a continuous, integrated, interactive basis.

The company's objective is to develop an IT mix that supports its strategies and differentiates it from competitors on a long-term, sustainable basis.
It has accomplished this by using IT to enhance existing strengths and to
create barriers while looking to functional and market gains to justify the
expense of customizing systems and integrating them into a single IT system
while training employees to use it.

By incorporating most of what the customer and head office need to know
in the e-commerce, order allocation (EDS), and accounting systems, independence of the mills has been increased, extending a process begun in
1993. That is, better monitoring and companywide commonality of decision-making criteria have reduced the amount of direct head office control
required as more things are done quickly and automatically on-line.

IT thus plays a key role in serving corporate goals such as enhancing the total productivity of all mills by improving production scheduling, reducing inventories, and strengthening customer relations. These systems are in turn coupled with marketing, production, customer service, new product development, and constant cost reduction that reflect Nippon Steel's understanding of its business, its industry, and its competitive strengths within this context.

Thus, Nippon Steel's actions serve to reinforce the view that major Japanese firms do particularly well in large, complex production processes such as steel that involve close coordination of myriad suppliers, multiple product variations, and different parts of the firm. Customized software has contributed to this kind of production integration and is an integral part of a global market advantage that is not easily replicated. Nippon Steel is thus a leader in implementing the totally integrated management paradigm.

Acknowledgments

Much of the material on Nippon Steel's IT development and use was gathered in briefings by its head office systems group and ENICOM in 1997, 1998, and 2000, and subsequent correspondence, as well as meetings with executives of NSSC and kouzai.com, the company's e-commerce initiative, in July 2001. In July 1998 the Sloan study team was briefed at the Kimitsu works on the introduction of the company's then new e-commerce strategy and its implementation in terms of customized casting. I wish to thank the many staffers who participated in my education regarding steel and IT's application to the industry, and to Nippon Steel in particular.

7

Automobiles

Toyota

This chapter looks at Toyota Motor Corp. (Toyota Jidosha) and the automobile industry.

Mr. Hiroshi Okuda, chairman of Toyota, knows "When the Ground Rules Change" (as he titled a 1998 speech at the Yale School of Management), and the implications that has for Toyota and the global automobile industry. He sees "three watersheds in the history of the automobile industry. Each time, a new business model changed the ground rules for the industry. Each time, the new model seemed invincible. And each time, it gave way to changing circumstances and a new business model. . . . Our old business model is breaking down for four main reasons. One, we need to decentralize our manufacturing and R&D activities. . . . Two, the product and process paradigms that Henry Ford established are themselves breaking down. . . . Three, information technology is transforming the inner workings of the automobile. It is also transforming the way we develop and make and sell our products. And four, the changing product paradigm and the growing role of information technology will open our industry to a vast array of competitors."

Gone are the glory days of the early 1980s when any Japanese car could sell in the U.S. market at a premium. A strong yen, the collapse of Japan's bubble economy, and a depressed Japanese auto market significantly changed the industry's structure, and now only Toyota and Honda remain as independent Japanese producers. Toyota's response is a strategy that, in the next two decades, will have significant impact on the global industry and on transportation and logistics generally, and will ensure the company's position as the industry leader.

Toyota clearly demonstrates that "old-economy" products such as automobiles and manufacturing processes such as assembly can be significantly transformed through sophisticated use of IT. This is seen in Toyota's development of its system to automate its traditional just in time (JIT) ordering from suppliers, its evolving intelligent transportation system (ITS), and its "smart" cars. These are presented in this chapter, showing how the company's IT strategy and overall management goals are integrated through mission statements and actions that explain IT's importance to achieving the firm's goals and long-term success.

Toyota's drive to use IT to control its competitive destiny has been motivated by a number of important developments in the Japanese and global automobile industries. The first two sections provide some understanding of the competitive context in terms of governmental policies, economic factors, and corporate dynamics. The third section looks specifically at Toyota's place in this environment.

Toyota's response has been to develop what it terms a "smart" strategy—smart design, smart production, and smart products—that offers customers an expanded range of customized products and services in ways not easily copied by competitors (efficient customization). Discussion of these, concentrating on IT's role in this dynamic process, comprises most of the chapter. A key component of this is a fundamental rethinking of the concept of an assembly line. The last part of the chapter summarizes Toyota's IT philosophy and provides an overview of how the company structures and selects IT.

Table 7.1 lists the world's major automobile groups, and table 7.2 ranks the 10 largest motor vehicle makers.

Competitive Landscape

Continued cost and quality improvements, changes in the types of vehicles demanded, and excess capacity were important determinants of the competitive environment in the 1990s, and will continue to be in the 2000s.

Lessening of the Low-Cost Producer Advantage

In the 1970s and early 1980s Japanese automobile companies were the world's lowest-cost producers (see Womack et al. 1990; Smitka 1991; 1993; and Fujimoto 1999). Japan's productivity advantage may have been double that of U.S. producers and triple European levels. At an exchange rate over 200 yen per dollar, this translated into an almost 50% cost advantage. However, by the mid-1990s the advantage for the average Japanese maker had been largely wiped out by the yen's roughly doubling in value after 1985 and Western (especially U.S.) producers' productivity and quality gains. This is why Smitka was basically correct in 1993 in predicting the Japanese industry's decline.

Still, averages can disguise substantial cost differentials among firms. Thus, although Western producers had matched the Japanese average, Fujimoto (1999) and others have estimated that Toyota's cost advantage over other Japanese firms was still at least several hundred dollars per car in the early 1990s. It is the relatively weaker Japanese firms (particularly Nissan) that have borne the greatest effects of these changes.

Table 7.1 Major Groupings of Automakers, Ranked by Size[1]

General Motors Corp (U.S.)[2]
  Adam Opel AG (Germany)
  Fuji Heavy Industries (Japan, 20% owned, makes Subaru)
  Isuzu (Japan, 49% owned)
  Saab Automobiles AB (Sweden, 50% owned)
  Suzuki (Japan, 10% owned)

Ford Motor Co. (U.S.)
  Aston Martin Flagonda Ltd. (U.K.)
  Jaguar (U.K.)
  Mazda (Japan, 33.4% owned)
  Volvo (Sweden, cars only, 100% owned from March 1999)[3]

DaimlerChrysler AG (Germany)
  Freightliner (U.S., 100% owned, heavy trucks)
  Mitsubishi Motor (Japan, 34% owned from October 2000)
  Hyundai Motor (Korea, 9% owned from September 2000)
  Kia Motors (Korea, 30% owned by Hyundai)

Toyota Motor Corp (Japan)[4]
  Daihatsu Kogyo (50% owned since 1995)
  Hino Jidosha Kogyo (50% owned from August 2001, trucks and buses)

Volkswagen AG (Germany)
  Audi (98.99% owned)
  Seat (Spain, 100% owned)

Fiat SpA (Italy)[2]
  Alfa Romeo, Ferrari, Lancia (100% owned)
  Maserati (100% owned directly or indirectly)

Renault SA (France)
  Nissan (Japan, 36.8% owned from May 1999)
  Samsung (Korea, from 1 September 2000)

Note: This list includes major ownership positions; joint ventures and cooperative agreements generally are excluded. An affiliate is based in the same country as the group parent unless indicated otherwise. Among 10 largest, Honda Motor Co. (Japan), and PSA Peugeot Citroen (France) do not belong to any group.

[1]Motor vehicle revenue of the group leader in 2000 (for which see table 7.2).

[2]General Motors and Fiat have a "strategic alliance" and cross-shareholdings.

[3]Having exited the car business, Volvo is an independent Swedish company that is a major producer of medium and heavy trucks and buses. Absorbed Mack Trucks (U.S.) and the Renault truck brands (France) in January 2001, owns 5% of Mitsubishi Motors.

[4]In July 2001 Toyota and PSA Peugeot Citroen announced a joint project for subcompacts to be sold primarily in Europe under each firm's name. As discussed in the text, Toyota has been increasing its long-standing equity interests in Daihatsu and Hino. In 1974 it owned 7.1% of Hino and 7.5% of Daihatsu, and now owns more than half of each.

Sources: Company filings. At ai-online.com (maintained by Automotive News) there is a more complete (19 printed pages) list of global joint ventures and affiliations as of some unspecified time in 2000. Especially heavy on providing information on which companies build or license other companies' models and technology, it apparently is not routinely updated.

Table 7.2 World's 10 Largest Motor Vehicle Makers, Ranked by Revenue, 2000[1]

Revenue[2]	All vehicles[3]	Company
185	8.56	General Motors Corp. (U.S.) [GM]
170	7.42	Ford Motor Co. (U.S.) [F]
152	4.75	DaimlerChrysler AG (Germany) [DCX]
106	5.61	Toyota Motor Corp. (Japan) [7203,TM]
81	5.06	Volkswagen AG (Germany)
54	2.35	Fiat Group (Italy)
52	2.54	Honda Motor Co. (Japan) [7267, HC]
49	2.23	Nissan Motor Co. (Japan) [7201, NSANY]
42	2.82	PSA Peugeot Citroen (France)
38	2.46	Renault (France)

Note: Ticker symbols are in square brackets for firms traded in the United States or Japan.
   [1]Data for Japanese firms are for the fiscal year ending 31 March 2001.
   [2]In billion U.S. dollars. Translations from other currencies are as reported by the companies.
   [3]In million units sold. Includes heavy trucks, buses, and coaches. A large percentage of what are called "light trucks" or "light commercial vehicles" in various sources are SUVs and pickup trucks that are used by individuals as passenger vehicles. It is impossible to meaningfully divide the market into commercial and noncommercial vehicles.
   Sources: Company filings.

Shift in Composition of Demand

In high-income economies, including Japan, there has been a shift from sedans to minivans to sport-utility vehicles (SUVs) and (in the United States) light pickup trucks as well. This benefited Toyota in the medium term because SUV margins are higher and Toyota uses many of the same parts in both its regular cars and SUVs. However, initially the U.S. firms that pioneered minivans and SUVs were able to arrest their loss of U.S. market share and to reap profits that have strengthened their competitive position as they started to apply Toyota's lean production system.

Vans, SUVs, station wagons, and light trucks have become very popular in Japan, too, going from 14.4% of the market in 1991 to 40.8% in 1997 and 51% in 1998. This shift particularly affected Honda, where such vehicles went from 0% to 64% of Japanese sales, and Mazda, where they went from 10% to 70%. Mitsubishi, which has always produced light trucks, saw them go from 32% to 63% of sales. For Toyota the impact was not as marked, reflecting Toyota's improved competitive position in traditional cars. Still, such vehicles' share increased from 11% to 35%. However, there has been increased competition from imports into Japan, which rose from less than 1% of the total market before 1985 to over 6% by 1996, and over 30% in the very profitable large-car segment that includes high-end BMW and Mercedes.

All participants have been able to follow these demand shifts. Moreover, with the support of their global groups, Toyota's domestic competitors should be able to continue to make such shifts, including increases in value added through new features and technologies.

Effects of a Strong Yen

In the wake of the September 1985 Plaza Accord, a strong yen made Japanese auto exports less competitive in world markets. This stimulated foreign direct investment (FDI) by Japanese producers, which further reduced export demand for Japanese cars. Indeed, despite the Asian market's rapid growth until 1997, local content and production requirements meant Japanese producers' high share did not help much in absorbing excess Japanese production capacity. In 1995, for example, of total sales of 3.9 million vehicles in the region other than Japan, only 600,000 were imported from Japan, an increase of just 100,000 from 1991. At the same time, some 3.5 million vehicles were produced in those Asian countries, including exports to markets outside Asia.

Excess Capacity

Japanese vehicle shipments (exports plus domestic demand) hit an all-time high annualized rate of 13.6 million units toward the end of 1991. Domestic production peaked at 13.5 million units in 1990, then fell to about 10.1 million in 1998, in reaction to the extended economic malaise. Exports dropped from about 6.6 million units in 1986 to 3.3 million in 1998, while domestic demand, which peaked in 1990 at 7.8 million, fell by about 1 million during the 1990s. Overseas production rose dramatically from very low levels in 1986 to several million units a year by 1998. Correspondingly, capacity in Japan peaked at 14.2 million units in 1992, with utilization at 90%. By early 2001 it was estimated at 12.6 million units with 80% of capacity used (Nomura Securities Company, quoted in the *Wall Street Journal*, 16 March 2001).

The combined, interactive effects of a strong yen and FDI on exports, plus the drop in domestic demand due to the prolonged recession, have created excess capacity in Japan estimated at 3 to 4 million units. It is unlikely to be absorbed by either a Japanese recovery or exports, because domestic demand is saturated at around 7 million units a year and overseas production is expanding. More plant closings thus are inevitable. The capacity overhang has put downward pressure on prices while increasing domestic and export competition. Thus, yen appreciation and Japan's economic difficulties have had a direct effect on profits and competition. There also have been indirect and strategic effects.

In a market with excess capacity due to weak demand, a low-cost, higher-margin producer has a large advantage. It is in a better position to continue investment in new model development, as well as in R&D and more productive equipment, compared to its rivals. In a capital-intensive, fixed-investment industry like automobiles, this situation yields tremendous operating advantages that tend to compound over time. Such a firm can afford to price lower in order to maintain market share, and to keep its factories operating profitably and close to its minimum efficient operating capacity.

In contrast, weaker firms often cut back in areas such as R&D, new model development, and plant upgrades. If the low level of demand is short-term, such actions may have minimal strategic effects. But when soft demand and excess capacity become protracted, as they have for Japan, the competitive effects can enable the low-cost, higher-margin producer to supply a vehicle that is both technically superior and less expensive. This appears to have been the situation for Toyota and Honda compared to Mazda, Nissan, and Mitsubishi.

Worse, excess capacity has not been limited to Japan and appears to have been growing. Globally, estimates for 1997 were 15 to 20 million units, and some analysts estimated excess capacity as high as 24 million units in 2000. The 1997 numbers are equivalent to a year or more of sales in the United States. Much of the excess plant is in high-income countries, but includes Brazil. Moreover, capacity is being added in developing countries. This means Japanese FDI in automobiles will need to be very efficient while being responsive to demand in terms of size, price, fuel economy, local conditions, and the environment.

The Emerging Competitive Environment

Several other important trends are affecting the automobile industry. First is that unit growth in demand is in developing economies. Second is the promulgation of stringent environmental and fuel-efficiency standards, especially in California. Third, the industry has been consolidating into global groups. Related to this is the weakness of many of Japan's and Korea's automakers.

Although exports of autos and auto parts have been an important source of demand for Japanese producers since the 1960s, Japanese cars no longer are in short supply or sell at a premium in the U.S. market. With over half of sales being in foreign markets, events external to Japan—such as wealth effects from the U.S. stock market and the 1997–98 Asian financial crisis—affect Japanese producers directly. In the global market, sourcing decisions depend principally on demand for specific vehicle types, exchange rates, and local-content rules.

Growth Markets

The fastest-growing vehicle market from the late 1980s to the late 1990s was Asia, and this is almost universally seen as the key region for future growth, although Latin America also has potential. Markets in high-income countries are simply saturated—there is one vehicle per licensed driver in the

United States, for example—but in developing economies there is one for every 10 or more drivers.

With about an 80% share into the mid-1990s, Japanese producers have dominated Asia. Although this partly represented early recognition of the potential, the firms also were pushed in this direction in the 1990s by the combined effects of Japan's recession and the strong yen. However, the size and growth of this market have brought strong challenges from U.S. and European auto groups beginning in the late 1990s.

Toyota's evolution reflects these trends, because overseas sales and production grew substantially during the 1990s. Indeed, sales growth is now mostly outside Japan, and the company expects that overseas sales eventually will be over 65% of revenues, compared to 48% in 1994. The company's top executives see Asian markets, where Toyota sold 433,000 vehicles in 1995—versus nearly 1.1 million in the United States and almost 2.1 million in Japan—as critical to the success of plans to boost global sales to 6 million units by 2010. Much larger sales in China and India are central to this strategy. Because of Daihatsu's strength in the Chinese market, Toyota increased its ownership in the company to over 50% in 1995.

Other Factors

Japan, several European countries, and U.S. states such as California (the fifth largest car market in the world) have introduced increasingly stringent environmental and fuel-efficiency standards. Because the regulations are frequently on a fleet-sold basis (the average performance of all cars the company sells in that regulated market), they affect producers' ability to meet them while still responding to the increased demand for SUVs, which tend to be less fuel-efficient. Therefore, automakers need to have more cars with better mileage and emission performance in order to sell more of their high-margin SUVs without paying large penalties. In addition, it is likely that many low-income countries such as China, which have long had serious pollution, will need to implement similar regulations.

The emergence of large global groups also is a major change in the competitive landscape. Group formation benefited from the 1997–98 Asian financial crisis and Japan's continued recession, because these forced the major Korean producers—Hyundai, Daewoo, and Samsung—and the weaker Japanese producers to restructure. Toyota's domestic auto revenues and profitability declined during the 1990s as competitors lowered prices to generate sales even at a loss. Still, due to its low-cost, higher-margin position, the company was able to maintain its minimum efficient production level and remain profitable. Now that these other Japanese firms (except Honda) have joined global groups, they will continue to exist, and will be stronger challengers in export and domestic markets because of better access to new designs and technical resources.

Toyota's Competitive Position

Throughout the 1990s Toyota and Honda remained profitable while their Japanese competitors faced losses and increased pressure to rationalize, as well as to minimize R&D and model changes. Toyota and Honda were able to bring new and improved products to the market, including truly innovative vehicles such as the hybrid car. This strategic approach helped Toyota maintain, and perhaps even improve, its competitiveness, but it did not raise production at Toyota's domestic plants. This is because Toyota had to lower domestic output and shift production overseas in response to a strong yen, weak domestic demand, and foreign government regulation and investment incentives.

Every 10 yen change in the exchange rate against the U.S. dollar affects the company's profits by ¥1 billion. This means the yen's weakening into the 120s in early 2001 will help profits, while the strengthening in early 2000 had a negative impact. This of course applies to other Japanese firms. Exchange rate concerns have encouraged Toyota to shift production outside Japan to hedge the impact on operating profits.

At the same time, Toyota wants its Japanese production to be about 13,000 units per day. This is because if production drops below 12,000, it would have to run less than eight hours a day, which it sees as its minimum efficient production level. Thus, it uses its production efficiency to lower prices to assure this level of demand, thereby raising its domestic market share and forcing competitors to accept a residual supply position. (In the fiscal year ending in March 2001, Toyota's domestic market share was 43.1%, compared to 42.2% the previous year.)

Toyota's Strategy

To supply a diverse, global market successfully, Toyota has developed an equally diverse and global strategic response. While there are many elements to this response, two are particularly important. One is to use IT to enhance Toyota's lean production and lean design strategy so that it evolves into an even more efficient and productive "smart" production and design strategy. The second is to design and develop vehicles that are "smart." The first aspect bears on the way Toyota produces its products, which in turn influences product design and production processes. The second aspect affects the products and services Toyota will be selling.

Many Japanese auto producers added capacity during the economic expansion of the late 1980s. Most was in highly automated plants that proved to be economically inefficient due to high capital and maintenance costs, as well as excessive downtime caused by the complexity of the equipment and processes. In contrast, Toyota, while experimenting with sophisticated automation off-line, stuck to its basic philosophy of keeping things simple and relying on its skilled labor. The emphasis was on total cost effectiveness and reliability. Equipment with "just enough" functions was preferred; technology for its own sake was avoided. Thus, for example, Toyota bought low-cost robots with payback periods of no more than two years (the equivalent of at most a year's labor cost).

This orientation led Toyota to develop a multipath design and production strategy, and to combine it with the strategic use of IT, to boost both organizational and product performance. To differentiate this from its traditional lean production strategy, Toyota refers to its "smart" strategy. IT's role in the smart design and smart production parts of the strategy is taken up in the following sections. (These are described extensively by Fujimoto 1999; however, he touches only briefly on the role of IT.)

The second part of Toyota's new approach—smart product strategy—has not received much attention in the literature. It is, however, the linchpin in Toyota's plan to extend the growing role of embedded software and electronics in automobiles generally in order to meet its twin initiatives in environmentally sensitive vehicles and intelligent transportation systems, respectively.

From Toyota's perspective the strategy is evolutionary. The company had developed a comprehensive lean production system by the early 1970s. As other Japanese producers emulated it, the whole Japanese industry began to achieve similar productivity and quality improvements, giving it a huge productivity and cost advantage by the early 1980s. This was eliminated only in the 1990s by foreign competitors' strong productivity improvements as they also adopted many lean production principles, aided by the yen's appreciation after 1985.

Toyota has some 30 years of experience with lean production, compared to less than 10 years for Western firms. In that time, lean concepts have been totally integrated into Toyota's organization and strategic thinking. Thus, as the company felt increased competitive pressures and the need for a new approach, it was in a good position to assess the strengths and weaknesses of its production system. By actually making such an assessment, it showed its ability to learn and think in an evolutionary manner.

Smart Production

Lean production approaches notwithstanding, final assembly at Toyota factories in the 1980s was simply a variant of the 1910s Ford-style sequential moving assembly lines, and the economics of such a system were breaking down. There were steps in the assembly process where Toyota had improved productivity to a point that further improvements were marginal. These bottlenecks bounded improvements to the speed of the entire line. Limits also were being seen in the benefits of assembling larger "black-box" units delivered from suppliers fully ready for inclusion in a vehicle. In addition, the labor force was aging and, despite the recession, Toyota has felt that longer term, there is likely to be a shortage of assembly workers, leading to more older workers, part-timers, returnees, foreigners, and women.

These points led to a complete rethinking of the assembly line. The new approach was initiated in a new plant in Kyushu in 1992, and then implemented at Toyota City in 1995 to produce the small RAV4 SUV. Success in these locations led to a 1999 revamping of the plant in Georgetown, Kentucky, as well as the Motomachi plant in Toyota City. The system retains many elements of Toyota's previous system, such as JIT parts delivery, but is a fundamental change in overall approach.

A New Assembly Process

The resulting dramatic productivity improvements are due to the concept of functionally segmented assembly. This is a direct application to manufacturing of critical path analysis, a project-scheduling technique which recognizes that some parts of an overall task can be done concurrently.

Assembly has been broken into 108 tasks, which have been grouped into segments. The process begins on two separate lines. One assembles the body. The second assembles the chassis, to which the power train (engine and transmission), which arrives from the engine factory almost ready to install, is added. The body then is added to the chassis and the vehicle continues down a single line, receiving the parts needed to complete the assembly process.

Different tasks require different amounts of time, and rather than a single line working at a constant speed, tasks in effect are done in small batches, with buffer stocks used to maintain a continuous pace for the overall assembly process. This has elements in common with "demand-flow manufacturing" as practiced by U.S. contract electronics manufacturers.

Functionally related tasks are assigned to subgroups so that each task is completed within a segment and quality is checked within a group of about 20 workers. Job rotation and training are conducted within each group of workers in a line segment. This has increased the function and responsibility of group leaders, because each leader is in charge of a semi-independent segment and has more discretion in managing it. For example, each segment can modify its line speed within limits.

Automated and manual assembly exist on the same line, and assembly workers, rather than off-line staff, are responsible for routine maintenance of all operating equipment. Such integration of human and machine elements with worker responsibility for improving performance is a Toyota hallmark, and is a natural outgrowth of its experience with lean production.

Importantly, improvement has been measurable. The lead time to master a job was cut in half, and a survey at the Kyushu plant indicated that most workers became more quality conscious and felt that their jobs were easier to understand. Also, because the buffer stocks absorbed the line-stop effects of other segments, overall downtime decreased. In this way the system helped workers focus and avoid being overwhelmed by the line's constancy, confusion, and complexity.

Because several operations are done in parallel, buffer stocks notwithstanding, actual in-process inventory has been reduced substantially compared to beginning with the chassis and having parts added in sequence. This is because an incomplete vehicle and its parts are in-process inventory whether moving along the line or sitting in a buffer.

The system retains JIT delivery of components to the factory. However, suppliers now are connected directly to Toyota's production information system so that they can automatically access the information they need for JIT delivery rather than just receiving a delivery schedule on a batch basis based on planned production. (Under the old JIT, parts were delivered to the assembly lines according to a production schedule sent to first-tier parts suppliers.) The *kanban* system, which originally was paper based, is now IT based.

JIT deliveries often have caused significant traffic congestion near plants. Indeed, Toyota told me that by the early 1990s, parts sitting on trucks were its largest inventory item. Smitka reports that, for some plants, traffic congestion had reduced auto-part truck delivery frequency from three times to twice a day and raised the cost of parts delivery (1993, pp. 21, 25). To rectify this, the company has developed a logistical and traffic-control system that has made setting delivery routes and times part of the ordering system.

The IT Support System

Behind this "simpler" assembly process is a very complex IT system. The tricks are making sure that the right chassis, power train, and body come together for a given customer order, as well as determining the quantity of buffer stocks. This might not have presented great difficulties for Henry Ford because all Model Ts were the same and all were black. However, for Toyota almost every car is unique. This requires sophisticated and complex real-time data management, and is why the new production system is "smart." For example, to keep buffer stocks from becoming excess in-process inventory, each segment must know in real time what the line speed and buffer stock levels are at each other segment. The system in fact goes further: Toyota knows where each car is in the production process at any point in time. This real-time system allows suppliers greater flexibility in planning their own production and the ability to respond quickly to any changes that occur. The assembly schedule usually is set about four days ahead of actual production.

The production system requires suppliers to make firm-specific IT investments in order to become part of Toyota's real-time, on-line network, including the logistical and navigation system needed to set and adjust delivery routes. Suppliers have been willing to do this, and in this way Toyota is institutionalizing the benefits of its supplier network for both itself and its suppliers.

Smart Design

U.S. and European auto producers traditionally have designed vehicles based on inputs from marketing and have left it to production to manufacture that design. Once manufacturing developed a prototype, the firm could cost the product and set the price. However, roughly 80% of a vehicle's costs are fixed in the first 20% of the design process, so it is very important that the product design can be made at the target cost or less. Thus, Toyota and, subsequently, other Japanese manufacturers intimately involve the production engineering group in the design process from the time when marketing first establishes a target market segment. (Product engineers are concerned with how the components operate, and they serve on new model and product-design teams. Production engineers assess how a car actually will be built.)

Design and engineering are done concurrently in an integrated process, an approach Sealy (1991) calls "design-for-manufacture." It makes use of an analytic design technique that rearranges or modifies already known designs to achieve specific goals or to lower costs. Computer-aided design systems facilitate such multiplicity, so they are integral to the process.

Toyota has moved toward larger modules delivered from suppliers fully ready for inclusion in a vehicle. As a result, parts suppliers are responsible for almost 70% of a vehicle's value added. Because of this, the design process includes working closely with suppliers. (Toyota estimates there are some 30,000 parts in one of its cars.)

In a process called "bundled outsourcing," some suppliers conduct detailed component engineering using "approved drawings" based on Toyota's specifications and initial designs. They thus supply "black-box" components that meet specified functional requirements without Toyota having to supply detailed drawings. IT greatly speeds and facilitates the interchange of such engineering and other information between supplier and Toyota with respect to the precise component, while 3D displays permit Toyota's engineers to quickly evaluate the part proposed within the context of the total vehicle.

Designing-in Buildability

Production engineering (PE) organizationally is a separate group within the company that has members at each plant. Toyota has standardized procedures and equipment at its plants for most processes, so it is relatively easy to shift model production among plants regardless of their location.

PE's project involvement has five major aspects. These cover design standards, design reviews, prototype builds, finalizing drawings, and designing the manufacturing process (including equipment). Early in the design process, PE engineers make data on the latest production standards and capabilities available to the design team. This is where close knowledge of what is happening in each plant is critical.

During design review, PE representatives informally suggest changes or solutions that can simplify manufacturing. This input becomes more concrete as a prototype is built. As sections of the design are finished, PE starts developing the necessary materials and equipment, including releasing drawings to parts suppliers. This significantly speeds the design-to-production cycle compared to the usual approach of waiting for the entire design to be finished before contacting suppliers.

The design team knows that if a design conforms to the currently published production process standards, it can be manufactured. This reduces the time needed to engineer a part because production engineering for it does not have to be repeated. Because the standards indicate a range of possibilities, there generally is sufficient flexibility for the team to meet its goals. This allows allocating more engineering effort to those items or features that are really new or different.

The newer the product or design, the more PE engineers are involved in the design process in order to ensure both producibility and cost efficiency. Because of cooperation and teamwork, and the fact that the PE personnel are assigned to new models for the life of the project, Toyota uses about half as many personnel on a design team as the typical U.S. firm.

The fact that design and manufacturing operate hand in glove from the beginning is a key aspect of Toyota's being and remaining the industry benchmark for production in terms of quality and efficiency. Also, because PE standardizes processes across the corporation and is constantly upgrading those standards, improvements in productivity are quickly translated across the corporation and positively affect the production of all vehicles worldwide.

Supplier Networks

The success of smart production and design is dependent on how Toyota manages its supplier relationships. The network has been cemented through the sharing and linking of IT systems, as well as cross-shareholding (which has continued even as other "vertical *keiretsu*" have been unwinding) and other interactions, such as exchange of personnel. There is a consistently high level of investment by suppliers in assets specific to their business with Toyota. This is a major reason behind the high quality levels, flexibility, and cost competitiveness that have made Toyota such a formidable global competitor. The system also has helped Toyota transfer technology to suppliers. The company's production IT group meets regularly with parts makers to ensure that the system is working along the entire supply chain.

Moreover, Toyota provides incentives for suppliers rather than seeking to extract profits just for itself. Still, it is significantly more profitable than its suppliers. In contrast, Nissan and Isuzu are not more profitable than their suppliers. Toyota has twice the return on assets of the second most profitable Japanese auto producer, Honda. Honda does not have a formal supplier group, being more arm's-length in its supplier relationships. It thus appears that Toyota is the leader in partnering and utilizing network benefits.

Indeed, using IT to enhance commitment and reciprocal benefits with suppliers is key to Toyota's achieving its twin goals of quality and efficiency. This is because Toyota recognizes that, with 70% of a car's value dependent on suppliers, cooperation is what allows it to drastically reduce new model development time, respond quickly to demand changes, and undergo endless rounds of cost-cutting. One role of IT in design and production has been to improve and speed the existing excellent communication and interchange of production data and engineering designs with suppliers without materially altering the relationships. Thus, IT's effect generally has been evolutionary with respect to its suppliers, in contrast to the large, industry-wide parts supply web site being organized by U.S. producers (discussed below).

Two projects are partial exceptions to this statement: parts delivery logistics and replacement steel. Toyota has begun a large IT development project with Nippon Steel to accurately estimate auto replacement parts and the required steel. This involves developing a massive database and complex analytical algorithm using factors such as where cars are located, the number being driven, accident and repair records, from where and when steel and parts were shipped, and parts commonality among models. This will allow Nippon Steel to lower its inventories of replacement part steel, with resulting cost savings shared with Toyota. Toyota's suppliers also are participating in Nippon Steel's e-commerce ordering system, which permits them to track their steel supply on-line in real time. (These IT projects are covered at greater length in chapter 6.)

How the System Works

The firm's on-line parts ordering system is global, but it is not yet on a 24-hour basis. Toyota still uses batch processing for parts ordering once the production schedule is set. In Japan ordering is done daily, but elsewhere it is weekly, which means Toyota must carry some inventory.

Each day the central computer specifies the car ID numbers that are going to be produced the next day. The server decides the best place to have each car produced, then, three hours before the assembly process is to begin, notifies parts makers, who are on-line, as to where the parts should be delivered. First-line suppliers have similar systems to notify their suppliers.

To support JIT and assembly functions, the company's IT group maintains a database listing which suppliers produced which parts for which cars. Thus, Toyota can trace particular parts in terms of warranty, insurance claims, and repair. Toyota also has a database for completed cars with data on factory, warranty claims, repairs, and marketing. Both of these data sets provide information for design and production changes that can improve reliability and quality, as well as for the replacement-part initiative described earlier. PCs are used to access the databases, which is why every staff employee has one. This has created security problems, as well as issues related to determining how different information is being used. But because information sharing is critical to the company's success, it sees no alternative.

Toyota's parts suppliers have strong incentives to reduce costs continuously. Their written contracts with Toyota contain no fixed prices; rather, twice a year, Toyota announces price reduction targets and renegotiates prices with each parts maker. A supplier that can reduce its costs below the new price without compromising quality can pocket the difference until the next round of negotiations. If it cannot meet its target, it may lose preferred status or even have to reorganize the way it operates. This extends even to allowing Toyota management to replace personnel.

Parts generally are highly customized by assembler and vehicle model, which necessitates considerable investment in assets specific to an assembler. This is seen in the concentration of suppliers around assembly plants—for example, Toyota suppliers in Toyota City and its immediate environs, and Mazda suppliers around Hiroshima.

There are large investments in specific human capital, too, because the suppliers' engineers are sent to an assembler's facilities to learn how the assembler manages the vehicle development process, down to the notes on drawings. There are informal networks linking suppliers and Toyota's managers and engineers that help get information and get things done. U.S. automakers have started adopting the form of such practices but, as Ahmadjian notes, they have been slower to adopt the substance of such relationships—especially the idea that an assembler has an obligation to protect its suppliers.

For more detail on the supply network, see Ahmadjian (1997, pp. 37–38) and Fujimoto (1999).

Web-Based Procurement

Toyota is taking a cautious approach to the suppliers' web sites proposed by U.S. auto producers, one for original equipment and another for replacement parts. Toyota has announced its own separate site, based in California, for replacement parts. It will compete against GM's TradeXchange and Ford's Auto-Xchange.

For original equipment parts, Ford and GM have merged their sites, and DaimlerChrysler and the Renault-Nissan group have joined. Originally called the Automotive Network Exchange (ANX), it is now called Covisint. Toyota and Honda may join, but they are expected to limit involvement to buying raw materials and simple parts. This is because although there may be benefits in such procurement, they develop parts with their suppliers and will not want to go through the joint industry site when such technical information might be exposed. Both software supplier Oracle Corp. and business-to-business e-commerce software and services firm Commerce One Inc. see opportunities for business and so have become partners in the venture.

Toyota, which has intranet links with 1,250 parts suppliers, will join only if it has freedom in how it uses the system and there are firewalls to protect confidential data. Also, Toyota does not support the trend toward universally available common parts because that undercuts its strategy to produce vehicles with unique features and exceptional quality. Further, there are operational risks because suppliers could offer low-ball prices during the first year to capture business, then hike prices in subsequent years. This would undermine the result of years of developing trust and capturing supplier network externalities.

Covisint

The U.S. assemblers' strategy and its potential impact are well described and analyzed by the Boston Consulting Group's Evans and Wurster (1999). Covisint (called Automotive Network Exchange when they were writing) involves over 5000 companies worldwide, providing a nonproprietary, global communications network built on the Internet. Covisint went on-line in late 2000 but in mid-2001 was still primarily an on-line auction site.

As described by Evans and Wurster, Covisint will support communications across all participating companies, with allowance for private networks for members that permit employees within and between companies to communicate securely. Over time, it will publish standards for different transactions that will be mandated by the major participating OEMs. Thus, production and logistics will become closely coupled across the supply chain, while automated bidding standards will enable contracts to be announced and bid among companies that are hardly acquainted.

Teams can share applications, so engineers from different firms in different countries can exchange CAD/CAM files and see each other's changes in real time during on-line meetings. Currently, OEMs and first-tier suppliers use proprietary networks to communicate. As these are replaced with a single open network, which means more commonality in interface and protocols, there should be fewer data-entry errors and communication will be faster and cheaper. In the early 2000s, specification changes from Detroit took about 90 days to be transmitted along the supply chain. Covisint makes reducing that to minutes feasible.

Covisint is expected to lower costs directly by intensifying competition within the supply chain. Standards will make it easy for buyers to post requirements, manage on-line bidding, and increase comparability among would-be suppliers. For some, this will mean an even more competitive market. For others, it will generate opportunities if they have genuinely better products or technologies. Developers say it will help small suppliers collaborate more easily by sharing resources and jointly designing products in real time. This could force a sea change in assembler and supplier managerial thinking.

Evans and Wurster believe Covisint provides the beginnings of an infrastructure that allows the rich, recombinant innovation Silicon Valley is famous for to flourish across barriers of geography, industry, and corporate culture. Toyota and Honda remain skeptical, based on their experiences and successful routines.

Evaluation

Expanding the range of potential suppliers that can bid on a producer's published standard is quite different from Toyota's intention of expanding its black-box parts strategy, which emphasizes larger modules, simplified assembly, and greater supplier interaction. This requires suppliers making even larger investments specific to Toyota, and even specific to a single model. Toyota thus needs to make its suppliers feel they will be fully supported.

Conversely, no matter what opportunities are built into Covisint for suppliers to cooperate more with assemblers, including participating in the design phase, under Covisint the risks actually have increased for suppliers that commit to undertake relationship-specific investment. Knowing that next year or the next model cycle they can be replaced, suppliers could well be reluctant to spend the money to offer specialized engineering. If U.S. assemblers feel the need to attract such a commitment, they will have to sign an exclusive arrangement that makes them dependent on the supplier. They then run the risk of being exploited in subsequent rounds if suppliers insist on cost-plus pricing to continue making firm-specific investments.

For these reasons, it will be difficult for U.S. producers to replicate the networking efficiencies of the Toyota system using annual competitive bidding on their web site. It thus is not clear that the benefits of Toyota's reciprocal commitment tradition can be replaced just by hanging an auto parts supply system on an e-commerce framework.

If a black-box strategy and the willingness to invest in relationship-specific assets, combined with periodic price reviews, is a superior sourcing strategy for continuous cost declines, improved productivity, and better quality, then the U.S. OEM parts supply web site is strategically flawed. This is true even if it moves the industry toward standardized parts used by several producers because Toyota and others can use it to the extent that such standard parts lower their costs. Standardized parts across makers by definition do not offer special quality or other enhancements to the completed vehicle. Thus Toyota gets cheaper standardized parts when that is strategically beneficial, and it can source proprietary parts when they add value. Toyota historically seems very good at this kind of mixing to get the optimum combination in terms of cost and quality.

In some respects the U.S. web site initiative is a step backward to annual low-cost bidding. Because they felt this worked for them in the past, it is an environment to which U.S. assemblers seem to want to return, hence the enthusiasm that has greeted the plan. However, starting with Womack, Jones, and Roos (1990), several studies have indicated that this sourcing strategy is not competitive compared to Toyota's approach. This may be just another demonstration that a bad strategy cannot be converted to a good one simply by giving it a "hi-tech" and "wave of the future" mantle. An IT initiative is successful only if it is used to enhance a sound business strategy.

Smart Marketing

It is not sufficient just to design and produce new products efficiently: this effort must be closely tied to actual demand and marketing. Thus, Toyota sees the need to create new marketing methods that will be effective in an information society, such as developing and introducing sales information networks and creating an information-receiving system that utilizes multimedia. Establishing ways to increase sales through the Internet also is part of this.

Since 1998 Toyota has been using the Internet to sell used cars in Japan. The company's web sites allow the customer to specify a configuration, and precise pricing information will be provided if such a vehicle is available. If it is not, the closest matches are offered. Beginning in 2001 Toyota has used data from the web site to proactively encourage trade-ins of used cars that are in demand. This has increased both used- and new-car sales. Because of registration requirements, the Internet cannot be used to sell new cars. Instead, a customer is referred to a nearby dealer.

In 1999 Toyota launched *gazoo.com* as a portal offering nonautomotive items, as well as links to various company web sites. From this, Toyota has discovered that most people using the Internet are doing searches.

In Japan, Toyota has established *toyota.co.jp*, an interactive web site and database oriented toward younger people, where these potential customers can introduce their own ideas for cars or get pricing on existing models. In addition, Toyota can track the kinds of cars or features that appeal to young people. It uses this information to design cars that are more appealing to the next generation, one of its prime strategic marketing programs.

Computerized ordering is found in all Toyota dealer showrooms in Japan: customers can order a car to their specifications with the expectation of three-week delivery. The goal is five days. The system significantly reduces the cost of dealer inventories (financing and floor space), as well as the profits lost to clearance through year-end sales and rebates. At the same time, customer satisfaction is increased because buyers quickly get the precise car they want. Cars can be modeled in 3D. Once configured, the order is entered directly into the computer controlling Toyota's production system.

In the United States, configuring can be done through Toyota's web sites (one for the Lexus and another for other Toyotas). The sites price the car and refer (potential) buyers to a local dealer that has that type car in stock (or can get it).

Responding to Demand Changes

For the developing-economies markets where Toyota sees its growth, it has had to develop smaller, simpler cars and techniques to meet local-sourcing mandates and buyers' initial ownership budgets. Toyota's solution in Asean markets has been especially creative, and complex. To support its top market share in the region (around 20%), Toyota has factories in Indonesia, Malaysia, the Philippines, and Thailand, generally in partnership with local interests. These factories cooperated to assemble just over 300,000 vehicles in 1995, almost half in Thailand.

However, Toyota does not produce minicars, and its subcompact (the Corolla) is relatively expensive for the Asian market and thus not a good entry vehicle compared to Suzuki's (GM Group) and Honda's minicars, so it has relied on affiliate Daihatsu at the low end. Daihatsu established a joint venture in China in the early 1990s. In 1995 Toyota increased its ownership of Daihatsu to over 50% as part of its long-term global strategy. This effectively consolidated an increasingly close relationship, which dated back to the early 1970s, when Daihatsu started making small cars for Toyota. Similarly, because of the importance of trucks to these markets, in August 2001 Toyota took majority control of Hino, which had long been the group's semi-independent truck maker. Toyota is integrating firms into its global IT system.

During the late 1990s about 20% of Toyota's sales in the ASEAN region were fully assembled imports, primarily from Japan. As of 1995, for ASEAN-produced vehicles, about 40% of the parts were produced somewhere in the region. Higher-value parts often are sourced from plants established in the area by big, traditional Toyota suppliers such as Denso Corp. Still others come from the company's own parts factories in ASEAN. These include gasoline engine blocks made in Indonesia, power steering gears produced in Malaysia, transmission parts from the Philippines, and diesel engine parts and body stampings sourced in Thailand. Under the brand-to-brand complementation plan initiated in 1988 by the governments of these four countries, as well as the successor ASEAN Industrial Cooperation Program phased in during the late 1990s, Toyota can ship parts among the participating countries at preferential tariff rates. Parts so traded count as locally made for local-content requirements.

This production and sourcing flexibility supports economies of scale and cost containment. However, to manage this complex arrangement, as well as to compute the optimal sourcing strategy based on tariffs, fees, and local regulations requires significant IT support.

Smart Cars

The ability to rapidly design and produce new cars for different markets is integral to Toyota's "smart" strategy. Perhaps nowhere has this been more apparent than in Toyota's leadership in the merging within the automobile of software, mechanics, and electronics. In the 1980s the Japanese coined "mechatronics" for the creating of electro-mechanical devices. Now, in areas like automatic focusing for cameras and controlling sophisticated computer peripherals such as printers and camcorders, they have added sophisticated software embedded in the product that controls the electronics and the mechanics. This will be an important aspect of Japanese industry's competitiveness in the 21st century, including vehicles and transportation systems.

The use of electronics and software in automobiles has been expanding steadily. Beyond improving such long-offered features as automatic transmissions, climate control, fuel injection, and cruise control, it has made possible antilock brakes, keyless entry, electronic air bags, vehicle distance regulation, and navigation systems, as well as engine management. Japanese firms have been leaders in introducing improvements to these features. Indeed, there is a close relationship between the electronics and automotive sectors in Japan.

Toyota feels that new generations of navigation and electronic control systems will become the car's brains and, in a few years, will be major criteria in a buyer's choice, so that lack of competence in this area could undermine a company's competitiveness. Developing the embedded software needed to instruct these devices requires understanding vehicle mechanics and the whole car. These are competencies only an assembler possesses, so strategically it became important to bring that competency in-house. Being directly involved is seen as the only way to keep pace and make sure new designs incorporate the latest electronics and IT, so Toyota has taken over development of chips and has built its own factories to produce them.

Toyota also recognized that it needed more software and electronics expertise in the parent company, and that it would need to increase affiliations with major consumer electronics producers. This led to several actions. One, it reduced dependence on Nippon Denso for electronic components. Two, it built its own electronic-related parts factory at Hirose in 1989, with electrical engineering capability covering electronic parts, antilock brakes, navigation systems and integrated circuits. Three, the company actively recruited electrical engineers, even those in midcareer, further emphasizing the important strategic nature of its move into electronics and embedded software. Four, it announced in 1996 the formation of a joint venture with

Texas Instruments to manufacture semiconductors at its affiliate, Toyoda Loom. Five, in 1998 it built an electronics parts factory in Miyagi.

Several specialized subsidiaries have been created to support this strategy. Toyota MACs develops, manufactures, and services specialized measurement-control systems and equipment. Nippon Idou Tsushin Corp. handles car telephones and Toyota Digital Cruise is classified by the government as a type-2 VAN (which means it leases telecom capacity for resale). Satellite Positioning Information Services provides navigation-related information. Toyota System Research develops and sells computer systems related to the development and manufacture of automobiles, including simulations. Toyota Soft Engineering develops and sells automobile-development-related computer systems, especially CAD/CAM. Also, to extend its CAD/CAM capabilities, there is a joint venture with Unix, which is now part of Novell. Toyota Caelum develops, sells, and services CAD/CAM software and hardware. Toyota System International, a joint venture with IBM and Toshiba, develops and sells business administration software. A joint venture with Fujitsu for pure software development rounds out these IT-based activities.

New Models

Toyota recognizes that increasing sales depends first on having products that customers will buy, and this means fresh models. Even during the 1997–98 Japanese recession Toyota announced the introduction of 15 new models globally, more than any other producer.

This is consistent with the strategic vision announced in 1996 as Vision 2005. Toyota indicated that responding quickly to market changes would be necessary to "survive and be a winner" given the new "intense global competition." This reflects the company's belief that a diversification of customer needs is shortening the product life cycle for vehicles, thus putting a premium on creating and producing new products faster than rivals.

The company sees a change in the very nature of competition. Earlier, being competitive simply meant having better quality and price. Although that is still important, establishing an accepted industry standard is now seen as key to long-term success. (Evans and Wurster observe "Once a standard achieves critical mass, the interconnectedness of *all* physically defined industries ensures that it will inexorably spread to fill the entire domain in which it is competitively advantaged" [1999, p. 180].)

While market changes in high-income economies are leading to more electronics and embedded software in every automobile, the rapid changes in those elements, along with changes in vehicle model demand, can be, and have been, emulated by competitors, even if with a time lag. In January 2000, Ford announced its "Internet on Wheels" concept car (24×7 vehicles) to meet the new competition that involves computer chips, sensors, Internet access, wireless communications, and the ability to exploit these devices and systems to sell more than just a vehicle. Even now, some electronics are dealer-installed options supplied by consumer electronics companies.

Thus, Toyota must run very hard to stay ahead. For this reason, another aspect of its strategy has focused on "smart car" technologies that are not easily copied. These efforts are related primarily to the environment and intelligent transportation systems.

Environmentally Smart Cars

In high-income economies, environmental regulations for vehicles have become stringent and there is continual pressure from many groups to increase the stringency. California, the world's fifth largest car market (some 8% to 10% of global demand in units, and more in value), often is copied by other U.S. states. It is seeking to reduce auto emissions by dividing autos into four groups, including ultralow-emission vehicles (ULEVs). Even in emerging markets where policy makers see the auto and auto-parts industries as economic catalysts, local demand will be affected by the pollution problems and traffic congestion plaguing their big cities.

As some of its 2001 advertising demonstrates, Toyota is seeking to identify itself as the number one auto company for environmental protection. Because just what that means is still unclear, Toyota is helping to define it, and then be it.

Toyota's development of more environmentally friendly cars initially was part of a three-year project begun in 1996. It proved strategically sound, as the Prius, introduced in Japan in 1997, sold out at 2,000 a month. Although not initially profitable, for 2001 it is expected to be. The Prius is a hybrid (gasoline- and electric powered) that can get up to 34 km/l (80 mpg) and creates significantly fewer pollutants. (The company advertises that the system "reduces smog-forming emission by up to 90% compared to the average car." Carbon dioxide and carbon monoxide are not smog-forming. Also, by using an average, it overstates the comparison to other new cars.) US sales began in August 2000.

As the 21st century began, only Honda had a competitive model. Ford and GM announced hybrids in 2000, but production will not be before 2003. Their entries are based on development work for which they and a consortium of U.S. firms and institutions received $350 million in U.S. government subsidies.

The Prius has qualified in California as a SULEV (*super*-ultralow-emission vehicle). This means it can substitute for a certain number of mandated electric cars, which are more expensive, and still meet the company's fleet mileage and emission targets under California rules. Toyota is experimenting with compact electric vehicles and direct-injection engines as well, but only the hybrid is assessed here, because it is currently produced and sold.

In June 2000 Fujio Cho, Toyota's president, announced that other hybrid models would be introduced, including an all-wheel drive minivan, as part of an effort to raise annual production to 300,000 units. Sales of the minivan began in Japan in mid-2001 and incorporate an innovative approach to all-wheel drive that uses a rear-mounted electric motor to drive the rear wheels. This eliminates the drive shaft, thereby decreasing weight and increasing cabin space.

Toyota and Honda hybrids require sophisticated software to control use of the electric motor and small gasoline engine. Coordinating the interplay between these two over the range of driving conditions is a complex task. Toyota calls its system THS (Toyota Hybrid System). THS computes the appropriate operating condition, as well as the current condition, of the engine, motor, generator, battery, and other components, and makes changes to move actual to appropriate. What is appropriate is a moving target under most conditions, so the task needs to be done continually in real time. Already Toyota is learning a lot about the new power system from real-world production models. It will have even more improved the models available by the time U.S. producers make their initial debut.

Intelligent Transportation System (ITS)

ITS is a concept being pursued in several venues rather than a well-defined term. However defined, it has two principal components: an onboard system for managing the car and an external traffic management system. In its ultimate form, which requires both components, actual driving is automated: the "driver" becomes a navigator, and then only to the extent of entering a destination or indicating the desire to pull over at a rest stop. There are many features that partially automate driving or provide navigational assistance short of this, and all can be termed aspects of ITS. As part of a larger strategy, Toyota has been developing a packaged system for each of the two principal components.

In Japan ITS is organized around VERTIS (Vehicle, Road, and Traffic Intelligence Society), an organization set up by the government, companies, and universities in 1994. In 1996 Japan passed a Transportation Efficiency Act. Similar legislation was passed in the United States in 1991—the Intelligent Systems Transportation Efficiency Act (ISTEA)—allocating $60 million a year for six years. The idea was that each country would do R&D and system research, then meet and exchange information on the status of their projects. The acts cover more than just ITS, but most government involvement relates to ITS.

This section looks at Toyota's overall ITS strategy, the navigation systems currently being deployed by a number of automakers, how Toyota plans to maintain its lead in navigation systems, and the onboard computer before turning to assisted and automated driving.

ITS Strategy

Toyota has been exploring the development and use of ITS since the mid-1970s (that is, from just after the first oil crisis). Hidekazu Ohe, manager of Toyota's ITS project, has worked on the system since its inception. However, it is only since the mid-1990s that ITS has become an actual part of its commercial products. As of 1998 Toyota had spent over $1 billion on the project (more recent data have not been released). By 2015, it expects the Japanese market for ITS-related products and services to exceed ¥60 trillion, with the rest of the worldwide market even larger.

Toyota wants to establish a transportation infrastructure through which the highway can sense and communicate with each vehicle. It will then be easier to introduce more advanced functions as they are developed or as permission to use them is obtained from governments. In 1993 Toyota summarized its evolving smart car approach as responding "to the needs of our information-oriented society" in which "automobiles are now increasingly equipped with navigation systems and sophisticated communication devices. Cars are gradually becoming 'intelligent vehicles.' Toyota is developing and introducing car electronics to enhance communication between people, automobiles, and society."

To make this vision a reality, the company has divided ITS into five basic work areas. By coordinating and managing the interactive relationships among them, Toyota intends to achieve growth and development as a "total mobility company." The first area is the intelligent car, a vehicle that incorporates sophisticated and complex systems and functions. These include the onboard computer, sensors, and other elements that control the car's various functions. It thus supports, and is the foundation for, the other areas. Second is multimedia for the vehicle—the "Internet on Wheels," which represents a new arena for mobile communications.

The third area covers support facilities that will achieve smoother traffic flow by coordinating vehicles and the transportation infrastructure. Fourth is business and organizational logistics, where Toyota will work with other firms to develop a comprehensive set of tools that will support more efficient transportation of goods and services through improved utilization of the existing road system. In the fifth area, new or radically improved transport, Toyota will work to develop transport systems for the next generation.

Matsushita and NEC are involved in building the electronics and computer systems for the project, including the navigation system that is part of the onboard computer. Nomura Research Institute and Mitsubishi Research Institute are involved in software development.

Reflecting the importance of communications to ITS, Toyota had an ownership interest in IDC Telecommunications (the company was purchased by Cable and Wireless in 2000). C&W will continue IDC's support of Motorola's cellular system in Japan. Toyota also invested in telecom provider DDI (now part of KDDI, having merged with IDO and KDD in December 1999.)

Navigation Systems

Japan has a high-level navigation system developed by the auto industry with Japan's Vehicle Information and Communication System (VICS), a public corporation. Planning began in 1990, and the system was introduced in 1996 in the country's three principal metropolitan areas: Tokyo-Yokohama, Osaka-Kyoto-Kobe, and Nagoya. Since early 2000 all of Japan has been included. The government allocated ¥370 billion for infrastructure investment. Traffic data obtained from the national and local police go to VICS for editing and are relayed to appropriately equipped cars.

Toyota has been a leader in navigational systems from the beginning, with a 45% share of the 2 million systems in 1997. By April 2000 the market had grown to 5 million units, and most new cars in Japan come with the capability.

During 1999, Toyota and its partners launched a second-generation system that added visual data on gas stations, convenience stores, and other facility locations to the traffic and weather data. Called "nav," it is a subscription service. An option, MONET, can arrange road service, supply data on events, make restaurant reservations, and the like. Nav also can be combined with a cellular phone that gives audio information in addition to the visual display.

VICS buys software and hardware from Toyota and its corporate partners. Toyota sells the hardware for this system both in its new cars and on a dealer-installed basis. An affiliate, Toyota Media Station, provides the interactive MONET service.

Related to this, Toyota has formed e-plat, a joint venture with NTT Data, an affiliate of the dominant telecom provider. The company makes the multimedia kiosks that are being installed in many convenience stores (FamilyMart in particular, but not 7-Eleven, which is working with its traditional IT suppliers, NEC and NRI; see chapter 8). The hardware is compatible with Toyota's navigation system, so that cars will be able to communicate with the kiosks to order and pay for concert tickets, make hotel reservations, and the like.

Toyota's proprietary system for Japan is called Nihon ITS. Several other automakers license it for use on their vehicles. In 2000–01 Toyota introduced a next-generation system in Japan with features such as two-way communications. Initially this is for automatic toll collection, but it can be extended to include automatic account debiting for parking, gas, and roadside services. These capabilities require only a one-way system (such as EZ-Pass, which is used for tolls in the United States), but Toyota sees an advantage to going directly to a two-way system—if only to provide a larger market for two-way services when they are introduced. With a system working in Japan, Toyota plans to proceed outside Japan. To that end, it has joined General Motors' North American geopositioning consortium.

Daimler-Chrysler's ITGS was the first sophisticated navigation system in operation, but Toyota believes it and Japan lead in developing and selling such systems. Comparable systems in the United States have at least two web sites: *smartTrek.org* and *smarttraveler.com*. Separate from purely navigational aids, "Help me" or emergency call systems are offered by Opel, Volkswagen, and DaimlerChrysler in Europe, and by Ford and General Motors (Northstar) in the United States. However, these systems do not have the customer-oriented features of Japan's version, nor are they building the basis for a full-fledged ITS using a multiple-function, two-way road communication system. With an installed base of 5 million units, Japan is clearly the global leader.

Staying Ahead

To maintain its lead in navigation systems and ITS, Toyota is working hard on three major pieces of ITS: an Internet application package, the onboard computer's operating system, and the hardware in the car. The project team is pursuing two major avenues in their approach to globalizing ITS. One involves discussions under International Standards Organization for harmonization of traffic information control interfaces. This initiative is composed of 15 working groups, and Japan is pushing to get a single international standard in cooperation with ITS America and Europe's ERITCO, which are the equivalents of VICS. The other avenue is a more flexible approach, because there are differences between countries on whether a real-time system such as Japan's or a request version such as in the United States is the more appropriate.

The U.S. situation is complicated by the fact that traffic- and automobile-related issues are handled primarily by states rather than the federal government. Toyota therefore is designing its system and introduction strategy to work even if there are multiple standards. This is similar to Nokia's approach to developing a phone that can be adapted easily to different technical and regulatory environments (chapter 11). Toyota believes that if it has a system that works and can be introduced anywhere, it has a good chance of becoming the de facto global standard, which is a key part of Toyota's long-term strategy.

Onboard Computer

In current vehicles, each feature has its own controller. Thus, brakes are controlled separately from fuel injection, and the navigation system, telephone, and radio also have their own controllers. If the car is going to be controlled as a whole, there needs to be a single computer directly managing all aspects of the vehicle. Under Toyota's ITS, there would be a single computer for the vehicle, directly linked to the servos that monitor and control the vehicle's various functions. It also will have the capability of displaying information to the driver and passengers. Nippon Denso will manufacture the onboard computer to Toyota's specifications, and Higashi Fuji is working with Toyota to develop the software to manage the car and communicate via the Internet. Toyota is building the controllers (two-way communications system) that will line the highways.

In developing the operating systems, Toyota has borrowed from existing systems. However, it is modifying them to make its own proprietary systems, based on its knowledge of the car in terms of both mechanics and electronics. The highway operating system will be externally based—supported and controlled by an Internet platform that Toyota is developing. It will communicate with the onboard computer, which has its own operating system, to run the car. The two operating systems are linked and integrated so that the information the highway provides ultimately controls the car's movement.

Toyota has found few people in Japan able to develop such software, so once it had developed the basic idea of what it needed, it went elsewhere in Asia and to the United States to get the programs coded. Toyota believes its competitors are significantly behind in developing onboard computers and Internet-based control and communication systems, with Daimler-Chrysler the closest.

Automated Driving

The technology for automated driving exists and is being used. An automatic driver system is being piloted in Australia and another in Essen, Germany. These cities have built dedicated roadways for buses driven automatically. Called dual-mode buses, when they need to be driven off the special road, a human operator takes control, as on a normal bus. Toyota is involved in the Australia project; DaimlerChrysler, in the German one.

Toyota calls its version an "intelligent multimode transit system" (IMTS) that "combines the advantages of trains and buses." IMTS includes the platooning of commercial vehicles. (That is, the system allows trucks to safely follow each other much more closely than would otherwise be the case.) Package delivery service Yamato Transport is said to be ready to use the technology for its intercity trucks once it is available in Japan.

Widespread implementation of automated driving requires construction of infrastructure and, particularly for individual drivers, settling of legal questions. These will take several more years. (See figures 7.1–7.3.)

Agreeing on how to set responsibility for accidents has delayed a large-scale test in Japan. Initial tests were held at Tsukuba in December 2000, and a full demonstration is set for Expo 2005 in Nagoya. The delayed test—really a full-scale implementation—requires building a special lane along the Tomei Expressway (which links Osaka, Nagoya, and Tokyo, and is Japan's most heavily traveled intercity route). Toyota does not expect the construction to be physically or technologically difficult, given the Japanese government's commitment to the project.

Despite the delays, Toyota and others expect widespread implementation at some point. With such a system "vehicle operation automated through interaction with the road infrastructure, so that braking and acceleration are

Promotion Plan for Intelligent Transportation Systems

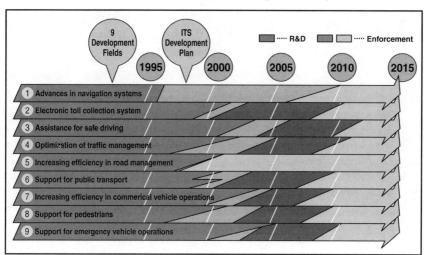

Figure 7.1

done automatically for safe and smooth driving." This requires markers in the road and sensors in the car to control steering. There also will be "intelligent intersections" that alert "drivers and pedestrians to approaching vehicles and give road information and instructions using programmable display panels." (This description is from an October 1999 Toyota brochure.)

Toyota's ITS Business and R&D

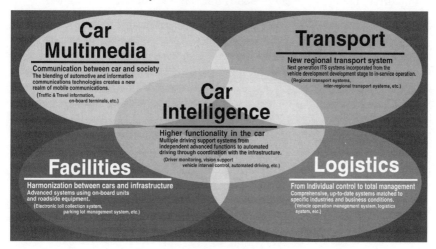

Figure 7.2

ITS Evolutionary Development

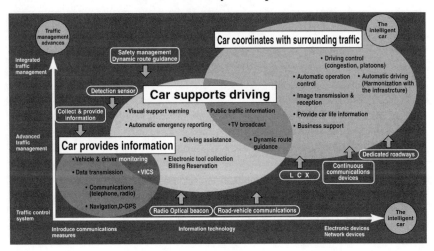

Figure 7.3

An overview of Japan's ITS and several associated applications are posted on *atip.org/public*.

More than roadways can be smart. Toyota sees ITS allowing an "intelligent parking lot" that provides data on parking availability, guides vehicles to spaces, and collects fees automatically. (A system in Vienna reports the number of spaces available in nearby garages on streetside display panels, but has no interactive features.)

While waiting for automated driving, Toyota will continue development of features that are entirely onboard the vehicle, such as automatic sensing and adjustment for distance between cars using radar. These are part of its Advanced Cruise-Assist Highway Systems program.

Offering IT-Based Services, Not Just Cars

Many mature old-line Japanese companies responded to the end of the high-growth era by diversifying into unrelated but "modern" industries. Toyota also has expanded its horizons, but primarily by moving into activities closely related to—indeed, usually involving—automobiles.

Drawing on its experience with its own parts delivery system, Toyota's ITS group has been working with Coca-Cola in Nagoya on a project to improve delivery times and driver productivity. This involves 140 vehicles and 600 vendors (customers). Toyota's "total delivery system" can establish a communications network among stores, vending machines, trucks, logistics centers, and so on, thus providing total management of goods distribution. Also, vending machines can automatically telephone when they need to be serviced or are out of a certain item. These data can be integrated with the logistics system for optimum delivery. The result is improved operating efficiency and better inventory control. Work also is being done on projects such as Toyota City taxis to improve their pickup and delivery of passengers by indicating the best route to a particular address, including avoiding points of congestion. Location information provided by cell phones linked to GPS systems makes passenger pickup more efficient.

In May 2000 Toyota joined in forming *famima.com*, an *e-retsu* which will operate web sites and place terminals in FamilyMart stores in Japan to offer tens of thousands of goods through the chain's on-line markets. This is a logical extension of Toyota's own diverse web portal, *gazoo.com*, where people can access the company's various sites, buy car-related merchandise, and access services. (The FamilyMart venture involves FamilyMart, 50.5%; trading company C Itoh, 14.5%; telecom NTT Data 10%; Toyota, 10%; Dai Nippon Printing, 5%; travel agency JTB, 5%; and Japan's largest ticket agency, PIA Corp., 5%.) The venture provides the opportunity for an additional pilot of Toyota's logistics systems in a different geographical location, with different stores and customers, as well as sales of multimedia kiosks. It also offers an even more intriguing possibility: using high-speed Internet connections to make the over 5,000 FamilyMarts virtual showrooms for Toyota cars.

IT at Toyota

Better communication, improved plant productivity, and increased client satisfaction (that is, better quality at a lower price) are the objectives when Toyota selects, develops, and implements IT. As Kensuke Nagane, head of the IT planning group, explains, the purpose of IT is not to change the system or operation strategy, which work very well, but to enhance them.

IT Philosophy

The basic IT strategy is to use systems to enhance existing strategies and organizational structures. Behind this is the company's core philosophy: "Since its establishment, Toyota's principle has been to strive constantly to build 'better products at lesser costs.' To this end, Toyota has developed its own unique production method. This system is based on the idea of 'just in time', the idea of Toyota Founder Kiichiro Toyoda. This system also seeks to thoroughly eliminate all sorts of waste in order to reduce prime costs. Toyota also places a maximum value on the human element, allowing an individual worker to employ his capabilities to the fullest through participation in the productive management, and improvement of his given job and its environment. With the motto 'Good Thinking, Good Products,' each individual worker is making his best effort to assure Toyota's customers the highest quality product, with an understanding that it is in his work process that quality is built in" (quoted from the company's booklet *Opening the Window*, p. 13).

Toyota shares common IT approaches with other leading software users. They include the creation of large proprietary interactive databases that promote automatic feedback between various stages of the design, order, production, delivery, and service process. Indeed, this kind of iterative routine is fundamental to its smart design and production strategy, and its Level 3 IT approach. Management recognizes that better cycle times between order and delivery reduce costs and improve forecasts. Similarly, more rapid design cycles mean quicker incorporation of new technologies. Customer satisfaction is improved through more timely completion of the sales process and constant product enhancement.

This outlook helped Toyota become firmly established in the late 1970s as the world's most efficient and lowest-cost producer of high-quality automobiles. Toyota has taken the lead in extending the lean production paradigm for automobiles into totally integrated management (TIM). Although it is unusual for the leader of one production revolution to lead the next, as indicated by Chairman Okuda at the start of this chapter, Toyota has clearly recognized the need for change and the role of IT in generating this new development. The company's TIM approach, using its new smart cars combined with its smart design and smart-production scheduling, has significantly improved productivity and market advantage through its monitoring, controlling, and linking of every aspect of producing and delivering vehicles and after-sales service.

IT Structure

Toyota's basic information system is a three-tier mainframe system involving hundreds of millions of lines of code, similar to most other large Japanese companies. The mainframes control the approximately 1000 servers, which control the networking system and communicate with the plants, with their equipment, and with dealers and suppliers. The mainframes schedule production and JIT delivery, as well as track orders. There are some 3000 CAD/CAM terminals. The company put a PC on the desk of every office worker in 1996, about 30,000 altogether, and networked them into the overall system. PC use has reduced paper use.

Because it is a real-time, on-line system, it has been totally integrated with Toyota's business operations, as is true for most large Japanese firms. It is completely managed and maintained by Toyota's internal systems group, with internal communication through its own fiber-optic system and with customized middleware providing the interface between users within the company.

Overseas operations have their own systems. These are not integrated extensively with the system in Japan, but they are networked for exchanging data on distribution and the total global supply chain in a preprogrammed format. This means, for example, that Toyota in Japan can send information to its U.S. dealer network regarding delivery of specific vehicles. Toyota also can send parts orders to overseas suppliers.

Ultimately, the company may divide IT into inside and outside Japan systems. Already, for example, Toyota uses almost 100% Hewlett-Packard hardware outside Japan, whereas inside Japan it does not use much HP equipment. Globalization is one area the IT planning group is working on, because it is often a problem getting domestic and overseas systems to communicate, especially in places where the communication infrastructure is weak.

Sourcing Software

Software selection is very pragmatic. It depends on the software's cost versus its contribution to increasing the overall value of the car, or to reducing the cost of designing and producing a car. Decisions to develop in-house or to buy are made case by case, based on experience. This is the same routine Toyota uses to decide between designing-in and ordering customized or standard parts for a car. It also is the decision process that led it to reduce "fat design" (the number of option choices Toyota allows a customer for items such as steering wheels) when it discovered replacement part inventories were becoming too high. Therefore, it represents Toyota's normal strategic routine for introducing new technologies and innovations, whether organizationally or in the car.

Except for the operating systems, Toyota has generally developed its own software and IT systems, and outsourcing has not been considered a real option, except to captive subsidiaries and for components that then typically are customized. This is because software is recognized as an integral element within an overall management strategy, and as such must be controlled directly by the company. Generally, integration is done by first assessing the possible business uses of the software or IT within the organization, its operations, or its products, with particular focus placed on IT's role in enhancing Toyota's ability to develop, produce, sell, and service different types of vehicles.

Outside packages are not totally rejected. For example, in 1998 the IT planning group was approached by PeopleSoft to buy an enterprise management package covering accounting, finance, and personnel. This was the first time they had considered purchasing such an outside package. They bought it, and adapted it to fit the overall system. This was because the package was cost-effective, and would allow creation of a global standard for the company in support areas. However, for the core of its operation— the production system (Total Production Factory or Toyota Production System)—Toyota continues to use only its own software.

Toyota's overseas operations are independent with respect to their IT systems, although Toyota is introducing a global standard for at least some software. Overseas factories are more likely to use packages for office support, but the systems that run the factories are basically the same as those used in Japan, which means they are company-developed.

Toyota decided in the late 1990s to reorganize its software development. As part of this, it spun out five software development subsidiaries, all Toyota majority-owned. The other owners mostly are Toyota-related companies or key suppliers to the venture.

Buying New Systems

Toyota has bought new PC hardware and software every five to six years, even though new versions are available much more frequently. This is in keeping with Toyota's philosophy of using the simplest way to achieve an objective, and to implement what works. This schedule allows it to get the functionality it wants, without so much time lost to retraining and transferring data. The PCs, which use a Japanese version of Windows, are primarily for e-mail and word processing; most workers do not use the features added in "upgraded" software. This approach reduces costs: a new PC plus software runs $2000 in direct costs. With 30,000 PCs, that is a $60 million purchase decision. The IT planning group estimates that the total all-in cost of a new PC system—including system integration, training, and support—is almost $7000 per PC, raising the total corporate expenditure to some $200 million. That said, if an employee needs an upgrade or a special computer, the request is evaluated on its merits.

The cycle for workstations and CAD/CAM systems needed for design and engineering is much faster, though still driven by the engineering group's actual requirements. Such changes require the IT group to work closely with Toyota's parts suppliers to ensure compatibility, so that design and engineering data can be easily exchanged.

Toyota's production IT group meets regularly with the makers of its computers. For mainframes these are Fujitsu and IBM. For backup support, fault-tolerant computers from Tandem (bought by Compaq in August 1997) are used. Sun, Hewlett-Packard, and Compaq (as the June 1998 buyer of DEC) supply CAD/CAM and engineering workstations. The IT planning group sees no reason to switch from UNIX, but would consider alternatives if UNIX ceases to meet Toyota's needs. PCs are from IBM, Hewlett-Packard, and Compaq.

Conclusion

Toyota's strategy is driven by its need to raise the efficiency and emulation bar for its rivals, whose cost-cutting and group market-share goals have increased competitive pressures in all markets worldwide. Toyota has dubbed its response to the global situation a "smart" strategy, reflecting its steps to build IT-based intelligence into the design, production, distribution, and servicing functions, as well as the car itself. To reduce potential emulation, it is working hard to establish its version of ITS and the hybrid car as global industry standards.

In its TIM approach to using IT strategically, Toyota is making specific tasks simpler while making specific jobs more skilled. The result has been a co-evolution of technology and work practices that has enabled the IT-supported system to evolve productively. Workers are happier because the system has led to productivity improvements that are generally correlated with higher wages.

By acquainting customers with its automated and customized ordering system, and constantly and rapidly increasing the number and quality of its services and products, Toyota is working to improve customer contact, reduce customer migration, and keep costs low. The new smart cars will take this to another level by familiarizing customers with the more sophisticated system and the de facto Toyota standard. Toyota thus is using IT to influence customer behavior and expectations in order to tie them to Toyota on an interactive basis. It has, of course, been doing something comparable with its supplier network for many years.

For the strategy to work, Toyota must efficiently gather and manage a wide range of information. And it must continually respond to the organizational and customer complexities that will evolve with smart cars and ITS. This is why trained personnel who understand all three fundamental strategic elements—automobiles, IT, and the company's auto production system—are critical.

Toyota seeks to do this in ways that establish beneficial IT loops with articulated goals and outcomes as part of the IT utilization process. For example, with smart design and supply capability, conversions of inquiries into sales should be greater. This reinforces dealer, supplier, and customer acceptance of the system and of the smart design, production, and product concept.

There are powerful benefits to such a strategy, especially in a capital-intensive industry that is vulnerable to diminishing returns due to rapid product emulation and economic fluctuations. Toyota's integrated strategy also extends the criteria for auto industry success beyond the lean production-related concept it developed. Toyota's managers are IT-fluent and consciously take advantage of the interlocking and complementary nature of investments in machines, IT, employee skills, human-resource practices, and organization.

This perspective includes recognizing that technology and organizational structure need to evolve and improve together. Thus, the company as whole has demonstrated the capacity to learn on an evolutionary basis, which Fujimoto (1999) calls "organizational evolutionary learning," in which strategy and implementation are aligned so that they support each other, and improvement is continuous. The results exemplify the paradigm and its impact.

Acknowledgments

Much of the material on IT structure and project selection is based on meetings with Kensuke Nagane, general manager of the Systems Planning Division, and Akikazu Kida in 1994 and 1998. The author visited Toyota in Toyota City, Nagoya, and Tokyo in 1989, 1994, 1998, and 2001, as well as while living in Japan in 1999 and 2000.

8

Retailing

Ito-Yokado, Seven-Eleven Japan

Ito-Yokado and Seven-Eleven Japan (SEJ), which IY controls, have used information technology to dramatically change many aspects of the way retailing is done. IT has enabled the companies' stores to respond more effectively to demand fluctuations from spot causes such as local events or variations in the weather, as well as to longer-term changes brought on by shifts in tastes and demographics. This has increased sales revenue per square meter and reduced inventory costs, probably the two most important metrics in retailing. To accomplish this, the companies have formed alliances and combinations with suppliers and others across a wide range of products and services. This, in turn, is motivating other Japanese retailers and suppliers to form strategic alliances to realize more profit from IT systems.

After an overview of the areas of retailing that IY is involved in, this chapter examines its use of IT and its supplier relations, including some innovative ways that have made SEJ Japan's leading purveyor of fast food, even ahead of McDonald's. IY's ventures into e-commerce are then taken up.

Japanese Retailing

This section outlines general trends in the two retailing sectors in which Ito-Yokado (IY) is involved: general-merchandise superstores (GMS) and convenience stores (CVS). Table 8.1 lists Japan's six largest retailers; note the absence of any traditional department stores.

General Merchandise Stores (GMS)

Two annual rates of growth show the performance of GMS: sales and floor space. Reflecting the decade's vibrant economic conditions, sales in the 1980s grew between 2% and 5% annually, while floor space grew between

Table 8.1 Japanese Retailers, Ranked by Size, 1999[1] (in billion yen)

Revenue[2]	Name and Category
3,224	Ito-Yokado Ltd. (diversified) [8264][3]
2,847	The Daiei Co. Inc. (diversified) [8263][4]
2,522	Jusco Co. Ltd. (supermarkets) [8267]
1,856	Mycal Corp. (supermarkets) [8269][5]
1,155	Uny Co. Ltd. (diversified) [8270][7]
1,120	The Seiyu Ltd. (supermarkets) [8268][6]

Note: Ticker symbols for Tokyo Stock Exchange-listed companies given in brackets.
  [1]Fiscal 1999, which ended during first quarter of 2000.
  [2]Consolidated revenue.
  [3]Includes Denny's restaurants, Seven-Eleven Japan, and 7-Eleven Inc. as consolidated subsidiaries, and York-Benimaru Co. Ltd. supermarkets under the equity method. Non-Japan revenue is about one-third of total, mostly from 7-Eleven Inc.
  [4]Includes Lawson, the second largest CVS.
  [5]Goldman Sachs Group owns 15.2% (as of May 2001). Goldman typically does not invest its own money in such situations, but is not required to disclose the ultimate owner. Formed as Nichii Co. Ltd. in 1963 by mergers of many small and medium supermarkets in the Kansai area. The name was changed in 1996.
  [6]Once part of Seibu-Saison group, which included Seibu Department Stores Ltd. The department stores declared bankruptcy in 2000. A chatty account of the group, which began in the 1920s with railroads, is Havens (1994).
  [7]Also sometimes spelled Unyu. Its group includes convenience store operators Circle K Japan and Sunkus & Associates.
  Sources: Company reports and Ito-Yokado Group Investors' Guide 2000, p. 14, which provides additional revenue and balance sheet data for fiscal 1998 and 1999.

2% and 4%. Then the bubble burst and things changed: 1991 was the last year that GMS had a positive spread between sales and floor space growth. Sales growth decreased rapidly in 1992, actually becoming negative, while floor space increased at a rate over 4%, and then jumped above 10% in 1993.

The reason was the liberalization under the Large Scale Retail Store Act, which began in 1990. In the 1980s the number of large retail stores grew slowly from 400 to 700. However, the number jumped above 1500 in 1990, and then rose steadily, reaching 2269 in 1996. With more large stores, individual stores began to experience heavy competition even as a weak economy was restraining sales.

In response, the firms have had to develop new strategies. There have been four aspects to this: pricing and merchandising, reducing operating costs, using information technology, and strategic site selection.

Pricing and merchandising strategies include efforts to sell more imported and private-label products. For example, imports accounted for 17.8% of IY's sales in 1996 and 19.5% at Jusco, while at Daiei, private brands accounted for 12.8% of revenues in 1995.

It has been more difficult to lower operating costs compared to convenience stores (CVS) or the discount centers that have moved into rural areas starting in the 1980s. This is because GMS have to bear almost all the initial investment cost of opening new stores, compared to CVS or discount stores, which generally are franchises and often are existing stores that have joined a chain. GMS also require relatively larger inventories. The primary cost-reduction strategy that remains is to find the best way for each store to control inventory. In particular, attention has been given to avoiding non-availability (opportunity loss)—that is, losing a sale because something is out of stock or not carried at all. This is why good IT is so important to retail profitability and success.

Point of sale (POS) information has been available in Japan for some time; what is important now is how to design a system that covers all aspects of a firm's business activities. Stores have found that such thorough command of IT systems can help avoid having shelves stocked with unpopular goods, as well as better identify what merchandise consumers really want at a given time. For example, demand at a specific store can vary depending on the time of the day and the weather. This information also can be used to identify the best time to order from producers or wholesalers. Just as manufacturing has moved to being "lean," so too is there "lean retailing." (For an insightful analysis of lean retailing and lean manufacturing in apparel and textiles, see Abernathy et al 1999.)

Good IT systems can help achieve the best balance among low inventory, high turnover, and few lost sales (low opportunity losses). Optimally managing these variables is the key to a GMS firm's success, and explains why IY's leading-edge IT strategies have contributed to its success in this highly competitive market despite Japan's economic malaise.

Convenience Stores (CVS)

CVS in Japan generally enjoyed relatively better performance than GMS in the 1990s. Sales rose from ¥3.89 trillion in fiscal 1993 to ¥6.18 trillion in fiscal 1998, according to Japan Franchise Association data. However sales fell slightly in fiscal 1999, to ¥6.13 trillion. The major players are listed in table 8.2.

While the GMS experienced declining sales due to increased competition and the economic downturn, sales at existing CVS dropped only 0.4% in 1995 compared to 1994. However, competition among CVS and against other retail sectors has been increasing, and the time is gone when the whole sector could enjoy huge growth opportunities. Now, only the better-managed CVS have a chance to grow faster. Several factors are important. First is merchandising strategy, including the services offered; second is the use of IT; third is strategic site selection; and fourth is owner development. In this regard, further deregulation definitely will increase the kinds of merchandise and services CVS can and will offer.

Table 8.2 Japanese CVS, Ranked by Size, 2000[1]

Sales[2]	Stores	Name
2,046	8,661	Seven-Eleven Japan [8183][3]
1,275	7,683	Lawson Inc. [2651][4]
960	5,812	FamilyMart Co. Ltd. [8028][5]
497	2,826	Sunkus & Associates [7557][6]
478	2,693	Circle K Japan [7437][7]
337	2,407	Daily Yamazaki[8]
232	1,469	MiniStop [9946]
6,737	35,693	Total[9]

Ticker symbols for Tokyo Stock Exchange-listed companies are in brackets. There are two other publicly traded CVS chains: Kasumi Convenience Network [7454] and Three F Co. Ltd. [7544].

[1]Fiscal years ended during first quarter of 2001.

[2]In billion yen. These numbers may differ from those reported for accounting purposes.

[3]Owned 50.7% by Ito-Yokado Ltd.

[4]Controlled by the Daiei Co., of which it was a 100% owned subsidiary until 1998, when shares began trading publicly. Daiei currently owns 21%.

[5]C Itoh group purchased 50.2% from Seiyu Ltd. in 1998. Through a subsidiary it currently controls 30.6%. Before 1998 FamilyMart was part of the Seibu-Saison Group. A brief history of the company is in Havens (1994, pp. 161–62).

[6]Part of the Uny group. Owned 25.54% by Uny Co. Ltd. and 25.53% by Circle K Japan Co. Ltd. (itself controlled by Uny; see note 7).

[7]Uny group owns 52.6%.

[8]A member of the Yamazaki Banking group [2212].

[9]The total is for the 12 months ending 31 March 2001 and thus does not exactly correspond to the individual company data because their fiscal years usually end in February.

Sources: Sales and store data for specific companies are from a survey of CVS companies by the *Nihon Keizai Shimbun* reported in the *Nikkei Weekly*, 30 July 2001, p. 2. Other data are from Ministry of Economy, Trade and Industry, *Monthly Report on the Current Survey of Commerce*, April 2001, p. 64. Ownership data from company filings.

The number of different products at a CVS are far fewer than at a GMS: over the course of a year a typical CVS has about 5,000 SKUs versus over 100,000 at a GMS. At any one time a CVS stocks about 4500 SKUs. (An SKU [stockkeeping unit] is a unique product as regards manufacturer and such characteristics as size, color, flavor, and the like. Visitors to 7-Eleven's web site will find the statement "2,500 different products" at its U.S. stores, but that is fewer than the number of SKUs, because size matters: 2% milk is a product, but quart and gallon containers each have a different SKU.)

According to SEJ the total number of SKUs it tracks for all its stores over a year is 30,000. This reflects a large number of seasonal and promotional items, geographical variations in what is carried, and the extensive and constantly changing fast-food offerings. This variety and SEJ's flexibility in supplying stores, especially with different food items during the day, are considered an important reason its sales per store are much higher than those of competitors.

Market Saturation

With the surge in the number of CVS, population per store fell to 2572 in 1996, which is below the 3000 then usually regarded as the critical viability level. In major urban areas the situation became even more unfavorable: in Tokyo, 2012; in Osaka, only 1819. However, the major chains feel it is important to distinguish between high-quality stores and lower-quality ones that are called CVS just because they are open 24 hours. The total number of CVS in Japan, 48,567 in 1996, includes every type that satisfies the minimum definition.

Of these, only about 32,000 were providing the other usual CVS services such as postage stamp sales, copiers, fax machines, video games, utility bill payment, and package delivery. Therefore, the population per high-quality store may actually have been around 4000. This means that, for quality operations, there was a chance during the late 1990s to add as many as 10,000 stores. In the event, the number of CVS actually declined by 9,000 to 39,627 in early 2001, and the general feeling is that saturation had been reached even for higher-quality stores.

Competitive pressures are indicated by the fact that low-quality stores that do not belong to a franchise have been closing or converting. In 1996 there were 1486 such closures, equal to 45% of the 3218 newly opened stores, which were virtually all franchises or owned by a CVS chain. Many of the mom-and-pop stores that once dotted neighborhoods also have closed or converted, but they are not included in these data unless open 24 hours.

Though the major CVS companies were doing some scrap-and-build of existing franchise stores, the number of scrapped stores per listed company was only some 100 per year, about 20% of new openings. Therefore, the share of stores related to the eight major CVS companies rose from the mid-1980s. It went from 21% in 1985, to 30% in 1990, to 40% in 1995, and to 43% in 1996. By 1996 their share was almost twice that in 1985. Reflecting a sharp shakeout, by 2000 the top six had 65% of stores and over 80% of total CVS sales. Now, even the major stores are reining in, with Lawson and FamilyMart in early 2001 announcing closures and relocations of hundreds of lower-performing stores, although planned openings in more promising locations mean there will be little net change in their total number of stores.

Merchandise Strategy

CVS have continually sought to add services to attract traffic, even if they do not contribute directly to profits. Thus, many have long offered copiers, fax services, and video games. Beginning in 1987 they have become payment points for electricity, gas, and water bills (SEJ was the first, and reports having 3% of the market in 2000). In February 1989, SEJ also became a payment point for Daiichi Seimei (life insurance). As deregulation has allowed, stores have added sales of money orders (June 1995) and postage stamps. Sale of rice also was allowed in 1996. Foreign exchange services started in April 1998. Package shipping began in the mid-1990s. SEJ works primarily with Yamato Un'yu (Black Cat), by far Japan's largest package delivery firm. In November 1999, SEJ began accepting payment for purchases made over the Internet. With these new offerings, sales of existing CVS began rising again.

Japan is still very much a cash-using society, and even those with credit cards are reluctant to give the number over the phone or Internet. This is demonstrated by the fact in the year ending February 2001, SEJ handled over ¥800 billion in third-party payments on behalf of 245 companies. This involved over 100 million transactions.

Reservation services for travel packages became available beginning in late 2000 and, looking ahead, stores may even be able to sell some prescription pharmaceutical products. One idea is to have them act as a pickup and payment point for an on-line pharmacy.

More banking and financial services will be offered as deregulation continues. Working couples needing financial services outside normal banking hours already have been targeted by firms such as Sanwa Bank (now part of UFJ; see chapter 10) in terms of its expanded automated branch network. Several CVS have announced aggressive plans to act as automated bank branches. IY has established its own bank, as discussed later.

SEJ and Sony have an agreement to offer high-speed downloading of games for PlayStation 2. This means the store can offer a total selection of games, but will have to inventory only blank CDs. Players will have an alternative to downloading over a slow (and expensive) residential telephone line. In addition, upgrades will be easy to provide for a small fee. The pressure on video game rental stores and software shops will be enormous.

In cooperation with Sharp (a major electronics company), FamilyMart is deploying Famiport kiosks in stores to allow downloading of game software and e-books. The kiosks were in over 20% of FamilyMarts by May 2001. The service is aimed at users of Sharp's Zaurus, a PDA with almost a quarter of the Japanese market. The kiosks are being made by e-plat, a joint venture of Toyota and NTT Data (an affiliate of Japan's dominant telecom carrier). The ordering and payment system connects to a communications and computer center run by Toyota. Actual settlement is handled by NTT Data in conjunction with IBM and the banks' clearing system. FamilyMart also is cooperating with Toyota to promote the automaker's *gazoo.com* web site (which is discussed in chapter 7).

Handling this wide range of services requires thought, support, and staff training. For example, when CVS started selling game software in 1996, the makers selected stores on the basis of distribution power. This relates to how extensive the franchise network is and how well the distribution system works to supply stores. The implication is that although a CVS can add items and services, not all chains may be able to do so well and profitably. Further, many of these new products and services, especially financial ones, are very IT intensive. The store ideally wants the customer to buy lunch, a snack and magazine for later, and a toiletry, while checking bank balances, making payments, or trading stocks.

Site Selection and Owner Development

"Area dominance" is considered the best CVS site-selection strategy by IY and many retail analysts. This means having a network of stores in an area that is dense enough to be, overall, more conveniently located than any competitor without cannibalizing one's own sales, and convenient to a distribution center. This is extremely complex on the ground, as it involves more than just a grid of stores. Traffic patterns and locations of complementary merchants are just two of the many factors, and there is a niche industry devoted to siting retail stores (at least in the United States; a convenient overview is the Urban Land Institute's *Shopping Center Development Handbook*).

Selection of franchisees is closely related to site selection, and is considered by IY and many retail analysts to be the most important aspect of CVS strategy. This is because the competition among CVS firms for new stores in promising areas has reduced the average quality of franchisees and CVS stores. (The U.S. literature on this is large, but there are many differences between the United States and Japan, especially in the legal system affecting franchises.)

At some CVS chains, the staff responsible for developing new stores and advising new franchise owners on store management is not very competent. Competence is very important when more complex services are added. SEJ's store-support staff of 1500 thus is a key competitive strength. Franchise-closing costs, are much higher than opening costs, so CVS firms have to pay careful attention to their relations, support, and contracts with franchisees. One listed CVS company and its franchisees have been struggling in court over interpretation of the franchise contract since mid-1996. Such rancor can adversely affect the whole franchise system.

The need to offer more services, liberalization of the Large-Scale Retail Store Act, and depressed economic conditions have created significant problems for small and medium family retail stores, and have given them strong incentives to become franchisees of a chain. Independents have not organized large cooperative marketing and buying organizations, as in the United States. A small family store licensed to sell liquor has a particular advantage, and the chains have offered good terms in such cases. As a result, more than half of new franchise stores have liquor permits.

IY has not utilized IT for site and franchisee selection. However, perhaps this is coming, or it may reflect good intuitive judgment in selecting franchisees, perhaps aided by a reputation that attracts better franchisees, which in part means having good locations and a liquor license. In 1996 SEJ had a net increase in franchise stores of 502, a record level.

The Ito-Yokado Group

The Ito-Yokado Group is Japan's largest retailer, comparable in size to The Kroger Co., the largest U.S. supermarket chain. Table 8.3 lists the group's principal components, and box 8.1 briefly describes U.S.-based Seven-Eleven.

The group dates back to a menswear store opened in 1920. The name Ito-Yokado was adopted in June 1965. The superstores and supermarkets use the same graphic logo, regardless of name, as do 7-Eleven stores, regardless of global location.

Alliances were formed with Wal-Mart in 1993 and Germany-based Metro Group (Europe's largest distribution group) in 1994 to share "information system and inventory control know-how while using their international networks to develop and import merchandise."

IT Strategies

IY's success illustrates the IT management principle that the implementation and design of each company's IT and IT strategy is unique to its competitive situation, industry, and corporate objectives. This is because such factors have influenced how IY measures success and how it chooses between packaged and customized software options. The company has linked its software strategies with its overall management goals through a mission statement that explicitly notes the importance of IT.

The next several sections look at how IY uses IT. A driving force in IY's use of IT has been Toshifumi Suzuki, and we begin with an overview of his philosophy and approach to IT. (For a detailed explanation of IY's IT strategy in the context of Japanese retailing see Hibara and Rapp 2000.)

Toshifumi Suzuki on IT

Toshifumi Suzuki, president and CEO of the IY Group since 1992 and previously president of SEJ, has always had a precise vision concerning how a retail business should be managed. He also knows that IT is indispensable to realizing IY's business goals, having spent his early career at SEJ, the most IT-intensive part of IY's operations. His important strategy decisions almost always entail the need for some IT input. Indeed, his management decisions often are in terms of what IT should be introduced. The types of IT that the IY Group has introduced since 1982 have corresponded to its business needs, and the level of IT has tracked its business requirements.

Mr. Suzuki regards retailing as a system-dependent industry, so he wants IY to be seen as excellent in using computer systems to meet the requirements the group, its suppliers, and its customers face every day. He emphasizes that retailing can benefit from using IT, but the IT must be a function of the retailing. To achieve this integration of retail and IT expertise, store

Table 8.3 Ito-Yokado Group

Percent of Sales[1]	
29.6	Superstores (GMS)
28.9	Ito-Yokado
0.4	Marudai
—	Cheng Du Ito-Yokado[2]
—	Hua Tang Yokado Commerical[2]
7.3	Supermarkets
5.0	York Benimaru Co. Ltd. [8188][3,4]
2.2	York Mart
—	Sanei
	Discount Store
2.6	Daikuma
	Department Store
1.1	Robinson's Japan
55.7	Convenience Stores
38.1	Seven-Eleven Japan Co. Ltd. [8183][3,5]
17.6	7-Eleven Inc. [SE][2,3,6]
2.6	Restaurants
2.0	Denny's Japan Co. Ltd. [8195][3,7]
—	Famil
—	York Bussan

Notes: There also are some small specialty stores (0.25% of sales).

Other activities not listed above provide 0.9% of sales.

Members of the IY Group had sales (net of intragroup sales) of 5,154 billion yen ($47.6 billion), making it comparable in size to the Kroger Co., the largest U.S. supermarket chain. Total sales figure given in table 8.1 is smaller because it is for the parent company and thus follows accounting conventions regarding how the revenue of affiliates and sub-sidiaries is handled.

[1]For fiscal 1999, which for most components (including the parent) ended 29 February 2000. For 7-Eleven Inc. data are calendar 1999.

[2]Operates outside Japan.

[3]Publicly traded. Ticker symbol in square brackets.

[4]Affiliate 28.6% owned by IY. Included in IY's consolidated financial statements under the equity method.

[5]Owned 50.7% by IY. In November 1973 an area licensing agreement was reached with Southland Corp. (then the owner of 7-Eleven) to open CVS in Japan. In December 1989 SEJ took over the 7-Eleven stores in Hawaii.

[6]IY directly or indirectly controls 72.6% (March 2001 proxy).

[7]Owned 51.6% by IY. Under license, Denny's restaurants were opened in Japan beginning in May 1973.

Source: Computed by the author from absolute data in Ito-Yokado Group *2000 Investors' Guide*, p. 1.

Box 8.1

7-ELEVEN INC.

The Southland Corp., founded in 1927, originated use of the 7-Eleven name for its stores in 1946. A 1987 leveraged buyout led to a bankruptcy filing in 1990. Since 1991, a wholly owned subsidiary of Ito-Yokado Ltd. (IYG Holding Co.) has owned the majority of the stock (72.6% per March 2001 proxy). The company's name was changed from Southland to 7-Eleven Inc. on 30 April 1999. Headquartered in Dallas, Texas, worldwide in 2000 the chain owned, franchised, or licensed some 11,500 stores excluding SEJ. Most, but not all, are called 7-Eleven.

---

operators and corporate managers make their own plans, then outsource the actual making of the hardware and software. Thus, IY people have to work out and exactly explain their needs to outside technologists. It is the dedicated units at Nomura Research Institue (NRI; the software provider) and NEC (lead hardware provider) that actually develop, implement, and manage the integrated software and hardware system.

Sharing information among all members of the IY Group—including business challenges and possible solutions—is something else Mr. Suzuki emphasizes. Each person in each section should have available the same insights with respect to specific business issues that top management has. Similarly, top managers' knowledge of IY's actual retailing situation needs to be current. Otherwise, Mr Suzuki feels, the company would be in trouble due to a lack of congruence between the urgent issues facing IY and their possible solutions. As part of this, once a week he gathers the 1500 operation field counselors engaged in advisory support for the franchise stores at IY's Tokyo headquarters.

How IY should control each store's daily inventory level is a primary focus of Mr Suzuki's. In the late 1990s he was constantly questioning why inventory per store exceeded ¥10 million while daily sales per store were about ¥400,000. To improve performance, IY has to measure it. That means knowing a lot about what is happening in each store. For example, which goods on the shelves are sold each day, in what quantities, and at what times? The company also wants to know what items tend to be bought together. For perishables, weather-related, and seasonal items, the questions are when an item sells out and how much must be discarded. These data are then assessed in terms of how and when merchandise is delivered to each store.

Mr. Suzuki thinks retailing should respond much more quickly to changes in customer demands, including demand for more variety. For example, the company's analysis shows that different age groups prefer different types of rice balls. The weather, neighborhood events, and many other factors also have an impact on consumer choice, and each store will have a different story about what is likely to happen tomorrow. Each store therefore needs to estimate for itself which items customers will want to buy in the next 12 or 24 hours, and order accordingly. Reviewing the results allows continuous revision of the data used to make the forecasts. IY believes this constant "estimation, ordering, and reviewing" is the only way to respond to customers' changeable demands on a store-by-store basis.

However, IY prefers to do this analysis retrospectively, albeit almost in real time. That is, it seeks to just catch up to changes in consumer demand rather than trying to forecast demand weeks ahead in a larger context. From Mr. Suzuki's viewpoint, the latter is just a gamble, whereas the former is based on the solid evidence gathered by IY's system. At the same time, the strategy does not suggest that ordering should be based only on past data. This is why IY is constantly assessing demand based on inputs from the stores concerning customer requests. As a result, approximately 70% of the items offered on IY's shelves change over the course of a year. This reflects weather and seasonality as well as changes in taste.

For Mr. Suzuki, product ordering is the most constructive and critical part of the retail business. He is suspicious of the automatic ordering systems that have been regarded as effective in the United States, arguing that they do not respond to rapid changes in the composition of consumer demand. From his experience managing 7-Eleven in the United States, he believes that the IT used in U.S. retailing lags behind SEJ's system in solving excess inventory problems and providing a more efficient ordering system. In particular, he thinks Japan has done a much better job of avoiding losing sales because of lack of merchandise.

IY's Use of IT

Because IT directly ties each store and franchise owner with corporate management, it is the primary link between the various strategic elements that affect the company. IY realized very early that maintaining and improving this advantage is the key to its competitive success against the other large GMS and CVS. This is why its corporate strategy and the IT groups at NRI for systems and NEC for hardware are so closely tied together on an interactive basis.

In 1982 IY decided to eliminate slow-selling goods from its shelves with an inventory control system developed in the United States. Because it did not have the IT staff internally to completely implement the project, it decided to transfer some of its staff to NRI and to work with NRI and NEC to develop the new system. Although it subsequently has outsourced much of its IT to NRI, it has retained IT planning and strategy within IY. As the relationship with NRI has evolved, it has brought many benefits to IY. (This is elaborated in the appendix to this chapter.)

The company has been a pioneer in using POS systems, including bar code readers, not only for generating sales slips but also for constantly checking on the popularity of every item in the store. In September 1982, SEJ installed what was then, according to the company, the largest POS system in the world. By December 1985, IY had a POS system in every one of its stores. Since that time, detailed, item-by-item information is uploaded to a central computer. In 2001 these data were being analyzed three times each day in a process that took about 20 minutes. The data also are sent to the wholesalers, distribution centers, and manufacturers supplying IY stores.

For the system to function smoothly, wholesalers and other suppliers need to have compatible information systems. IY has requested that suppliers invest in IT systems capable of meeting IY's continually evolving requirements. It has been difficult for many of them to make the large investments needed, but they cannot refuse if they want to keep IY business. Most who meet IY's high standards have benefited from the quick, automatic feedback of precise sales. Manufacturers, too, have benefited from more timely understanding of what customers want.

In 1990 IY felt it had gained sufficient control over its inventories to declare it would no longer return unsold merchandise, an unprecedented move for a Japanese retailer. Because IY was assuming inventory risk, it could ask for lower prices, and pass savings on to shoppers while still earning higher margins (if it handled the inventory risk well), a beneficial loop.

IY's functional gains have more than justified the expense incurred in developing customized software and hardware systems for its stores, including the related costs of integrating them into a single IT system for the corporation and the constant training of employees on how to use it. Management firmly believes that, at least for IY, IT systems are not generic and are best developed by closely affiliated vendors.

Besides a preference for customization, IY approaches IT in a number of ways that are similar to other leading software users. They include the creation of large proprietary interactive databases that promote continuous feedback between various stages of the order, supply, transport, delivery, and sales process. IY's ability to use IT to economize on traditional delivery systems and inventory practices also is similar. In addition, IY has created beneficially competitive feedback loops that increase productivity in areas such as customer service and product availability while reducing cycle times, improving supply channels, and increasing customer sales.

The Fifth System

Since 1978 SEJ has had five upgrades of its IT system. The new fifth system was in place in June 1999 after about three years of development, testing, and installation (which had begun in November 1997). IY invested some ¥60 billion (about $495 million at 1997 exchange rates) in its new system.

All SEJ stores have satellite and high-speed telephone links to the mainframes in Tokyo and Osaka. Using satellites typically is faster and less expensive than land lines, and provides more assured communications in the event of disruptions from earthquakes and typhoons. The network was developed jointly with NRI and NEC.

The company tracks the number of customers visiting the store at any time, using sensors at the door and occasional quick counts by the staff. Clerks key in gender and age range (there are three categories) when entering each sale.

POS data from each store generate reports in three standard formats. The first covers sales of each SKU for the previous 24 hours. A graphic screen displays the quantity on the vertical axis and the time of sale on the horizontal axis, revealing periods of peak sales. The second format looks at individual items in relation to their product groups and covers longer time periods. Take rice balls, which amounted to ¥80.1 billion in sales in 2000, as an example. The share of each SKU in a product group's sales for the past one week or four weeks is shown in a rank-order list.

The third format monitors items that, to retain freshness, are delivered to each store several times during the day (such as rice balls, which arrive three times a day). The goal is to balance wastage against sales lost to being out of stock. The graphic displays sales quantity, the time an item sold out, and the quantity, thrown away if an item does not sell out, between deliveries.

In addition to such processed POS data, headquarters provides stores with information on the weather, neighborhood events, and other external factors in order to increase each store's ordering efficiency.

Item-by-Item Control

IY describes its marketing strategy as "item-by-item control." This is expressed as "We formulate hypotheses about our merchandise mix and displays, and verify their accuracy against current sales data. Through this process, we aim to zero in on customers' ever-changing needs."

Such attention to detail reflects the fact that the demographic characteristics and shopping objectives of customers change according to time, day, and season, as well as weather and local events. In response, the company changes the merchandise being displayed and adjusts quantities. As a result of the constant change in product mix and the large number of local vendors SEJ uses, the company says it tracks some 30,000 SKUs in its inventory system over the course of a year, which is six or seven times the count for any one store at any given time.

Sensitivity to time is most applicable to fast-food and deli-type items (called HMR—home-meal replacement—items in the literature). Thus, as an example, research for one store found that senior citizens prefer one type of sushi lunch packages, while housewives prefer another, and the two groups have slightly different shopping hours. The seniors buy slightly earlier, so the deli case is stocked first with their preference, then restocked with the housewives' preference. In both cases these are single servings. In the late afternoon, larger packages (typically, three servings) are displayed for family dinners.

The overall process means stores can narrow the items and services offered to those that their customers actually want to buy at any specific time.
This makes space available for new products and services. The result is
shelves that always look attractive to customers. IY is in effect extending JIT
concepts to its customers' likely demand patterns, and it seems to work.

In this regard, local weather and events in the neighborhood are even
more critical to CVS sales than to those of a GMS, which makes detailed
sales data especially important. In part this reflects the more limited space
in a CVS, which makes the opportunity cost of shelf space higher. Moreover,
many items at a CVS are fast foods with a shelf life measured in hours. Thus,
the daily demand forecast is much more important for a CVS and must
differentiate among products precisely.

Because weather is especially critical, the company relies on private reporting stations that cover local areas and sends data to stores five times a
day. Topography causes significant differences in weather, so fairly specific
reports are important. The previous day's weather also is a factor, for different types of weather changes induce different buying patterns.

Faster data processing has allowed IY to move the ordering deadline from
10 A.M. to 11 A.M. for evening (after 4 P.M.) delivery. This gives each store's
staff more time to analyze the available information, and thus improves the
accuracy and precision of its ordering practices. Reflecting the importance
of sharing information between top management and the franchisees, all
1500 field counselors have laptops.

Delivery trucks are incorporated into the system by having the drivers log
in at each store, using a bar-coded card. This provides information for modifying routes to maintain schedules. There are frequent deliveries of fresh
food, using different trucks for frozen, chilled, warm, and room-temperature
goods.

The benefits of this sophisticated IT system have been reflected in SEJ's
business performance. Average daily sales per store were ¥890,000 in fiscal
2000, compared to ¥669,000 in 1997 and ¥356,000 in 1977. (Inflation in
Japan has been relatively mild over this time period, especially in the 1990s,
so this represents significant real growth.) From 1977 to 1997, average inventory turn went to 7.7 days from 25.5 days, and average gross margins
rose to 29.9% from 24.0%. In terms of per-store sales by CVS in 2000, the
average SEJ sold about a third again what Sukus, the next-best major chain,
did, and almost half again the average of Lawson, the second largest chain.

Average inventory turn has been relatively stable since 1991 even though
the fourth-stage information system was introduced in the early 1990s and
the fifth stage in the late 1990s. Average daily sales per store were relatively
unchanged during 1992–97 reflecting the adverse macroeconomic conditions from the bubble collapse, combined with the micro effects of increased
competition in the CVS sector. Just maintaining sales and turnover can be
considered a major strategic accomplishment. Although general economic
malaise continues in Japan, per-store sales have again begun to rise. Going

forward, SEJ's initiatives in on-line banking and e-commerce are intended to build store traffic, and thus revenue.

IY and SEJ have constructed a very sophisticated system that is largely independent of the Internet. This of course reflects the fact that it was largely in place by the time the potential of the Internet was widely recognized. However, the companies feel that the advantages of a proprietary network are such that they would not have made the system Internet-based even if that had been an option. This is not to say they are ignoring the Internet in areas they feel it appropriate, and they are monitoring its use by others. It is an element of its relationship with Wal-Mart. Lawson and Mitsubishi Corp., Japan's largest trading company, are constructing an Internet-based system intended to emulate SEJ's.

Supplier Relationships

Using various vendors and some packaged systems offered by firms such as Symbol Technologies, BA Merchant Services, BuyPass, Inter-Act, DataSage, and Systech, it is possible for U.S. and other retailers to introduce cutting-edge IT if they believe it can return high benefits. However, an advanced IT system, however defined, is far from sufficient to make a successful retailer, because the virtual must merge with the real. To have anything at all on the shelves and not have the benefits of IT competed away by others doing the same thing means retailers have to have well-functioning relationships with their suppliers.

Relationships between retailers and suppliers run along a continuum from predominantly hierarchical to mostly market-oriented. That is, retailers can control their suppliers fairly directly (contracting for private-label goods or even owning the production facility) or deal entirely at arm's length in spot markets. Relative size matters, but it is not the only factor in how the relationships work.

Reve and Stern (1986) created the following analytical framework to assess retailer and supplier relationships in terms of IT use and strategy.

1. Vertical interactions are the activity, resource, and information flows that take place between two organizations linked together in a distribution channel. Smooth progress and cooperation require that both share the belief that potential gains from cooperation can be larger than from not cooperating.
2. Formalization refers to the degree to which rules, fixed policies, and procedures govern inter-organizational flows, and how formal or informal contract rules on sharing possibly excessive returns can give each party enough of an incentive to keep cooperating.
3. Centralization of interfirm decision-making refers to the extent to which the power to make and implement interorganizational deci-

sions is concentrated in one of the two interacting organizations. In this context, either party may be more powerful in decision-making than the other, but power can shift, depending on the parties as well as on the performance of the relationship.

Table 8.4 shows a mapping, based on this format, of IY's interfirm relationships that might also be applicable to other retailers and their supplier relationships.

IT has transformed the relationships between retailers and suppliers, but in and of itself it has not shifted power. Retailers continue to be strong relative to smaller suppliers but weaker compared to larger suppliers that have established, especially must-stock, brands. IT has made it easier for retailers, and thus for suppliers, to spot slow-moving items more quickly and discontinue them.

Matching IT, Organization, and Strategy

An epochal event in retailing is the cooperation between Wal-Mart and Procter & Gamble (P&G) that started in 1987 and helped promote the concept of ECR (efficient consumer response, which was developed and named by the U.S. Food Marketing Institution). Under this arrangement, retailers provide POS data to suppliers through a computer network, and suppliers automatically deliver goods to the store to replenish stock. This sharing of data helps avoid both inventory accumulation and lost opportunities, providing a win-win-win for suppliers, retailers, and consumers. (The key characteristics of ECR are defined by King and Phumpiu 1996.)

ECR is similar to what SEJ has been doing since the 1970s, but there are two important differences: who controls the ordering and how shelf space is controlled and allocated.

Under ECR, an order is generated automatically when POS data indicate an item has fallen to a specified level. In contrast, SEJ applies "micromerchandising" under which each shop can order goods. The system authorizes clerks to predict near-term consumer demand resulting from, say, a change in weather or a special neighborhood event, and provides them access to a

Table 8.4 Intensity of Ito-Yokado's Supplier Relationships

Aspect of Relationship	SEJ and Daily Food Suppliers	SEJ and Large Food Producers	IY and Apparel Makers
Benefits to retailer	strong	strong	relatively strong
Benefits to supplier	strong	usually weak	relatively weak
Formalization	strong	weak	very weak
Centralization	strong	relatively weak	none

For explanations of formalization and centralization, see text discussion.

system that assists them to order accordingly. Truly effective ordering requires judgment, and that means training store employees (and working to keep them long enough to gain relevant experience). SEJ is helped in this regard by the fact most of its stores are franchises with owners active in operations. In other words, SEJ's approach is part of paying attention to its customers and watching the merchandise on its shelves and the services it offers on an item-by-item, store-by-store basis, using both IT and judgment.

Such differences may or may not matter for particular retailers' performance, but they probably affect how interfirm relationships with suppliers are designed, depending on the specific constraints affecting individual retailers. This is developed more fully in the section "Highly Perishable Goods."

Dependency

There is a potential for conflict between a retailer and a supplier when a very large percentage of the supplier's sales are through the retailer or the products are very important to the retailer. In the Wal-Mart—Proctor & Gamble example, 20% of P&G's U.S. sales are through Wal-Mart, while P&G items are a much smaller percentage of Wal-Mart's U.S. sales. Wal-Mart tried to leverage its buying power by proposing a comarketing strategy, which included P&G manufacturing private-label goods (at a profit advantage to Wal-Mart). P&G refused the request. It then began working to leverage its position of having many products that are ranked first nationally in their categories, while also developing ways to counteract, Wal-Mart's market power.

Thus, P&G has sought to develop new products that will be must-stock brands—that is, items so popular among consumers that retailers, even Wal-Mart, cannot be without them. Also, in 1994 it established several distribution centers to make it easier to supply products to small and medium retailers. In addition, P&G began to strengthen its relationships with other large retailers, such as Kmart. The goal was to reduce dependence on Wal-Mart. Still, Wal-Mart's continued expansion domestically and globally means it continues to be P&G's biggest outlet, so there is continued tension over profit sharing.

A similar situation has occurred in the relationship between SEJ and Yamazaki, Japan's top bread maker. Yamazaki's sales through SEJ have been estimated to be about 10% of Yamazaki's sales, while SEJ gets about 80% of the bread sold in its stores from Yamazaki. In 1993 SEJ proposed a private-label project, Just Baked Bread, to Yamazaki. For SEJ, the purpose was to provide high-quality bread at prices in SEJ's stores lower than in Yamazaki's own shops. SEJ was going to establish several new bakeries, which would cover nearby SEJ stores. Yamazaki was asked to invest in these bakeries and produce bread there. The system would have enabled quick provision of high-quality baked goods consistent with how IY supplies its stores with other perishable items.

However, Yamazaki's policy and position are similar to P&G's, as its bread market share in Japan is over 30%. It had never done private-label baking, and it saw no reason to put its national brands' market share at risk, let alone its technology and established distribution network. Yamazaki rejected the proposal, except for the island of Hokkaido, where the venture began in December 1993. However, Yamazaki, to protect itself from SEJ's market power, also began providing products to Lawson, the second largest CVS, from its existing bakeries through its own distribution network.

On the other hand, soon after SEJ announced its entrance into financial services (in cooperation with NRI, Sony, and NEC) three other financial service firms—Bank of Tokyo—Mitsubishi, Sanwa Bank, and Nikko Securities—agreed to invest as well. They saw SEJ's outlets as an easy way to extend their user base by linking their IT systems with IY's. None of these firms dominates Japanese banking or finance, so none has as much to lose by supplying private-label financial services to IY's customer base compared to Yamazaki in bread.

Team Merchandising

IY has made an effort with its GMS to sell more private-label or exclusive merchandise (called "team merchandising" or "team MD" by IY), especially in apparel. This has developed several popular products, such as polo shirts and 100% cashmere sweaters. Ideally, IY will be able to offer an exclusive design with a well-known brand. However, team merchandising often is only a spot transaction for a specific project, which means IY cannot promise to continue buying such merchandise on a long-term basis from one particular maker for an extended time period.

When large producers with well-known brands are involved, the overall performance of a private-label strategy has not been good. This is because such a supplier has little incentive to make the required investment or to negatively affect its own brand, which is a kind of investment. Thus, in dealing with apparel makers that are the top brands in their categories, IY generally has acquiesced in the suppliers' desire to sell products under their own labels, using IY as a major distributor. Thus, strong interfirm relationships in apparel have been problematic despite IY's retailing preeminence and IT sophistication.

As an example of SEJ's evolutionary learning, the company has implemented a clever strategy for private-label products. SEJ acquired the right to use the names of two famous noodle shops. It then went to Nissin Food Products, the top manufacturer of instant noodles, and contracted for production of a premium product solely for SEJ using the acquired names. This has been a triple win: not only has SEJ benefited, but the noodle shops receive licensing fees and Nissin is selling more instant noodles than it would otherwise.

Highly Perishable Goods

Close cooperation with suppliers in providing attractive fast food, such as box lunches, rice balls, and sandwiches, as well as fresh foods and fruits, has made SEJ the number-one fast-food purveyor in Japan. Indeed, in fiscal 2000 its fast-food revenue was more than 40% greater than McDonalds. (Over 60% of this involves cooked rice, including rice balls [almost 13% of total fast food] and sushi.)

This business has been quite profitable for SEJ even though all these items can perish during the day. The key has been in how it has overcome possible conflicts with or among its suppliers—the difficulties with Yamazaki appear to have been an exception. Most of SEJ's suppliers of fast and fresh daily food are smaller companies that don't make national-brand fast food. Although such firms may have less concern over joining with a specific retailer, other conditions still must be met to have cooperation work well in practice. This is because SEJ requires very timely delivery, as well as maintenance of quality and taste.

Yahagi (1994) has described some of the conditions needed to do this well, drawing on the arrangement between SEJ and its daily food suppliers, which he calls a "closed system." Such systems are characterized by relation-specific investments by suppliers, a high concentration of the suppliers' business with the buyer, and an open and fair reward system that shares benefits.

The daily food suppliers have been organized by IY in a formal way so that they can supply the same quality of food daily nationwide. For example, SEJ meets with box lunch producers once a week to discuss new products based on an analysis of its customer database. If, for example, it is decided to have three varieties of chicken box lunch, IY shares information on how to make these with all producers, requesting each to create the same menus and provide them to all SEJs.

IY's fast-food producers are required to bear the cost of building delivery centers and organizing delivery systems dedicated solely to their business with SEJ. From SEJ's standpoint this not only keeps its investment in bricks and mortar to a minimum, improving its asset turnover, it also firmly commits and ties the suppliers to SEJ's strategy, stores, and system. As part of tying the suppliers to itself and ensuring systems compatibility, SEJ rents out IT equipment. Whether a supplier decides to join an alliance with SEJ depends on whether the relationship-specific investment will benefit it. Almost one-third of SEJ's suppliers sell 100% of their output to SEJ (Yahagi 1994).

The reward system for participating suppliers is clear and stable. For a daily food product, the margin for suppliers is specified as more than 18% of retail. This is applied to all suppliers regardless of how much of the item they provide, the geographic area, or the product type. Such reliance on rewards based on a high degree of formalization gives strength to the cooperation between the suppliers and IY. This is a symbiotic relationship and beneficial loop in which IY's success contributes to its suppliers' success and conversely.

E-Commerce

E-commerce is definitely taking hold in Japan. Although it has been evolving differently than in the United States, it is changing Japanese retailers' strategies. Thus, with NRI's help, IY is moving quickly and decisively to have an impact on the development of e-commerce. In particular, it has been developing a customer-driven strategy in which the concept of convenience goes well beyond the types of items one normally has associated with CVS.

A key area in making e-commerce work is in developing convenient and secure payment mechanisms. Many Japanese do not trust giving a credit card number over the Internet or the telephone, and others simply prefer to pay cash. Teaming with a CVS allows e-commerce web sites to have people pay at a conveniently located store, as well as take delivery there. This also facilitates returns, which can be done on the spot.

It is common to order items such as books, video games, and CDs through the Internet, using the CVS for payment and delivery. In fact, IY has led this change. In 1999 SEJ established joint ventures such as e-Shopping!Books with Softbank, Tohan, and Yahoo Japan, and CarPoint Japan for car sales with Softbank, Microsoft, and Yahoo Japan. In addition, the 3 million customers of Japan's largest virtual mall, Rakuten Ichiba (*rakuten.co.jp*), can use SEJ stores to make their payments and pick up packages if they do not want them delivered. SEJ and NRI jointly have started providing clearing services for purchases made on the Internet. IY reports that about 75% of shoppers on its web sites pick up and pay at the store.

7dream.com

In January 2000, SEJ and NRI announced the formation of a new e-retsu (a company based solely on IT relationships) with capital of ¥5 billion. Called 7dream.com, SEJ intends it to be "one of the largest EC [e-commerce] businesses in Japan and operate at the forefront of its field."

7dream provides a range of services on its web site, which eventually will be accessible from the multimedia terminals currently being installed in SEJ stores. In keeping with NRI's recommendations that any e-commerce access strategy be "ubiquitous," 7dream also can be accessed directly over the Internet and other networks, including those open to mobile phones and direct TV.

The new firm is offering services related to travel, music, gifts, mobile phones, event tickets (including a tie-up with PIA Corp., Japan's largest-ticket agency), books (through an arrangement with e-Shopping!Books Corp.), car-related services (sales via CarPoint and, later, arranging auto inspections, repairs, driving lessons, and rental cars), and information services related to entertainment, digital photographs, and special examinations in partnership with firms such as Toppan Printing and JMA Management Center. Table 8.5 lists the owners and what expertise and services they bring to the venture.

As of August 2001 there were about 1,200 7dream terminals in 7-Eleven stores in the Tokyo area, with rollout elsewhere planned over the next few years. Meanwhile, anyone can order from the web site, or the call center, or in the store, using a monthly catalog available at all stores. The offerings in the catalog are nonbulky, because the stores have limited storage space for holding items until they are picked up. The catalog contains items not offered via the kiosks, which currently are more focused on tickets, CDs, and games. (This is currently true of the kiosks at all the CVS chains.)

SEJ expects start-up costs to be around ¥40 billion and projects annual sales of about ¥150 billion for 2002 and ¥300 billion for 2004. This obviously offers IY tremendous opportunities to enlarge the goods and services available at SEJ stores throughout Japan. It also significantly extends NRI's IT business and expertise.

Table 8.5 *7dream.com* Owners

Owner (percentage)	Expertise and services provided
SEJ (51%)	Principal organizer; provides places for kiosks to access the web site
NRI (13%)	Advises on structuring the business, as well as on developing and operating the e-commerce system
NEC (13%)	Built and operates the web site. Also designed and developed the multimedia terminals, all of which are connected via dedicated lines
Sony (6.5%)	Supplies technological support related to its mini-disk and integrated-circuit card technologies. including on-line packaged music
Sony Marketing (6.5%)	See Sony
Mitsui & Co. (6%)	A trading company, it provides information, general merchandising support, and distribution services
JTB (2%)	A travel agency (formerly Japan Travel Bureau)
KINOTROPE (2%)	A software firm it consults on Internet business design and systems development

IY Bank

Under Japanese law, only banks can have ATMs, so the other CVS have invited one or more banks to locate ATMs in their stores. That means the bank controls the ATM. IY and SEJ want to control the services available through the ATM, so they decided to organize their own bank.

IY was the first nonbank to apply for an on-line banking license, joined by Bank of Tokyo-Mitsubishi, Sanwa Bank (UFJ Group), NEC, and NRI as shareholders. It opened in May 2001. Nomura Securities, Nikko Securities, and Sony have joined the venture and three other banks (Asahi Bank, Shizuoka Bank, and Bank of Yokohama) have affiliated. The shareholding and affiliated banks have provided staff, as has SEJ. The bank's president is a former Bank of Japan official.

The participation of two securities firms reflects an expectation that on-line brokerage services will be provided at some point. Sony has affiliates offering life and auto insurance products, and also is planning its own e-bank. The banks expect to be able to close branches without sacrificing customer service. Depending on the store's location, the ATMs accept different affiliated bank cards as well as IY's.

By the end of July 2001 there were about 1000 ATMs installed, all in metropolitan Tokyo and adjacent areas. Installation costs have been about ¥2.5 million each. An ATM is a bank branch under banking rules, and accounts can be opened only at a bank branch (or by mail), so SEJ can open accounts only in stores with the ATMs. In the first two months about 10,000 accounts were opened. Not surprisingly, ATM use has been primarily on weekends and after 8 P.M. Besides 7-Elevens, ATMs ultimately will be placed in Denny's restaurants and IY's general-merchandise stores.

Conclusion

IY shows how IT in combination with physical location can be used creatively to expand store sales to include services that can range from package delivery, to banking, to downloading music and computer games, thereby increasing store revenues and customer traffic that can lead to additional sales. In IY's vision, IT is seen as enabling stores to expand product and service offerings in order to respond more effectively to fluctuating demand even while reducing inventory costs and increasing sales per square meter. IY recognizes that success requires it to establish a well-functioning delivery system between retail stores and suppliers, something IT can facilitate, along with close working relationships with suppliers of certain types of goods (highly perishable ones in particular), although the latter involves more than just IT. In effect, IY is extending JIT concepts to its customers likely demand patterns, and it seems to work.

In pursuing its vision, the company has become a leader in using totally integrated management (TIM) to change its competitive environment. This is because it has developed an approach that uses IT to capture significant improvements in productivity via a TIM system through which it monitors, controls, and links every aspect of supplying and delivering its products and services, including its external environment. IY also is using IT to influence demand and the competitive environment. Thus, the company is at the forefront in developing the TIM approach for food and convenience-store retailing.

Appendix:
The Role of NRI in Developing and
Implementing IY's IT strategy

One of Ito-Yokado's most important and successful interfirm relationships is with NRI, which operates like a captive IT subsidiary while delivering the benefits of a large, relatively diversified systems integrator. This appendix provides an overview of NRI and outlines its relationship with IY.

NRI considers itself to be "Japan's largest all-around information services company," comprising "think tank, consulting firm and SI [systems integration] vendor," and through 2000 it has been second only to NTT Data in total IT-related billings. However, it is not a think tank in the U.S. sense of an independently funded, often nonprofit, research institute providing policy recommendations. Rather, most work is done under contract for paying clients, some of which are public entities. In addition, the bulk of its revenues actually comes from its activities as a major software developer and systems provider, and it is definitely profit oriented.

The institute had about 3600 employees and almost $1.8 billion in revenues for the year ended March 2000. It is 100% owned by various members of the Nomura Group, which is centered on Nomura Securities, Japan's largest securities firm (although in 2001 there was talk of a public offering of part of the company which finally occurred in November.) This makes it very strong in providing financially related IT services, including systems development and operating support. The present NRI is the result of a merger in 1988 of the former Nomura Research Institute, founded in 1965, and Nomura Computer Systems, founded in 1966 (as Nomura Computing Center). NRI has offices and computing centers in Japan, the United States, and Europe, as well as offices in other Pacific Basin countries.

Not surprisingly, given its parentage, NRI's financial systems solution business is the most extensive part of the institute's activities, and it is particularly strong in back-office support for such tasks as account management, government reporting, and trading. These are just the sort of IT systems Ito-Yokado's bank will require both internally and to interface with the larger financial community.

NRI's intense relationship with Ito-Yokado began in the early 1980s when IY decided that it was better to develop a long-term, in-depth relationship with an outside IT systems provider than to continue to expand its internal

IT department or create its own software company. It chose Nomura because it felt that the kind of systems Nomura Computer Systems (NCS) had developed to support Nomura's branch office network was the closest to the kind of IT systems support it wanted for its stores.

IY transferred most of its IT department to Nomura to form the nucleus of what became a dedicated IY group within NCS. However, it retained a small IT planning and strategy section which manages the relationship with NRI and the implementation of IY's IT-based retail strategy. The arrangement, which has been extremely successful, thus effectively functions as a closely affiliated software supplier with legacy functions and understanding. NRI is an investor in IY's new IT-based ventures, such as IY Bank and *7dream.com*.

As Ito-Yokado seeks to use its convenience stores, bank, and IT systems to offer financial service or to connect to other firms such as insurance companies and brokerages, NRI's expertise and experience will become even more significant. IY's entry into on-line banking includes NRI and Nomura Securities as investors. In some cases, government rules state that a firm must have an "approved" system before it can offer a financial product to the public. NRI of course has existing approved systems and has a number of offerings to support asset management and trust banking activities.

NRI provides POS and consumer analysis systems support to "supermarkets, convenience stores, family-type restaurants, and other chain stores that supply a large variety of products in small quantities." Much of this is to IY and its group members, including Denny's Japan. To quote NRI marketing material, NRI will help identify a firm's IT needs and then build and operate the system so that the firm can assume an "aggressive management style." This includes building and managing interenterprise networks and large-scale database systems that help the client identify and manage consumer consumption patterns and behavior. This leverages the expertise NRI has developed through its work with Ito-Yokado. However, according to IY, their agreement precludes NRI's offering other users IT developed for IY for a least two years after deployment. This allows both NRI and IY to spread development costs.

Through its work in developing Ito-Yokado's supplier-linked systems, NRI has been able to extend its consulting and systems support into manufacturing fields such as apparel. But the idea in all cases is to provide "comprehensive system integration services, from systems design and development to the integrated operation of computers and networks," just as it does for Ito-Yokado and the Nomura Group.

For more details on NRI and its IT activities, see Rapp (2000).

9

Life Insurance

Nationwide Financial Services, Meiji Seimei

Greater affluence and longer lives have transformed the life insurance industry into being truly more about life than about death. The same factors plus deregulation have led to new products and caused new market niches to emerge, with more players in each. At the same time, on the supply side, market segmentation has been reduced. Mergers and affiliations within and across traditional segment lines are commonplace.

This chapter looks at two companies that illustrate these developments in the United States and Japan, and how IT can be used to achieve a competitive advantage in this context. They are Meiji Seimei Hoken, one of Japan's leading life insurers, and Nationwide Financial Services Inc., a major player in selected U.S. market niches. The two firms have chosen markedly different strategies for the competitive environment they face, and both differ in important respects from the approach taken by Citigroup (taken up in chapter 10).

The chapter is divided into two mega-sections. The first looks at Nationwide, and the second at Meiji. Nationwide is a Level 2 IT strategist that uses IT to support and strengthen its competitive position in niche retirement products that it sells through its own agents and a wide range of third parties. Meiji, in response to Japan's Big Bang and economic downturn, has developed an innovative Level 3 strategy based on a proprietary life-cycle model and laptop computer system that has significantly improved the performance of its 30,000 field agents and forced major competitors to respond with about an 18-month lag.

NATIONWIDE FINANCIAL SERVICES

Faced with a declining market and lower profits during the 1990s, Nationwide saw a need to change and to partially reinvent itself in terms of image and products. It has achieved this by employing IT as one important strategic tool. But, unlike many (usually larger) insurance companies and banks,

Nationwide has not diversified and expanded to offer a full range of financial products to its customers throughout their lives. Instead, it decided to specialize in an area closely related to life insurance. Thus, it offers three retirement-oriented products: annuities, variable life insurance, and defined-contribution plans.

Nationwide perceives that, even as other firms are seeking to become one-stop providers, many customers are interested in unbundled financial services and are diversifying their providers of financial products. It also has exploited the fact that some financial service providers who want to offer a full spectrum of bundled services are willing to sell products provided by another company.

The Company

Nationwide Financial Services Inc. (NFS) is a holding company that includes Nationwide Life Insurance Co. and various firms that provide asset management and other retirement-savings operations. The holding company was created in 1996 and started trading on the New York Stock Exchange in 1997 (with the symbol NFS). However, it is 81.4% owned by Nationwide Corporation, with which it is consolidated for tax and accounting purposes. Its ultimate parent is Nationwide Mutual Insurance Company. NFS believes that with this structure it gains stability and flexibility. Moreover, it can leverage the economies of scale generated by the overall Nationwide group as the group shifts its business and strategic emphasis away from being a mutual life and accident insurance provider toward being a for-profit firm offering retirement products. The Nationwide Group, based in Columbus, Ohio, traces back to the mid-1920s. Its web site is *nationwide.com.*

The combined entities posted 2000 revenues of $32.8 billion and had an $8 billion policyholder surplus. In December 2000, NFS itself had about $93 billion in assets. Marketing through direct agents, broker dealers, financial planners, banks, and web sites, it works with 2000 firms and 50,000 producers, and has 3.6 million customers.

NFS has sought to establish brand recognition for its products, using the slogan "Best of America." The product web site is *boafuture.com.*

The U.S. Market

Life insurers benefited in the 1980s from the rapid growth and popularity of universal life insurance, which is explained in box 9.1. However, the dramatic changes in financial services markets since that time have affected the industry. For example, many people have acted on the slogan "buy term and invest the rest." That is, instead of buying life insurance policies with savings features, consumers have unbundled and look to insurance only for death benefits, and primarily only through middle age. They no longer see

---

Box 9.1

UNIVERSAL AND VARIABLE UNIVERSAL LIFE INSURANCE

Universal Life (UL) is a variable-premium life insurance contract which accumulates cash value and adjusts the benefit according to the client's life circumstances. This contrasts to term insurance, where the customer pays a fixed annual premium in return for a specified death benefit.

With UL, the cash value can be used to pay part of the premium, or it can be reinvested. Policyholders also have the right periodically to adjust the death benefit without the issuing of a new policy, though medical proof of insurability may be required. In a regular UL policy, cash values accumulate at a market interest rate. In variable UL the cash value can be invested in securities (stocks or bonds), and the return on those securities affects the death benefit and future cash value of the policy.

Cash-value life insurance policies of any type are considered tax-advantaged investments in the United States, in that their increased value is not taxed as income and, using relatively simple arrangements, on the insured's death pass to beneficiaries free of exposure to estate taxes.

---

life insurance as a good savings and investment product. This is one reason the amount of life insurance in force in the United States is declining.

Term life insurance is the simplest and cheapest way to get death protection, and it is a highly competitive commodity with no special marketing spin. In addition, increased price competition in traditional nonterm life insurance products has been lowering profits.

It is a truism that life insurance generally is not bought, it is sold. In the United States most retail life policies are sold through independent agents, although many insurers employ in-house agents. Agents are the ones who can directly ask the client questions, explore different options, and thus influence choice. Most of the costs associated with administering a policy are independent of its size, so larger policies are more cost-effective and profitable.

Insurance is regulated at the state level, which poses some burden on companies in terms of having products approved, and thus gives some advantage to established companies compared to other financial service firms that might consider entering the business. This situation supports NFS's strategy of extensively selling its products through other financial service firms, such as brokers and banks, that want to offer such products to their clients but do not want direct involvement in the regulatory process.

NFS Products

The products NFS concentrates on are based on the same skill set as life insurance in terms of actuarial and long-term investment expertise. Thus, there is the potential for an integrated and interrelated approach to both marketing and investment management. Annuities are essentially reverse life insurance contracts with similar tax deferral and estate tax benefits, while variable life insurance contracts allow the customer to change the coverage, returns, and benefits as circumstances shift. Finally, 401(k)-type plans can be rolled into annuities or other retirement vehicles that depend on similar actuarial assumptions and tax deferrals.

While life insurance pays the face value of the policy at the time of death or, in the case of variable life, as adjusted for returns on the account, annuities pay an annual income (fixed or variable), usually until death. By definition, an investor cannot outlive a life annuity. Further, annuities or variable life (in exchange for reducing the death benefit) can be applied against nursing home care, while defined-contribution plans can be borrowed against or converted to annuities to provide cash flow. Therefore, all three are ways to provide for potential old-age expenses and retirement income. For this reason they have captured the interest of baby boomers and subsequent generations. Many in this group do not consider Social Security and Medicare likely to be adequate by the time they are eligible for benefits, so they are looking for alternatives to assure their retirement income.

Regulations governing private pension and benefit plans, pension scandals, and the reduction in benefits for retirees also have had an impact; people want pension and nursing care support that they control. Several tax benefits further encourage this development, because taxes on the earnings these products generate generally are deferred until there is a payout. Estate taxes also can be avoided with some products.

They thus have the benefits of traditional cash-value whole life insurance in that they provide spousal economic protection and capture tax-sheltered investment benefits. To this they add the benefit of flexibility over time, especially by tying in events related to health and retirement cash-flow needs. When combined with the aging of the population, it is no wonder that the growth of these products has been explosive.

Market Size

NFS sees the future market for retirement products as huge and growing quickly. By 2015 it sees preretirees controlling $9 trillion in pension assets.

Annual sales of annuities in the United States went from about $10 billion in 1985 to over $100 billion in 1998, which was equal to 10% of net mutual fund purchases that year. NFS is third in individual annuity sales. Variable life grew from 9% of U.S. life insurance in 1992 to 34% in 1998, while whole life's and universal life's shares declined. During the same period defined-contribution plans increasingly replaced defined-benefit plans: 401(k) assets rose from $500 billion to $1.4 trillion in 700,000 plans with 50 million participants.

With a 1999 market share of 20%, 7000 plans under management, and 1 million customers, NFS believes it is number one in providing defined-contribution plans to local public-sector employees. This reflects early identification of the market niche. Despite a significant decline in the equity markets during 2000, assets in NFS public-sector pension accounts declined less than 5%, going from $25.6 billion to $24.4 billion, and sales actually rose from $2.5 billion to $2.6 billion. Overall, NFS ranks third among U.S. 401(k) providers (some done on a private-label basis), administering over 17,000 pension plans. Total private-sector pension plan sales during 2000 were $4.8 billion, up from $4.1 billion in 1999.

The company sees an opportunity to use its multichannel approach to sell retirement-plan services to small employers. In 1998 fewer than a third of small employers had defined-contribution plans; NFS expects 72% will have them by 2002. This trend favors NFS's ability to track and manage a large number of small accounts with few participants. The company is the largest supplier of variable annuities through independent financial planning firms, and second through banks. About 40% of its annuities are offered through payroll deduction via employer-sponsored plans.

Strategic Issues

A key issue for firms selling life insurance and related products is controlling the underwriting cycle. A second large strategic issue is policy longevity—how long a policy remains in force—because this directly affects investable cash flows and the stability of the firm's investment portfolio. A third issue is the expense ratio—how much one has to spend to originate and administer a policy—which is a measure of marketing and office efficiency. It is in these three areas, as well as marketing and sales, that NFS has been at the forefront in using IT. The company was among the first to move aggressively into annuities, as well as in seeing the advantages of IT.

The underwriting cycle refers to the period from when an agent or intermediary calls on a potential client, to issuing of the policy, to payment of the premium. The ultimate goal is to have the agent sell the policy on the first call, issue it on the spot, and get paid immediately. More generally, the objective is to minimize the cycle time.

For a long time the underwriting cycle did not make much progress in terms of efficiency. This is especially true when a medical examination is required, as is generally the case for large life insurance policies. Usually, the extent of the exam relates directly to the size of the policy.

Because annuities pay clients benefits until they die, there is no moral hazard or adverse selection problem. Indeed, people who know they are sick may well apply proportionately less for annuities than for life insurance. Therefore, medical exams are not required. This greatly shortens the underwriting cycle. Also, it means the product can be sold through multiple channels, including banks and broker dealers, in addition to agents, because direct contact with an agent is not required. NFS has been very successful in exploiting these differences via third-channel intermediaries.

Sales Channels

In contrast to Meiji Life's use of its own agents, over 70% of NFS sales of individual retirement products and over 90% of individual annuities are through independent sources. The NFS approach has been to leverage its products by creating offerings that fit the models and plans of its clients or their advisers, thus directly linking its systems and strategy with theirs.

This creates a potentially difficult sales and servicing mix, as NFS wants to offer its products through a broad array of sales channels and thus cannot favor its own agents over independents, or the latter will migrate to other providers. At the same time, it wants to tie its support services and marketing tools as closely to NFS products as possible, so that the independent channels cannot easily substitute other firms' products using NFS marketing concepts. The strategy is to use IT to work with the agents to make it easier and more productive for them to sell NFS products.

To this end, the company provides wholesalers a CD-ROM with a continuing education course on the retirement products it offers. Completing the course earns a half-credit toward maintaining the insurance broker's license. NFS also provides CDs that can be used for a PC presentation on the benefits of specific Nationwide retirement products. Customers and prospects can access information on-line or via an interactive CD. These materials, while giving ideas about future retirement requirements under various scenarios, are not part of a comprehensive life-cycle model.

Marketing complex financial products usually requires hand-holding, which runs against the company's low-cost product strategy. The company thus tries to keep its ideas and presentations simple.

IT Use

The insurance industry generally is behind banking and securities firms in using IT. Most life companies during the 1990s focused on expenses. Costs can be divided into administration, back office, and selling and marketing. Insurers focused technology mostly on the first two in order to build scale in using their computers. As to marketing, techniques to give agents the means to educate consumers on choices in life insurance and annuities were just starting in the late 1990s. In this regard, Japan's Meiji Seimei is on the leading edge even relative to U.S. firms such as NFS.

There is continued reliance by the industry on paper and moving paper, which is why, even leaving aside the time for medical examinations, some firms take one to three weeks to complete the underwriting cycle for life policies. In contrast, for home equity loans and second mortgages applied for on-line, the time from application to approval often is less than 24 hours.

In contrast, NFS, like Meiji, uses IT to maintain a paperless relationship with agents, thus keeping costs low and better controlling the intermediary relationship. NFS also can electronically transmit product information directly to agents and corporate plan sponsors. Customers still get hard copy.

NFS's IT-intensive approach is even more important in the broker-wholesale distribution channel that the company has used to broaden and diversify delivery. These firms do not want to be burdened with paper either, but they do need easy access to documents in order to respond to customer questions and inquiries. This process becomes a beneficial loop that increases distribution and lowers costs: because agents and sponsors find it easy to deal electronically with NFS, they promote its plans, and so on.

Costs and return on investment of premiums are critical variables in profitability. Relatively small differences in administrative costs and yields can mean significant improvements in the final annuity payments when compounded over 20 or 30 years. NFS relies heavily on IT to keep costs low and to provide superior service and returns to customers and intermediaries. All its products are data-tracking-intensive, requiring active management and record keeping for many small accounts operating in a complex legal and tax environment. The database generated through its defined-benefit plans helps it to market related retirement products.

Administering plans with only a few participants and small accounts has frustrated many providers who have approached the small-employer market. Building on its early-mover advantage, NFS has accumulated significant expertise in efficiently and profitably managing such plans. Continuing success provides the company with even greater scale, and another beneficial loop.

Investment Management

In the mid-1970s Nationwide became the first insurance company to offer a multiple-manager approach to variable annuities. NFS offers a variety of funds among which clients can allocate and shift contributions, making their own selections or using an adviser. The result is a customized account for each client and a set of accounts for each provider. This discourages unbundling by clients and emulation by competitors. Fund managers see NFS customers as additive, because this sales channel does not compete directly with their regular mutual funds. Thus it is a win-win situation for NFS and the outside managers, and another example of the success of efficient customization as a marketing strategy. NFS uses IT to track managers' relative performance in order to ensure that its slogan "Best of America" is valid.

Fixed-income investments are managed in-house. NFS emphasizes private placements and mortgage-backed securities (MBS) because they traditionally offer higher yields than a bond portfolio. However, credit issues and refinancing of the underlying mortgages can create problems for such holdings. To analyze and manage these risks and otherwise manage the portfolio,

NFS has developed proprietary IT models. In MBS it invests primarily in the less volatile amortization classes.

Because clients can mix fixed income with equity investments, NFS avoided the generally negative impact a hot stock market had on interest in life insurance as an investment vehicle. Its traditional strength in fixed income should help it hold clients disillusioned by the 2000–01 "roasted pig" and bear markets.

Although clients usually are looking for better yields and a better future payout, they often also are risk-averse in their product selection because they are targeting a long-term future income stream. This is particularly true in terms of annuities, where individuals frequently are looking primarily for cash-flow certainty in their retirement years. That gives fixed-income assets some appeal. However, the company does offer a guaranteed minimum return even if a customer selects an all-equity option.

Conclusion

NFS once again illustrates the dual-strategy theme of using IT to achieve a business advantage through pursuing revenue enhancement and cost containment simultaneously.

By developing an edge in a select set of specialized high-growth products and offering them through a broad range of channels, the company has gained share and scale by getting less diversified providers, as well as individual insurance agents and financial planners, to offer NFS products directly or on a private-label basis. These intermediaries benefit because offering these products helps hold clients who otherwise might migrate to integrated providers such as Citigroup. They can safely deal with NFS because it does not compete with them. (At the same time, Citigroup is happy to be one of the fund managers NFS uses because the business probably would not otherwise be obtainable so easily.)

For this strategy to succeed, NFS's product, delivery, and after-sales service must be low-cost, effective, and high-quality even for smaller accounts. The clients of the independent agents, banks, and securities firms that sell NFS products must feel their needs are being met. To be a good, nonthreatening partner, NFS must be committed to a high-quality, low-cost outcome, because it is in this way that its interests are aligned with its distribution channels and the final customer.

NFS sees computers as a support tool for this overall strategy. Product flexibility and personal customization are essential elements, so the company uses IT to allow customers to tailor their own retirement solutions and to make adjustments as their life circumstances change. To achieve this in a personalized manner, it provides detailed IT support to its agents and third-party intermediaries on how to market this flexibility. Customers also can use the NFS web site for sales and after-sales support. The idea is to provide agents with factual marketing information on the target enrollment group. It leaves producing an integrated financial planning model to others.

NFS has a good Level 2 strategy. The company is using IT to effectively add value, create competitive barriers, and improve market share. However, unlike Meiji Seimei, NFS has not forced a change in its competitive environment, a Level 3 requirement.

MEIJI SEIMEI

Meiji Seimei Hoken (Meiji Mutual Life Insurance) is one of Japan's leading life insurance companies and its oldest. A member of the Mitsubishi Group, Japan's largest *keiretsu*, it has been a financial powerhouse for many years just on the basis of its group ties.

The life insurance industry in Japan, the company, and its approach to meeting the challenges of Japan's deregulation and economic malaise are taken up here. In particular, the focus is on how Meiji has been on the cutting edge of IT use by insurers in Japan by integrating its proprietary consumer life-cycle model with an innovative laptop computer-based sales and marketing program that is changing how life insurance and other financial products are sold in Japan.

The Company

Although individual and group life policies each account for about half of the face value of Meiji's total life insurance in force, individual (retail) clients represent the major portion of profits. It is in retail life sold door-to-door that Meiji is leading the way in the sophisticated integration of IT, life-cycle concepts, and business strategy. It is doing this by building on its organizational strengths and capturing the tacit knowledge residing in its huge sales force. The company has about 6 million clients.

Meiji's financial situation is strong. Thus, it has a solvency margin around 700, which is quite good. (The margin is a regulatory measure of risk-weighted assets relative to half of defined liabilities. At 200, regulators are required to take corrective action.) It also has significant unrealized gains even at current stock prices, and a relatively low exposure to foreign assets (between March 1993 and March 1996, Meiji had reduced foreign assets from ¥1.7 trillion yen to ¥582 billion).

However, it has suffered from stagnant premium income. Despite an almost 50% increase in total assets between March 1992 and March 1999, fiscal 1998 premium income of ¥2.5 trillion was essentially unchanged compared to the immediate postbubble period of fiscal 1991 and 1992. Further, during this period individual life policies, including annuities, fell from 66% to around 50% of total policies in force. So the share and value of group life premiums and policies relative to the more profitable individual policies have been rising sharply, though the rise also reflects the stability of group business due to the strength of the Mitsubishi group.

The Industry In Japan

After World War II the Occupation converted most Japanese life insurers from stock companies to mutual companies as part of a conscious policy to break up the *zaibatsu*, most of which had captive insurance companies. They could have been demutualized after the Occupation ended in 1952, but they were not. As former *zaibatsu* companies coalesced into *keiretsu*, the major life insurers again became part of groups, albeit as independent firms. As mutual companies, they were perhaps even more stable sources of long-term capital for the rapidly growing industrial sector than if they had been stock companies, because the managers did not have even nominal oversight by stockholders. The industry has been highly concentrated: through the 1990s, there were only 30 domestic companies, compared to 2000 in the United States. Table 9.1 lists the largest companies.

The firms profited significantly from quickly rising life expectancies because benefits actually paid fell well below actuarial expectations. As major investors in equities and property, they also were huge beneficiaries of the

Table 9.1 Major Japanese Life Insurance Companies, 1997 and 2001

Assets (in billion yen)[1]	S&P Financial Strength Rating		Company
	1997 30 April	2001	
43,205	AA	AA	Nippon Life
30,042	A	A+	Daiichi Mutual Life
23,683	BBB	BBB	Sumitomo Life
16,846	AA−	A+	Meiji Mutual Life
11,322	BBB	BB+	Asahi Mutual Life
10,077	BB	BB	Mitsui Mutual Life
10,080	A−	A−	Yasuda Mutual Life
7,082	BBB	A	Taiyo Mutual Life
5,734	A+	A+	Daido Life
188,417	—	—	Industry total

Through the 1990s, most Japanese life insurers were mutuals—that is, they were owned by their policyholders. As such, they did not have stock exchange listings. This began to change in 2000.

Ranking by premiums moves Yasuda ahead of Asahi. The three largest firms accounted for over 47% of net premiums written, and the nine listed here account for almost 80%.

[1]As of 31 March 2000.

Source: Standard & Poor's web site, *standardandpoors.com/ratingsdirect*

general rise in stock and real estate values that accompanied Japan's economic growth into the early 1970s.

Indeed, in the early 1980s Japanese life insurance companies were perceived as financial juggernauts and major sources of international capital. Changes in the foreign exchange law had made it possible for them to invest overseas relatively easily, and they were assiduously solicited by international investment banks. Many opened overseas offices to supervise acquisition of foreign securities and trophy real estate properties. Their massive portfolio acquisitions, especially of U.S. government bonds, combined with falling interest rates, weakened the yen and raised their capital gains. Then came the rapid appreciation of the yen in the wake of the September 1985 Plaza Accord, which caught the insurers by surprise. Not only did the benefits of asset diversification come to an abrupt halt, there were massive foreign exchange losses. Numbers in excess of $50 billion have been mentioned.

Burned once, in the post-Plaza period insurance companies channeled their increasing liquidity into Japanese assets, helping to inflate the bubble economy. Again, there were near-term gains as stock and real estate values soared—but the collapse in asset prices at the end of the 1980s has meant significant headaches since then. The industry has been experiencing many of the bad loan problems plaguing Japanese banks, even if it generally has escaped revelations of executive malfeasance.

Still, the firms grew in terms of assets during the 1990s. The peak in yen terms came in September 1998, when the Japanese industry had ¥193 trillion ($1.6 trillion at then-current rates) in assets, and 690 million policies in force with a face value of ¥1,900 trillion ($16.1 trillion). Most "policies" in Japan are endowment policies or are like certificates of deposit rather than life insurance contracts, so it is not quite so surprising to find an average of almost six per Japanese. Actually, this is many fewer than a decade earlier: the largest insurer, Nippon Life, alone had over 381 million contracts in March 1992 and Meiji had almost 175 million.

Deterioration of Asset Base

Since the 1998 peak, industry assets have fallen over 6%, to ¥181 trillion in February 2001. Until 1997 the deterioration of the insurers' stock and real estate portfolios was considered manageable, and bad loans were around 1% to 2% of assets for the top companies. However, by March 1999 the problem had grown considerably worse. Reported bad loans at Nippon Life, the world's largest life insurance company, increased 70% between March 1998 and March 1999. After writing off ¥800 billion in bad loans in fiscal 1998 (ended March 1999), using the same loan classification criteria as the banks (for which see Hoshi and Kashyap 2001, p 281–83), the eight largest life-insurers still had ¥1.1 trillion in bad loans on their books. That is the same level as a year earlier.

The collapse of Japan's stock market in the early 1990s and continued weak performance since has sharply reduced insurers' unrealized capital gains. (Such gains often are called "latent profits," and once were misleadingly called "hidden reserves.") As early as September 1997, several large insurers were reported to have losses on their stock portfolios at a Nikkei below 17,000, a level it has been below most of the time since, including during 2001.

Since the late 1990s firms have gone bankrupt or been sold to stronger players in lieu of bankruptcy. In June 1999, parts of Toho Mutual Life were absorbed by GE Capital, with the rest closed by the Financial Supervisory Agency. This added to the anxiety of both customers and officials that had been created by Nissan Mutual Life's bankruptcy in April 1997, because that had been considered an isolated occurrence. (For more on the industry in the 1990s, see Ostrom 1998.)

Falling Premiums and Contractual Mismatch

The deteriorating asset situation has been coupled with falling premium income, partly due to customer disenchantment with low investment returns and partly reflecting customer concerns with the industry's economic health. For example, in fiscal 1998 the top eight firms witnessed a 17.4% contraction in new retail life insurance and annuity contracts, and a 4.6% fall in contracts overall. Because contractual payments currently exceed investment income, the fall in premiums, which used to cover payments to beneficiaries, has forced some asset liquidation at precisely the wrong time in the business cycle.

The contractual mismatch (difference between what the insurers have guaranteed policyholders and what they are earning on their investments) rose from ¥128.3 billion in March 1998 to 1.3 trillion in March 1999 and 1.4 trillion in March 2001. Nippon Life reported that its guaranteed payment rates during fiscal 1998 ranged between 3.8% and 4.1% while its investment returns were less than 2%, a negative carry of about 2%. While Nippon Life and the other big insurers have other products and income sources, Nissan Life went bankrupt precisely due to the relatively large number of high-rate (5.5%) contracts it had written. The ability of even the large insurers to continue under such circumstances clearly is limited.

Some insurers have tried to solve the problem of declining premiums by raising premium rates, but this has led investors to seek other investment opportunities, thus lowering premium income even more. Insurers have realized that a better return on their assets is what is needed. One way to do that is to pare costs, including reducing employment. The first to feel the ax have been underperforming sales agents.

Underlying Problems

Large Japanese corporations can raise funds directly on their own credit more cheaply than by borrowing from intermediaries. This has been a problem for both the banks and the insurance companies. Continued economic weakness has further limited loan demand. To the extent that there is demand, it is from smaller, less creditworthy companies that the banks and insurers are reluctant to lend to. (In the late 1990s the credit crunch facing these firms was a major issue.)

Demographics that, for most of the postwar period, have been extremely favorable for life insurance providers are changing for the worse. Previously, premiums generally exceeded death payments, permitting insurers to build huge reserves. Now and for the foreseeable future, this effect is disappearing. Life expectancies are no longer rising faster than actuarial assumptions, and the proportion of older people is increasing rapidly. By 2025, more than 25% of Japan's population is expected to be over 65, more than in any other country. This compares to around 14% in 1993, the second lowest among the advanced industrial nations at that time.

Exacerbations

The life insurers' difficulties have in many ways been exacerbated by government policies to rescue the banks, which have been considered to have more severe and more urgent problems. First the insurers were forced to buy preferred shares to provide the banks with capital. (Meiji alone took a ¥35 billion loss from its forced investment in Hokkaido Takushoku Bank, which went bankrupt in 1997.)

Next, to create a positive funding spread for the banks to build capital and earnings, since the late 1990s and into 2001 the Bank of Japan has kept the discount rate almost at zero. This has lowered returns on the life insurers' loans and bonds, which are the insurers' principal source of income. Attempts to solve the mismatch by investing in higher-return foreign assets has exposed the insurers to foreign exchange risks. The yen's appreciation in the late 1990s meant losses, although the currency's weakness in the early 2000s has alleviated the situation somewhat.

Regulation and Segmentation

For almost five decades after World War II, Japanese financial markets were highly segmented and tightly regulated. Each market segment had a limited number of product offerings from relatively specialized providers. If one wanted to buy stocks or the Japanese equivalent of a mutual fund, one went to a securities company. If one wanted life insurance or an annuity, one went to a life insurance company. Because prices were regulated, choices often were based on nonfinancial factors such as the company for which one worked—for example, a Mitsubishi company. (A concise overview of the prederegulation financial system is Teranishi 1994.)

The Ministry of Finance (MOF) severely limited the life insurers' range of product offerings and even controlled pricing. The ability of firms to compete was highly restricted because the MOF's regulatory approach was the convoy system with a vengeance. (Under the system, referred to mainly in relation to banks but applied throughout Japan's postwar financial system until well into the 1990s, even inefficient financial institutions were helped to grow at the same speed, and protection was provided against failure. The term comes from the fact that, in convoys, all ships have to match the speed of the slowest ship, so that all reach their destination together. It also alludes to the fact the MOF provided escort [protection], the point of forming a convoy being that the cargo ships could be protected efficiently by warships. It should be noted this was not so much an explicit ex-ante MOF policy as an ex-post description by academics and journalists of what happened. See Hoshi and Kashyap 2001, p.111–12 and 271.)

Deregulation

Regulatory segmentation of Japanese finance by the MOF largely disappeared with the late 1990s Big Bang. What the director and managing director of the Sloan financial services center at Wharton, Santomero and Burns (1997, p. 2), noted for the United States has come to Japan: "Gone are the days when U.S. financial services firms were neatly segmented by regulation and practice—when international competition barely existed and information technology was in its infancy. . . . The traditional boundaries between industry segments are fading as new competitive pressures emerge. To adapt, industry players need to fully understand the evolving financial services marketplace and decide where their competencies offer the greatest advantage. New distribution channels, new products, and changing consumer behaviors mean providers must continually adapt their systems and procedures in order to ensure efficient and effective service delivery."

This means Japanese consumers must be helped both to understand these new products and why those being provided by a nontraditional provider might be superior, including the potential benefits of "one-stop" shopping. (An overview of the changing financial system is Hoshi and Patrick 2000.)

There was some hesitancy about including life insurance in the Big Bang, but the industry's problems led to sufficient political pressure on the government to include it. The companies are allowed to provide nonlife insurance products, securities, and "third-sector" insurance. (The third sector spans hybrid policies such as personal accident, cancer, and hospitalization. Only about 5% of the total insurance market, measured by premiums, foreign firms had about a 40% share before deregulation.)

To offer new products, life insurance companies have been allowed to create for-profit holding companies. But the legal obstacles are formidable, and thus the transformation will take time and could be expensive. In the meanwhile, the companies are relying on affiliations, joint ventures, and special unconsolidated subsidiaries.

Life insurers have sought new, more profitable business such as long-term health-care products that target the aging population. Meiji has even developed a product that allows clients to convert some of their life insurance to long-term medical care. Insurers also are expanding into nonlife products, brokerage, and money management. The introduction of 401(k)-type plans in August 2001 and of other asset management accounts has combined with rising retirement concerns to expand asset management opportunities. This focus on new products and businesses has led insurers into both acquisitions and affiliations, many with old *keiretsu* partners, but also with foreign firms.

The Competitive Environment

With all the companies facing a similar competitive environment, most have sought similar solutions. In addition, mergers among banks have put some of the cooperative affiliations in question. This is because an important strategic objective of such affiliations has been to offer the life insurers' existing customers, as well as new customers, an expanded product range, which is something the new banking groups are intending to do as well. Moreover, new competition in life insurance has emerged from affiliates of nonlife insurers and even from noninsurance parents such as Sony (which also is entering banking), Softbank, and General Electric. The weakening and mixing of *keiretsu* ties and pressure on lifetime employment have reduced many firms' (including Meiji's) access to almost automatic customers.

In investment advice and asset management especially, the field is crowded with Japanese and foreign financial institutions of every description. Many of the foreign firms specialize in this activity on a global basis and have significantly better records than any Japanese firm.

Diversification has both a benefit and a risk for Meiji and other life insurers. It is a benefit because they can expand into new markets and offer new products and services. It is a risk because of the influx of powerful competitors into their traditional bailiwicks. In addition, the greater flexibility being given to the Postal Savings System (box 9.2) and its insurance arm will contribute to competitive pressures.

In this competitive context, the strategic problem for Meiji in retail life insurance has been how to differentiate its product and services, including new ones, from those of all other firms while also creating a competitive edge in a deregulated financial market. Despite this adverse environment, Meiji believes that if it can successfully sell existing and new customers a wider range of products while avoiding more credit problems, its cash flow will be positive. This is the primary strategic issue that Meiji Seimei has sought to address in developing a new IT-based strategy.

Meiji's Strategy

By the mid-1990s Meiji recognized that it needed to develop a new strategic initiative to prepare for developments such as the Big Bang liberalization

Box 9.2
POSTAL SAVINGS SYSTEM

The Postal Savings System (PSS) has been one of the few truly nationwide financial institutions in postwar Japan, and as such it has had more deposit collection points than all the banks combined. (for example, in 1961, almost 16,000 versus about 11,000). Although generally discussed in terms of its competition with banks, it also is a competitor of the life insurers. PSS is managed by the Ministry of Public Management, Home Affairs, Post and Telecommunications, as successor to the Ministry of Post and Telecommunications, and has been jealously protected from the Ministry of Finance. The system's political constituency is extremely powerful. Attempts to reform it, let alone abolish it as no longer needed, have had been derailed repeatedly. In mid-2001 yet another attempt was under way, with some indications that the system actually may become an even more formidable competitor (see Cargill and Yoshino 2000; Suzuki 1987, pp. 170, 288).

During the 1980s the PSS directly contributed to the insurers' problems by offering high rates that, in the eyes of savers, were effectively government-guaranteed. This has been a factor in the subsequent mismatch problems between return on assets and payments on liabilities.

and Japan's rapidly aging population, as well as to address the issue of stagnant premium income. However, the strategy had to satisfy certain fundamental conditions. It had to use Meiji's huge sales force, help educate that sales force and Meiji's customers about new financial products and services, and establish a competitive advantage that could not be emulated easily.

With this situation in mind, Meiji set out in 1996 to develop its life-cycle model and to combine it with a delivery system that would assist its retail sales agents to deliver the related services in a more consistent and effective manner (efficient customization). That is, as it developed plans to compete across industry segments, the company's goal was to determine how it could best deliver traditional and new financial products to the existing customer base while protecting that base from encroaching competitors, including new providers.

The insurance strategy Meiji developed depends on integrating three fundamental parts of its business: its retail life insurance infrastructure, including its sales force, branches, and information network; its IT-based retail marketing strategy; and its detailed evaluation of Japanese lifestyles and patterns of personal development.

Emergence of the Life-Cycle Approach

In 1992, as part of an effort to understand customer requirements and potential new products and services, the company surveyed 50,000 randomly selected customers. Although at the time the pace and extent of the coming industry deregulation was still unclear—and expected by many to be slower than it proved to be—the company realized its traditional product offerings and approach to business had to evolve. It has long been known that customer needs change with circumstances, and that age is a good first-level proxy for many of the changes. It is this insight that has become the basis for cross-selling and the life-cycle models now employed in many industries (see the Introduction, subsection "Life-Cycle Models"). However, age is only a very general indicator, and efficient customization requires much more data and sophisticated analysis.

A key question is how to track changes by individual customer, and then to market and deliver the appropriate products and services in a timely manner. The company also needs to make sure that it develops and changes its products in ways that are responsive to changes in lifestyles and technology. Further, management needs to know how profitable each typical customer group is on a discounted basis and how easily the firm can retain the groups' members, through the life-cycle.

There are still more questions. These include when it is appropriate to start marketing a new product, how much effort should be made per potential customer, and what the most effective way to market and deliver each product or service is. These are complex issues that vary by product and customer group.

There is, however, a consensus among Meiji and its competitors about the best time to begin life-cycle marketing in Japan: just after students have entered the labor force. This is because Japanese consumers generally have great loyalty and most major financial institutions, such as Meiji, operate nationwide. Thus Meiji and its rivals find their clients have little reason to shift financial service providers as they pursue their careers.

Implementation

The goals of improving the productivity of the sales force and introducing the customer life-cycle model successfully are the primary drivers for Meiji in selecting IT and measuring the success of its systems.

The life-cycle strategy has been implemented by providing the sales force with laptop computers that have the life-cycle concept and related products embedded in the software. The delivery strategy is called the "mobile personal computing system for every agent." According to the company, the aims in implementing the system are to "strengthen the sales performance of the sales force; improve the quality and speed of customer service; restructure the information systems basis; improve the efficiency of service and desk work; [and] have a system with good cost performance."

Because Meiji is relying on its traditional sales force, its approach is somewhat different from a bank's. The company closely analyzes its agents' productivity in order to identify best practice. This can then be coupled with Meiji's software system to raise the performance level of all agents, a kind of iterative expert system based on an analysis of its own top agents. (Such techniques have a long, pre-IT history in Japan: something similar was done at the end of the 19th century to raise rice output.)

Meiji is very conscious of the expense of delivering products and services to different customers, so it tries to get as specific as possible in identifying different customer groups and their varying financial service needs. Thus categories are much more closely defined than simply saying "everyone in their 20s." Meiji also tries to assess the potential returns from new market segments, such as young people just starting careers, and the products most likely to appeal to them.

Meiji spends considerable effort evaluating costs and increasing agent productivity. Indeed, it believes it is now very good at implementing an IT-intensive strategy that combines cost containment with revenue enhancement. This is important because post-Big Bang increases in competition potentially will decrease premium revenues and policies in force while increasing marketing costs.

The Laptop Program

A key aspect of Meiji's approach has been to increase the independence of its agents through IT by incorporating most of what the agents need to market and deliver the company's financial products into its proprietary laptop system, including direct links to Meiji's central information system. This has reduced the need for local sales offices, permitting Meiji to extend the cost-cutting measures it implemented during 1993–97. The basic information infrastructure for the retail life division is now controlled from Meiji's IT center rather than locally.

Each agent has received a laptop loaded with software that incorporates all aspects of Meiji's life-cycle model, including links to various functional products and services groups. The software is constantly upgraded, and the agents are trained, as new products are introduced.

When an agent visits a customer and enters the client's basic data, information on the appropriate products is displayed graphically and in written form. The system also shows how the customer's requirements can be expected to evolve with changes in age, family structure, or lifestyle. The agent thus can explain the products and their relation to the client's life plan, including potential variations based on responses from the client. Clients are immediately able to see how variations in circumstances affect product recommendations. As a result, closings are faster.

Once a sale is made, the agent can enter the information electronically rather than going to a local sales branch. For some products, approvals can be obtained electronically, again speeding the closing process. The agent no longer submits paper except for forms requiring signatures (name seals).

The system was extensively piloted prior to its September 1997 launch in order to assure that both the agent and the customer could easily understand and respond to its nuances, as its effectiveness depends on a symbiotic integration of system, agent, and client.

As part of the pilot, Meiji evaluated a portion of its sales force and the agents' interaction with the system to establish a benchmark for the system's impact. It also solicited comments from the agents on possible improvements and problems. The company found that the top 20% of agents were very skillful: for them, even the laptop system was not sufficient, and this group has supplemented it with their own e-mail and computer use to add functions. (The company does not allow use of its laptops for external e-mail and Internet access because of potential security, virus, and similar problems. The firm does not want its agents to accidentally introduce an external element into its integrated system.) The middle 60% is the group whose productivity the system is intended to raise. The bottom 20% proved unable to use the system effectively despite training and support. These became candidates for termination or transfer to other jobs.

Logistically, it took three days to provide 40,000 Toshiba Libretto laptops loaded with the software to all sales units. The introduction went smoothly, except for some printer-related glitches.

Portable Printers

As a result of problems using printers at local offices, each agent has been issued a portable printer. After a client has approved a plan and an agreement is made, a draft is printed on the spot. If changes or corrections are needed to an insurance plan or contract agreement, the agent can immediately print a new version. The customer does not have to wait for a corrected copy to come in the mail. Mailing and printing charges have been reduced, as only the final policy is mailed, and this is now done directly by the host computer rather than the local office.

Before the new system, all insurance plans were printed in multiple copies, and Meiji had upward of 70 different forms using a variety of different colored papers and inks. This created significant design and presentation problems for agents and clients during the first stage of introducing the system because, at that time, Meiji was relying on local sales offices to print forms using data input from the laptops.

To address the printer bottleneck, the retail life group developed an overlay system, introduced in October 1998, that enables the agents' laptops to print any form in black (color is too slow and expensive on portable printers) on plain paper. It uses a Windows 95-based program called Sales Point. Although different from what Sales Point was written to be used for, Meiji's adaptation has allowed the company to use portable printers with the laptops. The program and all the necessary information on the forms are on a plug-and-play card that can be taken out of the laptop once printing is completed.

Continuing Modification

The retail life division's approach is dynamic in that it is constantly adding to the number of functions, products, and services that the laptops and sales force can deliver. This is part of the constant strategic upgrading and development of the company's IT and retail delivery system that has allowed it to increasingly shift away from local branches while upgrading and increasing the average performance of its sales force. The decision criteria in this respect have been to enhance the agents' capabilities with systems and machines, to expand the capacity of the delivery system, and to reduce costs, all through extending the use of electronics.

Meiji always keeps in mind its customers' various and changing needs, and works to make sure customers do not feel alienated by the shift in delivery structures. This was one reason for the extensive piloting of the laptop system before its launch in September 1997. It also is one of the reasons Meiji continues to modify the system to reflect agent and customer feedback.

The objective is to make the sales approach more congenial while gaining customer acceptance of the life-cycle approach to personal finance. This is critical, because success depends on the client and agent easily understanding and appreciating the information presented, and the customer's approval of the result. Personalized examples and the use of animated characters in laptop presentations illustrate this customer-focused method.

Meiji is not ignoring the Internet. Hajime Inomata, manager of Systems Planning and Development, sees more web-based delivery, with the software shared among companies. Beyond that, pending launch, the company was understandably reticent.

Benefits

Meiji has identified savings from the new system in the agents' work flow and contract cycle times. This results from simplifying desk work, assessment, and approvals; reducing and speeding paperwork; eliminating redundant inputs; and confirming and completing the transaction on site. One measurable benefit is the saving of two million sheets of paper per month, plus the cost of multicolor printing.

The simplification and improved data processing, combined with improved systems communications, have facilitated document retrieval in general and such things as entering address changes, invoicing, and claims processing. This improves customer satisfaction and increases productivity per customer or policy.

Because Meiji's IT sales system is based on the observed best practice of its top agents, the system has improved the consistency of performance and overall productivity of its agents. In turn, that has reduced the need for field agents. In April 1993 there were almost 50,000 agents and 1610 sales offices. In July 1997, after a series of cost-cutting steps and just before the laptop system was introduced, there were 40,000 agents and 1500 offices. In April 1999, reflecting the new system, the number of agents had been reduced a further 25%, to 30,000, with no loss in premiums or business. Moreover, it is easier to relate incentive compensation directly to sales results on a regular basis because the data exist on-line in a usable form. Managers monitor progress easily and react to situations quickly as they arise.

The new system also means it is no longer necessary to have cards with customer profiles at each branch. With almost 6 million clients plus another 3 to 4 million prospects, the 86 branches (administrative centers) on average each had over 100,000 cards under the old system (data as of April 1999). Databases and e-mail have eliminated a lot of paper and paper shuffling at the office locations from which agents work, as well as the branches. Clerical and back-office requirements and personnel thus have declined. Agents save time by telecommuting instead of making trips to the office to access data over the company's PCs, check paper files, or look for and print documents. All this has reduced the amount of office space needed.

Because they can easily connect to the firm's LAN, agents have direct access to information that generally had been available only through the branch manager, which means they are better informed about products and the company. This unanticipated increase in knowledge has led to additional sales, and demonstrates that agents are taking advantage of the system, resulting in evolutionary organizational learning. Further, it is easier for managers to assess each agent's sales by type of product and customer. This provides feedback that can help focus training and support.

Evaluation

Quite soon after it was introduced, there were indications that competitors were feeling the pressure of the laptop-based system. Daiichi Life introduced its system in June 1998, and Nippon Life only in January 1999. The time lag in their responses means Meiji achieved first-mover advantages.

Through direct marketing and electronic means, Meiji has built a structure that will support a long-term customer relationship. How Meiji takes the revenues or profits from this prospective relationship into account in determining the profitability of adding a new customer versus the cost of servicing and supporting that customer is proprietary information. But the company says it believes such new customers are profitable from the beginning, based on the size of their accounts and the lower cost of electronic support. Meiji is analyzing this assumption in detail, and expects to refine it by type of customer and product over time, reflecting its recognition that strategically using IT is a dynamic and continuous process.

IT Infrastructure

Meiji's basic information system structure is a three-tier system similar to those of most other large Japanese financial institutions. The mainframe (IBM) controls the servers (Toshiba), which control the networking system and communicate with the laptops (Toshiba). The mainframe has the task of scheduling operations, controlling security (especially document access), and program management. Meiji uses client servers for each group (such as asset management, actuary, marketing analysis, dealers, and agents).

The total-system software is IBM-based, while the LAN manager and laptop system run a Japanese version of Windows NT, and the rest of the networking (about 70% of the company's total networking requirements) is Novell- and UNIX-based. The company has about 8000 PCs on-line, not including the field laptops. These on-line PCs were still using MS-DOS V and Windows 3.0 in the late 1990s, a recognition that there was no need to buy newer versions for what were viewed as mostly needless features, especially as the existing system was working well.

IT Sourcing

Roughly 80% of the total system is customized, including virtually all the big application systems. Meiji's COBOL programs have hundreds of millions of lines of code. There are no plans to change the basic system. Thus, the laptop system was designed to work and interface with the existing, larger information system.

There has been selective use of packages, such as Excel spreadsheets, on the laptops as part of the field support system. In this way Meiji is trying to integrate its IT strategy with its competitive situation, industry, and strategic objectives. These factors influence how it chooses between various IT options to achieve its goals and how it measures the success of such choices. Because strategic success is the metric, retail life insurance MIS operations are incorporated into the business unit so that the two activities work together. IT work thus is not outsourced except to a captive subsidiary, Meiji System Service (MSS).

MSS works on mainframe-related software, systems, and databases, while Meiji itself focuses on more strategic software uses such as the laptop system. About 150 people work in Meiji's Information Systems Division and another 400 at MSS. Total EDP costs are about 0.5% of Meiji's revenues, with about 25% of its EDP needs purchased from MSS. These purchases by Meiji account for about 25% of MSS's ¥4.5 billion in revenues. MSS also works with nonlife firms such as Tokio Marine & Fire (which also belongs to the Mitsubishi Group) and Yasuda Fire & Marine.

IT Selection

The clear objectives of speeding communication, improving agent productivity, and increasing client satisfaction are the basis for selecting, developing, and using the software required for each function. In IT selection, Meiji looks first at technical merit and then at installed price, including the cost of adaptation and integration. IT management also will hire outside custom programmers to do coding, but Meiji, like Citicorp, will do the basic design and actual integration. Outside coders include the captive subsidiary MSS.

However, Meiji is flexible and utilizes different systems for different groups. It also sometimes will semi-customize a package. As an example, Meiji purchased Amtrade, a DEC workstation-based package for securities trading, because it was available quickly and there was little Japanese software development in the area. It would have been expensive to develop proprietary software, and there would be no strategic benefit. The mechanics of how trading is done are not important to Meiji once security selection has been determined. Rather, the key IT issue for Meiji was semi-customizing the trading system to integrate it with the firm's overall system.

Management's perspective is that functional and market gains justify customization expense, including the cost of integrating the customized application with the Japanese Windows NT packages, and then integrating the whole into the corporate IT system. Meiji has integrated both clients and agents into its strategic delivery system while formalizing their joint acceptance and use of the life-cycle model and service support mechanisms.

Any outsourcing would have put the firm and its IT support system at least one step away from this critical junction with agents and clients. Because the sales force and its automated support system are development-cost-intensive, the costs are subject to user-base economics.

Laptop Software

Meiji has developed its own applications for the laptops, although many of them are based on Excel spreadsheets as distinguished from totally customized coded programs. This is because the expert system in the laptop incorporates Meiji's own life-cycle model and integrates it with Meiji's own product and service offerings. However, developing a new laptop application takes one-fifth the IT staff time of the pre-laptop system and one-half the administrative and training time.

Because it is a real-time, on-line system, the laptops have been totally integrated with the firm's business operations and its customized mainframe system. That is, the laptops are fully able to communicate with the mainframe-managed system, sending and receiving information. This communication depends on customized versions of Japanese Windows NT work-flow and network-management packages purchased from Microsoft. In this way, Meiji has developed its own semi-customized middleware, which provides the interface or bridge between the NT system and Meiji's total proprietary IT system while providing its own method to manage the work flow efficiently.

Security

Meiji naturally is concerned with security, something that becomes more difficult as the company expands Internet usage and thereby exposes its database to potential unauthorized access. In addition, agents have concerns about giving up information, especially when the agent and client have had a long and close relationship.

To avoid access problems involving the laptops, besides an individual code number, each agent must sign in physically on the screen. (The laptop allows pen-based entries on the touchscreen; this capability was one reason the Toshiba laptop was chosen.) Agents are restricted to their own clients' data, plus corporate-wide information the company feels all employees should know. Meiji feels this approach helps prevent client information from leaking to unauthorized parties—despite the fact that almost 100 machines disappeared soon after introduction. The signature requirement definitely has helped prevent unauthorized entry, and the company believes no such entries have occurred.

Meiji has incorporated other protections. For example, simply turning off the laptop washes out data, and the laptop must be reconnected with the system server to refresh the information, or the data is permanently erased.

Competing in a Deregulated Market

Meiji's approach is achieving its strategic objective of enhancing its sales force's capabilities. It has no intention of abandoning the sales force because the service the agents provide is an important element of the company's competitive advantage. The company believes its main sales channel will remain agents, and that life insurance will be its main business, even as it introduces new products from other sectors. Still, the computerized system permits multiple sales channels. This is important if Meiji begins direct marketing by mail, call centers, or web site with no agent involved.

Affiliations with other providers is another part of the company's strategy. For example, Meiji and Tokio Marine & Fire plan to create a company to develop and market a Japanese version of pension and investment trusts. Also, by October 1996 Meiji had 18,000 agents separate from its life insurance sales force, plus 25 appraisers, working in a property insurance subsidiary. The company announced on 17 September 1999 that it had agreed to form a partnership with Nissin Fire & Marine and buy up to 10% of Nissin's stock (the maximum allowed by law), thus becoming Nissin's largest shareholder.

One benefit of alliances is that it is an easy way to expand both product offerings and the accessible client base. At the same time, it exposes existing clients to exploitation by partners. So a firm still needs low-cost, productive delivery into each segment.

The data-gathering and analysis made possible by its systems definitely have helped Meiji respond to the changes associated with the Big Bang and the entry of new competitors. In particular, its IT and lifestyle strategies have put the company in a good position to benefit from the proliferation of financial products it can offer and market segments it can enter.

New Product Possibilities

One competitive impact of the new system's introduction that Meiji has been able to quantify is the increased sales of a product that became available only with the introduction of the laptop and the life-cycle model. This is a life-cycle insurance plan that can be linked automatically with supporting products and that automatically shifts over time with the client's needs. Before the introduction of the new system, products were sold on the basis of an individual's specific needs at the time of sale. The new approach bases the products sold on the client's stated life plan and forecasted needs year by year. It also can be adjusted as specific events occur.

For example, looking at a family with small children, in the early years there might be need only for life insurance. As the children leave home, the amount of life insurance required falls, and the plan shifts to a retirement program based on an annuity amount, and later might shift to supplemental medical insurance or a long-term care program. In other words, once a payment level is committed, the company finds the most useful mix of products for the client, and changes that mix when needs change. There is a lot of flexibility in this policy, and variations are easily shown by using the laptops. The growth in sales of the product has helped Meiji mitigate the general stagnation in its traditional life insurance business.

Customer Relations

For Meiji, human-resource and client policies are closely aligned with its IT systems. Customers are getting the benefits of both automation and continued personal service from their agents. This facilitates the cross-selling that has been an important strategic goal in developing the system, as agents and customers otherwise would have difficulty understanding the wide variety of new products and how they relate to each other. Customer behavior is difficult to change, so by enhancing the existing field-agent system instead of trying to substitute electronics, Meiji is going with the market flow that emphasizes the need for human interaction, as well as efficient customization of client products and services. Meiji believes it is easier and more efficient to align its delivery and human-resource systems with its customers' psychology, goals, and interests than to try to get customers to align themselves with a different, perhaps totally automated, cost-driven strategy.

Conclusion

Meiji has developed a dynamic, integrated business and IT strategy to meet the challenges posed by the decline in corporate lending, the decrease in investment and premium income, and the Big Bang pressures of new competitors' entrance into retail life insurance. This strategy has succeeded in differentiating it from other insurers, as well as new competitors, while enhancing the strength of its sales force by arming it with laptops and a proprietary IT-based marketing system.

IT has been made an integral element in the overall strategy to sell more financial products to retail life insurance customers. At the same time, the company recognizes that for this to be productive, the IT systems must be coupled with an appropriate approach to marketing, customer service, and new product development that reflects a clear understanding of the company's business, industry, and competitive strengths.

This vision incorporating the life-cycle model is what has enabled Meiji to select, develop, and use IT to assist its 30,000 retail agents to operate at a higher and more consistent level of sales performance and customer service than a few years earlier, when it had 50,000 agents. The firm has integrated in-the-field support for its agents into its total support system for the company's overall operations. This has helped it to economize on traditional delivery systems and inventory, such as the number of agents and branch offices and storage of paper policy documents, while extending and expanding its customer base.

The system also has improved cycle times between client contact and financial contract, and between contract and document delivery, which reduces costs, quickens cash flow, and improves forecasts (which now need to cover a shorter period). Customer satisfaction also is enhanced through more timely completion of the process.

Similar to other leading IT users, Meiji has employed IT to enhance its existing organizational strengths rather than trying to adapt its organization to an IT system. This means IT is seen as a tool, so possible applications are assessed in terms of potential benefits to the business of being a life insurance company in a deregulated environment. There is a particular focus on IT's role in improving customer service, retail life insurance sales, and agent delivery, because these are the foundations of its business.

Meiji's computerized sales development system is helping it to continuously monitor and control various parts of its business environment, and the system itself has become an integral part of the way it organizes, delivers, and supports this business—from product development through delivery and after-sales service.

In targeting revenue enhancement as well as cost control, Meiji is behaving like the banks that emphasize not just the ratio of operating expenses to operating revenues, but also operating earnings per employee, as critical goals and as efficiency indicators. Such measures naturally focus on automation that complements Meiji's marketing strategy. However, given Japan's low cost of capital and relatively high personnel costs in financial services, heavy emphasis on such automation may be appropriate.

The IT system is designed to generate beneficial loops with articulated goals and outcomes. Using IT to monitor customer events means that when a customer event occurs, an agent can solicit related business. Agent success is likely to be greater under such circumstances, so this reinforces acceptance of the system and the life-cycle concept by both agent and customer.

By constantly increasing the number and quality of services and products based in part on feedback from agent interaction with customers, Meiji intends to reduce customer migration and keep costs low. By targeting and reinforcing the technical bias of younger Japanese, it also is using IT to influence customer behavior and expectations, and to tie them to Meiji on an interactive basis throughout their lives.

In other words, Meiji has been implementing totally integrated management (TIM), including using IT to influence its competitive environment by changing the way its customers look at their financial requirements, the kind of service and products they expect, and the way the competition must respond. The process should reinforce Meiji's position among life insurers and help it emerge as a leader in postderegulation Japanese finance.

10

International Retail Banking

Sanwa Bank, Citigroup

"Citicorp is in the forefront of technology in electronic banking and is testing the limits of regulation. It instills fear in the hearts of competitors." That observation was made by *Value Line* in September 1985, and it remains true today of its successor, Citigroup.

IT's role in consumer banking is the focus of this chapter, looking specifically at Citigroup's international retail banking and at Sanwa Bank's retail banking strategies in Japan. Sanwa, now part of the UFJ Group and Financial One alliance, has been the acknowledged domestic leader in using IT to achieve an advantage in Japanese consumer banking. It is the "domestic leader" because Citibank is the overall leader internationally, including among international banks in Japan.

Citi's drive to build market share in Japan receives special attention because it is an excellent example of how Citi is using IT to exploit and enhance its advantages in a large and rapidly changing financial services market outside the United States. Japan is Citi's highest growth consumer-market segment, with "core income" increasing 66% in 2000, compared to 22% for the overall global consumer segment. The number of accounts jumped 85% from 1998 to 2000, going from 1.5 million to over 2.8 million.

Structurally, the chapter has three mega-sections. The first two provide an overview of Japanese retail banking and a review of Sanwa Bank. The third takes up Citigroup and its consumer operations in the context of the financial services and banking industries, then outlines the company's global strategy and Level 3 IT support structure, with particular emphasis on its consumer business worldwide.

Table 10.1 lists the 14 largest public financial companies in the world in terms of assets.

JAPANESE RETAIL BANKING

The ramifications of the 1990 bursting of Japan's late 1980s bubble include major loan defaults for Japanese banks, especially loans collateralized by

Table 10.1 World's 14 Largest Publicly Owned Financial Services Companies, Ranked by Assets, 2000[1]

Assets[2]	Company (country)
1,295	Mizuho Financial Group (Japan)[3]
902	Citigroup (U.S.) [C]
901	Sumitomo Mitsui Banking Corp (Japan) [8318][4]
886	Deutsche Bank AG (Germany)[5]
775	UFJ Group (Japan)[6]
715	JP Morgan Chase (U.S.) [JPM][7]
699	Mitsubishi Tokyo Financial Group Inc. (Japan) [8306, MTF][8]
675	UBS AG (Switzerland) [UBS][9]
675	HypoVereinsbank AG (Germany)[10]
674	HSBC Holdings plc (UK) [HBC][11]
654	BNP Paribas SA (France)[12]
642	Bank of America Corp. (U.S.) [BAC][13]
613	Credit Suisse Group (Switzerland)
505	ABN Amro Holding NV (Netherlands) [ABN][14]

Notes: Because of the formation of four major groups by the seven largest city banks in Japan and mergers in the United States and Europe, the rankings for 2000 differ significantly from those in the late 1990s. In 1998 and 1999 only two Japanese banks—Tokyo-Mitsubishi and Fuji—were among the top 10. Several government-owned entities and mutuals are larger than some of these.

Ticker symbols are in square brackets for U.S.- and Tokyo-traded stocks.

[1]Calendar 2000 except for Japanese firms, where the data are for the year ending 31 March 2001.

[2]In billion U.S. dollars. Home-currency data as converted by the companies in their financial reports.

[3]Centered on Mizuho Holdings Inc. [8305], the group includes Fuji Bank, Dai-Ichi Kangyo Bank, and Industrial Bank of Japan, which are merging, and Yasuda Trust, a subsidiary of Fuji Bank. Mizuho means "fresh and fruitful harvest of rice."

[4]Sumitomo Bank and Sakura Bank are the principal components.

[5]Acquired Bankers Trust (U.S.) 1999.

[6]UFJ stands for United Financial of Japan. Centered on UFJ Holdings Inc. [8307], the group includes Sanwa Bank and Tokai Bank, which merged in January 2002, and Toyo Trust Co.

[7]Formed by the 31 December 2000 merger of Chase Manhattan Bank and J. P. Morgan & Co.

[8]Bank of Tokyo-Mitsubishi, Mitsubishi Trust & Banking Corp., and Nippon Trust Bank Ltd. are the principal components.

[9]Formed by the 1998 merger of Union Bank of Switzerland and Swiss Bank Corp.

[10]HypoVereinsbank acquired Bank Austria AG in September 2000.

[11]Hong Kong and Shanghai Bank is the primary component.

[12]Formed in 2000 by merger of Banque Nationale de Paris and Paribas.

[13]Formed by the 20 September 1998 merger of NationsBank with BankAmerica.

[14]Formed by 1990 merger of ABN and Amro banks, grew in the early 1990s by acquiring other banks and financial service firms in Europe and the United States. They included European American Bank in New York; in February 2001 it sold the consumer part of EAB to Citibank.

Sources: Company filings. Similar lists appear annually in the *Wall Street Journal* (end of September, covering 100 firms) and *Fortune* (August, covering three classifications of financial firms).

real estate and securities. This has resulted in massive write-offs and substantial inputs of government capital. Since the mid-1990s the banks' loan problems have been something that will take "several more" years to resolve. Indeed, by 2001 the number of more years had grown in some estimates to 5, extending the ultimate recovery to 15 years.

As these problem loans must be carried at a negative spread, they act as a drag on earnings and on the rebuilding of Japanese bank balance sheets. A further drag comes from stock holdings that are not paying dividends sufficient to cover carrying costs. This has encouraged banks to sell some shares in clients that had been held for relationship (rather than investment) purposes. Such sales were further fostered by the 2000–01 wave of large-bank mergers because a bank's holdings are limited to no more than 5% of a company's shares. (In the early stages of the crisis, shares sold to realize gains often were repurchased.)

Because banks were permitted under Bank for International Settlements guidelines to count 45% of their equity portfolios as part of tier-two capital, the collapse of Japan's stock market sharply reduced their capital even as it contributed to increased loan losses. This means that, as banks have realized gains from stock and other appreciated assets to offset loan losses, reserves in the form of appreciated assets have been diminishing significantly.

Eventual resolution of the problems depends on expanding bank revenues and earnings, so a recovery in bank balance sheets other than through government capital injections remains well in the future. Despite several mergers between stronger and weaker banks, real consolidation and rationalization similar to the U.S. experience have been severely limited by Japan's permanent employment system. That is, post merger, there has been little reduction in bank operating expenses and even a slight rise in costs due to a sevenfold increase in deposit insurance premiums.

Exacerbating these problems has been Japan's continued economic weakness, which limits domestic loan demand, combined with the fact large Japanese corporations can borrow directly on their own more cheaply than from the banks. Toyota, for example, in 2001 was the only AAA-rated Japanese entity; not even the Japanese government was so highly rated. Therefore, like their U.S. counterparts, Japanese banks have turned to overseas markets, derivatives, and retail banking in search of profits.

With all the city banks facing the same business and economic environment, most have sought similar solutions. Therefore, the strategic problem for Sanwa and its merger partners, Tokai Bank and Toyo Trust, has been how to differentiate its products and services from others, how to avoid more credit problems, and (very important) how to create a lasting competitive edge in Japan's banking environment.

Retail banking by city banks began to develop in Japan only in the mid-1970s as corporate loan demand began to slow after the first oil crisis. At the time, it was not easy for the city banks to shift gears from corporate to retail lending. Not only were they inexperienced, but entry into many areas was restricted by regulatory segmentation. With the late 1990s Big Bang, most restrictions have disappeared. Now banks can expand into areas such as money management, credit cards, and home mortgages. This is a benefit for Sanwa because of the new markets it can expand into and the new services it can offer. It also is a risk due to the influx of many powerful new competitors.

Although segmentation has been reduced significantly by deregulation, only from October 2000 has a company as broad-ranging as Citigroup become possible under Japanese law. That is when banks were allowed to operate insurance companies through a subsidiary, one of the last steps in the Big Bang process. (For a full account of the scope of businesses open to banks after the Big Bang, see Hoshi and Kashyap 2001, table 8.6. Good accounts of the banks' problems are Hoshi and Kashyap 1999, 2001, Cargill 2000; and Ueda 2000.)

SANWA BANK

Facing an even more daunting set of competitive issues than Meiji Seimei (chapter 9), Sanwa Bank also is combining IT and a life-cycle approach to customers in managing and navigating the competitive pressures of the Big Bang and the even bigger loan-loss problems. However, as a diversified bank with a long tradition of serving corporate clients, it is not relying solely on retail banking for survival.

Sanwa Bank Ltd. became part of the UFJ Group with Tokai Bank and Toyo Trust effective 1 April 2001. On 15 January 2002, it merged with Tokai Bank. The umbrella company is UFJ Holdings Inc. (UFJ stands for United Financial of Japan.) Before becoming part of UFJ, Sanwa was one of Japan's leading city banks, ranking sixth in assets during the 1990s. Based in Osaka, it was formed in 1933 by merger. Tokai was created by the 1941 merger of three Nagoya banks. Neither was part of a prewar *zaibatsu*.

Not only have Japanese banks been consolidating, they have been affiliating with established firms in other market segments to offer one-stop shopping. In July 1999, Sanwa agreed with five other firms to form an alliance in the retail market and asset management segments. Others have joined since, with several of the brokerage firms merging to create Tsubasa Securities Co. Called Financial One, "the Alliance for the Future," it includes firms from life insurance, property and casualty insurance, securities, trust services, and banking. The goal is to have "more regular customers with the alliance each utilizing the services of several alliance members."

Sanwa has about 17 million retail and consumer loan accounts (March 2000). Consumer lending of ¥5.9 trillion was about 24% of total domestic loans outstanding. The majority is for housing. In July 2001 the three UFJ Group members announced that in January 2002 they would completely merge their credit card operations. With 6.3 million customers, it will be the third largest issuer in Japan.

Retail Banking Strategy

The strategy Sanwa developed is continuing to be implemented by UFJ. This is to create a competitive advantage with what Sanwa calls "continuous relationship marketing." This involves emphasizing IT and automated branches to deliver an expanding range of services related to Sanwa's life-cycle determination of its customers' requirements. Because the retail market is less volatile and lower risk than traditional business lending or other banking areas such as derivatives, achieving a strong position can be very beneficial to Sanwa's, and UFJ's, future growth.

Success depends on how well Sanwa addresses two elements that connect its retail banking infrastructure with its IT-intensive retail marketing strategy. These are the appropriate stage in a customer's life cycle to start marketing a product and the most effective way to market and deliver a product or service.

To address the former, Sanwa's detailed evaluation of Japanese consumers' patterns of personal development requires collecting, managing, and analyzing substantial amounts of data. The second related and central concern is for the bank to use IT to control the costs of meeting the identified demands. This includes the expense of developing new customers, products, and services, and of delivering a service or product to a particular market segment. Sanwa's approach to addressing these issues has been to develop a matrix that identifies different customer groups and their banking needs according to current lifestyles. It cross-matches this with a set of products for which it carefully controls costs.

The costs and returns are closely analyzed in terms of the two major ways Sanwa can deliver products and services. One way is traditional full-service branches. The other is electronically, via the telephone, mobile phones, the Internet, ATMs, credit cards, mail, and convenience stores. ATMs and automated branches are system-intensive and thus are subject to user-base economics. That means their success can create a beneficial loop.

The traditional way is expensive. It is particularly costly relative to the potential returns from new customer segments such as young people just starting careers. Yet, Sanwa recognizes it is very important to capture these people as clients, because this segment is the fastest-growing retail banking market in Japan. Further, as these individuals progress through their lives, their economic needs and earning power will grow, and they will become more profitable customers for financial products ranging from mortgages to retirement products.

Target Market

Sanwa's main target is the mass of middle-class consumers, especially those it can reach electronically and through direct marketing campaigns. Within that group, its focus is those in their twenties and thirties, to whom it offers a particular set of products such as ATMs, credit cards, and telephonic banking. To those in their forties and fifties who have married, it wants to expand loans for housing, children's education, and weddings. For those entering retirement or who are wealthy, it offers products such as fund management and private banking.

Sanwa is competing for high net worth individuals through private banking in association with its Financial One affiliates, using a jointly owned company called Private Financial Management Co Ltd. This market segment also requires credit cards, ATM services, mortgages, funds transfers, and the like. That means a basic retail banking support structure is a necessary condition for successful private banking. Sanwa's extensive ATM and automated branch network thus is a plus in soliciting private banking business. Further, its system for tracking a customer's lifestyle can be extended to the requirements of its private banking clients. Private Financial Management has agreements with Morgan Stanley and UBS regarding provision of financial products. (According to the *Nikkei Weekly*, in Japan "rich" is generally considered ¥100 million in financial assets and ¥300 million in total assets.)

Specific Initiatives

Sanwa has increased banking by mail, phone, and Internet, as well as dramatically expanded the number of automated branches relative to competitors. It calls this "direct-to-consumer" banking. As part of this strategy, it also is experimenting with PC banking, and has announced a tie-up with Seven-Eleven Japan that will extend its ATM coverage significantly in terms of numbers and hours (chapter 8). Sanwa generated first-mover advantages in 1998 by offering 24-hour telephone and ATM banking accessible globally, as well as over the Internet.

This IT-intensive approach has directly supported the life-cycle concept in that Sanwa's research and database indicated that younger customers are busier and more technologically sophisticated. They thus prefer the longer hours and greater flexibility of automated branches with 24×7 ATMs. (Regulators consider an ATM a branch, and for a long time allowed operation only during regular banking hours, which generally are 9 A.M. to 3 P.M. on weekdays. Hours of use have become more flexible, but not all ATMs are on line all the time.) The tie-up with Seven-Eleven therefore is both IT-intensive and a direct extension of this concept, as convenience stores are heavily trafficked by younger customers who work.

Sanwa is creating a web bank with Hitachi, Japan Credit Bureau (the country's largest credit card issuer), and Recruit (a job-listing firm for graduating students) that will enable customers to pay for goods and services and buy mutual funds on line. It also will provide entry via Recruit to the young adults who are Sanwa's target entry market segment. In addition to settlement via the web, the bank's customers will be able to use Sanwa's 4000 ATMs to make deposits and withdrawals, as well as to arrange loans.

Sanwa cards also can be used at ATMs in 7-Eleven stores. Sanwa's goal for this bank is to have 1.5 million savings accounts and ¥1 trillion in deposits by March 2005.

A portal, *financialone.co.jp*, was established in May 2000, initially to provide a common link to alliance members' web sites.

Electronic Delivery Structure

Sanwa's approach to introducing its electronic delivery structure is customer-oriented in terms of basic strategy, even though it may evolve into a highly automated system. Sanwa has integrated clients into its strategic delivery system and has formalized this in its Consumer Direct Banking Center. It then tracks these clients in terms of its matrix management to offer them products and services as their life circumstances evolve and change. The alliance with Recruit is an obvious example.

This has aligned the bank's human-resource policies with strategic intent in that those segments that prefer automation are getting it, while those that prefer human customer service in terms of teller contact and cross-selling are getting that with respect to particular products and financial services. Permanent employment may be a benefit here, because the bank has personnel who are no longer needed in other activities who can be allocated to such tasks. For example, Sanwa seconded personnel to IY Bank to assist in its May 2001 launch.

Sanwa has increased share among its targeted customers (those in their twenties and thirties) in geographic areas where it has opened automated branches. Given the low cost of these branches, this business has been profitable while building the bank's relationship banking base. Thus, it sees its strategy during the late 1990s of adding some 700 of these branches in Osaka and Tokyo to its 360 full-service branches in those areas as having been very successful.

An indication of Sanwa's belief in the benefits of its approach is the announcement at the beginning of 2000 that it would close half of its regular full-service branches over the next few years. In contrast, major competitors had announced closings of only about one-eighth of their branches. This will give Sanwa and UFJ tremendous cost and operating profit advantages because this approach is extended to the combined bank. (Branch overlap from mergers accounts for many branch closings, but UFJ is going well beyond that.)

Automated branches require less space and less staffing (needing employees primarily only to replenish the cash and pick up the deposits). Sanwa estimates the costs at about one-fifth those for typical full-service branches. The bank is constantly adding to the number of functions and services the unstaffed branches can handle, as well as expanding the hours that services are available, which reduces its average transaction costs.

Sanwa began its unstaffed ATM strategy in 1989. In 2000 it had over 1000 such branches throughout Japan, more than any other bank. In addition, its regular branches all have Quick Lobbies so that they combine some of the convenience and efficiency features of the unstaffed branches and reduce the personnel needed at a full-service branch. Sanwa's participation in IY Bank is a direct extension of this strategy.

Conclusion

Sanwa's organizational structure and IT product choices help in understanding the bank's use of and demand for IT to create a competitive advantage in retail banking in Japan. These choices reflect its coherent business strategy and stated corporate goals, which are necessary conditions for its successful IT strategy. That strategy is based on management's recognition that the demand for particular retail banking products and services shifts according to age, job status, and other demographic variables. This view is central to their approach. It should carry over to UFJ, and Sanwa can be expected to encourage its Financial One alliance partners to follow its lead.

Evaluation of its competitive situation has guided Sanwa's management in using IT to economize on traditional delivery systems while extending and expanding its customer base and methods of delivering financial services. Such initiatives also have built beneficial loops in customer service, geographic coverage, and product availability while reducing cycle times and improving the production and delivery of services to the customer. This has enhanced customer satisfaction, indicating the importance of having IT development personnel as part of the retail division's decision-making structure and IT as an integral part of how Sanwa organizes, delivers, and supports its retail banking business.

All this makes Sanwa and UFJ strong Level 2 IT strategists. They fall short of being Level 3 in part because the alliance framework poses weakest-link risks to the one-stop shopping strategy Sanwa has committed to. Still, if Sanwa can use its IT and management acumen to set the standards for its affiliates, and the alliance successfully integrates its product offerings, each company can—like Nationwide Financial Services (chapter 9)—be a thriving niche player supported by a large synergistic organization (something NFS does not have).

It is this prospect that leads a number of analysts to rate Sanwa and UFJ among the banks likely to emerge from the current crisis and the Big Bang as a leader in Japanese finance, along with Meiji Life. This is true even though Sanwa faces a challenge from a very strong global consumer banking competitor, Citigroup.

CITIGROUP

One response to deregulation of financial markets has been to build large firms offering a wide range of services in insurance, banking, brokerage, and asset management. Citigroup has created the world's most diversified such company in terms of both range of services and geographical coverage. It is one of the most profitable financial groups, as well the largest in the United States. In its first full-year (1999) annual report, the company described itself as "A diversified holding company whose businesses provide a broad range of financial services to consumer and corporate customers around the world."

Created 8 October 1998 by the merger of Citicorp (the parent of Citibank) into Travelers Group, the new company took the Citi name. The Travelers Group was the result of a series of earlier mergers and acquisitions (and name changes). The original Travelers was a diversified provider of property, health, and life insurance, as well as other financial services, based in Hartford, Connecticut. Primerica acquired it on 31 December 1993 and adopted the Travelers name. Subsequent additions included investment banker Salomon Inc. (28 November 1997), which was combined with Smith Barney (acquired by Primerica in 1987), as well as, on 2 April 1996, the property and casualty insurance subsidiaries of Aetna Services Inc. Another major component was Commercial Credit.

Besides the global consumer segment considered in this chapter, Citigroup operates through three main divisions. The Global Corporate and Investment Bank serves corporations, financial institutions, governments, and other participants worldwide. Its services include investment banking, retail brokerage, corporate banking, cash management, and commercial insurance. Global Investment Management includes mutual funds and asset management services for institutional and individual investors. The Investment Activities segment includes venture capital activities.

In November 2000, Citi acquired Associates First Capital Corp. Inc. Associates provides various financial services to consumers and businesses, primarily in the United States, but it also has extensive operations in Japan and Europe. Over time its activities will be folded into Citi's similar operations.

Global Consumer Operations

Global Consumer comprises Citi's "global, full-service consumer franchise." This includes branch and electronic banking (e-Consumer), consumer lending services, and credit and charge card services, as well as life, auto, and homeowners insurance. It delivers "a wide array of banking and lending services, including the issuance of credit and charge cards, and personal insurance products in 57 countries around the world. Global Consumer creates products and platforms to meet the expanding needs of the world's growing middle class" (quoted from Citigroup's 1998 annual report).

With 146 million accounts worldwide, the segment represented just over 38% of Citigroup's "core income" in 1999 and 37% in 2000. Its assets grew from $235 billion to $271 billion. The non-U.S. component is the fastest-growing part of the company's consumer revenues and globally faces the least competition.

Citi offers MasterCard and Visa, Diners Club, and private-label cards. With the 1998 acquisition of AT&T's Universal Card Services, Citi accounts for approximately 15% of U.S. credit card receivables. Globally, at the end of 2000 there were about 100 million accounts, more than half of which were outside the United States. The company has begun to shift its diverse card portfolio to a common operating platform.

Prior to the merger with Travelers that created Citigroup, Citibank claimed (in its 1996 annual report) that it had the "best banking franchise in the world." This is because it provided "average people—that broad mid-sector of the market—with payment products, banking services and investment services that will help these customers achieve their personal objectives." Technology is a key aspect of this vision because "upgrading technology almost always achieves the dual objectives of improved customer service and greater cost control." The "intent is to use technology to remove work, errors, time and paper from our processes, and therefore be more focused on, and responsive to our customers." At the end of 1997, prior to the merger with Travelers, 54,800 of its total staff of 93,700 were outside the United States, and it had 3000 locations in 98 countries, in 57 of which it was offering consumer banking. At the end of 2000 Citibank offered some form of consumer banking in 100 countries.

Citi Within the Industry Context

While Citi recognizes that markets help define competitors, in pure international retail banking it has no competitors across the entire spectrum of products, services, and geography. Its strategic approach to market and competitive analysis thus takes a matrix structure. This views most of its retail banking competition in areas such as cards, checking services, and ATMs as locally or nationally based, such as in Japan with banks like Sanwa. However, in asset management, the set of competitors is wider and more global. Therefore the key to its global strategy is for it to efficiently, profitably, and interactively capture and transfer the benefits of its worldwide reach to other market segments in terms of scale and name recognition. In that way the whole of its global consumer business is truly greater than the sum of the parts would be independently.

The megatrends of liberalization, globalization, and technological change that help support this overall strategy began in the United States in the 1970s. The United States ended the gold exchange standard, forced the introduction of floating exchange rates, deregulated fixed brokerage commissions, eliminated regulated rates on retail bank deposits, and eliminated the interest equalization tax on purchasing foreign assets. It then helped extend these market-oriented developments globally in two ways.

First, the U.S. government continued to liberalize and deregulate the U.S. market. In response to the S&L crisis during the 1980s, itself partially the result of the liberalization of interest rates and financial services, it broke down restrictions on interstate banking. Citibank was a direct beneficiary of this trend, acquiring savings and loans in a number of states during 1982–83, including California-based Fidelity Savings and Loan of San Francisco, thereby establishing a major presence in the largest U.S. retail banking market.

Second, the United States began to push for similar market liberalization in other advanced markets such as Japan and the United Kingdom. Partly this reflected the Reagan administration's belief in markets as such. It also was driven by the strong feeling that foreign financial firms were benefiting from U.S. liberalization and deregulation, but U.S. firms were being deprived of profitable business abroad.

As an example, this policy led to the May 1984 Yen-Dollar Accord and changes in Japan's foreign exchange regulations that liberalized the international flow of capital. In the United Kingdom it contributed to the 1986 Big Bang that permitted freely negotiated brokerage commissions and the purchase of securities firms by banks and insurers, including foreign banks. That allowed Citibank to buy Vickers DeCosta, a British brokerage with overseas offices, including one in Japan.

Bank Consolidation in the United States

A wave of bank consolidations began in the United States in the 1980s. This led to formation of ever larger "superregionals" and, with the September 1998 combination of BankAmerica and NationsBank, to a near nationwide bank.

Historically, states have regulated banks within their borders and generally have restricted operations and branching to the state of origin. Thus, in the 1960s and 1970s the United States had upward of 16,000 banks. Changes in laws and regulations beginning in the 1980s, including allowing bank holding companies to own banks in more than one state, have cut the number to below 10,000, and the number is still falling. Not all the mergers have been geographically contiguous, so the bigger banks generally have different major competitors in different markets. Also, the traditional money-center banks, with greater emphasis on corporate business, continue to differ from the superregionals.

User-based economics suggests that the high fixed costs of maintaining and operating a merged bank's IT systems will be spread over more users, and there should be scale economies in such areas as credit card and account administration systems. But meshing systems and cultures has been a major problem that often has swamped prospective gains—at least in the short and even the medium run. In addition, because the emphasis usually has been on rationalization and cost savings, little in most U.S. bank mergers has been about building the business or developing new customers and products for the combined entity.

Citibank's Alternative

For Citibank, geographic expansion and mergers have taken a very different tack, with an emphasis on revenue generation in addition to cost savings. This is partly a result of history and partly conscious design. The state of New York for many years limited New York City banks to New York City. Thus, its predecessors, First National Bank of the City of New York and National City Bank of New York, both founded in the 19th century, expanded abroad aggressively at an early date and merged in 1955 to become First National City Bank in order to maintain critical mass in the New York City market. In 1975 it adopted the name Citibank.

Many of Citi's foreign operations date to the 19th century. Beginning in the 1980s, it decided to build on this presence to significantly expand its consumer business in these locations. Implementation has placed a strong emphasis on technology. As noted in its 2000 Annual Report (p. 6), the bank has a "focus on technological innovation, seamlessly delivering value to our customers across multiple delivery platforms." The idea is to provide clients increased access to its products. Citi has thereby captured two major trends in banking and financial services, globalization and technology intensification.

In the United States, other than the early 1980s special case of government-aided acquisition of savings and loans, Citibank did not try to keep pace with competitors in the expansion-via-acquisition craze. Rather, it focused on areas such as credit cards, mortgages, and student loans. By using call centers, direct mail and, later, the Internet, these could be offered nationally without owning a bank in each state or, by using call centers, even having a physical presence. The strong Citibank culture, with its international and money-center orientation, appears in retrospect to have been a major factor in developing this strategic approach.

Its choices have proven to have several advantages in terms of Citi's particular skill set. The product areas selected are large and require good technology support and database management. In addition, they have balance sheet, capital, and profit advantages because they can be easily securitized and sold, with Citi collecting a fee for loan origination and service. Fee income helps increase return on capital. In 2000 it was the number one provider of student loans and about 20% of its mortgage lending (in dollar terms) originated on line.

Citi's national expansion and use of telephone-based services, including national ATM links, began in 1983. In California it moved to gain market share by extending branch office hours and increasing the number of ATMs so that ATM lines were shorter than teller lines. It was a leader in both New York and California in developing a clearer set of ATM instructions to reduce the distaste for (and fear of) using ATMs.

Another major IT-intensive domestic consumer initiative has been Citi's dominance of electronic benefits transfer (EBT). Citi manages welfare and other payments for 27 states and the U.S. Department of Agriculture (food stamps), making it a major player in the market. While the business is profitable in its own right, it also provides a large database for pursuing additional consumer business with first-time financial service users.

Citi will continue to pursue activities in the United States that do not require a large nationwide branch network and play to its technical strengths. This is another important reason the Travelers merger made sense, because its products are not branch- or location-sensitive.

The Travelers-Citibank Merger

When the merger with Travelers was proposed in 1998, the primary motivator for both firms, but especially for Citibank, was cross-selling within the context of a life-cycle model (box 10.1 and the Introduction, subsection "Life-Cycle Models"). This revenue-generating motivation contrasts with the expectation of cost savings from branch closings, personnel reductions, and the like that have driven many US bank mergers. It was a friendly merger, with each partner bringing something to the table that the other

---

Box 10.1
LIFE-CYCLE MODELS AND CROSS-SELLING

A customer's needs change with time and can be quite diverse. That simple insight is the foundation for marketing and product development in financial services. Extensive cross-selling became possible only with the deregulation of financial services that allowed firms, especially banks, to sell a broader range of products. The life-cycle approach to marketing thus began to emerge in the 1990s as banks and securities firms were permitted to enter a wider range of activities. In public, the industry refers to cross-selling as "leveraging the franchise potential through relationship development, cross services, and integration of activities."

Citi gradually has evolved a modified life-cycle or life-event marketing model for the United States that it is adapting elsewhere. It differs from the Meiji Seimei model (chapter 9) and Sanwa Bank model, which are focused totally on Japan. Under Citi's marketing concept, the company seeks to capture college students through its credit cards and student loans, and then to track them as their careers develop, offering products such as car insurance, and car loans, then mortgages and homeowners insurance, life insurance, mutual funds, pension products, and so on. Certain colleges may even be prime marketing targets if they have large numbers of foreign students or students who travel, because Citi is particularly interested in internationally oriented customers.

This strategy can become intergenerational as a customer's children grow and have financial needs of their own. Each product not only can be profitable in its own right, it can supply an excellent database for cross-selling and very long-term customer development.

wanted. Travelers wanted access to Citibank's global consumer base, while Citibank wanted additional financial products that Travelers could offer. As a consequence, the large premium normally associated with a takeover or merger in the financial services sector was avoided.

Strategy

From a long-term perspective, a bank needs a strategic mix of market development, operating efficiency, and effective balance sheet risk management. Citi is using IT to help it manage these three important aspects of its global consumer business. In essence, integrated service delivery is viable only if the information delivery needed to support that service and related products is integrated and strategically aligned with the bank's business goals and objectives—including the balance between credit risk, revenue expansion, and cost reduction. Consistent with this dictum, Citi adds functions to the basic automated delivery structure. It does this as it becomes technically feasible and is demanded by the customer segments that the systems are designed to serve, either currently or over customer life cycles. In this way Citi is very customer-oriented in terms of its IT strategy.

Citi's approach to delivering and managing a wide range of products and services also is very technology-intensive. This is because a lesson learned in the early 1990s recession by Citi and other U.S. consumer-oriented banks is that diversification of assets and risks is important. The overall consumer business can remain profitable even when economic conditions become adverse because only some customer accounts will go bad. The trick is to screen out as many potentially bad accounts as possible, compute what percentage will slip through, then price the product accordingly. Citi has been doing this rather successfully, as indicted by the broad decline in consumer-related net loan losses across major market segments from 1998 through 2000.

Such analysis is what Citi is constantly doing with its global customer base, while trying to develop more sophisticated screens and market segment selection criteria. This process becomes especially important as the business cycle matures, because that is when business loans tend to get repaid and consumer loans, particularly the potentially riskier ones, tend to increase as consumers feel more confident about their employment and economic prospects.

Product Strategy

Given this perspective, the company's product strategy is driven by a focus on the overall customer relationship. For example, checking will be linked to credit cards and investment accounts, which might include brokerage or mutual funds. Loan, mortgage, and insurance products also will be linked.

Some of these links can be automated, such as transfers from the checking account for periodic purchases of mutual funds, as well as monthly payment of the mortgage, card balances, and insurance premiums. Citi hopes to be able to offer better interest rates or lower service charges for customers who agree to these linkages, sharing savings in processing costs. This should attract customers and decrease their desire to unbundle their financial services, with the associated benefits of greater client retention.

Thus, the company sees e-business as a way to integrate various financial services on behalf of the customer, such as individual cash management of accounts using the Web. This is the idea behind MyCiti, introduced in 2000, which permits customers to access all their Citigroup accounts, whether banking, brokerage, or insurance. "Citi on the Net" is viewed as a broad distribution channel that offers account aggregation and a range of services.

At the same time, Citigroup recognizes that many consumers prefer to unbundle their various financial services, using one or more providers for each service. If it is difficult to unbundle, some customers will go elsewhere for all the pieces, and all of the business will be lost. This is especially expensive if it is an existing customer who leaves. Not only is there revenue lost from the existing account, it is costly to generate a replacement in terms of marketing and account-opening costs. Thus Citi has organized itself to manage unbundled accounts. This approach extends the user base with resulting opportunities for cross-selling. It also means Citi lets each product and service stand on its own merits.

Delivering Product

In terms of product delivery in the United States, Citi's emphasis on technology is more a response to competitive developments, whereas abroad it is more due to economics and market segmentation. For example, one result of the wave of U.S. bank mergers, combined with changes in technology, has been an increase in the number of ways that products and services are delivered, including telephone, PC, staffed supermarket minibranches, Internet, customized voice response, and smart ATMs. In fact, branches are now a relatively small percentage of the total delivery channel.

Competitive pressures in U.S. banking are very intense. For U.S. banks, consumer customer attrition is 1.5% per month. So banks have to run hard just to stay even, which is what makes cross-selling strategically important. Although checking accounts are the anchor for the consumer relationship, banks have found that the more products they offer and that customers use, the better the retention rate. Thus, U.S. banks' marketing strategy is to aggregate individuals in a proactive sense, both to retain the customer and to get better profitability from the relationship. Thus, they are using IT to determine customer propensity to buy products.

Successful cross-selling is a double win for the bank, because it improves customer retention and generates additional revenue. But consumer banking tends to follow the 80–20 rule: 20% of the bank's retail customers account for 80% of the profits. And, on some customers, the bank is losing money. Thus, part of the aggregation and statistical analysis exercise Citi and other U.S. banks go through is to measure the net present value of certain customer groups, including the cost of getting a customer versus how long the customer remains. From this analysis, Citi has determined that it is worthwhile forgoing some earnings to keep a highly valued customer, such as periodic reductions in credit card rates, compared to the cost of trying to generate a new customer.

The drive to merge and cross-sell notwithstanding, U.S. consumer-related financial services remain very segmented and highly competitive in terms of payment mechanisms, distribution, convenience, choice, products, and services. This is well illustrated by the rapid decline in Internet brokerage commissions for retail investors. Thus, establishing competitive barriers that add value so as to make a profit has proven quite difficult.

However, Citi has the ability to segment the U.S. market in terms of those who are internationally oriented because it can offer actual overseas branches. (This is similar to American Express enhancing its travelers check and travel agency businesses by having offices in major cities worldwide.) This segment also generally is upscale, as it includes businesspeople who travel frequently and students and professionals going abroad. Overall, it has been growing with globalization. Conversely, within the United States, Citi probably had only kept even in the consumer banking area until the Travelers' merger, though now it is seeing better growth. To strengthen its position in the important New York City market, in February 2001 it bought the consumer part of European American Bank, with $11 billion in assets, 97 branches, and a strong, internationally oriented, client base.

Consumer convenience, globalization, and access in a variety of ways are driving Citigroup's IT strategy and philosophy, and this makes security a major concern. Security procedures are policies set at the corporate (Policy Committee) level. The idea is to do as much as possible through direct access without exposing the bank and customers to fraud or taking avoidable risks in any particular market segment. Such considerations have limited full global delivery of some e-services that Citi has developed.

The remainder of the chapter looks at Citi's use of IT and its international consumer banking activities, particularly those in Japan.

International Retail Banking

Citi's goal is to have a global customer base of 1 billion, primarily cards, by 2010, compared to 146 million at the end of 2000. While Citibank typically had 1% to 3% shares of overall bank activity in each of its non-U.S. markets, it now feels it needs 10% in certain markets. South Korea, Taiwan, Singapore, Mexico, Brazil, and Argentina are specified targets. Although some U.S. and European megabanks have substantial operations outside their home market, these are mostly corporate-oriented. In international retail banking, Citi is the only truly worldwide player and is defining the market.

There are only a few other banks that could play in this game (even if they decided to). Three are U.S. based products of mergers: JP Morgan Chase (formed December 2000), Bank of America (formed in September 1998 when NationsBank in effect took over BofA and its name), and FleetBoston Financial (formed October 1999). Fleet does 20% of its business overseas, mostly in Latin America where it has 250 branches. Bank of America actually has divested overseas consumer operations, selling Citibank its large branch network in Argentina relatively inexpensively in 1985.

Best positioned of all is London-based HSBC Holding, which has operations throughout Asia (where it originated as the Hong Kong & Shanghai Bank), and in the United Kingdom, United States, Canada, and (usually as minority interests) Latin America. However, in 2000 HSBC sold its consumer brokerage operations in Australia to Citi. Several Spanish banks have become major players in Latin America, but this is a regional strategy that has involved little cross-border integration. So, possibly except for HSBC, no one else has the reach or seems interested.

Citi has benefited from being seen as a safe haven in several countries that have been subject to financial crises. These range from Japan to emerging markets such as Southeast Asia and Mexico (where, in May 2001, Citi announced plans to buy Grupo Financiero Banamex-Accival SA—Banacci for short—parent of Banamex, the country's largest bank).

Technology and economics have affected Citi's expansion plans in emerging markets. Whereas once it might have bought a local bank, now it often expands electronically. For example, the 1997–98 Asian financial crisis hit Indonesia very hard, creating an opportunity for foreign banks to expand. But, instead of acquiring a distressed local bank with problem loans at a cost of perhaps $500 million, Citi installed more than 40 ATMs in Jakarta and expanded staff support at a cost of $5 million. It also began offering longer hours at its ATMs and existing branches, along with telephone banking. It thus has been able to extend service and exploit the flight to quality in order to expand its Indonesian market share with much lower capital and operating costs and fewer management headaches.

In all markets, Citi is moving to offer a standard consumer banking and financial services package. The idea is to provide a common worldwide experience to its consumer customers in terms of branches and products. Since the merger it has been adding Travelers' products to this menu. Subject to country and local regulations, these include mutual funds, annuities, and life insurance.

Emerging markets are a key aspect of the strategy, despite their problems. In 1996, 31% of Citi's card earnings came from emerging markets. This percentage has declined due to economic turmoil in these markets and the increase in total earnings from acquisition of AT&T Universal. However, it remains an important business that is expected to grow significantly.

The human-resource function for these activities, as well as other Citigroup businesses, is managed centrally at the corporate level. All the brokerage and foreign exchange business is in the corporate bank, but there are consumer and international consumer-related business synergies here as well through the group's mutual funds and foreign exchange dealings for card purchases and payments.

The Private Bank (for wealthy clients) is separate from the consumer bank, though Private Bank customers often want or need some consumer banking services such as credit cards and ATM access. Citi has designed an on-line aggregate account access package for such clients called SSB Access, which is similar to MyCiti for its regular bank clients. At the end of 2000 there were 1.6 million such accounts. Thus there are positive synergies between the international consumer bank and the Private Bank.

Citi in Japan

Japan has many of the world's largest banks (table 10.1) and has proved a difficult market for foreign banks to crack for most of the postwar period. However, the collapse of the Japanese bubble in 1990 and the continued weakness of Japan's economy and banking system have created opportunities for foreign banks and other financial service firms.

Citibank has had a presence in Japan since the 19th century and began expanding its retail banking activities in Japan in the 1980s as regulatory changes permitted. The initial idea was to take advantage of the bad retail bank experience of most Japanese depositors. For example, unlike the United States, until well into the 1990s Japanese customers did not have 24-hour ATM access, and sending funds abroad meant waiting two or three days even for U.S.-dollar-denominated checks, with the bank holding the yen funds. Bank credit cards also were nonexistent.

Citi began by opening branches and developing a branch support and back-office infrastructure, including an affiliation with Dai-Ichi Kangyo Bank (Japan's largest at the time) to supply ATM services. It also introduced bank credit cards. Initially it experienced problems attracting customers, because there was no perceived need for the cards. Cash and charge accounts where one regularly shopped, ate, or drank predominated.

In the late 1980s and early 1990s, Citibank had major financial difficulties of its own that distracted it from Japan and raised concerns in the minds of potential Japanese clients. In 1991 Masamoto Yashiro was recruited from Exxon Japan, where he had been chairman, to head Citi-Japan. Because of Exxon's gas stations, he had good retail branch experience. He also knew about positioning a foreign company successfully in a retail business in Japan. In addition, his political instincts were excellent because he had dealt with the Japanese government on energy and oil issues for many years.

Mr. Yashiro saw there was a need both to re-establish Citibank's credibility and to have a large local distribution channel with a set of products. He came up with the idea of affiliating with the Postal Savings System. The Ministry of Post and Telecommunications (MPT) was interested because defined contribution plans were coming to Japan, and it wanted to have part of this asset management business. This was something it did not have the capability to do, but Citi did. In addition, postal savings customers would have international ATM access through Citibank.

By the mid 1990s Citibank had recovered financially, but there still was a perception among Japanese consumers that it was weak. However, the MPT recognized the recovery and struck an arrangement giving Citi access to the MPT's ATMs in post offices. This gave the impression that the Japanese government was vouching for Citi. As a result, Citi's consumer banking activity gained immeasurably during 1994–95. At the same time, Japanese banks were experiencing severe problems, causing a shifting of funds into postal savings. Besides credibility, Citi gained an extensive distribution network (there are more than 20,000 post offices in Japan) and a potential distributor for its asset management services as Japan's defined-contribution plans come into place. (Authorizing legislation finally passed in June 2001, with implementation in August 2001.)

The key to implementing this strategy on a practical basis was a full ATM support system, which requires efficient and reliable IT. With ATMs, Citi could completely bypass creating a branch network. Once the bank had a customer, it could begin to market other products, such as credit cards and mutual funds. To make the IT connection seamless, Citi sent its own team of software engineers and programmers to work with MPT to create and manage the interface between the two systems. Japanese banks complained about being excluded and so were permitted to access the postal system's ATMs, but their customers have to pay a fee.

The Japanese consumer bank used to report to corporate headquarters through the regional headquarters in Singapore, but because of size it has gained more autonomy. It now reports directly to the consumer bank headquarters in New York for most activities, while working with Singapore on regional issues and IT support.

Building a Franchise

To increase its Japanese consumer banking business, Citi has used physical branches, strategically placed ATMs, IT, affiliations, Internet and telecom delivery, and global products targeted at middle-class customers who are interested in the bank's international reach. This approach has been complemented on the corporate side through asset management, brokerage, and foreign exchange support.

Having established a bricks-and-mortar distribution channel through its branches and the arrangement with the Postal Savings System, Citi's marketing emphasis has been on nonbranch access—that is, using the Internet, telephone, ATMs, call centers, and mail. It wants customers to feel comfortable not coming to the bank. Studies indicate that already about half of all Japanese bank customers do not go to their banks, even in population centers where branches are close. The ratio is about the same for Citi customers.

Remote banking is the way Citi plans to blanket Japan. But only in the physical sense and for those who choose that: when a customer comes to a branch, Citi wants the experience to be pleasant and productive. To facilitate this, Citi has developed a model layout for branches that it applies globally. Automated service areas are at the entrance, and the actual branch is farther inside or even on a different floor.

Often it will develop retail banking ideas in other markets, then import and adapt them to Japan. The biggest market segment from Citi's perspective in this regard is charge cards, and it is working diligently to expand this business. All customers who open an account are asked if they want a card. Indeed, the application form for the card is on the same form as the application to open an account. It also has cobranded cards. For example, it issues cards in Japan with Northwest Airlines with a mileage incentive.

Despite the immediate emphasis on charge cards, the larger thrust of Citigroup's strategy in Japan is to build a loan- and investment-related business, rather than a transaction-payment related one. This includes asset management, mutual funds, and brokerage services. This is because Citi's analysis indicates that asset-based products are inherently more profitable than transactions in the current competitive environment.

The company has used focus groups to learn the kinds of financial services customers would like for certain events (such as college, weddings, and retirement). This is the beginning of adapting Citi's life-cycle model to Japan and developing a set of life cycle profiles based on its Japanese customer base.

Focus on the life-cycle model extends Citi's perspective beyond cards and ATMs to asset management. Indeed, many foreign financial service firms see a tremendous opportunity in Japan as a result of the unfunded pension liabilities of companies and the low returns Japanese managers have provided savers, even in years when the domestic stock market has performed well. There thus is a direct connection between Citi's retail bank business and its global asset management business through the mutual funds that Citi manages and sells.

Citi has collected over $3 billion in mutual fund assets from its Japanese customers, spread over eight funds. These include a global fixed-income fund (denominated in U.S. dollars) and a yen bond fund. Citigroup also is involved in the brokerage business directly through a relationship with Nikko Securities, which began operating in early 1999. As part of this, in August 1998 Citi purchased 9.5% of Nikko's equity and, through the exercise of convertible debentures, raised that to 20.7% in March 2000. Citigroup is marketing wrap accounts that include mutual funds through both Citibank-Japan and Nikko Salomon Smith Barney.

IT Support

Citi's coherent business strategy and, especially, its international consumer strategy are important determinants of the nature and evolution of its IT strategy. They influence how it chooses among IT options for achieving specific goals, and how it measures success in different business environments.

Citibank has been quite good at using IT to enhance the organizational strengths of its extensive international branch network and to capture the expert knowledge that resides there after decades of doing business in many different countries. This is done through a combination of packaged and customized software. The combination used in a particular situation depends on what is needed to support its business strategies, markets, and organizational structure on a timely basis in a specific environment.

A common (global) solution is not imposed if a local situation requires a different IT approach, and Citi makes an effort to understand local conditions. The only truly global requirements are that a local system is capable of being integrated into, or efficiently linked with, Citi's existing systems and that adequate security arrangements can be made.

Sometimes, when the company wishes to initiate a new product or service in a specific market, no packaged software product or solution exists because industry demand has not yet developed. In such cases, it will develop or adapt the needed software.

Citigroup's mission statements for the global consumer bank explicitly note the importance of information technology to strategic success worldwide. Thus, Citi's IT support group for the consumer bank is part of the decision-making structure. Consistent with other leading users discussed in this book, this is one reason why Citibank's international retail bankers have pursued IT outsourcing only in a very limited way. When they have, it has been mostly with firms that possess proprietary technology that Citi believes will work well with its existing systems, and particularly will support a specific product or service.

IT also plays a major role in enhancing branch and function productivity through improving credit decisions, reducing errors, and strengthening customer relations. In fact, these IT systems are coupled with marketing, product design, customer service, innovations, and constant cost reduction in ways that reflect Citi's clear understanding of its business, its markets and its competitive strengths within its evolving global industry context.

Citi uses some of the IT strategies seen for other leading users, such as creation of large, proprietary, interactive databases that promote automatic feedback between various stages of the product marketing and account service process. Further, it has built its IT systems to create and exploit beneficial loops. This is one reason it expanded its relationship with America On Line (AOL) and its 27 million customers by becoming a preferred financial service provider. For AOL, it is a way to extend its client, product, and market reach at low cost.

Citi's global consumer banking group appears to be the leader in implementing totally integrated management (TIM) in international retail banking. Indeed, the group has even coined a term for its leading-edge effort: "Cyber Marketing." The group's strategy of "globalizing" retail banking is leading the changes in international retail banking that are a function of a continually changing global economic environment; evolving customer needs; and shifting account relationships.

Citi is consciously influencing and stimulating many of these changes. For example, in 2000 40% of its new student loans were originated via its web site, compared to 16% in 1999. It is helping to spread use of on-line payments with the c2it program, which was launched in October 2000. It permits anyone to transfer funds by e-mail to anyone with an e-mail address. The sender registers a debit or credit card with Citi to arrange the transfer, which means the recipient does not learn the card number. The service can be reached directly at its own web site (*c2it.com*), through AOL's Quick Cash, or from other web sites of Citigroup services.

Support Structure

R&D to support the IT for the consumer strategy, which is managed by the e-Consumer group, is concentrated in a subsidiary, CTI (Citi Technology Inc.). This unit is the "business responsible for developing and implementing Global Consumer Internet Financial Services products and e-commerce solutions." The unit spent $497 million in 2000, and $295 million in 1999.

Based primarily in Los Angeles, a group within CTI helps operations in each country balance local standards, consistency with Citi's system, security standards, and relevant law and regulations (including, sometimes, U.S. law on encryption). This group is the interface with the Corporate Policy Committee, which sets the rules governing these trade-offs. Once a system addition or initiative has been agreed on, the local operation is responsible for implementation, but CTI is responsible for making sure it is compatible with the rest of the Citi system.

In each country, Citi seeks to build a systems network managed by a regional computer center, which provides economies of scale without sacrificing local autonomy. Singapore houses the computer center that supports consumer banking for Asia, including Japan. An IT country head manages IT for Japan and the connection to the Singapore regional center. All Japanese data are consolidated in Singapore.

Being offshore provides protection against earthquake damage. This is important: during the January 1995 Kansai earthquake Citi-Japan was one of the few banks that could continue operating without disruption. In contrast, the JCB Alliance could not respond for 72 hours. Because people often need to travel and buy supplies during a crisis, earthquake issues related to available banking or credit card services are serious.

IT Selection

Development and system integration begin with a business unit, wherever in the world it may be, assessing the possible merits of using software to solve a problem or meet a requirement relative to its organization, operation, and products. Because the requesting unit is charged with the costs, a manager will not undertake or approve an IT development program unless there are expected bottom-line benefits, and the manager will work to assure that those benefits are realized. All outside vendors have to comply with Citi's rules and protocols with respect to connecting to its system, and have to build this requirement into their offers.

This corporate routine results in strong focus being placed on IT's role in enhancing the consumer group's ability to do its job. The routine is thus both unit- and customer-focused. In this way IT selection is based on the Global Consumer group's needs, the IT project's cost, and what is available both internally and from outside vendors.

Management looks to functional and market gains to justify the expense incurred in customizing certain systems, including the costs of integrating new customized and packaged software into Citi's total IT system, and training employees to use it.

Outsourcing

IT services are outsourced by most major U.S. banks. By 1995, 84% of U.S. banks with more than $4 billion in deposits outsourced (*American Banker* 17 April 1997). However, Citibank has done this only for small pieces of its systems, and not for strategic initiatives, so it generally is seen as an outlier.

One prominent example of how Citibank closely manages this process even when using packages or outside programmers is a $750 million project in the mid-1990s to link and completely integrate Citi's 60,000 PCs and 2000 LANs worldwide into a common global network and systems infrastructure. This really was "insourcing" because, from the beginning, Citi controlled the system architecture and the tools used, and had done a pilot on 5000 of its own PCs in order to establish the prototype system. The contract, which went to DEC and Electronic Data Systems (EDS), thus was for execution. The company had worked with DEC since beginning development of a distributed processing network several years earlier. By contracting the operational and computer-servicing tasks, Citi freed internal IT resources to work on technology strategy and to make sure the project results met its objectives (*American Banker*, 27 June 1996).

Internet Initiatives

Citi's goal is to develop and implement an integrated strategy that tries to do as much as possible electronically, but recognizes the need for physical branches and call centers to provide human contact. It is Citi's ability to combine clicks and bricks that is enhancing its competitive advantage in global consumer banking.

The e-Consumer unit manages the global consumer group's Internet strategy and execution, including the creation and delivery of electronic financial services and e-commerce initiatives. This includes Citibank Online, c2it (a person-to-anywhere (P2A) online payment service), and MyCiti (an online account-aggregation site), as well as a strategic alliance formed in 2000 with AOL.

Citibank was not quick to embrace the Internet, and did not form a unit—dubbed e-Citi—primarily charged with using it until 1996. In 2000 a restructuring created the corporate Internet Operating Group, with a unit paralleling each of the main business lines. The consumer-related activities of e-Citi became part of e-Consumer while e-Citi continues to handle development activities not limited or related directly to individual businesses. Certain other support activities were transferred to Citi Technology Inc.

During the late 1990s e-Citi studied what existed and where success and failures had occurred. It next developed a five-year plan to identify what the bank would like to deliver to the consumer and how it would do that. This included prioritizing products and services based on what was technologically feasible. Working with the Los Angeles-based technology group, it set a price and time-to-completion for the IT related to each product and service. This price and IT package then was compared to offers from outside vendors, as well as to the expected revenue, profit, or cost saving on the product or service after introduction of the IT system. Similar procedures are followed by the various units that have succeeded e-Citi.

Citi negotiates alliances and sometimes invests in outside businesses or vendors that it feels will help the corporation generally—although typically not just to develop a one-time product or program. Examples of such strategic IT investments are 7/24 Solutions Inc and Phone.com (now Openwave Systems Inc). These are all minority stakes. A number of initiatives and investments have been discontinued and written off as Citi has refined its approach, the technology has evolved, and some things simply did not work as envisioned.

Hub and Spoke

The Internet support group feels that the bank sometimes can take too long to introduce a new product or service, so it has tried to facilitate generic solutions where outside entities or services can easily connect to the bank's IT system. In addition, its system must accommodate unbundled service providers and access by multiple Internet service providers (ISP).

To facilitate this, e-Citi and 7/24 Solutions have developed a generic connection at the bank (termed a hub). The hub is plug-compatible to outside providers, who can access it (as spokes). The connection and access specifications are totally open. However, given Citi's size and scope, it is beginning to define the standard for such access. This approach is consistent with Citi's willingness to unbundle its services, as other banks and financial service providers can connect to Citi's hub.

Los Angeles is responsible for managing the hub. This includes making the protocols available to other systems that need to access it. That is, it is responsible for opening and managing the standards, as well as for getting reciprocal information from other organizations. This means Los Angeles manages those IT interfaces, as well as the human relationships associated with outside systems, such as the technical personnel at other financial institutions and ISPs.

Using IT to Target Customers

Citibank uses IT as a way to solicit international consumer banking business. For example, the Japanese consumer bank's marketing campaign has been targeted at people who will keep an account balance of over ¥100,000, with ¥500,000 as minimum to be eligible for free banking services and full access to the Postal Savings System ATMs.

Initially, the campaign to increase the number of customers was untargeted across the perceived marketing base, with no real discrimination among groups. But subsequently the bank has worked with the marketing department on a more focused approach that relates product introductions to perceived weaknesses in the local competition, combined with an analysis of how customers actually behave. This involves extensive database development combined with a statistical package to analyze the data. Account officers, administrators, and marketing people all have access to the data on-line in real time. This allows managers to access and generate reports by type of customer and product, helping them manage the product marketing strategy by segment.

SAS, a privately held U.S. software company, provides the on-line statistical and data analysis software. Officers can specify content, but the SAS software helps create the reports and make them meaningful. Also, there are templates that extract certain information that managers and senior managers routinely want to see. These also ensure that the format has some commonality, allowing comparisons and aggregation between officers, branches, products, countries, and regions.

To do this well, Citi's Japanese consumer group needs a combination of people and IT. The group seeks to link people and ideas more closely with what is learned from Citi's database about actual customer behavior. Thus both standard and ad hoc reports are produced. The latter are usually associated with product upgrades or new initiatives. The former are done daily so managers have timely information by class of customer, as well as for target customer groups, along with a statistical analysis of what is occurring with respect to penetration, product use, profitability, credit, fees, and timing.

The group spends considerable time analyzing spending patterns of segments of card customers over a year. This is a huge data history that helps Citi to know its global and Japanese customer base. Further, because Citi has more than one type of card, including 1 million worldwide Diners Club members, which is usually a business card, it can do a wide range of market segment analyses, country comparisons, and targeted marketing. In comparing countries, for example, it can explore differences in spending patterns due to levels of economic development or regulatory regimes. This might suggest future changes or opportunities to introduce products or services in a given location.

These data are a key benefit of Citi's global reach. No one else has the data to do this type of analysis. This advantage helps Citi extend its worldwide lead, which in turn builds its international consumer base, and that leads to better information, as well as more cross-selling. All this is interactive and tends to compound over time, a beneficial loop.

Market Segment Analysis

To analyze market segments in Japan, each product market segment that is changing as a result of deregulation, increased competition, or economic pressure is identified as a "bucket of opportunity." This helps identify competitors' potential vulnerabilities. These opportunities are then compared to the products Citi has or could create. This actually works whether the group looks first at a competitive bucket or at a particular product. That is, the question can be posed as what particular additional product is best to offer an existing customer group or as what customer group would want this product. The SAS software package helps in this process.

Citi's consumer marketing group uses a number of screens or criteria when assessing a campaign or product, especially as the group wants to avoid campaigns that are likely to be unsuccessful or, if successful, too expensive. The latter usually reflect a customer-service issue. That is, if the campaign or product requires a lot of information to be delivered on a full-service basis to give customers what they want and expect, then it is likely to be too expensive.

The breakdowns of Citi's various customer bases into categories it feels are meaningful, as well as the database itself, are proprietary, and are constantly being modified. In Japan the group's normal approach for a new product or service is to start small in order to gauge customer response. It may even send different messages to different groups, depending on the analysis of each segment. Customers contact a customer service representative (CSR) if they are interested, and Citi tracks responses by segment.

Breaking customers into smaller market segments means the bankers need to be more involved in analyzing these segments and the bank's database, and in creating the rules for the CSRs that apply to managing each client group. Once the rules are in place, the bankers can iteratively program them and build consistency into the system and its application before proceeding to the next level of analysis and segmentation. This progression is important, because each marketing program builds on the previous one.

For example, Citi knows which customers, using which cards, are buying certain products and services, in what volume and where. That means Citi can offer to send a defined set of its customers a targeted message from a vendor (for example, offering a Hawaiian vacation package to people who have used cards for overseas travel). This does not give up any customer data, as the vendor merely supplies the message. Citi also can encourage customers interested in buying a given product to use Citi to find them the best deal. Thus the global consumer bank sees itself acting as a facilitator in transactions between merchants and customers.

Citi is ahead of the curve in some areas and countries, so it still has to be patient regarding the emergence of standards to make some of these things possible. Thus, it is constantly making choices and trade-offs between what it has the capability of doing, local standards, and consistency with Citi's system. One principle that overrides all these is that Citi will not compromise on security or the integrity of the customer's account and account data.

Call Centers

Citi's proprietary software and caller ID mean it can very quickly identify a caller and the campaign being responded to (if applicable). This means information on the account relationship and the campaign can be brought up as the call is being answered. To the extent this is not automatic, Citi's target is to key in a minimum of data so that the CSR can identify the customer within five seconds of receiving the call. Once the customer is identified, the CSR has the customer's entire relationship with Citi across all products and businesses on screen.

The CSR has the authority to make certain changes, market specified products, and solve particular situations and issues on the spot for any account. If a change is being made, such as an address or phone number, all accounts are changed with the one call. This saves both the customer and the bank time and money compared to multiple calls to different call centers.

Fees can be waived based on the customer's total relationship with the bank. CSRs are given parameters on this in terms of how good the total relationship has to be to justify a fee waiver, but within those guidelines they use their own discretion.

The benefits of this to the firm go beyond any specific campaign or customer. This is because studies have found that CSRs given a list of customers and asked to cross-sell incremental products are more likely to stay with the bank. This reduces staff turnover and training costs while increasing revenues through more product sales, a double win. Citi's experience is consistent with work on education and banks' human resource practices at the Wharton Financial Services Center (box 10.2).

IT systems that generate information, as opposed to just automating exist-

---

Box 10.2
THE INTERACTION OF STAFF AND IT

A large research project on U.S. retail banking and software systems (Prasad and Harker 1997; Everson, et al. 1999) has mapped IT and management processes across parallel functions, such as opening an account, buying a CD, and changing an address. In a finding pertinent to more than just consumer banking, the study concluded that efficiency matters in terms of cost and customer perception, but how it matters depends on who controls the system. If it is the line person, the customer comes first; if it is the person managing IT, then system cost per unit predominates.

For firms in the best-practice sample, such as Citibank, the two perceptions and functions are integrated: system costs are balanced against customer value and revenues. This is possible because product managers and consumer bankers control the retail IT process through their budgets. To the extent this is not true at competitors, they are at a competitive disadvantage.

Maintaining such a balance necessitates understanding how and why something is done. Such understanding allows the best-practice firms to make choices for rational, explainable reasons.

---

ing tasks, tend to support high-involvement or high-performance work practices (Hunter and Lafkas 1998). These practices are *employee enhancing* because they improve existing skills, create new skills, and lead to greater worker autonomy. In turn, the IT system usually evolves and changes in tandem with the work practices, so there is a coevolution of technology and practice. This is seen at Citi. Because such developments are based on the firm's original choices, this supports an evolutionary approach to understanding Citi's use of IT and how it is achieving best practice.

A direct result of greater CSR efficiency is that more products and services meet Citi's profitability test, thus offering more potential to expand the total global consumer banking relationship, increase client retention, and further improve profits.

Mobile Phones and the Internet

From Citibank's perspective, in Japan and several other European and Asian countries, the mobile phone is the direct-access device of choice, though of course users of PCs and other devices also will be served. In Europe this has been dubbed m-commerce, short for mobile e-commerce, and Nokia (chapter 11) is helping to lead the way.

The user base and capital investment cost numbers are straightforward and compelling. Outside the United States, at the end of 1999 the installed PC base was less than the number of digital mobile phones sold that year alone. Digital mobile phones are much cheaper and handier than PCs and their processing capacity is growing quickly. Over 60% of the population in Finland have digital phones, in Australia and Japan, over 50%; and over 40% in the United Kingdom, Germany, Italy, and Hong Kong.

With short message service (SMS) text can be displayed on a screen. This allows sending wireless messages via the Internet. By the end of 1999 about 350 million SMS-enabled phones had been sold worldwide and upward of 90% of new phones being sold in Europe and Asia handle SMS. Because the United States has lower digital penetration rates, it cannot be used as a model for the potential of mobile retail E-banking globally.

In Japan, though, the situation is quite different. The name given the leading mobile internet service is i-mode, offered by NTT DoCoMo, the country's dominant mobile phone provider. Introduced in February 1999, in early 2001 almost 60% of DoCoMo's 35 million mobile phone subscribers had the service.

Citibank has worked with telecom providers to offer services using i-mode and is ready for DoCoMo's migration to G3 capability. For Citi this is straightforward, because its hub-and-spoke connection strategy allows migration to G3 standards, and the access system is flexible enough to work in the United States.

Citi's research indicates that its consumer customers are interested only in moving data and are not interested in contextual presentation, including colored web sites with advertising. Transactional capability and moving data do not require the sophisticated processor that essentially defines a computer. Even skeptics with respect to the mobile phone as a data transmission device acknowledge that for stock prices, money transfers, and similar requirements, phones can be highly efficient.

What is needed is security, privacy, reliability, accuracy, and reasonable speed. Fancy graphics are not required or expected. Indeed, not having graphics, advertising, or other contextual content greatly increases transmission speed and reliability, because fewer bytes need to be sent. Translators pull out the essential information. The resulting reduction in data transmission requirements is astounding because as much as 95% of what one sees on a web page is not substantive content. Plain text can be sent at 10 kilobits per second, but graphics can be transmitted at only 100 bits per second, just 1% as fast. (Encryption adds 50% to 100% to transmission times.)

Introducing direct access and digital cell phone technology has been a two-step process. First, Citi developed a system of direct access for customers calling on a voice line or by modem from a PC. Access then was extended to the Internet through a Citi web site. Citi definitely sees a move toward an international standard that everyone accepts or can interface with. The operating systems most mobile phone makers and telecom providers believe will be used are Psion's Form Factor and Palm Pilot. (Windows CE is too big.)

PC users will have access to all their Citi accounts and data, including the peripheral context lost on a mobile phone. In this way Citi's customers decide how they want their information delivered and through what kind of device. Citi will facilitate access to its site for any of these devices. However, by emphasizing the digital mobile phone, it expects to influence and service the largest part of the global consumer financial services market. These are businesspeople, international travelers, and young, upwardly mobile professionals—and they are a larger proportion of the mobile phone market than of the total retail banking market. They also represent Citi's target international retail market.

Supporting Internet Access

Easy access and customer flexibility in moving funds create significant security and customer support issues. In particular, the bank has to be able to say "Stop" when something is not in order. However, this frequently leads to a client call or branch visit. Often the customer cannot explain the problem to the CSR without referring to what is happening on the screen. To address this issue electronically and reduce customer complaints, Citi wants to be able to show data on the mobile phone at the same time the customer is talking to the CSR. This dual streaming of voice and data is a priority project for Citi because the technology also should simplify resolution of credit card disputes, currently a very costly activity. Such dual streaming is an aspect of 3G mobile phone technology, so it is coming, if more slowly than expected in 2000.

Citi gets many calls related to problems that are actually with the customer's system or browser software or at the ISP. But, as this is part of the customer's total experience with Citi, the bank needs to help fix the problems. Therefore, the company works hard to make sure the data are getting to the customer and that the links are reliable, which means the group works with ISPs on their access to the Citi hub. Further, just as telecom companies do, Citi imposes reliability and security requirements on ISPs if they want to have access to Citi's hub for their customers. Because financial services are a big part of demand for ISP services, and Citi is a big provider, Citi generally can impose these criteria on ISPs. This is one way it is forcing suppliers to make firm-specific investments and to comply with standards that are part of Citi's TIM strategy.

Substituting IT for People Successfully

A big trick in using IT successfully and competitively is to know when there is a need for human contact and when technology can be substituted. Balancing these considerations is critical to competitive success. There also is a need to understand the form that the substitution should take, as well as how to sell it to the customer. The practical test of whether the mix is working properly is if Citi is attracting customers to new products and they are profitable. This is why the company uses focus groups and is developing a life-cycle marketing model that will help it anticipate and service needs as they appear. It is a continuous process: client product and service requirements are changing, and so are the available products and technical delivery systems.

In the late 1990s Citi found there was more demand for its voice response system in Europe than it had anticipated. Specifically, there were surges in call volume in two periods each month. Analysis found that the activity was directly related to people calling to see if their wages (typically paid bimonthly) had been deposited because they wanted to know when they could start paying bills. Some customers called several times in a day. A call center can be very expensive to establish, and there are ongoing personnel costs. Absent the peaks, capacity was adequate, so e-Citi looked for alternatives.

It hit on the possibility of sending a message to a customer's mobile phone as soon as the deposit was credited, and it worked with telecom companies to do this in a secure manner. The plan was piloted in Poland, which involved making an arrangement with the Polish phone company regarding the charge for sending the message to Citi customers' mobile phones, and permission was solicited from customers to authorize having the message sent. The service was then expanded, and 67% of customers in Europe had signed up by December 1999. The results have been dramatic. Call volume dropped and is now level throughout the month. Moreover, customer satisfaction has risen, and Citi has the possibility of sending other messages that might be of interest to the customer. It thus plans to implement the idea even more broadly, including in Japan.

Additional IT Initiatives in Japan

Citi is working with merchants and suppliers to speed payments. If successful, this will affect both its customers and the distribution of goods.

In May 2000 Citi-Japan joined Fujitsu (a major computer company) and DDI (now KDDI, a telecom service provider) in a pilot settlement service. Similar to Citi-Wallet, the system works by registering clients' credit card or bank account numbers with Citi in advance. Customers can then order products anywhere (keying in a set code for the item), using an Internet-capable mobile phone. Citi manages payment from the registered account.

Customers can access the product codes through the Internet, newspapers, or even a restaurant menu (if they want to pay for a meal using their mobile phones). Receiving goods at home, the office, or a convenience store can be chosen from a menu displayed on the phone. The system also permits bank transfers. The goal is 12 million customers by 2004, a substantial addition to Citi's consumer base, in addition to being a good test for introduction elsewhere in the world. The program is an open standard.

Given its strategy, the priority IT development areas for the company in Japan include security (working with telecom provider NTT) and brokerage-reporting software (working with systems house NRI). The latter is important, because Citigroup wishes to extend, link, and integrate its corporate relationship with Nikko Securities to its consumer banking activities, such as the relationship with Ito-Yokado's on-line bank through that bank's investment from Nikko.

Conclusion

The strategic problem facing Citibank in the 1990s was how to make the bank more profitable in the face of intense competition in the United States and abroad in all areas of financial services. Citi's solution took three forms. The first was to aggressively increase its international consumer franchise. The second was to develop and expand a set of products with national and international potential, such as credit cards and mortgages, that are IT-intensive rather than branch-intensive. The third was to extend this strategy by merging with Travelers in a transaction that created an expanded range of products to sell through its domestic and, even more important, its international outlets.

Now Citibank is using its global delivery capability in combination with a worldwide IT strategy to define the future of international consumer banking. It is doing this through adaptation of its proprietary life-cycle model and marketing strategy to a country's level of development and Citi's target customers. The approach has emphasized its existing international presence and branch network. The conception and implementation of Citi's strategy also are closely intertwined with telecommunications, and particularly with developments in mobile telecom. This also is true for several of the other leading IT users examined in this book (Toyota, Ito-Yokado, Meiji Seimei).

To accomplish its goals, Citi systematically collects, manages, and analyzes customer and market data, and links the results directly to its IT delivery systems. Citi's strategy thus is leading and benefiting from the continuing megatrends in finance: globalization, liberalization, consolidation, product proliferation, and technology intensification.

Success in turn has depended on Citi's timely marketing and delivery of products using IT and other means. By getting the customer acquainted with Citi's automated life-cycle products and account services at an early date, and by constantly increasing the number, convenience, and quality of its services and products, Citi expects to improve customer contact, reduce customer migration, and keep costs low. This is a beneficial loop in that less customer migration reduces costs and implies greater customer satisfaction, which opens the door to further customer contact, and so on. Further, by targeting and reinforcing the technical bias of younger consumers especially, it is using IT to influence customers' behavior and expectations, and tie them to Citi on an interactive basis.

Citi is trying to move as many transactions as possible to electronics and to expand the number it offers electronically. However, it recognizes that branches and ATMs are not going to disappear and the desired shift will occur only to the extent that customers see it as a way to get more convenient, faster service for themselves. Thus, all Citi's consumer banking and IT strategies are centered on creating common multiple access points for the customer, from the model branch experience to Internet banking.

Management is seeking a lifelong relationship and wants the customer to see it that way, too. Citi thus is trying to use IT to influence the way customers look at their financial requirements and the kinds of service and products they expect from a financial services provider, given these perceptions. This reflects a totally integrated management (TIM) approach to consumer banking worldwide.

Acknowledgments

In preparing this chapter the author especially benefited from the guidance given by the Wharton Financial Services Center, a Sloan industry center, as well as the staffs at Citibank and Sanwa Bank, who were very generous with their time.

11

Wireless Telecommunications

Nokia

IT strategies rely on good telecommunications and some companies, such as Toyota and Citibank, expect wireless communications to play an increasing role. Many see mobile telecommunications as an important part of how IT fits in our futures, and Nokia is perhaps the most successful major firm in the industry. Hence, a chapter on Nokia. While the other chapters focus on firms' use of IT, here attention is on the strategies and technologies of a company whose products are a facilitator—indeed, a crucial link—in the strategies of several of the leading IT users examined.

In addition, Nokia represents, in its own strategic evolution and use of IT, the same totally integrated management (TIM) paradigm that is found in the practices of other Level 3 IT strategists. This is seen in its partnering strategies with suppliers and customers, its adept negotiation of open industry standards it can influence, and its end-to-end global supply chain management.

Following an overview of the convergence of IT and telecommunications, the chapter outlines how Nokia's history has shaped its success. This is followed by an examination of its end-to-end demand and supply management system, which uses proprietary IT. The company's commitment to open standards and extensive use of partnering to develop products for itself and to help others create reasons to use its products are then taken up, including overviews of many of the technologies involved.

IT and Telecommunications

The convergence of computers and telecommunications has been expected since computers began widely appearing in offices in the 1960s. Almost immediately, computers were sending data among themselves across telecom links and IBM bought Rolm, a telephone switch maker, in the 1980s. However, it was not until telecommunications began to become digital that significant convergence could occur. Since the 1980s the switches that route telephone calls have moved from being electromechanical to software-directed electronics.

Moreover, information itself increasingly is digital. That is, audio and video, when transmitted, become just another stream of binary data. For individuals, this especially means the Internet. Internet traffic is handled by different types of switching and routing hardware than traditional telephone traffic. For this and other reasons, full convergence has yet to arrive across the board. However, it is no longer just over the horizon because Internet-enabled digital mobile phones are here now, especially in Japan.

Worldwide, there were around 700 million mobile phone subscribers at the end of 2000, compared to 500 million a year earlier and 300 million at the end of 1998 (one-third of whom had analog phones). The 60%-plus annual increases in sales of the late 1990s are gone. So, too, are the explosive growth prospects predicated on early rapid deployment of third-generation (3G) systems. These have been dashed by the rollout expense and the weakened financial condition of many operators. Still, Nokia expects a billion users by the end of 2002. The annual growth of 20% to reach that is still very rapid, but, it can be reasonably expected as new functions (even though short of full G3) entice new users.

Nokia Corp. is a major presence in global mobile telecommunications. It is the world's largest maker of mobile phones, and has widened the gap between itself and its major competitors, Motorola Inc. and Telefon AB LM Ericsson. Thus, it held over 30% of the handset market in 2000, 35% in the first quarter of 2001, and even more in the middle half of the year. This has been achieved through aggressive introduction of relatively inexpensive digital phones that have attractive software features, as well as ever-lighter weights, smaller size, longer talk times, and (to attract younger users) changeable colored faces. (It has been aided by major competitors' mistakes, and has done well despite some mistakes of its own, from which it has learned.)

Mobile phones have become a commodity, but Nokia believes it can differentiate its phones in ways that are difficult to emulate, at least quickly. It intends to do this by continual early introduction of new features, especially Internet access, and by keeping its supply chain lean and closely responsive to changes in demand and supply via TIM. The company's approach is very complementary and supportive of life-cycle concepts, Citibank's m-banking, and m-commerce more generally.

Nokia, the Company

Firms that see the "opportunity to shape the future by proactively supporting the building of both standards and constellations of actors working together, in its transactional environment" have been termed prime movers by Ramirez and Wallin (2000). Nokia has been doing this since the 1970s by combining proprietary technology with the acceptance of open standards. This is one reason why, in a study of competitive fitness of major companies worldwide, INSEAD researcher Jean-Claude Larreche found Nokia to be among the top firms, and ahead of or even with its likely competitors on all measures (Marucca 2000).

Yet, just 15 years earlier Nokia had been a hodgepodge conglomerate, evolved from a pulp and paper mill started on the banks of the Nokia River in 1865, struggling to identify its corporate mission.

The company's transformation began in the wake of the 1973 oil crisis and encompassed the tenures of four CEOs, each of whom seemed to perceive the emergence of a new economy that would require a new kind of Nokia. All four were considered highly controversial for flouting the conventional industrial wisdom of the day. Only in retrospect does their direction seem obviously right. In implementation they were pragmatic, a characteristic they share with other IT innovators. Further, their visions were consistent with the rapid increase in IT-related business activity. The company's strategic approach correctly gauged some of the key criteria to competitive success in such a superhigh-growth environment.

As with Nippon Steel and Toyota during the 1960s and 1970s, aggressive capacity expansion, gaining market share, and rapid price reductions in line with (or in anticipation of) productivity improvements were critical to success. The company similarly has done an excellent job relative to competitors in managing its supply chain to reduce costs and increase its client base.

The company's web site is *nokia.com*.

Structure

Nokia, incorporated and headquartered in Finland, operates worldwide. It is composed of three groups: mobile phones, telecommunications, and other. Sales in 2000 were $28.7 billion, compared to $8.4 billion in 1996. Europe accounts for over half of revenue, with the Americas and Asia-Pacific each a little less than a quarter. Principally listed in Helsinki, since July 1994 its shares have traded on the New York Stock Exchange (with the symbol NOK).

The mobile phone group is the world's largest producer. Its worldwide market share was over 30% at the end of 2000 and growing. In 2000 the group represented 72% of revenue, up from 66% in 1999 and 54% in 1996.

The telecommunications group is one of the world's largest suppliers of mobile network equipment and systems, and also makes fixed-line and radio-access network products. It provided about 25% of revenue in 2000, down from about 30% in 1999 and 33% in 1996 because of even faster growth in mobile phones. Products previously were mostly for the GSM standard, but have shifted to 2.5G and 3G standards. Within the telecom group there is an Internet division. Formed in 1998, it has grown in large part by acquisitions. The division seeks ways to make mobile connections to the Internet more secure, more reliable, and faster. That will provide reasons to buy Nokia mobile phones.

The industrial group produces digital satellite cable, network terminals for broadcasting and multimedia applications, and workstation monitors, as well as battery chargers, filters, and antennas for mobile phones.

Early Telecom Ventures

Nokia's venture into electronics and telecommunications began in the 1950s when Scandinavian countries started radio telecom services on a commercial basis to link their many remote areas. The business had about 100,000 subscribers in 1980 and represented an extension of the radiophone business Nokia had helped to start in the 1960s. The business has been superseded by GSM mobile phone service.

One early supplier was Finnish Cable Works (FCW). It primarily produced power and phone cables, but in 1960 entered the electronics business centered on telecommunications and subsequently started to develop radiophones. Some were exported to Russia or sold to private businesses, but most were sold to the Finnish government for military and emergency use, particularly in sparsely populated areas. (Box 11.1 describes the evolution of the Finnish telecom market.)

In 1967 FCW, along with Finnish Rubber Works, merged with Nokia to form the Nokia Group. The combined company had four operating groups, with electronics representing only about 3% of revenues. The new firm began to develop its own pulse code modulation (PCM) phone switch. This was an early form of digital telecom technology (box 11.2).

In the 1970s the Finnish government created a new mobile radio network, audio-radio-phone (ARP), which was followed in 1975 by a joint decision by all the Scandinavian countries to establish Nordisk Mobile Telephone (NMT), the world's first multinational cellular network. Although Nokia

---

Box 11.1

TELECOMMUNICATIONS IN FINLAND

For historical reasons Finland has had around 40 relatively small phone companies, each serving a different geographical area. The Finnet Association, a cooperative formed in 1921, provides interconnection and, since deregulation in the mid-1990s, has expanded into offering mobile and international service as well. Finnet subsidiary Radiolinja is the second largest mobile operator. Sonera, 53% government-owned, is the largest. It previously was known as Telecom Finland. Originally part of the government's post and telecom (P&T) service, its predecessors supplied long-distance services to sparsely populated areas, as well as international telephone service and telex. In 1987 the Ministry of Transportation assumed regulatory responsibility and P&T created the partly privatized Telecom Finland for its operating functions.

Box 11.2
PULSE CODE MODULATION (PCM)

Transmission systems based on pulse code modulation (PCM) were created in 1967. In PCM, analog sound signals are converted into digital form. This technology substantially increased the capacity of telephone cables. In 1969 Nokia was the first company to introduce PCM transmission equipment that conformed to CCITT (Consultative Committee on International Telegraphy and Telephony) standards. Nokia views this early involvement with digitalization as one of its most important strategic decisions ever.

PCM also is used for the compact discs that dominate the recording industry, although a superior digital recording technology has become feasible and in 2000 was being introduced (in a way that is compatible with existing players).

---

had lost the ARP competition to Salora, the resources required to develop the new system led to a cooperative effort in which Nokia developed the base stations and Salora the mobile phones. The effort was a great success, because the joint venture became the market leader.

NMT opted to set key specifications (create a standard) and open bidding to all vendors. Open standards meant competitive bidding that reduced service costs by 75%. NMT began full operation in 1981 and quickly became heavily used thanks to competitive pricing and features such as international roaming. Other countries—including Spain, Russia, and Thailand—subsequently adopted the technology. This increased demand expanded scale led to more orders and even lower service costs, a beneficial loop. For example, in 1983 NMT demand was just 73,000 but had risen to 1 million in 1990.

In the late 1970s Nokia also began cooperating with the state-owned electronics company, Televa, in a 50–50 joint venture called Telefenno, to develop a digital telephone switch (the DX100), which evolved into the DX200 equipped with Intel microprocessors. The DX200 was quite successful, gaining half of the Finnish market by the mid 1980s. Its development helped form the base for Nokia's digital network technology.

Salora and Nokia had agreed in 1979 to combine their radio telephone activities into a 50–50 venture, Mobira. Then, in 1983, Nokia bought Salora, including its television business, and in 1987 increased its electronics, computer, and communications activities by buying the other 50% of Telefenno. Turnover at Telefenno was about 49% of Nokia's 1987 revenues, and other telecommunications was about 17%.

In 1987–88 Nokia added other pieces to this strategic emphasis on telecommunications and electronics by acquiring Diversicom Cue (a U.S. paging company) and Standard Elektrik Lorenz's consumer electronics business (thus gaining a brand name well known within Europe). It bought Ericsson's Information Systems business in 1988, creating Nokia Data. These acquisitions made Nokia a leading U.S. paging company, the third largest TV producer in Europe, and the largest IT firm in Scandinavia. The acquisitions also provided distribution and access to local manufacturing in the protected markets of central Europe.

However, given excess European TV capacity, a less well-known brand than Philips or Thomson, and heavy Japanese competition, Nokia's consumer electronics business started spilling red ink. In addition, Ericsson's Swedish IT experts had difficulty adapting to the Finnish market. These problems were compounded in 1988 when Nokia's CEO committed suicide.

The new CEO, Simo Vuorilehto, began the task of consolidation and focus, and in a short period sold the paper business, the chemical business, and Nokia Data. He retired in 1992, after appointing Jorma Ollila to replace him. Ollila had come from Citibank in 1985 as Nokia's VP of international business development and had subsequently been made senior VP for corporate finance. He has provided much of the vision that has made Nokia the international power in mobile communications it is today.

The Shift to a Mobile Emphasis

As Ollila tells it, the transformation of Nokia to being centered on mobile phones was partly accidental. In 1990, when Vuorilehto was strategically reviewing Nokia's businesses, he sent Ollila to manage the mobile phone unit. Representing about 10% of Nokia's turnover, it was losing money due to the global economic downturn, the Soviet political collapse, and stiff competition from Motorola and Ericsson. Part of Ollila's mandate was deciding whether it could be revitalized or should be sold.

Outside factors were unfavorable, as continued turmoil in eastern Europe and the Gulf War in early 1991 dampened sales. However, with cooperation from the workers, Ollila was able to reduce capacity without a strike. (When the situation improved, the redundant workers were rehired.) He also rectified R&D problems and got the mobile phone R&D group to begin tracking the new GSM digital standard. In 1991 the mobile phone business expanded its production base by purchasing a U.K. manufacturer, Technophone, and by 1992 it was profitable.

The rest of Nokia was not so fortunate: the firm reported losses for 1991 through 1993. However, the growing emphasis on telecommunications helped make 1993 continuing operations profitable, although a write-down of the picture tube business created another overall loss. Thus, by the mid-1990s, Nokia felt ready to concentrate on mobile communications. Ollila shut four TV factories during 1992 and a fifth, in Germany, in 1996. However, the sixth, in Finland, was kept open because it was involved in the production of multimedia units. In 1995 Nokia sold its tire and cable machinery units. In 1997 90% of turnover came from telecommunications, and only about 6% was within Finland.

The venture into TV was not a complete loss, because the company learned a great deal that has been critical to its current success and evolving competitive advantage. This includes the acquisition of video display and multimedia technology, which have become critical components in mobile telecommunications, including 3G systems. Among the soft lessons learned was better appreciation of foreign (especially Asian) markets, including the variants in culturally based consumer desires that can affect technology development and applications.

Nokia now understands that, from a company or manager viewpoint, consumers and markets can behave "irrationally." Such consumer behavior can have an impact on the appropriate R&D trajectory. Sometimes this means abandoning what the firm believes is the best technology for what the consumer perceives as important.

(The fate of Sony's Betamax in the face of Matsushita's VHS standard is often cited as a "better" technology losing out, although there is considerable argument as to whether Betamax actually was better. In any case, VHS offered longer recording times sooner, and that was the determining feature for the consumer. Learning from that experience, in the mid-1970s Sony and Philips compromised sound quality when applying PCM to CDs, apparently so that disc size would meet automakers' specifications regarding available dashboard space and so that [most] entire symphonies could be recorded on one CD.)

Ollila established the company's strategic objectives as "Focus, Global, Telecom-oriented, and High Value-Added." To achieve this, he formed a strong cooperative team at the top of the company that many observers see as responsible for propelling Nokia to the forefront in mobile telecommunications. In common with other leading IT users, Ollila also sees the value of setting precise, quantifiable goals.

The company moved to establish Nokia as a brand rather than relying on OEM sales. Customers had included Radio Shack, with which it had formed a partnership in 1984 as part of its strategy to penetrate the U.S. market, and Matra, with which it partnered in 1986 to commercialize mobile (especially car) phones in France and other parts of Europe. This approach combined its traditional competence in partnering with a holistic strategy toward the Nokia brand.

GSM

Its historical strengths stood Nokia well when, in the late 1980s, the European Commission for Post and Telecommunications established a commission to examine mobile telecommunications. Called Group Special Mobile (GSM), it had the authority to establish a common standard for Europe's mobile telecom industry. GSM quickly decided on a digital standard, also called GSM (for global system for mobile communications). In contrast an analog approach was being used extensively in the United States. The technology was designed to allow such services as packet switching, which can transmit data at high speeds over wireless networks. It also decided that construction of the network should begin in 1992, so time was of the essence.

GSM has spread from Europe to Asia and even partially into the United States. At the end of 1996, GSM had been selected as the standard by 208 carriers in 105 countries. Such global penetration made both Nokia and Ericsson stronger versus their major rival, Motorola (which had remained committed to the analog technology dominant in the United States, where it was the market leader).

Due to the magnitude of the task of developing a new technology, Nokia quickly turned to forming alliances, joining Alcatel Altshom SA (France) and AEG (Germany) in the European Cellular Radio 900 consortium in 1987. In parallel, Nokia formed Nokia Cellular Systems to develop and sell systems, while it planned for Mobira (later renamed Nokia Mobile Phones) to manufacture handsets. When Nokia realized the new digital system would dramatically increase the demand for new handsets, it acquired U.K.-based Technophone in 1991 to enlarge its production. In July 1991 Finland got the world's first GSM service, offered by Radiolinja and using a Nokia system and handsets.

Nokia also used partnering to expand its European market share quickly, working with new cellular providers such as Orange plc in the United Kingdom and E-Plus Mobilfunk GmbH in Germany. It also signed an agreement in 1989 with AT&T Corp. to cooperate in the development of a new generation of microcircuits for mobile phones, which would be customized digital signal-processing components for the Europea-wide GSM network.

As subscribers switched from NMT to GSM, operators had to write off their investment in the older network. This gave Nokia an understanding of what was involved when new technology meant scrap-and-build even though the existing equipment was not fully amortized (depreciated) on a company's financial accounts. Therefore, it learned how best to market new products and technology not only in Europe but globally, because many telecoms worldwide have faced such costs, and will again, as newer technologies such as 3G are introduced. This in turn has helped Nokia to influence the global market's evolution, as well as to manage the next change in the global standard.

Demand Supply Management

Nokia visualizes a "demand-supply" network that includes customers, not just suppliers. Such customer focus and the desire not to leave any business on the table is similar to Ito-Yokado's concern with lost sales and Merck's with drug availability. If Nokia can do this efficiently, including good inventory control, the benefits are clear.

The emphasis on logistics and IT management grew from a particular event. In 1995 there was a downturn in cellular sales, leaving Nokia stuck with high-cost chip inventories. Its initial reaction was to cut inventories massively, but it also shortened its chip order-to-delivery time from 12 weeks to 8 weeks, trading a decrease in the risk of carrying obsolete inventory for the risk of lacking chips. Looking longer term, Nokia began in 1996 to integrate its supply chain into its management structure.

A purchasing system from SAP AG (box 2.1) was installed to specifically track parts in real time so that they could be routed to the factories needing them. The result was a reduction in inventory requirements from 80 days to 40 days, a fall in inventory value by 35%, and a 300% increase in the inventory turnover rate. The goal was a demand-pull system, what Nokia calls "execute to order," whereby components have to correspond to products consumers want.

In 1998, this logistics system was amplified by a supply-chain management system from Manugistics that was integrated into Nokia's overall IT system. The need for this was driven by the fact that by 1997 some 59 telecom operators in 31 countries were using Nokia's GSM systems. The company also was selling 40 mobile phone products in 130 countries from 12 plants. This requires some 100 billion components each year, delivered in the right amount at the right time in the right place, a situation that necessitates a well-tuned JIT operation and is heavily dependent on a customized proprietary IT system.

Suppliers operate through a private Nokia network which its customers also can access. The company asks suppliers to make firm-specific investments in time, money, and organization so that Nokia will have an integrated and coordinated end-to-end solution. It does not use compulsion in this effort, but instead indicates how it will be mutually beneficial, which it has. This is similar to Ito-Yokado's and Toyota's experiences, and creates a beneficial loop of lower inventories through a better and quicker balancing of demand and supply shifts. The efficacy of the system compared to competitors has been amply demonstrated in the downturn beginning in late 2000 and extending into 2001, when Nokia did not build inventory that became obsolete and unneeded, while Ericsson and Motorola did.

Nokia's experience is that by working toward such a joint understanding and mutually beneficial experience, it builds trust with its suppliers and in turn with its customers, because everyone runs their businesses better. Nokia even works with second-line suppliers when a first-line supplier thinks that would be helpful, as do Toyota and Ito-Yokado.

Ollila recognized that production in various locations and markets in many countries requires complex logistics to operate efficiently in supplying the plants with parts and components, and in supplying customers with finished products and systems meeting their specific requirements—that is, efficient customization. Thus, for him, logistics and the supporting IT have become the most important aspect of demand-supply chain management and the key to global market success. So this aspect of Nokia's success, and the use of IT to support it, is driven from the top to meet the demands of global sourcing and marketing.

Importantly, Nokia's approach is an application of TIM. The company's supply chain management is a fundamental part of its strategy. This is because Nokia sees itself as an extended enterprise involving customers and suppliers, and organizes itself around this principle. The primary focus is on the customer and the customer's needs. IT remains only an enhancer or enabler of the management strategy.

The "performance metric" for whether the strategy and related IT are working depends on Nokia's version of total cost analysis (explained generally in the Introduction). One key variable is the date of supply. To the extent the company can reduce the inventories needed to support a given date of supply, it can reap substantial savings. Nokia calculates the impact on operating profit of reducing inventory holdings by 10 days as equivalent to a 1% increase in sales.

Sourcing IT

In structuring the IT support for its end-to-end demand-supply chain management structure, once Nokia had decided what it wanted, it used external consultants to create about 40% of the system. The rest it did internally. The company is application-driven, in that it does not let the IT package determine the organizational structure or demand-supply strategy. Further, the IT needs to add value through improvement of operating structures while discouraging emulation.

Now that the system is established, the company operates and upgrades it completely by itself because it wants to assure with a "99.999% probability" that product is available globally when and where it is needed. This can be done only when the IT operation and the organization are completely integrated and the interests of the IT and operating personnel are totally aligned. Nokia does not feel any outside operator will have the knowledge and commitment to do this.

This view extends to production. Thus, the company considers Ericsson's move to outsource manufacture of handsets as difficult to manage, and therefore a competitive plus for Nokia.

Marketing

While managing the demand-supply chain is key to controlling costs and responding rapidly to demand shifts, one must still generate demand. Thus, creating an advantage and resources through alliances or partnering not only has been important to developing the supply chain and new network products and services, it also has been beneficial to Nokia's business plans in terms of the production of, demand for, and distribution of handsets.

In 1984 Nokia formed a joint venture with Tandy Corp. (operators of Radio Shack, which is now also the company name) to build a production facility in Korea. Eventually Nokia took over ownership of this plant, along with two in Texas. (Nokia's U.S. headquarters is in Irving, Texas, near Radio Shack's headquarters and the plants.) Combined with the U.K. and Hong Kong plants of Technophone, Nokia gained a large global production capability. It also achieved good distribution through Radio Shack's 6700 outlets in the United States, which was particularly important, given both the size of the U.S. market and the ability it gave Nokia to track competitive developments, especially vis-à-vis Motorola, at that time the world's leading producer of mobile phone sets.

A marketing relationship with the trading company Mitsui & Co., starting in the early 1990s, allowed Nokia to monitor technology developments in Japan. By maintaining a sharp focus on the Japanese customer, Nokia was able to build brand credibility better than any foreign supplier, despite intense competition from major domestic producers such as NEC, Sony, and Matsushita. The experience in Japan also has been beneficial to Nokia in other ways, as box 11.3 outlines.

Nokia was aided in its international marketing by the knowledge and expertise accumulated from working with the earlier NMT standard, because it was adopted by other countries but then was replaced by GSM. This experience meant Nokia was able to anticipate many technical developments. It also provided significant experience working with major telecom operators, who both were buyers of Nokia's systems and influenced users' choice of handsets.

In 1991 Nokia decided to develop a phone that would work globally— that is, not only with the new European standard, GSM, but also with TDMA (U.S. standard), PDS (used in Japan), and GSM 1800(PCN) (Japan). While the electronics inside each phone are somewhat different, the appearance was to be consistent worldwide.

Box 11.3

STRATEGIC BENEFITS FROM NOKIA'S CONTESTING JAPAN

Although Nokia is not the leading supplier of digital handsets to NTT DoCoMo, Japan's leading mobile telecom operator, it is the leading non-Japanese supplier. DoCoMo, together with Matsushita, NEC, Mitsubishi, and Fujitsu (its four major suppliers), created the de facto mobile phone standard for the Japanese market during the 1990s. Outsiders to this group, including other Japanese manufacturers such as Sony, have had to work hard to gain access to the market.

The Japanese market has been very demanding regarding weight, size, and talk times. Nokia's involvement in Japan pushed its ability to improve these features globally. Japan also has been on the cutting edge of advanced features delivered on wireless phones. This includes the first truly mobile Internet-ready system, DoCoMo's i-mode, which entered service in February 1999. I-mode was developed by DoCoMo itself, in cooperation with Japanese electronics companies.

Involvement in Japan also has shown Nokia how important it is to supply features through software rather than hardware, as multiple handset platforms raise costs sharply (as a number of suppliers, including Motorola, have discovered). Fox (2000) discusses Nokia's management style further in the broader context of how simultaneously meeting the requirements of customers in different markets can lead to unexpected benefits.

This project eventually led to a phone that was designed with maximum modularity and as many common parts as possible. The external appearance of each model is the same, regardless of the systems it works with. This is analogous to Toyota's approach to different potential ITS systems.

Establishing 3G and CDMA Standards

Initial European discussions for the third-generation (3G) standard began in the early 1990s within ETSI (European Telecommunications Standards Institute) and mostly were managed by the large operators (telecom providers).

As the GSM standard and cell phone gained market strength, manufacturers such as Nokia began to increase their influence on the subcommittee where the technical standards for 3G phones would be decided. The major candidates were TDMA (time division multiple access), CDMA (code division multiple access), and TD-CDMA (a combination of the two). In deciding which to support, Nokia opted to be market- and partner-driven. However, although it could produce phones for any new standard, the shorter the path from GSM to the new global standard, the more advantage Nokia would possess in network development, given its experience base. It thus resisted having the U.S. choice become the standard because GSM would not easily migrate to it.

Nokia therefore began discussions in 1996 with Mitsui & Co., a major Japanese trading company, and NTT DoCoMo, Japan's dominant cell-phone operator, to achieve a common standard for Europe and Asia. By 1997 it was apparent, however, that DoCoMo and other Asian countries had settled on CDMA, while the Europeans had opted for a combination of CDMA and TDMA called FMA (frames multiple access). Because it was in Nokia's interest to have a common Asian and European standard, it supported CDMA for Europe. This was despite the fact that shifting from GSM to TDMA was much more straightforward than moving to CDMA.

Nokia was joined in this approach by Ericsson, and was opposed by Siemens, which wanted a U.S.-European standard that it would develop with Nortel and Motorola. Siemens's idea was that this would help it gain market share from Nokia and Ericsson. However, through the Finnish government, Nokia was able to get U.K. support for its approach, and that tipped the balance. Thus, in January 1998 a compromise 3G standard favoring the Nokia-Ericsson proposal was adopted by ETSI.

In the months that followed, Qualcomm, Motorola, and other U.S. companies entered the fray along with the U.S. government, as some U.S. firms became concerned that they would be left behind in the development of a truly international 3G standard. For a while the possibility of reaching a global agreement appeared small, because operators, suppliers, and governments championed their own approaches. Ultimately compromises were reached. A key step was the decision to abandon attempts to have a single standard. This came in January 1999, and was ratified in March at an ITU (International Telecommunications Union) meeting in Brazil. Also in March, Qualcomm and Ericsson settled a battle over intellectual property rights regarding CDMA, clearing the way for licensing. Qualcomm receives licensing fees and royalties on all CDMA-based infrastructure, handsets, and modules, as well as CDMA chips (which it also makes). Further, Ericsson acquired Qualcomm's network business and related product development.

CDMA will be the basis for the 3G standard worldwide, but each individual operator can select the CDMA variant it wants. This is very close to the original Nokia—Ericsson suggestion. In June 1999 there was further harmonization when the different approaches to 3G CDMA became, nominally, a single standard with "three modes." UMTS (Universal Mobile Telecommunications Systems) is the name given the 3G technology being implemented in the EU. Based on WCDMA-DS (the W is for wideband), this was formalized when the European Council of Ministers and the European Parliament adopted a Common Position and Decision in December 1998.

Having an open system based on a global CDMA standard, but with variations by country, means different configurations of elements to meet national criteria. This plays to Nokia's strengths in modular design.

The 3G and 2.5G Market

In April 1999, DoCoMo ordered 3G mobile phones from Nokia, as well as phones and base stations from Ericsson. From that point forward, cooperation regarding standards gave way to competition for orders—in which, in the case of phones, Nokia is doing well. This is true even though handsets are more of a commodity product than base stations or network systems, and the competition is intense because it includes Japanese and Korean producers. Nokia has achieved success by providing customized features that add value to using a Nokia phone and that cannot easily be emulated by others, the essence of a recognizably successful IT strategy.

A pragmatic approach has yielded benefits as Nokia helps clients to manage the transition from GSM and other second-generation systems to 3G. Operators worldwide are upgrading their networks to what is being called 2.5G. Based on the number of contracts won, as of late 2000 Nokia was close . to Ericsson, which is the world's leading wireless-network vendor. Nokia claimed 40 contracts, compared to 44 for Ericsson and only 7 for Motorola. Also, Nokia has signed some of Europe's leading operators, including Spain's Telefonica Moviles, Germany's Viag Interkom, and France's Cegetel.

Contracts for 3G (as of March 2001) are six for Ericsson and four for Nokia. Ericsson won the two largest, Vodafone AirTouch in the United Kingdom and NTT DoCoMo in Japan. Both Nokia and Ericsson have Japan Telecom as a customer.

Competing in the Evolving Market

Sales to large network providers often are relationship based; for Nokia, even its handset clients are seen as relationships rather than merely transactions. Competition for every client within Finland taught the company this lesson early in its development and taught it to compete on an interactive basis rather than relying on a government-encouraged and-enforced monopoly, as was true for many of the telecom equipment providers elsewhere in Europe and Japan.

Now that a CDMA-based global standard is set, the challenge for Nokia is to develop and efficiently supply phones with features that will attract users, and to work with operators and their suppliers to ensure that their systems can provide the features.

Success means targeting the right segments as m-commerce and m-technology expand and various niches covering data, voice, and multimedia emerge. Such targeting involves determining how to relate to different age groups, how to relate to different customer interests and responsibilities, and how to supply such a diverse market on a global basis. In sum, this involves efficient customization. To respond to the expectations of one important target group, the affluent young, Nokia believes it must develop a cost-effective media phone with user-friendly multimedia features and moving pictures.

To address these considerations, Nokia again is turning to partnering, as outlined in the next section generally and in the remainder of the chapter more specifically as regards operators and suppliers, tools, content, and services. The results are expected to be powerful beneficial loops in which market share, experience, and earnings compound to consolidate and strengthen leadership positions for Nokia and its partners. It also will play to Nokia's strength in managing its global demand-supply chain.

Partnering: General

Nokia views the environment for its business of supplying digitally based services as dynamic, with rapid technology convergence—or integration—of telecommunications, networking, and computers, built on supplying digitally based services. Because the technology is changing quickly and the markets are attracting new competitors, Nokia must consider and enter alliances and partnerships to access hardware, systems, and content technologies and their related markets if it is to pursue its overriding goal of combining the mobile phone and the Internet. In other words, working with other companies is a key part of Nokia's strategy, and its ability to do so is an important aspect of its success.

The company sees a difference between leveraging the expertise of its partners and just having a joint venture. So, although working with the right firms is important, how one works with them also is important if one is to reap the benefit of their firm-specific investments and expertise. This is similar to Toyota's differentiation between firms that might supply it with standard parts through the North American e-commerce supply network and those that will supply it with parts modules specially designed for a certain model car.

Managing the alignment of interests, as well as the business activities, is crucial. Therefore, in each undertaking Nokia tries to keep the number of activities, goals, and partners relatively small. This helps keep interests aligned and competitively focused.

Nokia partners on a global basis because its markets are global. But of necessity it must, like Citibank, allow for local differences, because telecom providers and regulators in each market have their own agendas and regulatory environments, which must be accommodated. This makes efficient customization, combined with fast delivery times, a key aspect of its competitiveness.

Operators and Suppliers

Nokia's network equipment business is significantly smaller than its handset business, but it has been profitable in its own right and the two divisions are synergistic (that is, can create beneficial loops for each other). Nokia can benefit from providing vendor financing for network infrastructure because newly built systems offer services available on new Nokia handsets.

In April 2001 deals with two major operators—Hutchinson 3G UK and Orange plc (for a Swiss project and for a project covering France, Germany, and the United Kingdom)—were announced in which the financing exceeded the value of the Nokia equipment being sold. Because Nokia does not make a full range of equipment, in order to get the system up and running, the company apparently is willing to help finance complementary gear. It feels it has a sufficiently strong balance sheet to do this, and an incentive, since the rapid loss of momentum in the wireless arena from late 2000 has created significant disarray. The company is seeking to exploit this to the detriment of its major competitors, which have been competitively and financially weaker during the 2000–01 zapping of the telecom sector.

For field trials of its WCDMA technology, Nokia has partnered with M1, a leading mobile operator in Singapore. The purpose is to test advanced mobile applications such as Internet access. The results will help Nokia evaluate its technology in a real operating environment. M1 firmly believes "that the transactional aspects of the Internet will be predominantly carried over wireless networks within the next three years." Thus Nokia's and the operator's vision and strategic intent are consistent, something Nokia recognizes from experience as usually being a critical ingredient in a successful strategic partnering. The trial includes features from the RealNetworks partnership, showing Nokia's integrated strategy.

Nokia has implemented similar WCDMA field test systems with other partners, including in China, Finland, and Japan. In addition, it has built 3G demonstration centers for its partner operators in Europe to use for a complete evaluation of 3G applications under working conditions. Nokia customers thus can evaluate and comment on such mobile applications as location-based services and Internet access at 384 kb/s.

Nokia also is working to strengthen its position as a leading supplier of TETRA (Terrestrial Trunked Radio System) networks and terminals. These are radio-based systems used primarily in remote locations such as northern Scandinavia. Nokia has supplied Finland's Ministry of the Interior a nationwide TETRA network that enhances the ministry's ability to meet all situations, especially rescue services, and replaces current radio networks. During 2000 Nokia introduced mobile IP packet data and wireless access protocols (WAP) functionalities for its TETRA networks. This offers users the ability to handle different data applications such as on-line access to databases, location routing, and emergency services. Nokia's TETRA network also contains special features that are attractive to the ministry, such as prioritizing emergency calls.

As early as 1996 the company anticipated that Asia would become its largest regional market. Nokia has been selling telecom equipment in China since 1987, when it delivered a DX200 exchange. China is Nokia's third largest market (after the United States and Europe), and its investment there had surpassed $1.7 billion by early 2001. It then had over 5500 employees in over 20 representative offices, seven joint ventures, one wholly owned manufacturing plant, and one R&D center.

A key partnership in supplying lighter, smaller, more powerful handsets has been with Ultralife Batteries (UB), based in the United States. As of 2001, UB's standard battery weighed about 28 grams and had a talk time of up to 3.3 hours and a standby time of 6.5 days. A higher capacity battery weighed 85 grams, and had a talk time of 10 hours, and standby time of 22 days.

Because Nokia sees mobile telecommunications and handsets as an integrated operation driven by user applications, it is working closely with a long list of developers. It sees this activity as crucial in expanding the market for mobile value-added services, and especially standard wireless Internet-related technologies such as WAP. That is because telecommunications, information technology, content, and mobility are all converging. In this evolution, Nokia is taking a lead role and the various content developers play an important part because Nokia wants to stimulate the creation of new tools and standards, as the next section shows.

Tools and Standards

In keeping with its commitment to open standards, Nokia is a member of a number of forums and committees. It also promotes standards and tools it has developed, and works with various partners to create more proprietary technologies. A few of the more important are described here. Box 11.4 outlines approaches to wireless Internet access and box 11.5 looks at ways to make such access faster.

Forums

Nokia is part of the Wireless World Research Forum, formed in December 2000 to formulate visions on future strategic research directions for wireless phone systems and services. In this way the group—which includes Alcatel, Ericsson, Nokia, and Siemens—hopes to identify and promote research for mobile and wireless systems while closely cooperating on standardization. There are three working sessions and a workshop each year. The effort furthers work started in 2000 on the Wireless Strategic Initiative by Alcatel, Ericsson, Nokia, and Siemens as an EU Information Society technologies project, which invited experts to three roundtables to develop concepts for a wireless world.

Symbian is a consortium formed in 1998 by Nokia, Ericsson, Motorola, and Psion to advance 3G technology, including accelerating development of higher-speed networks and making wireless Internet access ubiquitous.

RosettaNet, a consortium of about 300 major IT firms formed in February 1998, is working to create open industrywide standards for e-business and m-business—the "lingua franca for eBusiness" is its slogan. Nokia is a board-level participant. RosettaNet is particularly focused on IT users, but Nokia also will benefit as a supplier. Its web site is *rosettanet.org*.

Nokia seeks to further its firm-specific, low-cost production advantage by more closely integrating its production processes with its suppliers. RosettaNet can help extend this integration via the Internet because its open standards offer Nokia the chance to build and leverage more flexible solutions to manage relations with its global suppliers. Nokia can then create e-business supply frameworks that cross individual company boundaries but still provide a common set of properties for business transactions.

Wireless Mark-up Language (WML)

Having a familiar tool facilitates creating wireless web-based content, so in June 2000 Nokia entered an alliance with Macromedia to provide Nokia's WML Studio to developers using Macromedia's Dreamweaver or Flash. Macromedia is a leading provider of software for programming web sites and, like Nokia, is part of the WAP Forum, the industry association that has developed WML.

The availability of WML Studio software on-line enables developers to use Macromedia's free software tools to program WML content for delivery to Nokia and other WAP wireless device customers. Developers using Dreamweaver, which is a powerful web design program, will be able to work within the Dreamweaver interface they are familiar with. Further, WML Studio helps them preview their work on Nokia's phone simulator

---

Box 11.4
INTERNET ACCESS

In Japan wireless access to the Internet via DoCoMo's i-mode microbrowser already is a booming market, and access elsewhere will grow rapidly with the introduction of 3G systems and devices. Here are the major technological pieces in wireless Internet (except those relating to speed, which are covered in box 11.5).

WAP (Wireless Access Protocol)

Wireless Internet access and advanced telephony services on digital mobile phones, pagers, digital assistants, and other wireless terminals initially were standardized by WAP. A de facto worldwide standard, WAP allows multiple-supplier solutions for consistent and reliable end-user access across digital networks. It is compatible with a variety of operating systems currently running mobile devices. The technology enables the design of interactive real-time mobile services such as mobile banking, ITS, and Internet news services using digital mobile phones or other mobile devices such as Toyota's car-based systems.

The WAP Forum was founded in June 1997 by Nokia, Ericsson, Motorola, and Unwired Planet (later called Phone.com, now Openwave Systems Inc.) to develop an open standard for handsets to communicate with the Internet or a computer application. The Forum had some 600 members in mid-2001.

Both Nokia and Motorola began shipping WAP handsets at the end of 1999. WAP was not well received at first and subsequently was reworked. Working with the GSM Association, Openwave developed a new WAP browser launched in mid-2001. Then, in August 2001 the WAP Forum announced WAP 2.0.

XHTML

Internet protocols do not cover wireless connections, and the screens on most mobile phones are not efficient at displaying web pages in HTML, which is used for creating most current web pages. A principal immediate goal has been to make it easier to transmit just text, as firms such as Citibank need to send only a written message or data in connection with a financial transaction. More broadly, the goal is to facilitate EDI systems in general, and e- and m-commerce in particular, by making it easier to analyze data content automatically.

Initial work to create a wireless standard has merged, under the auspices of the World-Wide Web Consortium (W3C), on XHTML as the mark-up language to create all content.

---

directly from Dreamweaver, as well as to debug and validate the WML code created.

Automotive Tie-ins

Nokia was early in considering ways to marry mobile communications and the automobile. In 1988 a venture with Volvo was proposed that included

---

Box 11.5

THE QUEST FOR SPEED

At just 9.6 kb/s, using the technologies generally available, wireless access to the Internet was impractically slow for most uses in 2001. Several ways are being developed to boost transmission rates, including using a mark-up language such as XML that reduces the amount of data to be transmitted. But, as of mid-2001, optimism had dampened significantly from a year earlier because deployment of 3G has been postponed. Even when it does come, the typical 3G connecting speed now is expected to be in the 64 kb/s to 144 kb/s range (as reported by the *Wall Street Journal*, 16 March 2001, after surveying operators and equipment makers). Some analysts' earlier estimates (or hopes) had been for the megabit speeds consistent with streaming video.

In the meanwhile:

HSCSD (high-speed, circuit-switched data) aims to enable GSM to operate at up to 57.6 kb/s (comparable to the current common dial-up, wire-line modem).

In the future:

GPRS (general packet radio service) is intended to increase speed on TDMA networks to as much 172 kb/s and allow continuously open connections that are billed only when actually used. (From the operator's standpoint, the latter means several users will share a channel concurrently, which effectively increases capacity.) This is touted as a 2.5G technology and is being implemented in Europe. Field trials of Ericsson and Motorola systems began at the end of 1999. But in practice it appears initial connections with GPRS will be at 20 kb/s to 40 kb/s.

EDGE (enhanced data for global evolution) is intended to boost speeds on GSM and TDMA networks to 384 kb/s (that is, equivalent to a low-end, wire-line DSL connection).

---

the concept of "an office in a car" with a data terminal and printer in addition to a radiophone, all digitally based. Nokia's board ultimately decided not to pursue the project, although Volvo wanted to proceed.

Nokia worked with Volvo and Swedish Telecom to develop the world's first data management, planning, and monitoring system for use in road haulage. This is similar to what Toyota has done with Coca-Cola distributors and taxis in Nagoya. In 1995 Nokia acquired a stake in Geoworks, a U.S. software firm developing applications for mobile computing situations such as automobiles.

These early contacts bore fruit in 1998 with the Volvo S80 mobile phone system, which Nokia helped develop. In this innovative system, the display is in the dashboard, the controls are between the seats, the speakers are in the seats, and the microphone is in the sun visor, yielding a user-friendly operation that allows all occupants of the car to participate in a conversation.

Other Tools

Nokia entered a multiyear agreement with AOL in January 2001 to develop a WAP microbrowser for mobile devices that would be a Netscape version of Nokia's microbrowser with AOL features. This provides AOL brands and services to on-line customers anywhere, anytime, through non-PC devices, and also accesses Nokia's huge customer base. Nokia gets access to AOL's customer base while working with another Information Age leader. Under the arrangement, AOL is licensing Nokia's WAP browser source code and will work with Nokia to establish the open-standard technology Nokia has made available to various manufacturers, chip-set vendors, service providers, and operating system integrators to foster easier mobile data access.

As a direct extension of this strategy, in January 2001 Nokia acquired a 5% ownership interest in, and signed a licensing agreement with, U.S.-based InterTrust Technologies Corp., a leading developer of peer-to-peer, distributed digital rights management (DRM). DRM is a crucial element in digital media distribution solutions because media consumption increasingly is through digital devices, and it is important to content providers that they get paid (protect their intellectual property rights). InterTrust's version is highly regarded and works on both mobile and stationary computing platforms. Thus, it represents a key part of Nokia's strategy to cooperate with other industry players so as to define the technical architecture for the mobile Internet.

Nokia and InterTrust plan to offer customers entirely new services in terms of mobile content distribution by providing content owners, application developers, and service providers worldwide the most advanced solution on which to base products and services. Further, they want to establish InterTrust's DRM as the de facto standard for seamlessly offering rights-enabled products and services in the mobile market.

In 2000 Nokia successfully demonstrated the world's first wireless Internet synchronization using the SyncML protocol, which is the first global standard for data synchronization. Initiated by IBM, the SyncML alliance of over 250 companies includes Lotus, Motorola, Palm, Psion, and Starfish Software as well as Nokia and IBM. The point is to simplify access to management information systems, e-mail, and databases, including web-based documents, that are spread across multiple networks, platforms, and devices.

Wireless Financial Transactions (M-Commerce)

A key development to encouraging the use of mobile phones for Internet access is its use in financial transactions. One goal is to have the mobile phone itself be a payment device. This involves not only assuring security but also making the system easy to use. Nokia has a number of m-commerce partnerships and investments, some of which are covered here. (Also see the discussion in chapter 10.)

To make the mobile phone a payment device, Nokia has been working with U.S.-based 2Scoot since 2000. Nokia's 5100 smart phones can become a payment device through 2Scoot's network simply by using a cover with a special chip. The chip broadcasts a short-range radio frequency to a 2Scoot scanner at the cashier. This technique already is used for toll booths, baggage tracking, parcel delivery, electronic airline ticketing, and car anti-theft systems. Using 2Scoot's system, payment is made with the user's credit card.

Wireless payment methods that are both simple and secure are essential elements of m-commerce. To this end Nokia also has been working with two Dutch companies, KPN Mobile NV (a network operator) and Interpay Nederland (a payment processor). In April 2001 they reported a successful test using a wireless identity module (WIM). WIM is an open standard, independent of network, operator or financial services provider that enables a digital signature (in the form of the user's PIN.) The companies pilot-tested WIM on a smart card using the SET (secure electronic transaction) protocol designed by Eurocard/MasterCard and Visa as an open standard for electronic payments. Another pilot program is being launched to further test the system.

To promote security for wireless financial services Ericsson, Motorola, and Nokia formed the MeT Initiative in April 2000. Siemens, Matsushita, and Sony joined later. The purpose is to develop an open and common industry framework for secure mobile electronic transactions. Security is managed via digital signatures and cryptographic encoding that verify transactions and ensure confidentiality for information such as credit card numbers. In this way, MeT works to assist the development of new services and applications related to m-commerce that benefit customers and service providers. It is doing this using existing and possible new standards as appropriate.

Existing standards include WAP, WTLS (wireless transport layer security), Wireless Identification, PKI (public key infrastructure), and Bluetooth. Bluetooth is a short-range radio technology that expands wireless connectivity to personal and business mobile devices, thus enabling users to connect their mobile phones, computers, printers, digital cameras, and other electronic devices to one another without cables. Fast becoming a de facto worldwide standard, its development is overseen by the Bluetooth Special Interest Group, with over 1300 member firms. Nokia was a founder.

In a related move, Nokia acquired California-based Ramp Networks for $127 million in January 2001, strengthening its IP network security offerings with Ramp's small-office security products. Nokia thus is extending security for its mobile networks to businesses of all sizes, adding another important element to expanding the market for mobile communications and M-commerce.

Businesses and consumers are unlikely to use their mobile phones for commercial transactions unless they feel completely comfortable that the data exchange is fully secure and that any intellectual property issues are satisfied. Thus, Nokia will continue to develop a significant position in the growing network-security market. It will do this through its IP Network Security Solutions Group, which is integrating leading security software such as Check Point with the routing functionality of Nokia's security platforms to achieve high but user-tailored network security.

Content

Nokia is not itself going to be a content creator, but it recognizes that the availability of content is important to sales of its equipment. This has motivated Nokia to seek partnerships to provide content that its customers want, in ways that are compatible with Nokia's products, services, and technology.

Success of 3G generally is seen as depending on user access to exciting Internet content. This relates directly to Nokia's view that the mobile phone is very much a consumer-oriented product, which means it must appeal to the individual consumer. It thus is hardly surprising that entertainment and games form a key part of its strategy. This approach has proven very effective for NTT DoCoMo, the dominant Japanese mobile phone operator.

Entertainment

Nokia believes most mobile network operators ultimately will offer games to their customer base, as DoCoMo has done in Japan since 2000. Thus games are another element of the company's integrated global 3G strategy. To that end, the company created a web site in Europe, ClubNokia, that allows members (some 5 million in 26 countries in mid-2001) to download games and music into their handsets.

Activision was one of the first game companies to work with Nokia. Net Entertainment, a Swedish developer, has been working since 1999 on games for WAP-enabled mobile phones, and Oxford Softworks is cooperating with Nokia to enable 10 board games on WAP handsets. Altogether, Nokia's Mobile Entertainment Service has over 300 registered developers for its Mobile Entertainment Developers program.

The strategic concept behind the development tools Nokia supplies is to provide game application developers and online content publishers with a simpler way to create interactive entertainment—"entertainment on the move"—for Nokia's new WAP-capable phones. The program provides software tools and support for developers to create new commercial products or WAP versions of existing games. Nokia is constantly trying to add to the total number of interested developers and has two Web sites for potential developers (*forum.nokia.com* and *nokia.com/wap*).

RealNetworks, the technical and market leader in broadcasting audio and video over the Internet, will include its RealPlayer in the next generation of Nokia's phones under a June 2000 agreement. Customers with the devices will easily be able to access and download the huge amounts of RealAudio and RealVideo content from web sites worldwide. The phones are scheduled to be available in 2001 and are supported by EPOC, an operating system for small, handheld devices developed by Psion plc, a U.K. firm which also is a Nokia partner. Psion competes with Palm Inc's Palm Pilot system and Microsoft Corp's Windows CE and Pocket PC. RealNetworks software will help Nokia respond to the spread of higher-speed and broadband Internet connections, which allow better-quality pictures and sound to be sent wirelessly.

This cooperative agreement also gives Nokia access to RealNetworks' more than 130 million registered users and gives Nokia's customers access to RealNetworks' Real.com Message Service. The service enables users, at their option, to be notified when special entertainment or news programming is available.

Media Terminal

To leverage its partnering to create entertainment and other content for its handsets, Nokia plans to introduce a media terminal in the United States by the end of 2001. It is a home media center that combines the Internet and digital TV so that users can have one central device to organize and store media-related information through integrating digital video broadcast, Internet access, and video recording. The browser will thus offer a real transition from the TV to the web. Using this terminal, home viewers at their own direction can see a TV/Internet split screen; video-on-demand; interactive games; high definition digital TV; and much more. The viewer also can use the device to browse the web, or receive and send e-mail. It also will connect to printers, scanners, digital cameras, and game controllers.

Although competing with some aspects of Sony's Play Station II and Microsoft's X-Box, Nokia is applying its open standard partnering strategy as part of the competitive mix by incorporating Linux and HTML, for which a wide number of applications are already available. Further, by giving potential partners and developers access to its source code, Nokia creates a situation where software and systems developers can easily create applications for the terminal, because it is based on Intel architecture in combination with Nokia's existing receiver module.

Other Content Ventures

To access the frequent traveler, Nokia has entered an agreement with SABRE Holdings Corp., a leading provider of IT services to the travel and transportation industries that started as an airline reservation network for travel agents created by American Airlines.

To penetrate the market for wireless solutions in professional areas such as law and medicine, Nokia is working with a number of firms. Wireless-MD is a leading U.S. provider of services for on-line wireless retrieval of medical data. Through its systems, medical practitioners can quickly and remotely connect to a base system to access data such as patient records, insurance requests, test results, authorizations, medication, and possible allergies. Other firms are designing similar programs for lawyers to wirelessly access documents, client records, and case law.

Clouds

In June 2000 Jorma Ollila, the firm's chair and CEO, estimated there will be 1 billion mobile phone subscribers globally by the end of 2002. To succeed in growing and servicing Nokia's share of this market, he recognized that the firm needs to remain aggressive, flexible, and nimble. Thus, he wants "decision-making to stay quick" because "we are not as quick as we were six years ago," when Nokia had 28,000 employees (compared to 56,000 in 2000). "You start to believe that what you created three years ago is so good, because it was good two years ago and 18 months ago, and you continue to make money, and then there's someone in Israel and Silicon Valley just loving to kill you with a totally new technology. I think the problem in a big organization is that it starts to feed information internally that sort of supports its own internal truths and doesn't believe all the signals that you are getting. . . . I think that is a big problem. . . . I'm not overly worried. But I am worried because human nature is like that" (Dow Jones 2000).

In fact, during the following year, there was a rapid deceleration in growth and an industrywide lowering of expectations. Financial markets therefore have completely revamped their valuations of all types of telecom companies, including Nokia. Yet, the fundamental story remains in place, even if it is being realized at a slower pace. Thus, Nokia's financial results through mid-2001 show it is executing its plans well, at least relative to its competitors. The company continues to work toward the transition to the 3G technologies and beyond, including continuing to buy and to partner with companies having appropriate technologies.

Several Japanese firms are mounting a challenge to Ollila's conviction, and they may prove more formidable than Motorola and Ericsson have become in handsets. Indeed, in late April 2001 Sony Corp. and Ericsson reached a preliminary agreement to merge their mobile phone handset businesses in a 50–50 joint venture. Phones sold in Japan are among the most sophisticated in the world for size, weight, and function. The expertise of Japanese companies in producing components, especially screens, is expected to help them be serious competitors. Matsushita Communication Industrial Co., Japan's largest handset maker and part of the Matsushita group that is a global powerhouse in consumer electronics (sold under the Panasonic brand), expects to double its 5% world market share by 2003. However, both will have to overcome Nokia's integrated global strategy, as well as their own missteps, including large and costly handset recalls in Japan in June 2001.

As the size of the wireless market and the speed of its growth have become more uncertain, the various players are poaching on what had been each other's segments. Thus, although the company would describe it as helping independent content providers, others consider ClubNokia, a web site with games and music that can be downloaded to handsets, as a move onto their turf. In Europe, many Nokia phones have a direct link to the site. Telecom providers also are offering direct links to select or in-house content providers. Thus, Virgin Group has a "VX" key on some British models built specially for it.

A more immediate threat to Nokia, or at least its profit margins, is telecom providers using private-label handsets. Nokia has agreed to identify Orange plc (a unit of French Telecom) on Nokia-made handsets, and it provides SBC Wireless an exclusive color. Other makers are willing to provide handsets customized to a telecom provider and bearing only the provider's name. Going even further, Motorola in July 2001 announced it will sell chip sets to anyone.

Conclusion

A firm can benefit from historical accident and competitors' mistakes, as Nokia has. However, building on such advantages means having a good strategy in place, proper positioning, and continuing to do things better and more competitively than rivals. This involves the adoption and adaptation of new technologies, including IT, in ways that enhance and extend competencies in existing markets and in response to new markets and opportunities.

Open standards and cooperation set a pattern that strategically has served Nokia very well in terms of its approach to new technology. Combined with an early involvement in digital technology, this approach positioned the company well for what was to come, although there have been false starts as well as successes. The company also believes that its focus on customers and their evolving needs, and its early planning regarding issues such as "availability, price and usability," contributed to its strategic success as "mobile phones began to become a realistic choice for more and more people." This has been complemented by its TIM approach to both product and demand-supply management.

Nokia recognizes that to continue to grow faster than the market it must increase capacity, install newer machinery, and otherwise improve manufacturing to attain higher volumes with greater total factor productivity. As part of this, Nokia has been integrating its design and production strategies so new products can be manufactured more efficiently. Such actions to increase market and cost leadership in turn create a beneficial loop of learning, scale, and scope, leading to more price reductions and additional gains in market share. Price reductions attract more demand, justifying further capacity expansions. They also reduce customers' costs, making those customers more competitive and increasing demand for Nokia's products, another beneficial loop.

The company's perspective, which is driven from the CEO, is for the customer to have an easy "plug-and-play" experience built on a business platform that Nokia can reconfigure to different environments, just as can be done for the automobile. That is, anyone who drives a car in one country can, with a little adjustment, drive in another.

To constantly achieve this kind of personal customization of handsets efficiently at mass-produced costs, which Nokia believes is necessary for success in the 2.5G and 3G markets, requires creative partnering with firms that can provide IT features and services more easily and cheaply than Nokia. The strategic concept is to share expertise and market position to evoke firm-specific investment that favors Nokia. This will build a mobile-systems software portfolio that will provide network and handset support for the mobile Internet while working with service providers to put the required components in place. In this way, Nokia is changing the competitive nature of the wireless industry by moving customers and suppliers in a direction that will make the mobile phone *the* all-purpose communication device whether one wants to access the Internet, make a phone call, or pay bills.

PART III

CONCLUSIONS

12

Gaining a Leading Edge or
Leaving a Bleeding Tail

What matters is whether a firm understands and creatively uses IT to improve how it does things, be that making a product or providing a service. The Level 2 and Level 3 firms described in this book are evolving and implementing strategies that add value and build competitive barriers, thereby pressuring rivals and gaining an edge in their industries. This concluding chapter highlights what can be learned from them.

A fundamental point is that basic strategic principles still apply, and there is every reason to believe this will continue to be true in the "new" new economy. This will be a relief to the world-weary middle-aged. It should not be too disappointing to the young who thought they could outflank everyone by changing the rules. As entrepreneurial hotshots said in the 1970s: "If this doesn't work, we can always get real jobs."

Another element from the past that is ignored at one's peril is that while Japanese firms and management style may be out of vogue, they are not completely discredited. Several leading IT strategists are Japanese, and they have attained this position by evolving their corporate cultures in ways that retain many elements of the "traditional" Japanese firm. Indeed, their success often has reinforced the perceived benefits of these practices, such as the long-term employment system that allows them to train and retain the vertical-application specialists needed to implement their IT strategies on a sustainable basis. This is not what the research project initially expected to find.

If Japanese firms absorb the IT strategy lessons and best practices from U.S. experience faster than their competitors can synthesize Japanese best practices, they will be even more formidable competitors than when they were focused more on market share than on profits. Steel and automobiles are two industries where this appears to be the case. Indeed, in both industries the leading strategist is using IT to improve profits and gain share.

The most condensed statement of the message of this book is that if the basic business strategy is sound and is supported by an aligned organization, IT can be used to significantly enhance a company's strengths through a mix of customized and packaged software that can add value and create real barriers to entry and emulation. If these strategies are being pursued by a competitor, especially one using a Level 3 IT strategy, then a firm must seek to counter by building on its own strengths first, and then using IT to enhance them. Trying to re-engineer a business or organization while running to catch up is unlikely to succeed, and can put a firm even farther behind, at great expense.

Basic Strategic Principles Still Apply

The competitive environment of the new and "new" new economies has important continuities with the old economy. Probably the most important is that basic strategic principles still apply. Indeed, applying them is even more critical to survival and success.

One such key principle is pursuing and implementing cost controls and revenue enhancement in an integrated and interrelated manner. Companies doing this are more likely to do well than companies that do not, because they are working with two sides of the profit equation rather than one. Further, this focus is more customer oriented, an important element in leading strategists' basic business approach. Although beyond the scope of this book, a growing literature indicates that overemphasis on cost-cutting, especially slashing staff, can be counterproductive. Even more intuitively obvious (though heavily discounted in the dot.com bubble) is the need to get paid.

To add value and create competitive barriers through a combination of cost and revenue benefits, firms and their management still must pay attention to, and balance, various established business concepts. These include quality, customer focus, competitive awareness, evolutionary development, tacit knowledge, innovation routines, supply chain management, market segmentation, and risk management.

The strategies of leading IT users recognize IT as one tool in their kit to achieve their objectives: while versatile and essential, it is best used in concert with others. Thus, their strategies incorporate both "clicks and bricks," and some firms are so good at combining these that they are significantly changing their competitive environments to their long-term advantage.

Point List 12.1
Basic Principles

- Physical production and delivery integrate IT use.
- Cost control and revenue enhancement are pursued simultaneously, in an integrated manner.
- Quality still counts.

Partnering

If a service or IT support can be strategically best offered via a partnership, leading firms will do it as a way to implement the basic principles. This means being able to manage such partnerships is an important, probably essential, skill for a company to have. Leading firms are not caught up in a "not invented here" mentality. Thus, one well-developed IT routine is their ability and experience in searching out, creating, and utilizing commercially based partnerships. The result is the emergence of company groupings jointly organized by several leading IT users either to work together on a cooperative IT project or standard, or to create a new e-commerce company. I have termed these IT arrangements in Japan *"e-retsu"* or, more generally, e-groups (box 12.1).

Joining an *e-retsu* is consistent with a strong preference for customized and semi-customized IT systems. The leading strategists understand that no company can cover all new business areas and initiatives. Thus, they look to their partners to implement the pieces of the larger business puzzle where the partners have expertise and a competitive advantage.

The purpose is to access the skills and technologies each firm needs to exploit e-business markets. This allows them to move more quickly into e-commerce than might otherwise have been possible, while containing costs and reducing the business and financial risks as well. Further, given some partners' strong financial position and worldwide reach, the group is not dependent on a hot stock market to fund growth and global extensions.

Some of these groupings are a type of multivendor purchasing system. Examples are Ito-Yokado's relationships with its lunch-box suppliers and Toyota's management of its JIT network. In both cases suppliers have made

---

Box 12.1

E-*RETSU*

E-*retsu* are groups of firms that have come together to work on a cooperative IT project or standard, or to create a new e-commerce venture.

Within an industry, cross-licensing of technology is routine and, especially in Japan, collaborative early-stage research is not uncommon. However, there was no reason for the project to anticipate cooperative IT-based relationships among various companies from different industries or (in the Japanese case) *keiretsu*. In fact, the various e-*retsu* noted were announced well after the original project was under way.

Of the 17 leading IT users studied (not all of which are included in this book), 8 are in an e-group with at least one other studied firm. Among the 7 firms pursuing Level 3 IT strategies, 5 have developed close IT-based connections, in some cases with more than one other studied firm. The table in the introduction to part II indicates which firms are in e-groups.

firm-specific IT investments. In addition, some groups contain multiple IT suppliers, such as NRI's and NEC's participation in the IY bank and Ito-Yokado's e-commerce venture, 7-dream.com. Toyota also is using a multi-vendor IT approach for an "intelligent transportation system" that includes, among others, NRI, Matsushita, and Nippon Denso. Both of these methods (firm-specific and multiple IT suppliers) provide other ways to control IT costs and yet expand solution flexibility.

Other IT-centered business developments include Toyota's joint steel for auto parts project with Nippon Steel; Nomura Securities, Sanwa Bank, and Citigroup (Nikko Securities) helping Ito-Yokado create its on-line bank; and Nokia's work with Unisys on introducing 3G.

Customization and Market Segmentation

IT, especially in the United States, initially led to significant standardization, and while there are many areas in which this is useful and beneficial, such as operating systems, it sometimes means customers are forced through price or availability to buy from a predetermined set of products even if none meets their business needs. This is the downside of a producer-driven, sometimes monopolized, IT industry structure.

Further advances in IT have meant that firms can deliver high-quality products and services to cost-conscious customers at mass- or lean-production costs, something we have termed "efficient customization." This makes possible a marketing approach that targets consumers with total product or service flexibility—the ultimate segmentation of the market. This applies to both the final-consumer and intermediate-goods markets, as is shown in several of the case studies (Nippon Steel, Toyota, Ito-Yokado, and the financial service companies).

The idea of offering greater variety and customized products from a single source, at little or no price premium, is a very powerful one. Once a firm knows how valuable a customized product is to particular customers, and therefore how easily it can retain them on a long-term basis, the firm can determine the most effective way to market, price, and deliver its customized products and services.

This is not an easy task. It means constantly amassing and managing large amounts of data to better understand, and even develop, market segments. Further, it involves complex issues that vary by product and customer group. However, sophisticated algorithms and IT databases help the leading strategists address these issues. Firms do this in an established manner, using sets of rules and routines that emerge in an evolutionary way and build on the company's strengths and existing business strategy.

In order to quickly cost the customized offerings at lean-production prices, several of the leading IT strategists have used IT to develop total-cost accounting systems. These specifically identify different customer groups and the costs of supplying them. (Nippon Steel and Sanwa Bank are excellent examples.)

Gathering and Using Data

Leading users have become very good at gathering, managing, and systematically analyzing a wide range of information about their clients and potential customers. This is essential when offering customized products and when the entire process—design through after-sale service—is integrated. For such strategies to work, a firm not only must have good IT systems, it must be good at managing the related organizational, supplier, and customer complexities.

Using IT-based analysis of the data, leading firms develop and promote what they believe is demanded by each customer segment while constantly testing this view and the system in the market. Examples range from Citi's global consumer bankers continually assessing credit card holders' spending habits to Ito-Yokado's analysis of each store's sales of different items at different times and under different conditions, to Sanwa's detailed response to particular life events.

Doing this well requires a tremendous attention to detail in data gathering, analysis, and use. That is, effective implementation is an important strategic input. Thus, it does not help Citi or Sanwa to know that a life event is occurring if the customer service representative does not respond properly to the customer's inquiry.

Effective data-gathering and use can reduce and help manage business risk. This can be done directly, as in the case of Citibank and its assessment of probable loan losses on its consumer portfolio. It also can be less direct, as in Ito-Yokado's obsession with lost sales opportunities or Merck's business options approach to R&D investments.

Because the data often are unique to the firm, they are usually critical to creating system benefits that will not be competed away and therefore the firms want to use them for decision-making across the firm.

Setting Goals

Setting goals and disseminating information are essential elements of achieving a firm's strategy. Goal-setting processes have been important ingredients in developing IT strategies and initiatives at NEC, Meiji, Sanwa, Ito-Yokado, Nippon Steel, Citibank, and Merck because everyone buys into the goals and the way to achieve them.

There is a definite benefit when managers are able to explain and articulate the firm's goals and how they are being implemented through IT and other means. This means a conscious effort to reduce and manage organizational complexity as a way to manage business technology, financial risk, and IT complexity.

It also means that all managers and divisions are committed, and agree on what is to be done and how it is to be achieved. This is a Japanese-style decision-making process in that many potential problems are identified and worked out at the start of the project rather than as it proceeds, and diverse business groups from R&D to manufacturing to marketing all are involved in the assessment.

Japanese firms therefore appear, not surprisingly, to be particularly good at such goal setting and at using the process to manage technical and implementation complexity. If these skills indeed help in managing technical complexity and developing IT systems, several Japanese firms on balance will continue to be very good users of IT to achieve competitive advantage for the foreseeable future. This is especially true if the process takes many iterations, involves considerable trial and error, and depends on a good understanding of the firm, the industry, and IT technologies.

U.S. and European managers should take warning. This is especially so for firms that currently have conflicts among managers and employees in goal setting, because this creates development and implementation problems. In the extreme, it can subvert the overall quality- or IT-improvement efforts because employees will not work to find or implement solutions.

Managing Change

Leading users have established procedures and organizational structures to continually improve performance and capture tacit knowledge. If existing structures or strategies need to be changed, this is done on its own merits and before trying to implement a new initiative. IT is used as a way to enhance existing organizational strengths, and not as an agent of organizational change.

Change usually involves trial and error: a new system will require testing, training, and modifications in structure and use. However, because the commitment to quality and IT systems improvement must be continuous, the idea is to establish a beneficial loop. This loop means that after the initial change, future changes come naturally and lead naturally to further improvements. When such changes are culturally supported by the whole firm and its customers and suppliers as well, all benefit.

At leading firms there is little internal resistance to a new system because it is aligned with the firm's strategic direction and its managers are IT-fluent. Moreover, the metrics are clear, and these ultimately influence and drive the organization because workers at lower levels can then identify and implement actions related to improving these measures. Further, there is a realistic time frame for implementation.

Hoshin Kanri

Many leading Japanese IT users apply the concept of *hoshin kanri* (policy direction). An important aspect of this is focusing on three or fewer priorities at a time. Each focal point has relevant metrics. (Examples include improving operating earnings per employee, on-time delivery, cycle times, new model development, and the return on risk-adjusted assets.)

The priorities (goals) should have network externalities. That is, they should have a cascading impact, positively affecting multiple aspects of the business as they are implemented. Another *hoshin kanri* principle is active top management leadership in linking and integrating IT and long-term quality with decision-making.

Examples are Ito Yokado's weekly meetings to assure product and service consistency among stores, and Merck's planning and resource allocation committees that hold IT development and drug R&D projects to the same system in terms of man-hours, rates of return, and budget commitments per dollar spent.

IT and Human Resources

Leading users are very conscious of the interconnections between IT, quality, and human relations.

When routines are well understood and every person knows every other person, consultative processes take less time and there is significant tacit understanding of corporate objectives and how to get things done. This implies that long-term employment gives firms an advantage in developing and implementing an IT strategy. It is becoming a less common practice even in Japan, so the fact that the best Japanese firms are especially good at the interconnections may put them under less pressure relative to competitors to rationalize employment. This creates a beneficial loop because their more experienced work force makes it easier to develop and implement their strategies, further improving their competitive position. Toyota and Ito-Yokado are good examples of this.

U.S. and European companies have been successful when they have clearly stated goals and work at integrating strategy and organization. Merck's and Citibank's review and IT project management systems, for example, do this by making IT part of the budget process and requiring all IT projects to meet both corporate strategy and corporate financial goals. Nokia seems to be good at developing and managing IT-based alliances with important outside software and hardware companies that are helping solidify its long-term competitive position in mobile telecommunications.

Tacit Knowledge

There typically is an appreciation of the role of tacit knowledge within a leading strategist in both creating and maintaining its strengths. Various IT initiatives are undertaken to enhance this knowledge and the related competencies.

Merck sees its ability to manage the FDA approval process as a key variable in managing the drug pipeline and speeding time to market. It therefore has undertaken several IT initiatives that have made the approval task easier for any one drug, thereby allowing the firm to manage a larger pipeline of drugs. Similarly, the strategy behind Meiji's laptop-based life-cycle system is to capture the expertise, experience, and capabilities of its best agents in a self-developed evolutionary expert system that upgrades the performance of the rest of its agents.

Metrics

Leading firms have IT review committees. They do not look at IT in isolation, but see it as part of the system that supports basic business functions such as product development and marketing. Each recognizes that the firm's various parts operate as a whole and need to succeed as a whole for the business and IT strategies to work. Thus they insist that each IT project have some metric identified and agreed to in advance as part of a contract that specifies what is going to change if the project is successful. Moreover, leading firms consider it important to identify and learn from failures.

Good IT management committees make people aware of the externalities across the various functions that IT affects. Firms then are able to capture these externalities through organizational changes and systems support in which employees can see and understand the impact. Such spillovers further justify the firms' control over IT development, because strategic success is the ultimate metric.

Software selection is pragmatic, with an emphasis on the value of what it does versus its cost, whether purchased and adapted or developed internally. Decisions are made case by case, based on evolutionary learning and using the same rules and routines as decisions on introduction of new technologies and organizational structures. Business requirements are not modified to accommodate a system. Rather, it is recognized by leading IT strategists that even if creating systems tailored to one's needs initially is more expensive than buying packaged IT, the customized software often provides advantages that cannot be emulated and thus justifies its cost. So, for them, competitive considerations determine software development and purchase decisions.

Because the number of objectives is limited, it is easier to identify and fix any problems. For similar reasons, the characteristics used in evaluating software performance are application specific and depend on the area in which the IT is employed.

Easily understood and measurable goals for IT systems help employees achieve business success. They also keep IT part of the solution by institutionalizing and organizing the process of using IT so that it is integrated and aligned with the firm's business direction. Internal resistance to new and better systems then does not occur. Such IT management includes a realistic time frame for implementation, which the leaders build into their goal-setting and review process because they know unrealistic timetables can discourage employees and lead to premature scrapping of worthwhile IT projects. Indeed, such realism is essential for developing real-time on-line systems that are totally integrated with business operations.

Time and Quality Management

Intertwining IT with basic strategic principles and a firm's total business strategy and competitive vision is especially important in time and quality management. There are obvious interactions between quality and IT management. Certainly, given the size of IT budgets, mission-critical applications, and organizational integration, it is important that quality standards be applied to IT systems themselves.

For leading firms, time is a strategic issue. That is, reducing the time it takes to complete a task is part of the competitive equation. Time to market for new products can be especially important. Thus, leading users employ IT to significantly speed the design-to-production cycle by standardizing processes across their companies and their suppliers. This is illustrated by Toyota's initiatives to get its designs rapidly produced and Merck's efforts to complete clinical trials faster and with more patient information.

Speed must be accomplished with a full attention to detail or the strategy will fail. Nowhere is this important truth more apparent than in the need to align IT and quality. The best IT systems are of no avail if the product or service is not what potential customers want, is of poor quality, or does not work. For this reason the next section relates IT strategies and quality. Indeed, regardless of national culture, it appears that leading users have developed quality and IT feedback loops that are similar.

Quality Is Still What Counts

For leading IT strategists, concern with quality has always been central. Their IT systems are so complex and tightly integrated with their organizations that developing them and making them work necessitates strong attention to quality and detail. This is important because e-commerce and e-business have become management obsessions in the way quality was in the mid-1990s. Managements often ignore the previous focal point as they concentrate on the current one. That is a huge blunder, because the information revolution means quality and other strategic mistakes are quickly amplified.

News about poor service or product problems can be transmitted globally in seconds, with expensive consequences. Intel discovered this when it tried to ignore a glitch in an early Pentium processor. The damage to the firm's reputation was as significant as the direct costs of the product recall it ultimately was forced to accept.

Efficient delivery of a poor-quality product will not generate a beneficial loop of greater customer satisfaction and repeat sales. Citigroup states this clearly: "Quality is primary. We save money when we don't have to correct errors, and we build revenues with superior products and services." The adage "If you don't have time to do it right the first time, when do you have time to do it over?" still applies.

Several leading IT practitioners examined in this book (Citibank, Merck, Nippon Steel, Nokia, Toyota) want parts of their IT systems accepted as industry standards. Indeed, they have shown that establishing a de facto standard can be an important lever for controlling the competitive environment. However, it clearly will be difficult to gain this position if the system does not work or is unreliable.

Shared Characteristics

Leading IT users have many characteristics found in firms good at creating quality (Easton and Jarrell 1997). Thus, in the following summary of Easton's and Jarrell's work, "IT" can be substituted for "quality."

At the best firms, responsibility for quality and efficiency on a global basis is closely integrated or aligned with strategic planning. The point of stressing quality is to benefit the business: providing quality is a means to an end, not an end in itself.

Successful firms insist on using metrics to establish the actual results of specific quality initiatives. The metrics may be financial, physical, or qualitative, but improvement must be identifiable. In addition, there is responsibility; so after priorities and their associated metrics have been set, someone is responsible for managing the initiative and making it work. The operating units thus are stakeholders, and in many cases have bottom-line responsibilities as well.

If there is an effective system to start, making it better is easier: less has to be changed, and one has a better idea of what can be improved and why. Improvements arise from a dynamic, continuous, and iterative process. Initiatives generally are ways to enhance and make the existing culture stronger rather than to change it.

This is why senior management commitment and involvement must be a part of the process. Otherwise, credibility and focus are lost. The involvement of top management is how one moves from a firm with pockets of excellence to one where the whole firm develops a culture of excellence.

Beyond these points, there is no "typical" process for making quality improvements; the "how" is unique to each firm. It is driven by the ability to combine a good understanding of the businesses and the strategies required to be successful. In short, planning and operational excellence are keys to quality.

A Variety of IT Options

Based on these principles, the study of leading IT strategists demonstrates that what a firm does in using IT to enhance its strategic position can take various forms. It can improve a process or improve the product or service itself. Both approaches relate to the fact all Level 2 and Level 3 firms have a very strong customer focus that determines most aspects of their larger business strategies as well as the specifically IT component. Point list 12.2 spotlights some major things IT is being used to do by leading users, with reference to some of the relevant case studies.

Point List 12.2
IT Options

• *Improve Processes*

Nippon Steel's accelerated production times for customized steel orders and Toyota's faster design and production cycles for new models are examples.

• *Improve Products and Services*

Nokia's smart phones, Ito-Yokado's expanded 24-hour services, and Merck's rational drug design, as well as life-cycle models such as those used by Meiji Seimei, Citigroup, and Sanwa Bank that anticipate customer needs and facilitate the tailored delivery and use of their expanded range of products and services over their customers' life times illustrate this.

• *Track the Competition*

Merck's inventory policy for pharmacists directly considers the availability of a competing drug and balances this against the cost of carrying larger inventories

• *Better Manage Supply Chains*

To lower costs and improve quality, leading firms generally have suppliers directly connected to their production or sales information systems, so that the suppliers can automatically access the information they need for JIT delivery. Toyota, Ito-Yokado, and Nokia exemplify this.

• *Improve Quality*

Merck's tracking of potential side effects even after FDA approval and Toyota's effort to reduce warranty claims by analyzing repair and replacement records by model and country illustrate this.

• *Help Keep Human Contact Cost-effective.*

In customer service, leaders have a willingness to retain access to real people while using IT to enhance the speed and ability of customer service representatives in addition to providing electronic access to those who want it. Citigroup is a leading example.

By incorporating these principles in their corporate cultures through the use of rules and routines, leading IT strategists have created a dynamic, evolutionary model for using IT to gain an edge.

Conclusion

Firms that have a good understanding of their strengths, strategic advantages, and corporate direction, including quality issues, are better able to efficiently deliver quality to their customers. Moreover, they are likely to align their human resources and IT with quality objectives. All the leading firms recognize that some human element is necessary for an effective and successful quality strategy. Getting the human-IT mix right in terms of use and expense is key.

Good IT, by institutionalizing tacit knowledge and tracking important data, helps to manage detail, and thus to ensure quality. This is a beneficial loop that one's firm always should seek to create, even if it does not attain a Level 3 IT strategy. Even if one cannot gain an edge from applying the lessons presented in this book, at least one should be able to understand the competitive challenges ahead.

Appendix: The Principles of Using IT Strategically

It is through the intense interaction of business and IT strategy with the firm's organization, suppliers, and customers that IT is used to create the long-term firm-specific advantages that give value and build barriers. To summarize some of the lessons derived from the case studies, here are some fundamental principles that Level 2 and Level 3 strategists employ.

• Look at the business and its needs to determine what is expected of IT, then choose what will do what is required efficiently.

- Educate the firm's IT users to be able to identify ways in which IT can work for them.
- Let user needs and budgets drive IT selection.
- Use IT to implement solutions that are not possible otherwise, such as using large databases to manage R&D or embedding software that adds or enables product functions.
- Judge IT by actual realized gains in revenue, quality, or productivity.
- Focus MIS departments on supporting IT users and ensuring compatibility of various system components on an integrated basis.
- Use IT to make jobs both easier in the mechanics and more challenging in the initiatives or tasks that can be undertaken. (That is, simplify specific tasks while increasing the skills of each worker as an individual.)
- Use IT to support quality management by codifying tacit knowledge, as well as more explicit rules and routines, thus facilitating application.
- Use IT to establish and strengthen beneficial loops that have articulated goals and outcomes, thus adding value and building barriers.
- Use IT to facilitate production and delivery of customized products and services at mass- or lean-produced costs and prices, improving both choice and quality. This we have termed "efficient customization."
- Promote time management through IT systems that improve production cycle times (for example, the time needed to produce a steel coil or integrated circuit) and time from design to market.
- Maintain and routinize an attention to detail using IT, so that faster speeds do not confound correct implementation or product and service quality.
- Limit outsourcing to generic tasks (such as payroll or the software from a manufacturer to run specific equipment), while recognizing that for some firms—in both manufacturing and services—payroll IT can be strategic in costing customized products.

Appendix

Sloan Industry Centers and Their Web Sites

Apparel	Harvard University *http://www.stitchintime.org*
Automobiles	Massachusetts Institute of Technology (MIT) *http://web.mit.edu/ctpid/www/imvp*
Computers[1]	Stanford University *www.stanford.edu/group/scip*
Food Services	University of Minnesota *http://trfic.umn.edu*
Financial Services	Wharton School (University of Pennsylvania) *http://fic.wharton.upenn.edu/fic/*
Pharmaceuticals	Massachusetts Institute of Technology (MIT) *http://web.mit.edu//popi/index.html*
Semiconductors[1]	University of California (Berkeley) *http://esrc.berkeley.edu/csm*
Steel	Carnegie-Mellon University *http://steel.ucsur.pitt.edu/steel/index.htm*
Telecommunications	Columbia University *www.citi.columbia.edu*

Publications, directors, and information on purpose, history, and funding can be found on respective web sites.
[1]Includes related software.

Bibliography

Abernathy, Frederick H., John T. Dunlop, Janice H. Hammond, and David Weil. 1999. *A Stitch in Time: Lean Retailing and the Transformation of Manufacturing—Lessons from the Apparel and Textile Industries*. New York: Oxford University Press.

Ahlbrandt, Roger S., Richard J. Fruehan, and Frank Giarratani. 1996. *The Renaissance of American Steel: Lesson for Managers in Competitive Industries*. New York: Oxford University Press.

Ahmadjian, Christina. 1997. *Japanese Auto Parts Supply Networks and the Governance of Interfirm Exchange*. Working Paper 129. New York: Center on Japanese Economy and Business, Columbia University.

Anchordoguy, Marie. 1989. *Computers Inc*. Cambridge, Mass.: Harvard University Press.

Cargill, Thomas F. 2000. "What Caused Japan's Banking Crisis?" In *Crisis and Change in the Japanese Financial System*. Edited by Takeo Hoshi and Hugh Patrick. Boston: Kluwer Academic Publishers.

Cargill, Thomas F. and Naoyuki Yoshino. 2000. "The Postal Savings System, Fiscal Investment and Loan Program, and Modernization of Japan's Financial System. In *Crisis and Change in the Japanese Financial System*. Edited by Takeo Hoshi and Hugh Patrick. Boston: Kluwer Academic Publishers.

Davidow, William H, and Michael S Malone. 1993. *The Virtual Corporation: Structuring and Revitalizing the Corporation for the 21st Century*. Harper Business.

Dempster, Prue. 1969. *Japan Advances: A Geographical Study*. Methuen & Co.

Dixit, A. K, and Robert Pindyck. 1995. "The Options Approach to Capital Investment." *Harvard Business Review*, June, pp. 105–115.

Dow Jones Online News. 2000. "Nokia Chief Wants Decision-Making to Stay Quick."

Easton, George S., and Sherry L. Jarrell. 1997. "Using Strategic Quality Planning More Effectively: Lessons Learned from NSF Project Research." Presentation at Columbia Business School Conference on Quality, New York, September.

Evans, Philip, and Thomas Wurster. 1999. *Blown to Bits: How the New Economics of Information Transforms Strategy*. Boston: Harvard Business School Press.

Everson, Ann, Patrick T. Harker, and Francis Frei. 1999. *Effective Call Center*

Management: Evidence from Financial Services. Working paper 98–25B. Philadelphia: The Wharton School, University of Pennsylvania.

Fox, Justin. 2000. "Nokia's Secret Code." *Fortune*, 1 May, pp. 161–174.

Friedman, Milton. 1957. *A Theory of the Consumption Function*. Princeton, N.J.: Princeton University Press.

Fujimoto, Takahiro. 1999. *The Evolution of a Manufacturing System at Toyota*. New York: Oxford University Press.

Fujitani, Yoshitaka. 1995. *Challenges Facing Japanese Steel in Today's Global Economy*. Occasional Paper Series 21. New York: Center on Japanese Economy and Business, Columbia University.

Godfrey, A. Blanton, and Richard C. H. Chua. 1997. *Integrating Quality and Productivity with Strategic Business Performance*. Wilton, Conn.: Juran Institute.

Gurley, J. William. 1998. "Creating a Great E-Commerce Business." *Fortune*, 16 March, pp. 146–148.

Harker, Patrick T. 1997. "High-Performance Workplaces in Services: The Case of Retail Banking." Lecture at Wharton School, University of Pennsylvania, Philadelphia, September.

Havens, Thomas R. H. 1994. *Architects of Affluence: The Tsutsumi Family and the Seibu-Saison Enterprises in Twentieth-Century Japan*. Harvard East Asian Monographs, 166. Cambridge, Mass.: Harvard University Press for the Council on East Asian Studies, Harvard University.

Hibara, Nobuhiko, and William V. Rapp. 2000. *Food Retailing: Ito-Yokado Group*. Working paper. New York: Center on Japanese Economy and Business, Columbia University.

Hoshi, Takeo, and Anil Kashyap. 1999. "The Japanese Banking Crisis: Where Did It Come from and How Will It End?" In *NBER Macroeconomics Annual 1999*. Edited by Ben S. Bernanke and Julio J. Rotemberg. Pages 129–201.

Hoshi, Takeo, and Anil Kashyap. 2001. *Corporate Financing and Governance in Japan*. Cambridge, Mass.: MIT Press.

Hoshi, Takeo, and Hugh Patrick, eds. 2000. *Crisis and Change in the Japanese Financial System*. Boston: Kluwer Academic Publishers.

Hunter, Larry W., and John J. Lafkas. 1998. *Information Technology, Work Practices, and Wages*. Working Paper 98–02. Phildelphia: Financial Institutions Center, Wharton School, University of Pennsylvania.

Imai, Masaaki. 1986. *Kaizen: The Key to Japanese Competitiveness Success*. Random House Business Division.

King, Robert K., and Paul F. Phumpiu. 1996. "Reengineering the Food Supply Chain: The ECR Initiative in the Grocery Industry." *American Journal of Agricultural Economics* 78: 1181–86.

Lynn, Lenard H. 1982. *How Japan Innovates: A Comparison with the U.S. in the Case of Oxygen Steelmaking*. Boulder, Colo.: Westview Press.

Marucca, Regina. 2000. "Competitive Fitness." *Harvard Business Review*, July, p 24.

Myers, Stewart C., and Christopher D. Howe. 1997. *A Life Cycle Model of Pharmaceutical R&D.*" Working Paper 41. Cambridge, Mass.: Program on the Pharmaceutical Industry, MIT. Available at *mit.edu//popi/index.html*

Nelson, Richard. 1991. *Why Do Firms Differ and How Does It Matter?* New York: Columbia University.

Nelson, Richard, and Sidney Winter. 1982. *An Evolutionary Theory of Economic Change*. Cambridge, Mass.: Harvard University Press.

O'Brien, Patricia. 1992. "Industry Structure as a Competitive Advantage: The History of Japan's Postwar Steel Industry." *Business History* 34, no. 1: 304–335.

Okuda, Hiroshi. 1998. "When the Ground Rules Change." Lecture, Yale University.

Ostrom, Douglas. 1998. "From Colossus to Casualty: The Transformation of Japan's Insurance Industry." *Japan Economic Report*, 16 January.

Porter, Michael. 1980. *Competitive Strategy: Techniques for Analyzing Industries and Competitors*. New York: Free Press.

Porter, Michael. 1986. "Competition in Global Industries: A Conceptual Framework." In *Competition in Global Industries*. Edited by Michael Porter. Boston: Harvard Business School Press.

Prasad, Baba, and Patrick T. Harker. 1997. *Examining the Contribution of Information Technology Toward Productivity and Profitability in Retail Banking*. Wharton School Working Paper 97–09. Philadelphia: Wharton School, University of Pennsylvania.

Ramirez, Rafael, and Johan Wallin. 2000. *Prime Movers; Define Your Business or Have Someone Define It Against You*. New York: John Wiley & Sons.

Rapp, William V. 1973. "Strategy Formulation and International Competition." *Columbia Journal of World Business* 8, no. 2: 98–112.

Rapp, William V. 1995. *The Future Evolution of Japanese-U.S. Competition in Software: Policy Challenges and Strategic Prospects*. Final report. New York: U.S.-Japan Friendship Commission, Center on Japanese Economy and Business, Columbia University.

Rapp, William V. 2000. *Nomura Research Institute: Gaining and Sustaining Long-term Advantage Through Information Technology*. Working Paper. New York: Center on Japanese Economy and Business, Columbia University.

Reve, Torger, and Luis W. Stern. 1986. "The Relationship Between Interorganizational Form, Transaction Climate, and Economic Performance in Vertical Interfirm Dyads." In *Marketing Channels: Relationship and Performance*. Edited by Luca Pellegrini and Srinivas K. Reddy. DC Heath and Co. Lexington, Mass.: Lexington Books.

Santomero, Anthony, and Peter Burns. 1997. *Financial Institutions Center*. Philadelphia: Wharton School, University of Pennsylvania.

Schwartz, Eduardo S., and Lenos Trigeorgis, eds. 2000. *Real Options and Investment Under Uncertainty: Classical Readings and Recent Contributions*. Cambridge, Mass.: MIT Press.

Sealy, Michael. 1991. "The Global Design Strategy of Japanese Automobile Manufacturers." Seminar paper, Columbia University.

Smitka, Michael J. 1991. *Competitive Ties: Subcontractors in the Japanese Automotive Industry*. New York: Columbia University Press.

Smitka, Michael J. 1993. "The Decline of the Japanese Auto Industry: Domestic and International Implications." Japan Economic Seminar paper.

Suzuki, Yoshio, editor. 1987. *The Japanese Financial System*. Oxford: Clarendon Press.

Teranishi, Juro. 1994. "Japan: Development and Structural Change of the Financial System." In *The Financial Development of Japan, Korea, and Taiwan: Growth, Respression, and Liberalization.* Edited by Hugh T. Patrick and Yung Chul Park. New York: Oxford University Press.

Trebartha, Glenn T. 1965. *Japan: A Geography.* Madison: University of Wisconsin Press and Methuen & Co.

Ueda, Kazuo. 2000. "Causes of Japan's Banking Problems in the 1990s." In *Crisis and Change in the Japanese Financial System.* Edited by Takeo Hoshi and Hugh Patrick. Boston: Kluwer Academic Publishers.

Womack, James P., Daniel T. Jones, and Daniel Roos. 1990. *The Machine That Changed the World.* New York: Rawson.

Yahagi, Toshiyuki. 1994. *Convenience Store System no Kakushin-sei.* Nihon Keizai Shinbunsha. In Japanese.

Yoshida, Kenichiro. 1996. *Tokyo Steel Manufacturing.* Tokyo: Salomon Brothers.

Yoshida, Kenichiro. 1997. *Japan's Steel Industry Outlook, Blast Furnace Companies' Fiscal 1997–98 Prospects.* Tokyo: Salomon Brothers Japanese Equity Research.

Index